Karl Barth in Conversation

Karl Barth in Conversation

Edited by
W. Travis McMaken
and David W. Congdon

PICKWICK Publications · Eugene, Oregon

KARL BARTH IN CONVERSATION

Copyright © 2014 Wipf and Stock Publishers. All rights reserved. Except for brief quotations in critical publications or reviews, no part of this book may be reproduced in any manner without prior written permission from the publisher. Write: Permissions. Wipf and Stock Publishers, 199 W. 8th Ave., Suite 3, Eugene, OR 97401.

Pickwick Publications
An Imprint of Wipf and Stock Publishers
199 W. 8th Ave., Suite 3
Eugene, OR 97401

www.wipfandstock.com

ISBN 13: 978-1-60899-677-3

Cataloguing-in-Publication Data

Karl Barth in conversation / edited by W. Travis McMaken and David W. Congdon

xviii + 314 p. ; 23 cm. Includes bibliographical references and index.

ISBN 13: 978-1-60899-677-3

1. Barth, Karl, 1886–1968. I. McMaken, W. Travis. II. Congdon, David W. III. Title.

BT111.3 M151 2014

Manufactured in the U.S.A.

New Revised Standard Version Bible, copyright 1989, Division of Christian Education of the National Council of the Churches of Christ in the United States of America. Used by permission. All rights reserved.

Scripture taken from the New King James Version®. Copyright © 1982 by Thomas Nelson, Inc. Used by permission. All rights reserved.

Scriptures taken from the Holy Bible, New International Version®, NIV®. Copyright © 1973, 1978, 1984, 2011 by Biblica, Inc.™ Used by permission of Zondervan. All rights reserved worldwide. www.zondervan.com The "NIV" and "New International Version" are trademarks registered in the United States Patent and Trademark Office by Biblica, Inc.™

Scripture quotations are from The Holy Bible, English Standard Version® (ESV®), copyright © 2001 by Crossway, a publishing ministry of Good News Publishers. Used by permission. All rights reserved.

Contents

Preface • xi
—By W. Travis McMaken

Abbreviations • xix

Section 1: Past Conversations

1. Promise and Command: Barth and Wesley on Matthew 5:48 • 3
   —By John L. Drury

   Barth, Wesley, and Revolutionary Christianity: A Response to John L. Drury • 20
   —By Christian T. Collins Winn

2. Schleiermacher and Barth: On Theology as the Science of the Divine Word • 26
   —By Matthew J. Aragon Bruce

   On the Critical Science of Theology: A Response to Matthew Bruce • 38
   —By Matthias Gockel

3. Dietrich Bonhoeffer in the Theology of Karl Barth • 46
   —By Matthew Puffer

   Response to Matthew Puffer on Dietrich Bonhoeffer's Influence on Karl Barth • 62
   —By Andy Rowell

4. Pauline Apocalyptic and Political Nihilism: Jacob Taubes and Karl Barth • 70
   —By Benjamin Myers

The Missing Enemy & A Missed Opportunity: A Response to Myers's Pacification of Political Theology in Taubes and Barth • 83
—By Derek Alan Woodard-Lehman

Section 2: Present Conversations

5 "You Wonder Where the Spirit Went": Barth and Jenson on the Hiddenness of God • 91
—By Peter Kline

The Spirit Is in the Details: A Response to Peter Kline • 109
—By William Barnett

6 Dueling Ecclesiologies: Barth and Hauerwas in Con-verse • 116
—By Halden Doerge

A Response to Doerge on Barth and Hauerwas • 125
—By Ry O. Siggelkow

7 Christ vs. Mammon: Tanner and Barth on Economics and Theological Method • 129
—By J. Scott Jackson

Following the Deacon Jesus in the Prophetic Diaconate: Toward an Apocalyptic "Third Way" Beyond Barth and Tanner • 143
—By David W. Congdon

8 Beauty, Glory, and Trinity in Karl Barth and David Bentley Hart • 152
—By Keith Starkenburg

Beauty, Glory, and Trinity in Karl Barth or in David Bentley Hart? A Response to Keith Starkenburg • 165
—By Han-luen Kantzer Komline

Section 3: Expanding Conversations

9 On *The Monstrosity of Christ*: Karl Barth in Conversation with Slavoj Žižek and John Milbank • 171
—By Paul Dafydd Jones

An Analysis and Diagnosis in Response to Paul Jones's "On *The Monstrosity of Christ*" • 189
—By Sigurd Baark

10 Karl Barth in Conversation with Pauline Apocalypticism • 195
—By Shannon Nicole Smythe

Apocalypse Ellipsis: A Response to Shannon Smythe • 211
—By Andrew R. Guffey

11 Barth and Kegan: Theological Anthropology and Developmental Psychology in Lived Experience • 216
—By Blair D. Bertrand

Kegan and Barth: A Response to Bertrand • 230
—By Katherine M. Douglass

12 No Country for Old Man: Barth Calls the Coen Brothers • 234
—By Jon Coutts

A Response to Jon Coutts on Barth and the Coen Brothers • 247
—By Brad East

Afterword: The Future of Conversing with Barth • 255
—By David W. Congdon

Appendix: Become Conversant with Barth's Church Dogmatics: *A Primer* • 279
—By David Guretzki

Bibliography • 299
List of Contributors • 315
Index of Names • 319

Preface

—By W. Travis McMaken

KARL BARTH IN CONVERSATION—NOT the flashiest title, but a significant one. When asked about the prodigious nature of Barth's *oeuvre*, the sympathetic scholar might well be inclined to place tongue firmly in cheek and state simply that Barth was a bit loquacious. That Barth felt a commanding need to communicate is indisputable, but he seems to have enjoyed it as well. His *Gesamtausgabe* contains three volumes of *Gespräche* from the last decade of his life, full of discussions and interviews with everyone from other scholars, students (both Protestant and Catholic), media outlets, and church folk.[1] These volumes belie the picture often painted by Barth's detractors of a doctrinaire, inflexible, and insular theological egoist. Far more compelling is the picture of Barth as a lively conversationalist. Furthermore, Karl Barth has been brought into conversation from the very beginning. Two of the very earliest writings about Barth put him into dialogue with other thinkers. In 1924, Martin Werner wrote his polemical work, *Das Weltanschauungsproblem bei Karl Barth und Albert Schweitzer: Eine Auseinandersetzung*, and in 1925, Anders Gemmer and August Messer published their three-hundred-page study, *Sören Kierkegaard und Karl Barth*. The present volume builds on this history and attempts to put Barth into conversation with various other thinkers and subjects from before, contemporary with, and after his own lifetime.[2]

Continuing with the theme of conversation, this volume comprises the revised and expanded proceedings of the 2010 Karl Barth Blog Conference

---

1. See Barth, *Gespräche 1959–1962*; Barth, *Gespräche 1963*; Barth, *Gespräche 1964–1968*.
2. There is a great deal of interest in conversing with Barth's theology. In 2004, Mike Higton and John McDowell edited a volume with the title, *Conversing with Barth*. And in 2013, the annual Karl Barth Conference at Princeton Theological Seminary was on the theme: "Karl Barth in Dialogue: Encounters with Major Figures."

(KBBC), hosted on my blog, *Die Evangelischen Theologen* (DET).[3] Many of the authors that contributed to this volume are more or less active theology bloggers, and such blogs have performed an important role over the past years as a new generation of theological scholars has worked to find their voice in a digital age.[4] The present work is something of a symbolic apex of that endeavor, at least for one theo-blogging community. Consequently, I begin what follows with a short history of the KBBC before moving on to preview this volume's contents. I will conclude by briefly acknowledging debts of gratitude that have accrued during this project.

1. History of the Karl Barth Blog Conference

When I organized and hosted the first KBBC back in 2007, it was not the sort of thing that could profitably be published as a book. That undertaking was much more parochial, informal, and immature. Students at Princeton Theological Seminary (PTS) during my tenure there in the Master of Divinity program had the habit of establishing—as (over?)eager students will do on any campus—informal reading groups as a way to more deeply engage thinkers and texts outside the bounds of the formal classroom setting. That first KBBC was intended as an online, blog-y version of such a group. I simply solicited a number of my friends, including one whom to this day I know only from theo-blogging, to write up comments on various chapters of Barth's *Protestant Theology in the Nineteenth Century*. Although these posts are still indexed on DET, I have long lacked the courage to look back at them. Most of us were only masters-level students then, I believe, and my fear is that it shows. Nonetheless, we had a lot of fun putting it together and learned a bit along the way to boot. Many thanks to David W. Congdon, Daryl Ellis, Andrew R. Guffey, Jason T. Ingalls, Benjamin Myers (who was kind enough to offer some concluding remarks), Michael Pailthorpe, Chris TerryNelson, and Shane Wilkins for being there at the beginning.

It became clear to me rather quickly after the first KBBC that I should organize a second installment. At the most basic level, it had been enjoyable and informative the first time around, so why not do it again? At a deeper level, I was interested to discover whether the KBBC could develop into a more communal activity in the theo-blogging world. The 2008 KBBC

---

3. URL: http://derevth.blogspot.com. The name of the blog at the time of the 2010 conference was *Der Evangelische Theologe*. It has now taken on a more decidedly collaborative character.

4. My co-editor for this volume and I have reflected elsewhere on the significance of theology blogging. See Congdon and McMaken, "Theo-Blogging."

consequently featured a number of repeat participants and PTS folks, but also a strong cadre of folks from elsewhere in the theo-blogosphere. A further development was that although this KBBC also took a primary text as its guide, Jüngel's *God's Being Is in Becoming*, the various contributions now bore their own titles and did not slavishly labor to discuss the text on a chapter-by-chapter basis. In other words, they began to look like real academic conference papers even if not at that level in terms of quality—although I have heard conference presentations that were worse than some of 2008's KBBC contributions. For taking a part in this important stage, my thanks go to Sergi Avilés, Matthew J. Aragon Bruce, Congdon, Halden Doerge, Ingalls, Jon Mackenzie, Adam McInturf, TerryNelson, and Wilkins.

The KBBC took on something like a life of its own during that second, 2008 installment. Traffic surged and commenting exploded. Even though traffic and commenting numbers continued to surpass previous KBBC marks through the 2010 installment, the latter growth was incremental while the jump from 2007 to 2008 was of an entirely different order. It was immediately evident that there was a sizeable (at least in terms of theo-blogging metrics) and engaged audience for this sort of thing. Further, and led by the 2008 contributors, this audience showed itself to be interested in aspects of Barth's thought related to the possibility of natural knowledge of God or, more generally, natural theology. The 2009 KBBC thus took as its theme the intersection of Barth's thought and the first chapter of Paul's epistle to the Romans. Once more the contributors diversified, with a combination of new writers and old stalwarts who justly deserve my thanks: Lynn Cohick, Congdon, Kevin Davis, Doerge, John L. Drury, Nathan Hitchcock, Ingalls, Shannon Nicole Smythe, and Wilkins, the last of whom especially deserves credit for the commenting burden he shouldered as the principle dissenting voice amidst a sea of "Barthians."

Traffic and commenting continued to surge, but the work that went into organizing the KBBC was becoming a bit onerous for me. I was sure of two things: first, I had not yet exhausted the KBBC's potential; and second, that I desperately needed a break from the organizational burden. Thus it was that—before the 2009 KBBC ended—I enlisted my good friend and colleague, David Congdon, to help me organize the next installment. We decided to see how far we could take the 2010 KBBC. As I mentioned previously, the present text is the result. This volume is not identical to the 2010 KBBC, however. On the one hand, the blog event contained more contributions than we were able to accommodate in published form, so I encourage you to visit DET and pursue them. My deepest thanks go out to those who participated in the blog event but are not represented in this volume:

- Andrew Esqueda writing on Barth and Herman Bavinck, with a response by Joel Esala.
- Derek Maris writing on Barth and Paul Tillich, with a response by Tripp Fuller.
- Michael Jimenez writing on Barth and Alain Badiou, with a response by Geoffrey Holsclaw.
- Adam Kotsko writing in response to Paul Dafydd Jones on Barth and John Milbank and Slavoj Žižek.

Of course, the blog version also contains scores of comments on the various contributions. On the other hand, the contributions that did find their way to this volume have been revised and expanded to allow the authors greater opportunity to make their cases and respond to cases made. In addition, Drury's contribution on Barth and John Wesley—with a response by Christian T. Collins Winn—is new to the volume, as is the afterword by Congdon and the appendix by David Guretzki.

2. An Overview of Karl Barth in Conversation

Far be it from me to spoil the fun and prematurely divulge the arguments, assertions, and ripostes that await in the following chapters. But I do want to briefly exercise my editorial right to comment upon the volume's contents. Those contents are divided into three categories—Past Conversations, Present Conversations, and Expanding Conversations. Each of these categories contains four essays on different figures and/or themes, and each essay is followed by a shorter response.

To begin, the Past Conversations category sets Barth in conversation with important thinkers who have also passed from the scene. Drury leads-off by putting Barth into conversation with John Wesley. While recognizing that these two thinkers diverge significantly, Drury focuses on their respective interpretations of Matthew 5:48 to advance the claim that Barth and Wesley share a basic commitment to challenging Christianity's cultural captivity. Collins Winn responds to Drury by suggesting a shift from the language of overcoming Christianity's cultural captivity to that of Christianity's revolutionary character. Drury uses, and Collins Winn quotes from Drury, the language of "perpetual revolution" and this undoubtedly allusive reference to Marx's "permanent revolution" is instructive. Bruce next writes on the conversation between Barth and Friedrich Schleiermacher on the nature of theology and its relation to science. Although he spends most of his time on Schleiermacher, Bruce exposits both thinkers and concludes with four theses on their similarities and dissimilarities. For instance, he argues in his third thesis that Barth was mistaken in his understanding of Schleiermacher on theology's scientific character. Matthias Gockel provides three points of response that serve to bring Barth and Schleiermacher even more closely together. In chapter three, Matthew Puffer delves into the conversation between Barth and Dietrich Bonhoeffer. While much ink has been spilled on how Barth influenced Bonhoeffer, very little has been dedicated to discerning how Bonhoeffer influenced Barth. Puffer takes up this task with reference especially but not exclusively to Barth's doctrines of creation and reconciliation. Andy Rowell's response begins by reflecting on the methodological difficulties of Puffer's endeavor before concluding with a reflection on how the political situation of the 1930s and 1940s complicated relations between the two theologians. Finally for these Past Conversations, Myers takes up the conversation between Barth and Jacob Taubes. Taubes appropriated for his political thought aspects of Barth's early work on Paul's epistle to the Romans, and Myers works to highlight the apocalyptic tenor of both. Derek Alan Woodard-Lehman problematizes Myers's readings of both Barth and Taubes in his response, focusing especially on what Barth means when he talks about "not-doing" (*Nicht-Handeln*).

Present Conversations is the next category, and it sets Barth in conversation with significant theologians who are still with us. Peter Kline begins this category with a long essay on the conversation between Barth and Robert Jenson concerning God's hiddenness and the doxological character of theological knowledge. He aims at a reading of Barth's theological position that prioritizes concrete ethical enactment here and now of the love that God revealed in Jesus Christ at the expense of conceptual knowledge of God. William T. Barnett's response analyzes how such conceptual knowledge of God is in fact necessary for the ethical task. Or to crystallize matters in the terms that loosely structure Barnett's response, *pathos* is insufficient unless joined to both *ethos* and *telos*. Doerge addresses the conversation between Barth and Stanley Hauerwas, and highlights the fundamentally antithetical character of their respective ecclesiological visions. Ry O. Sigglekow's response builds on Doerge's analysis by addressing how Barth and Hauerwas think about sanctification and especially the church's proper visibility. The conversation between Barth and Kathryn Tanner on the subject of theological economics occupies J. Scott Jackson in his essay. He shows that Tanner's concrete economic proposals are continuous with Barth's own more suggestive comments while also noting that Tanner's thought might benefit from deeper engagement with Barth's reflection on the "lordless powers." Congdon responds by highlighting this theme and offering a rather creative sketch of the church as a "prophetic diaconate." He also provocatively but rightly singles out the Occupy Wall Street movement as a "parabolic" witness to the socio-economic demands of the gospel. Concluding this Present Conversations category is Keith Starkenburg's contribution to the conversation between Barth and David Bentley Hart. Starkenburg argues that Barth accomplishes under the aegis of "glory" what Hart accomplishes under that of "beauty." Han-luen Kantzer Komline's response raises questions about this sort of comparative methodology.

Expanding Conversations is the third and final category, and its pairings of essays and responses engage Barth in conversations somewhat off the beaten Barth-studies path. At the very least, these are not typical theological conversations. Jones begins this section by putting Barth in conversation with Slavoj Žižek and John Milbank, specifically with reference to their book, *The Monstrosity of Christ*. He suggests that the christologies on offer from Žižek and Milbank are not monstrous enough, on Barthian grounds, since they do not take seriously enough the deep horror of sin. Sigurd Baark provides a penetratingly critical response to Jones, emphasizing the importance of attuning oneself to the dialectical character of these thinkers' work. Rather than setting Barth in conversation with a figure, Smythe next puts him into conversation with the thought-world of Pauline apocalyptic. She argues that while Barth's earlier work is rightly characterized as consistent with Paul's cosmic apocalypticism, his later work is best described as characterized by forensic apocalypticism. Guffey's response, while appreciative, calls for the discussion of Barth's apocalypticism to be grounded more carefully in the literature of Second Temple and New Testament studies. Blair D. Bertrand furthers Barth's appropriation by the practical theological field by placing him in conversation with developmental psychologist Robert Kegan. He endeavors to show that Barth and Kegan's work is complimentary by focusing on a case study involving a young man's dismissal as a counselor at a Christian camp. The reader might be forgiven for thinking that Katherine M. Douglass's response represents Bertrand's essay as more critical of Barth than it is. She argues that Barth's theological anthropology excludes from full personhood those who are not capable of typical adult relationships, especially if this is a permanent disability. For my own part, I wonder how Douglass's criticism might change in light of Barth's soteriological universality and vocational particularity. Furthermore, it is clear that Barth does not really have such a high standard; e.g., he is perfectly willing to countenance the baptism of children ten years of age, provided those children "would like to be baptized ... [and] belong to the [Christian] community."[5] Finally, Jon Coutts imagines eavesdropping on a late night

---

5. Barth, *Gespräche 1963*, 90.

telephone conversation between Barth and the Coen brothers about their work, especially their film adaptation of Cormac McCarthy's *No Country for Old Men*. This essay circles around the nature of sin and evil, and Brad East's response furthers that reflection.

This volume offers two concluding pieces that stand apart from the architecture that I have now briefly sketched. Congdon's afterword comments on all that came before by reflecting on the task of conversing with Barth. He begins by noting important conversations that are unfortunately absent from or underrepresented in this volume—of which there are many—before moving on to point out a number of barriers to fruitful engagement with Barth in the contemporary theological climate. Congdon concludes by elaborating some basic principles and insights to guide fruitful conversation with the Swiss theologian. Finally, the volume concludes with an appendix by Guretzki entitled "On Conversing with Barth." This piece is a primer of sorts for those who are interested in engaging with Barth, but who feel overwhelmed at the thought. Guretzki spends considerable time introducing Barth's work, especially the *Church Dogmatics*, providing a number of helpful tips on what we might call the mechanics of reading such an expansive work. He also supplies three metaphors that help to give a picture of Barth's work as a whole—Barth as a theological architect, a theological composer, and as a fractal theologian—before concluding with a brief annotated bibliography of secondary sources on Barth. I strongly encourage any readers who are not independently knowledgeable of Barth's theology to read this appendix before moving on to the conversations that populate this volume.

3. Acknowledgements

It remains for me to repay some debts of gratitude. To begin, many thanks once again to all those who wrote for the KBBC over the years, and especially those who contributed to the 2010 iteration whose offerings we could not include in these pages. Thanks to all those who read the KBBC over the years, and especially to those who joined the conversation by posting comments. The burden of publishing this volume was made considerably lighter by the many people who donated freely and graciously from their monetary resources to help cover the typesetting costs, for which I am deeply thankful. Nathaniel Maddox performed some very helpful library legwork. Bertrand and a blessed sister from his congregation, who wishes to remain unnamed but who nonetheless deserves my deepest thanks, labored over the bibliography. Paige Davis, teaching assistant to the Lindenwood University religion department, was instrumental in compiling the index.

Of course, this volume would not have come together if it was not for Wipf & Stock's willingness to take a chance on making this jump from a blog conference to traditional publishing. Our editors—Christian Amondson, J. David Belcher, and Robin Parry—have exercised great patience as we worked to get this volume to print amidst a great number of personal and professional life changes. We are most thankful for their support, and that of the publisher as a whole. And finally, just to remind folks that the editors of this volume are mainline Protestants, all biblical quotations are taken from the NRSV unless otherwise noted.

Abbreviations

Barth, Karl. *The Christian Life: Church Dogmatics IV, 4: Lecture Fragments.* Grand Rapids: Eerdmans, 1981. Abbreviated as *ChL*.

Barth, Karl. *Church Dogmatics.* Edinburgh: T. & T. Clark, 1956–1975. Abbreviated as *CD*.

Barth, Karl. *Die kirchliche Dogmatik.* Munich: Kaiser, 1932; Zürich: Theologischer Verlag Zürich, 1938–65. Abbreviated as *KD*.

McCormack, Bruce L. *Karl Barth's Critically Realistic Dialectical Theology: Its Genesis and Development, 1906–1936.* Oxford: Clarendon, 1995. Abbreviated as *CRDT*.

Revised translations are signified through the notation, "rev."

Section 1

Past Conversations

1

Promise and Command

Barth and Wesley on Matthew 5:48

—By John L. Drury

IN ADDITION TO THE standard-issue metallic ones provided by my University, I have a pair of nice wooden shelves in my office. These two shelves are set aside to house texts from the two most important sources for my theological work: John Wesley and Karl Barth. Although the traditions that flow from these figures have shaped me deeply, I must admit that they are an odd couple indeed. I am repeatedly asked by Wesleyans and Barthians alike how it all fits together. My initial and admittedly cheeky answer is to say, "Just look at how I practice theology; if you like what you see, then that's all the proof I need." But a more systematic answer ought to be expected from a systematic theologian. So, here's one small step toward making explicit the connections I perceive between these two great streams of theological reflection.

My central claim is that *John Wesley and Karl Barth, for all their genuine differences, share a common orienting concern: overcoming culturally-captive Christianity.* As such, they both participate—each in his own way, but with remarkable compatibility—in what I call the perpetual revolution for real Christianity. I will advance a series of four theses in order to substantiate this claim. To begin I offer a detailed exploration of Wesley and Barth's strikingly similar interpretations of Matthew 5:48, "Be ye perfect as your heavenly Father is perfect." The subsequent three theses try to make sense of this similarity, each of which identifies a deeper level of common concern between Barth and Wesley. In keeping with this "archaeological" pattern of thought, the latter theses are increasingly more exploratory in character.

But taken as a whole my argument opens up a fresh way of reading both theologians that highlights their common cause—a cause I regard as worthy of participation.

1.

My first thesis is that *Wesley and Barth both interpret Matthew 5:48 not only as a command but also and primarily as a promise.* Such remarkable similarity from two such divergent thinkers deserves sustained comparative analysis. Out of chronological deference, I begin with Wesley. In his entry on Matthew 5:48, Wesley says,

> *Therefore ye shall be perfect; as your Father who is in heaven is perfect*—So the original runs, referring to all that holiness which is described in the foregoing verses, which our Lord in the beginning of the chapter recommends as happiness, and in the close of it as perfection. And how wise and gracious is this, to sum up, and, as it were, seal all his commandments with a promise! Even the proper promise of the Gospel! That he will put those laws in our minds, and write them in our hearts! He well knew how ready our unbelief would be to cry out, this is impossible! And therefore stakes upon it all the power, truth, and faithfulness of him to whom all things are possible.[1]

At first, we should note what Wesley does *not* say about this verse. He does not say that Jesus is ratcheting up the demand of the law in order to evoke a sense of helplessness that leads to faith in him and his atoning work. Such an interpretation is common in both Lutheran and Reformed traditions. Wesley does not even consider this alternative, and setting it aside coheres with his collateral commitments. He shares in Pietism's immanent criticism of the Reformation: that in its correct insistence on justification by grace through faith, it explains away the ethical teachings and example of Jesus. Wesley's position is clear: Matthew 5:48 is *not* reducible to a law that kills in order to drive us to the cross.

On the other hand, Wesley also does not interpret this passage as a command *per se*. He sees it as a summative and sealing *promise* that the happiness and holiness described and commanded in the preceding verses are not out of reach. According to Wesley, Matthew 5:48 asserts the divine possibility promised to us that underlies the divine necessity commanded to us. He even identifies emphatically that this is "the proper promise of the

---

1. Wesley, *Explanatory Notes*, Matt 5:48, emphasis original.

gospel!"[2] A command followed on the basis of a promise believed—that is what it means to have the law written in our hearts.

Where does Wesley get this? Is not Matthew 5:48 quite obviously an imperative? First of all, Wesley corrects the AV's translation "be ye perfect," replacing it with the future tense "ye *shall* be perfect." "So the original runs," he asserts. Although this translation is contestable, it at least shows that Wesley regards this interpretive move as exegetically warranted.[3] But we need not hang too much on this grammatical observation, for Wesley does not directly deny the command character of this text. In fact, the coinherence of promise and command is a recurring theme in Wesley's interpretation of the Sermon on the Mount. As he says in his comment on Matthew 5:2: "Observe the benevolent condescension of our Lord. He seems, as it were, to lay aside his supreme authority as our legislator, that he may the better act the part of: our friend and Saviour. Instead of using the lofty style, in positive commands, he, in a more gentle and engaging way, insinuates his will and our duty, by pronouncing those happy who comply with it."[4]

So pitting promise and command against each other will get us nowhere with Wesley. The point is that the call to be perfect is not *only* a command, but *also* and *primarily* a promise. This fits with the general teleological pattern of Wesley's thought.[5] As can be seen in his comment on Matthew 5:48, Wesley treats happiness, holiness, and perfection as nearly interchangeable terms. This interchangeability only works because each is conceptualized teleologically, i.e., in terms of its end or goal.[6] Happiness, holiness, perfection—this is what is promised us. This is where we are headed. And so happiness, holiness, and perfection are also commanded of us, as our way of living into our future with God.[7]

---

2. Ibid.; emphasis added.

3. Although Wesley is technically right that the verb is in the future tense, it is a case of what grammarians call the "imperatival future." It is used throughout Matthew 5 to quote OT commands, following the Septuagint rendering of the same.

4. Ibid., Matt 5:2.

5. The teleological character of Wesley's theology is set forth in Bence, "John Wesley's Teleological Hermeneutic."

6. Bence demonstrates that happiness and holiness are consistently paired in Wesley's thought: ibid., chap. 2.

7. Each of the six direct references to Matt 5:48 in Wesley's *Standard Sermons* either concur or are compatible with Wesley's interpretation of Matt 5:48 in his *Explanatory Notes*. The six references are in "The Marks of the New Birth" (#18), IV.1; "Upon Our Lord's Sermon on the Mount, Part IV" (#24), II.2; "Upon Our Lord's Sermon on the Mount, Part III" (#23), III.13 & IV; "Upon Our Lord's Sermon on the Mount, Part X" (#30), 15; "Catholic Spirit" (#39), Intro.1; "Circumcision of the Heart" (#17), I.1. This evidence corroborates the notion that Wesley's interpretation of Matt 5:48 in his *Notes*

With Wesley's interpretation of Matthew 5:48 before us, let us turn now to Karl Barth. In contrast to Wesley, Barth is firmly planted in the Reformed tradition. So we might expect an interpretation of Matthew 5:48 that follows his forebears. Surely he will say that this passage is an unreachable goal that drives us to confession and perhaps also inspires us to make small steps in this life.[8] But this reading is precisely what we do not find. Instead, he takes the command to be perfect as seriously as any radical reformer or puritanical pietist ever would. And he does not do so in passing, but rather gives it pride of place in his ethics. In fact, Matthew 5:48 is the very first biblical passage cited in his general ethics.[9] And he cites it to support the central thesis of his mature ethics, i.e., that the Law is the form of the Gospel: "The Gospel itself has the form and fashion of the Law. The one Word of God is both Gospel *and* Law . . . As the one Word of God which is the revelation and work of His grace reaches us, its aim is that our being and action should be confirmed to His. 'Be ye (literally, ye shall be) therefore perfect (literally, directed to your objective), even as (i.e., corresponding to it in creaturely-human fashion as) your Father which is in heaven is perfect (directed to His objective)' (Mt. 5:48)."[10]

With this theological claim and accompanying biblical citation, Barth begins his lengthy discussion of ethics as the Command of God in general, which in turn sets the terms for the forthcoming ethics of creation, reconciliation, etc. Three characteristics of this passage are immediately noteworthy.

(1) Barth agrees with Wesley that the verb should be translated as a future indicative rather than an imperative, i.e., not "be ye perfect" but "ye *shall* be perfect."[11] The command of the true, living God—the triune God who elects humanity in Jesus Christ—is first of all a *promise*. As such, God's command is primarily a permission and invitation, and only then a demand and requirement. In other words, the law is the form of the gospel.

---

is not anomalous, but rather fits within his broader theological perspective. Although cited by their internal numbering system, all quotations of Wesley's Sermons come from the Jackson edition of *Works of John Wesley*.

8. The Reformed "third use of the law" permits an alternative reading of Matt 5:48. In fact, Calvin himself offers a rather positive reading, cf. *Calvin's Commentaries*, 16:308. But the subsequent Reformed tradition commonly reached for this "Lutheran" interpretation of Matt 5:48.

9. Cf. CD 2.2, §§36–39.

10. CD 2.2:511–12.

11. Interestingly, Bultmann corrected Barth's exegesis in a letter pre-dating CD 2.2, saying that the future tense in Matt 5:48 should be taken as an imperative, cf. *Karl Barth–Rudolf Bultmann Letters*, 83. Clearly Barth did not heed his advice.

(2) Like Wesley, Barth takes seriously the "as" clause, which he takes to mean "corresponding to it in creaturely-human fashion."[12] *Correspondence* is a key term for Barth's ethics, and it is conceptually foreign to Wesley's thought form.[13] But both assert that there is a genuine connection between God's own ethical activity and ours.[14]

(3) Both Barth and Wesley offer a *teleological* interpretation of Matthew 5:48. Barth interprets "perfect" as "directed to your objective."[15] The teleological character of the command explains the aforementioned correspondence: you are "directed to your objective . . . as . . . your Father which is in heaven is . . . directed to His objective."[16] However, in this passage Barth only formally indicates the teleological character of the divine command. For the material content of this claim, we must turn to his next citation of Matthew 5:48. But already at this point we find significant convergence between Barth and Wesley in their interpretation of Matthew 5:48.

Barth cites Matthew 5:48 again fifty pages later, and once again we find it in a prominent place in the argument. At the beginning of a crucial sub-section entitled, "The Form of the Divine Claim" (§37.2), Barth inserts the following brief exegetical excursus: "The well-known passage at the close of Mt. 5 shows us almost word for word what we have to say about the teleological character of grace. In it the *teleotēs* of the heavenly Father (*the teleotēs* of grace) is revealed in the fact that He vouchsafes rain and sunshine to all men, and therefore loves even his enemies. This shows that the peculiarity of those who know and receive His grace, in contrast to what

---

12. *CD* 2.2:512.

13. For the centrality of correspondence to Barth's ethics, cf. Nimmo, *Being*, and Neder, *Participation*. In his review of Nimmo's book, published in the *International Journal of Systematic Theology*, Neder points out that "correspondence" need not be so sharply contrasted with "union" and "communion," for the concept of correspondence explains the content of these important but often ambiguous terms. But both Nimmo and Neder agree on the centrality of the correspondence in Barth.

14. Hunsinger analyzes the relation between the "dominical as" and the "evangelical as." The "dominical as" refers to the Synoptic golden rule, while the "evangelical as" refers to the primarily Pauline injunction to forgive as Christ forgave. To these should be added the "teleological as" of Matt 5:48, as it does not seem to fit either category precisely. It is a sort of hybrid—a "dominical" form of the "evangelical as." On account of its prominent placement in *CD* 2.2, Barth seems to regard Matt 5:48 as a fitting text to support the transition from dogmatics to ethics. See Hunsinger, "After Luther."

15. Barth's reference to the common "object" of divine and human action sounds very similar to Calvin's interpretation of Matt 5:48, in *Calvin's Commentaries*, 16:308. So Barth is not completely original in this move. As we shall see, his originality comes through his combination of this move with a series of other more radical moves.

16. *CD* 2.2:512.

the publicans do, must and will consist (*esesthe*) in the fact that they, too, love their enemies, and are therefore *teleioi* like their Father in heaven."[17]

The teleological character of grace! What does Barth mean by this pregnant phrase? At a minimum, it means two things: (1) that God's eternal election of grace fulfilled in Jesus Christ includes by way of anticipation a corresponding human action in which we, in our own way and in our proper relationship to him, participate in God's gracious self-revelation; and (2) that God's command is not an alternative to God's word of grace, but an outworking of that very grace. God's command to us is simply the "go and do likewise" implied within the "he has made all things new."

Barth expands on this idea a few pages later in the same sub-section:

> All the New Testament passages so far adduced speak of definite acts and attitudes in which this imitation of God and Christ must take shape. They are all in line with Mt. 5:48. Our aim must correspond to the distinctive aim of our Father in heaven, who meets both the good and the evil with the same beneficence. It must be a readiness to forgive one another. It must be persistent in kindness even towards persecutors of the faith. It must be a humility in which we do not look at our own things, but at the things of others. It must be a love which is directed even—and especially—to our enemies.[18]

The teleological character of grace means that enemy love is the substance of Christian ethics. Although ontologically distinct, God and humans share a single *telos*: loving the world. As God loves his enemies, so we also love ours.[19]

So, on numerous counts, Barth interprets Matthew 5:48 in a way remarkably similar to Wesley. They use different concepts and place the accent differently, but they both interpret Matthew 5:48 teleologically, i.e., not only as a command, but also and primarily as a promise. But is this just a lucky coincidence? Could it be that I have simply stumbled onto a mere surface commonality? Perhaps Wesley and Barth are like two lines heading

---

17. *CD* 2.2:567.

18. *CD* 2.2:578.

19. Outside of the general ethics (§§36–39), there are only eight direct citations of Matt 5:48 in Barth's *Church Dogmatics*: §18, p. 396; §56, p. 649; §59, p. 190; §64, p. 167; §66, p. 551; §68, p. 805; §74, p. 17. In nearly every case, Barth interprets Matt 5:48 as a promissory command in a manner consistent with *CD* 2.2. In no case does Barth adopt an opposing interpretation. Furthermore, the same interpretation of Matt 5:48 can be found in Barth's famous essay "Gospel and Law" in Barth, *Community*, 78. All this evidence demonstrates that Barth's interpretation of Matt 5:48 in *CD* 2.2 is not uncharacteristic.

in opposite directions that just happen to intersect at this one point. If so, then this comparative analysis is of limited constructive value. We must move deeper in order to ascertain whether their similarity at this point is indicative of a shared concern. The comparison must move from the interpretation of Matthew 5:48 to the assumptions that make this interpretation possible.

2.

I begin the more exploratory portion of this essay by widening the scope of comparison from Matthew 5:48 to the whole of the Sermon on the Mount. What status does each figure assign to the Sermon on the Mount? What function does it perform? Where does it fit within their respective theological projects? In brief, my thesis is that *both Wesley and Barth assimilate the "radical" reformation rediscovery of the Sermon on the Mount within a "magisterial" reformation framework*. Since Barth's work more readily lends itself to this sort of "architectonic" analysis, I will begin with him this time.

The material analyzed above appears within Barth's general ethics (§36–39). The Sermon on the Mount plays a prominent role at two key points in the general ethics: as an expression of the *content* of the divine *claim* (§37.2) and of the *definiteness* of the divine *decision* (§38.2). In both cases, the Sermon on the Mount is simultaneously relativized and lifted up. It is relativized insofar as Barth refuses to regard it as a collection of absolute principles. But it is lifted up insofar as Barth treats it as a central locus for discerning the nature of the divine command as a living encounter between God and humanity.

In §37.2, Barth asserts that the singular content of the divine claim is the summons to accept God's action in Christ as right.[20] In the covenant fulfilled in Jesus Christ, God has asserted his right over against us and made us right with him. This act of grace includes within it a claim on our lives: that we would accept this right and live in accordance with it. "The grace of God . . . determines man to existence in this covenant. It determines him to be the partner of God. It therefore determines his action to correspondence, conformity, uniformity with God's action."[21] Among various other ethical passages from the New Testament, Barth cites the movement from divine action to corresponding human action in the Sermon on the Mount to substantiate this argument. Structurally, Barth consistently begins with God's

---

20. CD 2.2:575: "The concern in the divine claim is that man's action should become and be always that of those who accept God's action as right."

21. CD 2.2:575.

action for us in Jesus Christ, then—and only then—he follows with a clear affirmation of the ethical imperative it entails. Here is where the Sermon on the Mount fits within Barth's train of thought.

In §38.2, Barth asserts that the divine command is a living, sovereign decision that is always *definite* and *concrete*. The biblical witness does not contain general principles for which we find particular applications. No! The Bible is the story of God's particular dealings with particular people, and every command recorded in it is a definite one directed to a particular person or group. Nevertheless, "this concrete commanding to be found in the Bible must be understood as a divine command relevant to ourselves who are not directly addressed by it."[22] Barth unfolds this dialectic by means of a detailed exegesis of the Ten Commandments (pp. 683–88) and the Sermon on the Mount (pp. 688–700). In both passages, we find a record of concrete commands that bears witness indirectly to God's living decision regarding the concreteness of our lives.

The significance of this move is that Barth does not simply place divine action in the past, to which corresponds a present, human action. Divine action perpetually precedes human action, so that we hear the voice of Jesus anew in the words of the Sermon on the Mount. With this move, Barth once again relativizes the Sermon on the Mount while simultaneously lifting it up as central to the Christian life. And he does so *structurally*, weaving it into the very fabric of his thought. Consequently, it cannot be dismissed as merely incidental.

Barth's dialectical incorporation of the Sermon on the Mount into the structure of his theological ethics is a classic case of the unrelenting assimilative power of his thought.[23] Barth is a truly "catholic" thinker inasmuch as his theology is both thoroughly committed to its central claims and able to include a vast array of alien claims. The "radical" reformers (in)famously asserted the centrality of the Sermon on the Mount over against the Paulinism of the "magisterial" reformers. Barth's christocentrism radicalizes the Reformation insistence on *solus Christus*. So, at first glance, this should make it even harder for him to appreciate the positive function of the Sermon on the Mount than his forebears. And yet he finds a way to affirm the Sermon on the Mount, and to do so more clearly and resoundingly than his forbears. His view is necessarily dialectical, and certainly would not placate the protestations of the radical reformation. But on his own terms he has

---

22. *CD* 2.2:627.

23. Assimilative power is the third of Newman's seven notes of a true development of doctrine in, *Essay*, 183–89 and 355–82. For more recent literature on assimilative power, cf. Christian, *Doctrines*, 145–218; and Marshall, "Absorbing the World," 69–102.

found a way to systematically incorporate the positive significance of the Sermon on the Mount.

When we turn to John Wesley, we find someone who ends up with a very similar position despite his very different conceptual apparatus and habit of thought. It is well known that Wesley incorporated the insights of both the "magisterial" and "radical" wings of the Reformation. This he shares with the wider Puritan and Pietist movements that form his direct theological antecedents. What is seldom recognized is the extent to which this incorporation is expressed structurally in his *Sermons*. Like Barth, he systematically assimilates the "radical" reformation rediscovery of the Sermon on the Mount within a "magisterial" reformation framework.

To make such structural claims with regard to Wesley meets with immediate resistance, for it is a deeply ingrained habit both within and without the Wesleyan tradition to say that John Wesley was not a systematic theologian. For Wesleyans, this is usually intended as a compliment. Now such an assertion is certainly true if one takes a modern, philosophically overdetermined system of deduced propositions as definitive of the practice of systematic theology. But such a definition would also result in Barth not being a systematic theologian, along with nearly every pre-modern theologian—at which point one would be right to ask for a more flexible definition. A more pliable definition of systematic theology would include organized presentations of Christian doctrine that aim to be relatively comprehensive and coherent, e.g., Calvin's *Institutes*. But even so loosely defined, many Wesleyans would still regard Wesley as unsystematic.

I consider the assertion of an unsystematic Wesley to be not only misleading, but misguided. In his four-volume *Sermons on Several Occasions*, Wesley grouped sermons together by theme and then ordered them in a loose but logical pattern. It does not follow a typical loci structure, and its organizing principle is never made explicit. But it follows a pattern nonetheless: that of Wesley's *ordo salutis*. And what is striking for our study is where he places his thirteen discourses on the Sermon on the Mount. The Sermon on the Mount is central to his account of the Christian life, but it comes into play *after* a clear statement of justification by faith and assurance by the Spirit.[24]

Wesley begins with a programmatic statement on salvation by faith (#1), which sets the tone for the whole. He then describes how this salvation unfolds: awakening (#2–3), justification (#4–7), assurance (#8–12), ongoing

---

24. Donald W. Dayton was the first one to highlight for me the structural patterns in Wesley's *Sermons*. The following analysis is inspired by many conversations with Don, who has been a mentor to me and a small cadre of "holiness Barthians." In fact, this entire essay is unthinkable without his pioneering work.

repentance (#13–15), and the means and marks of regeneration (#16–19). Over the course of these sermons, Wesley's movement of thought can be detected: *from* the utter graciousness of God in justification *to* God's gracious empowerment for a new life of obedience. Once this turn has been completed, Wesley proceeds to describe the concrete content of this new life of obedience by means of thirteen discourses on the Sermon on the Mount (#21–33). At the head of these discourses he places a sermon entitled "The Lord Our Righteousness" (#20), which recapitulates the entire movement from Christ's righteousness to ours described in the preceding sermons. Wesley's discourses are then immediately followed by a discussion of the Law's establishment by faith (#34–36), unity with other believers (#37–39), and Christian perfection (#40–43), which round out his *ordo salutis* before turning to over a hundred other sermons on topics varying from divine attributes to the proper use of money.[25]

The significance of this structural analysis is that Wesley, not unlike Barth, places the Sermon on the Mount at the center of his concrete description of the Christian life while bracketing it within a framework determined by the doctrine of justification by faith. I do not mean to suggest that Wesley and Barth have identical doctrines of justification. In fact, they diverge sharply at that very point at the level of specific dogmatic claims—Wesley having reigned in the reformation doctrine of alien righteousness while Barth radicalizes it. But there is a *structural* compatibility between them, insofar as they both enclose the "radical" reformation rediscovery of the Sermon on the Mount within a "magisterial" reformation framework. In other words, both Barth and Wesley take the ethical teaching of Jesus seriously without undermining justification by grace through faith.[26]

3.

I have been arguing that the exegetical similarity between Wesley and Barth on Matthew 5:48 is not a mere coincidence, but an indicator of a deeper level of shared concern. The first layer of this shared concern is expressed in their structural compatibility with regard to the Sermon on the Mount.

---

25. I do not think it is an accident that Wesley places his sermons pertaining directly to the doctrine of God in the back half of his collection. This does not entail that the doctrine of God does not matter to him. Rather, it is consequence of his decision to pattern his sermons around the way of salvation. Teaching on the divine being is logically basic, but in the narrative of Christian conversion and growth its necessity is not felt until further down the road.

26. Such a reading of Wesley overlaps significantly with Collins's interpretation in *Theology*, 1–18, 155–236, 279–312.

But this in turn is itself an indicator of an even deeper level of convergence concerning the law. *Wesley and Barth both assess the law in primarily positive terms.*

Here again we see that Wesley and Barth deploy different conceptual tools and make divergent dogmatic claims. Their positions are certainly not identical, and genuine tension remains. What intrigues me is that they continue to pursue a common cause despite this deep disjunction. They share the instinct that a positive assessment of God's law is precisely what the church needs to hear. Their vastly different accents and inflections should not distract us from this shared instinct.

It is uncontroversial to assert that John Wesley has a positive assessment of the law. What is interesting is *how* he expresses this assessment. In his fifth discourse on the Sermon on the Mount (on Matt 5:17–20), Wesley says, "every command in holy writ is only a covered promise."[27] This statement combines two claims: (1) the primacy of promise over command and (2) the coinherence between promise and command.[28] As we saw, both claims are present in Wesley's interpretation of Matthew 5:48. But in this sermon they are lifted up as a hermeneutical rule for all of Scripture. The primacy of promise and its coinherence with command cannot be dismissed as an accidental property of the literary style of the Sermon on the Mount. The pattern is characteristic of all divine speaking.

These two claims conspire to support a positive view of the law.[29] The law has this positive function not independently of the gospel, but as integral to the gospel. God's commands are simply covert promises. All the good that God expects from us he commits himself to enact. "Does he command us then to 'pray without ceasing?' to 'rejoice evermore?' to 'be holy as

---

27. Wesley, "On Our Lord's Sermon on the Mount, Discourse V," II.3.

28. The movement of thought in the preceding paragraphs corroborates my strong interpretation of this phrase. He makes a series of three assertions, each of which is stronger than the one before it. First, he asserts the *non-contradiction* of law and gospel: "that there is no contrariety at all between the law and the gospel" (ibid., II.2). Second, he asserts their *interconnection*: "There is, therefore, the closest connexion [sic] that can be conceived, between the law and the gospel" (II.3). Third and finally, he introduces his claim "that every command in holy writ is only a covered promise" with the clause, "We may yet further observe," indicating that this is the highest level of positive relation between law and gospel.

29. Wesley explicitly correlates promise with gospel and command with law: "Yes, the very same words, considered in different respects, are parts both of the law and of the gospel: If they are considered as commandments, they are parts of the law; if as promises, of the gospel" (ibid., II.2).

He is holy?' It is enough: He will work in us this very thing: It shall be unto us according to His word."[30]

At this point, Wesley is within shouting distance of Barth's famous inversion of law and gospel.[31] But the different paths they take are crucial to trace. Wesley operates with a Platonic conception of the moral law.[32] For Wesley, gospel and law are so closely intertwined because they are understood as expressions of the timeless divine attributes of truth and goodness. This can be seen in the paragraphs leading up to the famous "covered promises" line. He begins by introducing the classic distinction between the ceremonial law and the moral law. The moral law "stands on an entirely different foundation from the ceremonial or ritual law." It is "from the beginning of the world" and "must remain in force upon all mankind, and in all ages; as not depending either on time or place, or any other circumstances liable to change, but on the nature of God, and the nature of man, and their unchangeable relation to each other."[33] According to Wesley, the moral law is a permanent feature of divine-human relations. As such, it is to be assessed positively, as an expression of God's eternal good will, not a response to human evil.[34]

---

30. Ibid., II.3.

31. Barth's first and most well-known reversal of the Lutheran law-gospel pattern can be found in "Gospel and Law," in Barth, *Community*, 70–100. Barth wrote this essay in the Fall of 1935 as a farewell address during the height of the German church struggle. Therefore, the connection between Barth's gospel-law thesis and his rejection of natural theology should come as no surprise. Although "Gospel and Law" predates the final steps in Barth's development of a revised doctrine of election, it was written less than a year before the 1936 Calvin Congress, after which he began rethinking his doctrine of election. Furthermore, Barth's discussion of gospel and law in §36, which immediately follows Barth's fully revised doctrine of election, is nearly identical in substance to the argument of "Gospel and Law." So his understanding of gospel and law is also positively related to his doctrine of election.

32. Cf. Collins, "John Wesley's Platonic Conception." Wesleyan constructive theology has yet to catch up to the implications of this magisterial contextualization of Wesley's thought.

33. Wesley, "Sermon on the Mount V," I.2. He goes on to manifest his eighteenth-century Enlightenment context by asserting that Jesus "has not introduced a new religion into the world, but the same which was from the beginning;—a religion, the substance of which is, without question, as old as the creation" (I.4). Tindal's *Christianity as Old as the Creation* was published in 1730.

34. Wesley also deploys numerous Aristotelian tropes alongside these Platonic ones: cf. Long, *John Wesley's Moral Theology*. Although I am inclined to follow Collins in accenting the generally Platonic character of Wesley's concept of law, these lines of interpretation are ultimately not incompatible. The interweaving of Plato and Aristotle is itself a recurring feature of Wesley's antecedent intellectual tradition. Wesley's contrast with Barth on this point consists precisely in the extent to which he takes for granted what Barth sets his sights against.

Barth would fully agree with the last sentence of that paragraph. But he completely rejects the argument that leads up to it. Barth's thesis that the law is the form of the gospel inhabits a fundamentally different field of discourse. His tropes are far more Kantian and Hegelian than Platonic and Aristotelian.[35] And Barth's primarily positive assessment of the law is rooted in his supralapsarian Christology, rather than an eternal moral law that at best coincides with a *logos asarkos*.[36] For Barth, the gospel is also law because God has only one word to say to us from and to all eternity: Jesus Christ. Therefore, God's word in its mode as law can be no other than the concrete form which grace takes as it encounters us.

But this deep conceptual divergence between Wesley and Barth makes their similarities on this point all the more striking. "Every command is only a covered promise" and "the law is the form of the gospel" are eerily resonant. As hermeneutical rules, they are compatible. And in them comes to expression a shared instinct: that the law must be both subordinate to the gospel and positively related to it. Both Wesley and Barth assert the primacy of promise over command and the coinherence between promise and command.

The resonance between Wesley and Barth on the law does not necessarily commend their respective proposals. They may have simply slid down two different slopes into one and the same pit. Surely the worst fears of Barth's Lutheran critics are confirmed by placing him in the company of the legalistic Mr. Wesley. Both have been sharply criticized for their high views of the law, even by some of their most sympathetic interpreters.[37] By asserting the coinherence of gospel and law, do they not turn Jesus into the purveyor of a new law and so undermine the gospel of grace? How is a gospel that takes the form of law genuinely *good* news?[38] Replying to this

---

35. This need not be substantiated given the last few decades of Barth scholarship. But it seems prudent to reference one work that thoroughly documents Barth's relationship to his German idealist heritage: Macken, *Autonomy Theme*.

36. Barth's reversal of the Lutheran law-gospel pattern is of a piece with his career-long assault on the false gods of natural theology. There is no God behind God. It does not matter whether this hidden God is terrifying (e.g., Luther) or true, good, and beautiful (e.g., Wesley)—it is still a second thing alongside Jesus Christ. The integration of Barth's gospel-law thesis into the very fabric of his most core commitments is masterfully set forth in Jüngel, *Karl Barth*, 105–26.

37. Deschner argues that Wesley's assertion of the law's eternity risks idolatry in *Wesley's Christology*, 102–8. Jenson argues that Barth's account of God-in-history leaves insufficient room for the paradoxical duality of God's word and work in *Alpha and Omega*, 151–71. Jenson develops his own constructive alternative in his *Systematic Theology*, 2:153–64.

38. This is only one side of the objection, for it can also be asked: "How is an eternal gospel and its correspondingly eternal law good *news*, i.e., something that actually

objection allows me to assert one last comparative thesis before concluding with some remarks on the significance of this inquiry.

4.

My final claim is *that the positive assessment of the law found in Wesley and Barth operates within their respective visions of God's economy of grace, which—though sharply divergent—are not fundamentally incompatible.* The circumspection evinced by the double negative and qualifying clause is intentional, for this is the most exploratory of my comparative theses. The evidence for such a global comparison is necessarily the least secure, and the connections at this point are the most tenuous. But our excavation of the ground beneath their similar exegesis of Matthew 5:48 cannot stop at their views of the law. It must proceed to the bedrock: their respective visions of God's economy of grace. Some measure of compatibility is required at this deepest of levels in order to sustain the claim that Wesley and Barth share a common orienting concern.

The objection raised above provides an apt point of entry. How is a gospel that takes the form of law genuinely good news? For Wesley, the coinherence of promise and command is good news because it operates within the context of his *sacramental theology*. For Barth, the coinherence of promise and command is good news because it operates within the context of his *doctrine of election*. After a very brief summary of each, I will explain why I believe these sharply divergent visions are not fundamentally incompatible.

Throughout his career Wesley fought against the tendency of his followers to neglect the manifold means of grace that God provides through the church. His two most famous sermons on the subject ("The Means of Grace" and "The Duty of Constant Communion") consist almost entirely of replies to objections against the necessity of attending to these means. Although he advances a vast array of arguments, most of them appeal to one of two claims: that Christ has *promised* to be present in these means and that Christ has *commanded* that we attend to them. The promise is more dominant in "The Means of Grace," while the command is more dominant in "The Duty of Constant Communion." But these two claims are ultimately united, for the core of Wesley's vision is that God has ordained

---

happens, takes place in a sequence of events?" This side of the objection is especially put to Barth, whose supralapsarian Christology invites it. Although Wesley thinks in more straightforwardly sequential terms, the same objection could be put to him as well. Responding to this objection would require analysis of their respective theologies of time. Perhaps said analysis would provide another case of compatible concern amidst conceptual divergence, but it would take us far beyond the purview of this study.

this particular economy of grace, promising to be present there and so also inviting us to meet him there. We are command to *wait*—wait on Christ to fulfill his promise. Our duty is "waiting in the way God has ordained, and expecting that he will meet me there, because he has promised so to do."[39]

Wesley's high view of the law, his appropriation of the Sermon on the Mount, and his interpretation of Matthew 5:48 do not appear in the least bit legalistic when placed within the context of his sacramental theology. Instead, we have a vision in which God's moral expectations of us are *internal* to the logic of his gracious presence with us. Our duty is not to do something alongside or independent of what God does. No! Our duty is to act in accordance with the fact that God has promised to be present in a particular way. Our duty is to be present where God has promised to be present, and to wait on him to fulfill his promise. This same pattern is at work in Wesley's interpretation of Matthew 5:48: just as the promise of presence underwrites the duty to commune, so the promise of perfection underwrites the command to pursue it. In all our dealings with God, Wesley calls on us to wait patiently—but expectantly and so actively—on God.

Once again we are a far cry from the conceptual universe of Karl Barth. Whereas Wesley relies heavily on the antecedent tradition of sacramental reflection, Barth reconstructs his doctrine of election from the ground up. Jüngel puts it deftly when he says, "Barth's own theology develops out of such basic questions, aimed at previously obvious presuppositions, making them not so obvious. A break with what is all too obvious through penetrating, basic questions is the motif which animates and frees Barth's thought."[40] Barth does not share Wesley's confidence that divine providence has preserved an institutional process of mediation that relates us to Christ. Barth thinks in more restricted terms of Jesus Christ as God's singular presence in the world. This christological concentration grounds his positive assessment of the law.

According to Barth, God only has one word to say to the world: Jesus Christ. The eternal will of God simply *is* the election of Jesus Christ.[41] The election of Jesus Christ is the act of God's self-giving.[42] God's command is not another word alongside this act of gracious self-giving but rather its mode of expression when it encounters us. Soon after citing Matthew 5:48,

---

39. Wesley, "The Means of Grace," IV.2. Wesley goes to great lengths earlier in this sermon to block any mechanization of the means (cf. II.3).

40. Jüngel, *Karl Barth*, 94.

41. Cf. CD 2.2, §33.2.

42. CD 2.2:161: "The eternal will of God in the election of Jesus Christ is His will to give Himself for the sake of man as created by Him and fallen from Him . . . The election of grace in the beginning of all things is God's self-giving in His eternal purpose."

Barth says, "What God wills of us is the same as He wills and has done for us. God wills Jesus." Because Jesus Christ is the one word of God, "Obedience to God always means that we become and are continually obedient to Jesus."[43] God's promise and God's command have one and the same content: Jesus Christ. God graciously elected to be present fully and truly in Jesus Christ and God graciously commands that we live a life that corresponds to Jesus Christ.

Although he deploys sharply divergent thought-forms, Barth's vision of God's economy of grace is not fundamentally incompatible with Wesley's. They both agree that God is an agent, and so fellowship with this God requires human agency. For both, fellowship with God is the *content* of the divine will for humanity. But for both this fellowship takes the *form* of moral action. The differences are deep. Barth conceives of the fellowship in terms of his christocentric doctrine of election, while Wesley defines it in terms of holiness and happiness. And Barth understands human agency in terms of witness, while Wesley thinks in terms of the mediation of grace through instituted means. But a similar pattern emerges amidst these genuine differences: God promises to be present in a particular way, and the very nature of this promise entails a command to act in correspondence with his presence. "You shall be perfect, as your heavenly father is perfect."

5.

The cumulative effect of the various levels of compatibility explored above is a sense that John Wesley and Karl Barth, for all their genuine difference, share a common orienting concern. They are both fueled by a desire to overcome culturally-captive Christianity. They identify the root cause of the problem differently and use different tools to solve it. But they are working on the same problem. We ought not overlook this joint project in our appropriate attention to dogmatic detail.

---

43. *CD* 2.2:568. Barth goes on to cite positively one of Wesley's contemporaries: "The concentration and intensity with which this was continually said by Nicolas von Zinzendorf was amply justified. He said it in opposition not only to a secularized orthodoxy, and not only to the Enlightenment, but also to the moral and mystical ambiguities of the Pietism of his time. In so doing, he reestablished not merely a Reformation but a New Testament insight. We may be astonished at baroque features in the way in which he said it. And we may argue that, entangled in certain Lutheran ideas, he did not say it universally enough. But we must give him credit that he was one of the few not only of his own time but of all times who have said it so definitely and loudly and impressively" (*CD* 2.2:568). Given Wesley's own complex relationship to Zinzendorf, he may provide a useful third party to the conversation between Wesley and Barth.

Culturally-captive Christianity manifests itself in its continual evasion of the "hard saying" of Matthew 5:48. The history of interpretation of this verse, along with the Sermon on the Mount as whole, is the story of a death from a thousand qualifications. But Wesley and Barth stand out as theologians who take this passage with utmost seriousness. Both treat Matthew 5:48 as a model instance of the commanding grace of God in Jesus Christ. This commanding grace disrupts a seamless relationship between Christianity and culture. As commanding *grace*, God's one word disrupts the social, political, and legal arrangements—both old and new—by which we try to sustain ourselves, for it promises something genuinely new that only God can bring about. As *commanding* grace, God's one word disrupts the divisions we try to put between creation and redemption, with which we attempt to delay the radical transformation God is already bringing about. Understanding the gospel as commanding grace is essential to the perpetual revolution for real Christianity against its cultural captivity.

Important differences remain between Wesley and Barth at the level of execution. Wesley frames the problem of cultural captivity primarily in terms of *antinomianism*. In his polemical writings, Wesley accuses nearly every one of his interlocutors of antinomianism—a fact that reveals Wesley's overall orienting concern to overcome nominal Christianity.[44] Barth, on the other hand, frames the problem primarily in terms of *natural theology*. The subtle intricacies of Barth's dogmatic corpus are at every point weapons in the fight against Christianity's inner pagan.[45] Undermining the identification of Christianity with Western culture is Barth's orienting concern.[46] But these different diagnoses of the problem should not obscure the shared orientation against culturally-captive Christianity underlying them.

Important differences in their respective contexts should also be noted. John Wesley fought his battle for real Christianity *within* the classical Christendom arrangement. He therefore takes for granted the metaphysical, political, and sacramental givens of Western culture, as can be seen in his Platonic conception of the moral law and his Anglican sacramental theology. He does not set his sights against these givens, but uses them in his fight for real Christianity. Barth, on the other hand, fought his battle for real Christianity *after* the collapse of Christendom. He therefore cannot take for granted its givens, but rather reconstructs his dogmatics from the ground up. Of course, he carries over much of the classical tradition. But he does

---

44. Cf. Park, "Theology."

45. Cf. Jenson, *God after God*.

46. This explains why the theology of Ernst Troeltsch was so disturbing to Barth, and also why Barth continues to be a resource after the global turn in academic theology.

not take it for granted, and at many points sees it as part of the problem.[47] Nevertheless, these differing contexts should not conceal the extent to which they were fighting the same battle. In fact, their contextual differences help to explain how such different ways of thinking could be used for one and the same purpose. For where the battle rages, there the soldier is tested.

Barth, Wesley, and Revolutionary Christianity

A Response to John L. Drury

—By Christian T. Collins Winn

JOHN DRURY HAS PERFORMED a much needed service by bringing together arguably two of the most influential Christian personalities of the modern age. John Wesley's work and witness sparked the Methodist revival in England in the eighteenth century, contributed to developments in North America especially in the nineteenth century, and his influence can still be felt globally in movements that directly and indirectly identify with his particular catholic vision and ecclesial organization. Karl Barth, the great twentieth-century theologian from Switzerland, made an indelible mark not only on academic theology but also on the life of churches around the globe. Indeed, I myself have not escaped the influence of these two seminal figures, having grown up in the United Methodist Church in North Carolina, and having written a dissertation on Karl Barth under one of the great Wesleyan interpreters of Barth, Donald W. Dayton.[48]

---

[47]. This way of contextualizing Wesley and Barth invites the participation of a third party: Søren Kierkegaard. Whereas Wesley fought for real Christianity within Christendom and Barth after it, Kierkegaard fought *against* it. As such, he is half-way between Wesley and Barth, both historically and theologically. Perhaps this way of putting the matter can help to reopen the question of Barth's relationship to Kierkegaard—a relationship that has been rightly deemphasized in recent Barth studies, for it was wrongly overemphasized a generation ago. The time is ripe to revisit this relationship. But that is a conversation for another time.

[48]. It would be ungrateful if at this point I also did not indicate my deep appreciation for and debt to Dayton's influence, not the least in how to think about the relationship between Barth and Wesley. In fact, the current response owes much to Dayton both in the general direction pursued and the particular evidence adduced.

Drury's essay embodies a larger conversation that has been going on for some time between Baptist, Pietist, and Wesleyan theologians and Barth.[49] One might also add Pentecostals to this mix as well.[50] Aside from the specific fruit of his analysis, Drury's essay demonstrates that bringing Barth into dialogue with "non-traditional" interlocutors can be very illuminating and productive for understanding dimensions of Barth's thought that are overlooked or missed by more "traditional" approaches. And Wesley—as well as Pietist, Baptist, and Pentecostal figures—would have to be considered "non-traditional" in relation to Barth, who is more often compared to Calvin, Luther, Schleiermacher, or some other great luminary from the Reformed Protestant world.

Rather than engaging the specific results of Drury's analysis, I would like to further his basic thesis: "that John Wesley and Karl Barth, for all their genuine differences, share a common orienting concern: overcoming culturally-captive Christianity." Like soundings, what is offered below should be taken as an unsystematic attempt to note additional areas of commonality which, if given the attention and systematic analysis they are due, would ultimately vindicate Drury's thesis.[51] Following on his analysis of Wesley and Barth's theological ethics, I propose a supplemental change to Drury's thesis, which when factored in, would read as follows: "that John Wesley and Karl Barth, for all their genuine difference, share a common orienting concern: *the recovery of revolutionary Christianity.*" Drury is already pointing in this direction when he notes that both "participate . . . in what I call the perpetual revolution for real Christianity." My argument is that this second, interpretive statement deserves to be brought into the thesis, in order to make that which is implicit explicit and to further radicalize Drury's analysis and claims. My argument is formulated as follows: both Wesley and Barth, in their respective ways, emphasize the radical-revolutionary nature of the Christian life through their emphasis on Jesus'—and therefore the Christian community's—identification with the poor and outcast. This identification with those on the underside, so to speak, represents a revolutionary posture toward the world "as it is."

On first glance, my suggestion that John Wesley, the life-long Tory, would have anything in common with Karl Barth, the "red pastor" from

---

49. Along with Dayton, one could mention here the work of Kimlyn Bender and Kurt Anders Richardson, among others.

50. I am thinking here especially of the work of Frank Macchia and Peter Althouse.

51. Other areas of conversation could and should also be explored, such as the relationship of Wesley and Barth to Zinzendorf and Pietism, or Barth and Wesley's conceptions of freedom, or Barth and Wesley's relationship to the Enlightenment. All of these, and not a few others, deserve attention.

Safenwil, on the topic of the revolutionary nature of Christianity would seem absurd. This perception, however, rests on a misunderstanding as to what we, and Barth, mean by "revolution."[52] To be clear, and to the relief of Wesley, "revolution," as theologically defined by Barth, does not mean the simple overthrow of the established order by human means so that another might be set up. Rather, first and foremost, it refers to the history of God embodied in Jesus Christ, in whose life-act the world "as it is" was judged and found wanting, and simultaneously redeemed and placed on a different footing. As Colossians so eloquently states, the powers and authorities—those forces, divisions, and categories that divide and destroy human life—have been disarmed, overthrown, and made a spectacle through the power of the cross (see Col 2:15). Or as Barth would say: "that Revolution which is the impossible possibility . . . [the] forgiveness of sins and the resurrection of the dead . . . [or] Jesus Christ—He that hath *overcome*—who is the true answer to the injury wrought by the existing order as such."[53] The real revolution, therefore, is the overthrow of the world "as it is" in the crucifixion and resurrection of Jesus Christ, which means that all other revolutionary movements and events are at best mere shadows, or at worst, usurpers destined only to destroy and not to make alive.[54] This "revolutionary root" is the revolutionary act of God in Christ, which makes "real Christianity" revolutionary.

The crucifixion and resurrection of Jesus is *the* revolution. However, the life-history of Jesus also evinces a corresponding radicalism. In his discussion of Jesus as "The Royal Man," Barth notes four concrete aspects of this correspondence.[55] First, Jesus is the One whose power is expressed in powerlessness and weakness. Second, Jesus "ignored all those who are high and mighty and wealthy in the world in favor of the weak and meek and lowly."[56] Third, Jesus lived in conformity with God, which consisted in the

---

52. It also rests on our understanding of the biography of Barth and Wesley and their respective political leanings. What I am suggesting is that notwithstanding the importance of their respective political stances, these should be bracketed for the sake of clarifying what it might mean for Christianity to be "revolutionary."

53. Barth, *Epistle*, 481; see also Barth, "Christian's Place," 298–99.

54. This is a point that Barth makes especially in his exegesis of Romans 13 in the second edition of his Romans commentary: see Barth, *Epistle*, 475–92.

55. See *CD* 4.2:166–92.

56. *CD* 4.2:168. See also the following: "Throughout the New Testament the kingdom of God, the Gospel and the man Jesus have a remarkable affinity, which is no mere egalitarianism, to all those who are in the shadows as far as concerns what men estimate to be fortune and possessions and success and even fellowship with God . . . In fellowship and conformity with this God who is poor in the world the royal man Jesus is also poor, and fulfills the transvaluation of all values, acknowledging those who

"pronouncedly revolutionary character of His relationship to the orders of life and value current in the world around Him."[57] Fourth, and finally, as this man, Jesus was for humanity and not against it. The first three form a single composite concrete description, such that "we do not really know Jesus (the Jesus of the New Testament) if we do not know Him as this poor man, as this (if we may risk the dangerous word) partisan of the poor, and finally as this revolutionary."[58] Most critical and decisive, however, is the final point: that *this* Jesus, and no other, is *for* humanity. The whole life of Jesus is revolutionary and of decisive importance is his identification with the poor.

Moving from Christology to ecclesiology and ethics, for Barth, "revolution," though only properly applied to the work of God in Christ (i.e., the revolution of God), includes or elicits a corresponding human action which is described as "revolutionary" in character. As Barth notes elsewhere, "all ecclesiology is grounded, critically limited, but also positively determined by Christology";[59] and this is no less true for "Christian ethics," especially as concerning Christian identification with the poor. "He whom the Bible calls God is on the side of the poor. Therefore the Christian attitude to poverty can consist only of a corresponding allegiance."[60] In an even more precise formula: "The Church is witness of the fact that the Son of Man came to save the lost. And this implies that—casting all false impartiality aside—the Church must concentrate first on the lower and lower levels of human society. The poor, the socially and economically weak and threatened, will always be the object of its *primary* and *particular* concern."[61] One can find similar passages throughout the *Church Dogmatics*.[62] In an especially succinct formulation, which gathers up the various forms of Christian solidarity with humanity in all of its misery and deprivation, Barth describes all this as the "revolt against disorder." "Christians are summoned by God's command not only to zeal for God's honor but also to a simultaneous and related revolt, and therefore to entry into conflict."[63] Christian solidarity with the dispossessed, the poor, the outcast, the refugee, the sick, those rightfully or

---

(without necessarily being better) are in different ways poor men as this world counts poverty" (*CD* 4.2:169).

57. *CD* 4.2:171.
58. *CD* 4.2:180.
59. *CD* 4.3:786.
60. Barth, "Poverty," 245.
61. Barth, "Christian Community," 36; emphasis mine.
62. See, for instance, Barth's discussion of the "Diaconate" in *CD* 4.3:889–95, where Barth comes close to describing solidarity with the poor as one of the *notae verae ecclesiae*.
63. *ChL*, 206.

wrongfully imprisoned, is nothing less than a revolt against the prevailing system and its judgment as to human worth, dignity, and life.

One would have to imagine that Wesley, the political conservative, would have found it difficult to identify "revolution" with "Christianity." Nonetheless, though lacking the same systematic grounding,[64] Wesley shares in Barth's convictions regarding the necessity of Christian solidarity with the poor and the dispossessed. Furthermore, his writings also reveal a radicalism toward the prevailing order that comes close to the spirit of Barth's "revolt against disorder."

Wesley's work with the poor is well-known, but what is less well-known is that Wesley made solidarity with the poor constitutive of the maintenance of one's salvation. "The walking herein is essentially necessary, as to the continuance of that faith whereby we 'are' already 'saved by grace,' so to the attainment of everlasting salvation."[65] Commenting on Luke 7:22, Wesley went so far as to argue that the preaching of the gospel to the poor was "the greatest mercy, and the greatest miracle of all,"[66] and noted in his *Journal* that he would prefer to preach to the poor rather than the rich.[67] Wesley's emphasis on ministry to the poor was so central to his ethical praxis and ecclesiological vision that one commentator has gone so far as to argue that the later splits within the Wesleyan movement can be interpreted as fights over whether the Methodist movement would remain committed to Wesley's own "preferential option for the poor."[68]

But can Wesley's emphasis on solidarity with the poor be described in the language of revolt, as with Barth? I believe it can, especially when paired with Wesley's protest against slavery. In his arguments for Christian solidarity with the poor and the oppressed, Wesley offers harsh criticism not only of the specific practices which produce poverty and slavery, but also shows a budding concern for the legal and social structures that would make such

---

64. There is some debate in the literature as to whether or not Wesley's ethics can be said to be systematically grounded at all. Dayton in particular notes that discerning the theological grounding of Wesley's emphasis on solidarity with the poor is difficult: see Dayton, "Good News," 79. On the other hand, Jennings, Miles, and to some extent Marquardt, argue that Wesley's ethical praxis is grounded theologically in Wesley's soteriology: see Jennings, *Good News*, 139–56; Miles, "Happiness," 207–24; and Marquardt, *John Wesley's Social Ethics*, 87–101.

65. Wesley, "On Visiting the Sick," in *Works of John Wesley*, 3:385–86. All sermon citations come from the bicentennial edition of *Works of John Wesley*.

66. Wesley, *Explanatory Notes*, 227.

67. See, for example, Wesley's journal entry for November 17, 1759, in *Works of John Wesley*, 21:233, as one of the many passages where Wesley demonstrates this orientation.

68. See Dayton, "Good News to the Poor," 77–108.

practices possible.[69] This is nowhere seen more clearly than in his 1775 tract, *Thoughts Upon Slavery*, wherein Wesley asks: "But can Law, Human Law, change the nature of things? Can it turn Darkness into Light, or evil into good? By no means. Notwithstanding ten thousand Laws, right is right, and wrong is wrong still. There must still remain an essential difference between Justice and Injustice, Cruelty and Mercy."[70] Generally understood to be expressed in the categories of natural law, Wesley's pamphlet ought to be interpreted as nothing less than a protest against the legal and social order which sanctions the practice of slavery, which Wesley described as "man-stealing" and "murder."[71] Solidarity with the poor and the oppressed meant acting on their behalf, which meant raising the question as to the legitimacy of the social order. Though Wesley would not go so far as to call this a "revolt against disorder," it does come close to the spirit of Barth's own understanding of the struggle to establish human righteousness.

I have only been able to offer a sketch of how Barth and Wesley might be brought into conversation regarding the revolutionary nature of Christianity. Others must take up the deeper analysis, where the connections between Barth and Wesley can be given fuller treatment and the real and serious divergences between them can come to light. The pointed question that both theologians raise, however, is whether a Christianity that does not take seriously Jesus' identification with the poor really deserves to be called such. Both are searching for a form of Christian communal existence that conforms itself to Christ, "the partisan of the poor." One can only hope that this common question and search will inspire the contemporary church not only to think about the poor, but to be with them, and in so doing join the revolution of God.

---

69. This is obliquely demonstrated in Wesley's *Journal* regarding his embrace of field preaching, a practice which would have been considered out-of-bounds in the social order of eighteenth-century England. Wesley remarks that he determined to make himself "more vile" through field preaching, and chose as his text Luke 4:18–19, which he believed was fulfilled in "every true minister of Christ." See Wesley, *Works of John Wesley*, 19:46.

70. Wesley, *Thoughts Upon Slavery*, 16.

71. Often overlooked by commentators on Wesley's tract is his appeal to theological themes, especially toward the end of *Thoughts Upon Slavery*. The sudden appearance of these themes, and their decisive role in Wesley's appeal to certain classes of individuals, calls into question whether *Thoughts Upon Slavery* can *only* be read as an argument based on natural law.

2

Schleiermacher and Barth

On Theology as the Science of the Divine Word

—By Matthew J. Aragon Bruce

IN HIS *THEOLOGY OF Karl Barth*, von Balthasar wrote: "Schleiermacher gave Barth a powerful intuition into the unity, grandeur and totality of theology as a scientific discipline."[1] With this, von Balthasar proposed that Barth's thought exhibited a degree of genetic dependence upon Schleiermacher at both a formal and material level. The concern of this essay is not to inquire into such genetic dependence. Rather, it is concerned with the phrase "theology as a scientific discipline." How did these two modern theologians conceive of theology, and dogmatics in particular, as a "scientific discipline"? What is the nature and task of theology under the conditions of modernity, conditions prominently marked by the ascendancy of "science" and the modern research university?

1. Schleiermacher

In §1 of his *Brief Outline* (1830), Schleiermacher writes: "Theology . . . is a positive science," i.e., "a compendium of scientific elements which have their common bond not as if they form a necessary component of the organization of the sciences by virtue merely of the idea of science, but only in so far as they are required for the accomplishment of a practical task."[2] With the

---

1. Balthasar, *Theology of Karl Barth*, 199.

2. All citations from *Brief Outline of Theology as a Field of Study* will be abbreviated and by *Leitsatz* number (e.g., *BO* §#); citations are to the 2nd 1830 edition unless otherwise noted. This will allow readers to make use of the various versions available

adjective "positive," Schleiermacher defines theology as a practical science, i.e., a critical inquiry that cultivates human knowledge for the purpose of addressing practical individual and social needs. The elements of theology (Schleiermacher has in mind all aspects of the four traditional theological disciplines and not simply systematic theology or dogmatics) are bound together as a science not by virtue of the idea of science but rather by the task that theology pursues, viz., the training of church leaders for the task of proclamation. His conception of "positive science," though having earlier precedents, emerges in large part amidst the educational reforms that revolved around the foundation of the University of Berlin, an event in which Schleiermacher played a central role.[3] Moreover, the question concerning the scientificity of theology has continued to be shaped in conversation with the role of theology in the contemporary (secular) university.[4] Thus in this essay, Schleiermacher's notion of science will be examined in light of the developments surrounding the formation of the modern university and the reform of the German educational system in the early 19th century.

Schleiermacher borrows the definition of a "positive science" from F. W. J. Schelling. In his 1802 *Lectures on the Method of University Studies*, Schelling develops a philosophy of education founded on the notion of science as an "organic whole," i.e., a collective undertaking involving all members of the scientific community.[5] This is in marked contrast to what English speakers often understand with the term "science," i.e., the distinct, relatively independent fields of inquiry classified as the natural sciences. For Schelling and Schleiermacher, on the other hand, there are not sciences *per se* but only science, for "the more something is treated in isolation, the more incomprehensible and convoluted it appears."[6] Each member of the academic community contributes her part to the whole, i.e., to the collective development of scientific knowledge. Schelling contended that it was only under the guidance of the philosophy faculty that this vision of the unity of thought could be brought about and impressed on young minds. It is no

in either German or English translation. All translations are my own from Schleiermacher, *Kurze Darstellung*.

3. For Schleiermacher's role in the founding of the University of Berlin and the place of theology in the new university, see Pannenberg, *Theology and the Philosophy of Science*, 242–356; Howard, *Protestant Theology*, 130–211; and Ziolkowski, *German Romanticism*, 218–308. The reader will note my extensive debts to Howard and Ziolkowski.

4. See, for example, Bayer, *Theologie*, 487–500, 528–31.

5. Schelling, *Vorlesungen*, 4.

6. Schleiermacher, *Gelegentliche Gedanken*, in Anrich, *Idee der deutschen Universität*, 223.

surprise then that theology and other "positive" faculties of the German universities, law and medicine, were considered scientific not in themselves but only in their relation to philosophy. Philosophy, in this sense nearly synonymous with science, was considered the pure pursuit of knowledge for its own sake whereas the other faculties were designated "positive," i.e., their unique fields of inquiry were undertaken out of practical concerns, viz., for the spiritual, moral, and physical health of the state. Schleiermacher's treatise, *Occasional Thoughts on Universities in the German Sense* (1808), written specifically to address the foundation of the University of Berlin, contains, for our purposes here, only insignificant differences with Schelling. Both give the three positive faculties a place in the university, because the state has an interest in the training of "instruments for the state" (viz. pastors, lawyers, and doctors); the common good depended on these *bürgerlich* social roles.[7] The training of the individuals who will serve the state in such roles, so contended Schelling (and Schleiermacher agreed), should be shaped by science: "Without doubt such instruments should surely be formed by science... but science ceases to be science as soon as it is reduced to a mere means rather than promoted for its own sake."[8] Their common argument is that the state should provide for and promote scientific knowledge pursued for its own sake, divorced from utilitarian concerns including those of the state. In so doing, the state will, contrary to common wisdom, gain the very good it desires from the university: citizens formed by science and as such equipped to be the very best of civil servants.

Both Schleiermacher and Schelling give theology a place in the collective whole of science, but some of their contemporaries sought to severely reduce the role of theology in, if even exclude it from, the new university.[9] Schleiermacher's defense of theology as scientific must be understood in this light; he appeals to the common understanding of science as an organic, collective whole in order to argue for a place for theology in the university. Thus his definition of what constitutes science is external to theology, and

---

7. See Schelling, *Vorlesungen*, 17; Schleiermacher, *Gelegentliche Gedanken*, in Anrich, *Idee der deutschen Universität*, 257–59. The language "instruments of the state" points to the primary inspiration behind both Schelling and Schleiermacher's treatises on university education, viz., Kant's *Conflict of the Faculties*, in Kant, *Religion*, 247 (7:18). The positive faculties as understood by Schelling and Schleiermacher were what are today referred to as professional schools.

8. Schelling, *Vorlesungen*, 251.

9. See Anrich, *Idee der deutschen Universität*, for a selection of the essential texts (Schelling, Fichte, Schleiermacher, Steffens, and von Humboldt). There exists significant disagreement as to the role and content of the theology faculty in the texts of Schelling and Schleiermacher, let alone those writers who sought to exclude theology (e.g., Fichte).

moreover theology is one part of the collective human enterprise of science. Barth and others will find resultant problems in this conception. Before turning to Barth, however, it is still necessary to set out the particulars of Schleiermacher's understanding of theology as a science.[10]

In *BO* §5, Schleiermacher writes: "Christian theology is therefore the compendium of scientific knowledge and techniques, without which the possession and application of a united leadership of the Christian Church, i.e. a Christian Church governance, is not possible." Much criticism of Schleiermacher attacks at just this point. Troeltsch, with whom Barth's criticism shares much, argued that Schleiermacher's understanding of theology and especially dogmatics was merely an expression of the contemporary theologian's personal belief undertaken in order to inform the preaching and teaching of the church; as such, it cannot be designated scientific, since "science . . . is concerned only with the general and universal."[11] This is also the seed of Pannenberg's criticism, who contends that Schleiermacher's definition reduces theology to the practical task of church leadership and that this is tantamount to making the educational needs of church leadership determinative of the content of the Christian faith, at least as taught in the university.[12] Pannenberg counters that the opposite is actually the case and that in fact the content and even the form of Schleiermacher's work proceeds on just this basis contrary to his own definition. The danger Pannenberg sees in Schleiermacher's supposed reduction is the risk that theology will be understood not as the search for the truth about God and God's relationship with human beings, but rather as an ideology that defends the existence and interests of the church and the educational needs of its leaders in a bourgeois society. Pannenberg's interpretation is understandable as such *Ideologiekritik* justly takes to task much later 19th-century theology

---

10. Because Schleiermacher's notion of theology as a science is inseparable from the question of the role of theology in the university (or if it belongs at all), and the university in question is a state university, the question of the relationship between the church and state inevitably arises. In Schleiermacher's day, and if perhaps less so, in Barth's (and many contemporary European nations), pastors were considered servants to the state because they provide a necessary social service. This provision of social service justifies the state's support (especially financial support!) of the study of theology and theological research. Taking up the question of the state's support of theological studies would be necessary in a full treatment of the question of theology as a science in Barth and Schleiermacher but is beyond the limits of this investigation. The interested reader is advised to begin with the aforementioned texts of Pannenberg and Howard. See also Gerrish, "*Ubi theologia, ibi ecclesia?*," 249–73, and Barth, "Wort Gottes," 144–75.

11. Troeltsch, "Dogmatik," 516; see below for Barth.

12. See Pannenberg, *Theology and the Philosophy of Science*, 250–55.

on the matter; I argue that Schleiermacher is not susceptible to this charge, however.

In the explanation of *BO* §5 Schleiermacher says that its content is already contained in §1. What he means by this is far from obvious and thus requires unpacking. Recall in §5: "theology is . . . the compendium of scientific knowledge and techniques." Schleiermacher explains further that the Christian faith has no need for such a compendium but the church does; this is supported by §3 where Schleiermacher states that theology is not the responsibility of everyone in the church but rather those in leadership. Theology in the sense of critical inquiry—and this is the sense Barth has in mind in the discussion below—is essential for the life of the church but not for the faith of the individual Christian, insofar as faith is given while theology is human reflection on this faith. Does this not support Pannenberg's criticism? It does not if Schleiermacher understood church leadership, as with the Reformers, as the calling to a spiritual office rather than as a legal hierarchical office for the establishment (sacramental or otherwise) and management of the institutional church.[13]

Such an interpretation enlightens our understanding of the *Brief Outline*, e.g., §11: "Every treatment of theological subjects as such . . . always belongs within the province of Church leadership." All theological work is properly called "theological" only if it is undertaken for the sake of the church. Theology for Schleiermacher is an ecclesial undertaking. It is the church's critical self-reflection on its own being and experience. Theology is the church's reflection on its own history in order to understand its present location and to guide it into the future. The theologian, be she a professor or pastor, is called to understand the place of the church in history. This involves both knowledge of the past of the church and also its contemporary form and doctrines, understood as the product of the historical development of the church.[14] These two aspects, the past and present of the church, are when taken together the sum total of historical theology, "the actual corpus of theological study" as well as "the indispensible condition of all reflective effort toward the further development [of Christianity],"[15] i.e., the future of the church.[16]

The reason for Schleiermacher's placement of dogmatics within historical theology should now be clear: "Dogmatic theology is the science of

---

13. See Redeker, *Schleiermacher*, 104. See also *Confessio Augustana*, §28; and *BO* §13.
14. *BO* §26.
15. Respectively *BO* §28 and §70.
16. See *BO* §81.

the system of doctrine prevalent in a Christian ecclesial community at a given time."[17] Historical theology is divided into three sub-divisions: exegesis, dogmatics, and church history. Theology makes uses of the various historical tools available to other sciences in order to investigate the primal church in which all ecclesial communions are rooted. Inquiry into the further development of the church after the Apostolic age is undertaken by church history (the history of the church as community) and the history of dogma (the history of the writings and teachings of the church).

Dogmatics is that aspect of Christian theology that explicates the contemporary doctrinal content prevalent in a particular ecclesial communion through critical inquiry into the history of dogma, exegesis (Schleiermacher unfortunately includes the New Testament and excludes the Old, a feature for which he must be faulted), and church history—the three of which when taken together form the sum total of the historical experience of the church. Dogmatics is a descriptive discipline, which traces the development of the history of doctrine to its contemporary state. It is "the systematic presentation of the doctrine that has currency at any given time."[18] The emphasis on the empirical, descriptive task of dogmatics, let alone its definition as "the science of the system of doctrine prevalent . . . at a given time," once again brings the Troeltsch and Pannenberg line of criticism to the fore. Is dogmatics concerned with the truth, with the reality of God and God with humanity, or is it merely a description of what the church believes at a given time, rightly or wrongly? In other words, if dogmatics is primarily descriptive, does it have the ability to criticize and correct "the system of doctrine prevalent in a Christian ecclesial community at a given time"? And if it does, how does it do so, and on what basis?

According to Schleiermacher the historical material of Christianity is the basis of theology and, in particular, dogmatics.[19] Thus, knowledge of the present moment is the most significant aspect for church leadership, for the very reason that it is that from which the future church will develop. Historical theology is the discipline that, when it functions properly, exerts a "right and appropriate influence upon both the healthy and diseased conditions" of the contemporary ecclesial community.[20] The present state of the church, however, can only be understood from its past. Since the church is

---

17. *Gl.* §19; see *BO* §97 and §195. By *Gl.* I refer to Schleiermacher, *Der Christliche Glaube*, which is titled *The Christian Faith* in English translation

18. *BO* §97.

19. In the 1831/32 student notes, Schleiermacher is recorded to have said, the "Christian faith refers back to fact. This factuality is always the final basis and not anything that is speculative," cited in Schleiermacher, *Brief Outline*, 3.

20. *BO* §81.

"occupied in the process of expansion," and continually comes to contact with other social forces, it is necessary to ascertain the purest perspective possible of its distinctive nature. This is possible only through knowledge of "primitive Christianity."[21]

Schleiermacher's development of the tripartite form of historical theology is in large part behind the 19th-century obsession with the "essence of Christianity."[22] Schleiermacher approaches this issue through ecclesiology. Some explanation is needed here. The science of theology as a whole is also organized triadically; the three sub-divisions are philosophical theology, historical theology, and practical theology. In his treatment of philosophical theology, Schleiermacher lays the ground for his ecclesio-centric theology. The task of philosophical theology (we must set aside most contemporary meanings of the term) is to determine the nature of Christianity by contrasting it with other religious communities.[23] In addition, philosophical theology has the task of determining what developments in the historical expression of Christianity are in accord with its essence and what developments are derivations and therefore "diseased conditions." Philosophical theology is thus neither a purely scientific nor a purely empirical practice; rather, it proceeds critically by comparing what is historically given in Christianity both to other religions and, in light of the current division of the church, to the theologian's own confession in comparison with other confessions. Philosophical theology is then also a historical discipline, for it "presupposes the material of historical theology as already known; its prior task, however is to lay a foundation for the properly historical perspective on Christianity."[24] This feature of philosophical theology is made explicit in *Glaubenslehre*, §11: "Christianity is a monotheistic faith ... and is essentially distinguished from other such faiths by the fact that in it everything is related to the redemption accomplished in Jesus of Nazareth."

The essence of Christianity, the Christian form of piety, is then faith in Jesus Christ as the redeemer: the historical fact upon which the church is founded, the concreteness of the Christian experience, is faith in Christ the redeemer. Or perhaps better put, the material principle of Christian theology is the feeling of absolute dependence upon Christ. This feeling is what makes a person a member of the Christian church. The often misunderstood "Introduction" to the *Glaubenslehre*, and its "borrowed propositions," are better

---

21. BO §84.

22. Though the degree to which the later nineteenth-century theology is faithful to him remains an open question.

23. BO §32.

24. BO §65.

understood in this light. Schleiermacher is not trying to base the veracity of the Christian faith in either speculative deduction or rational proof. Rather his aim is to give a description of the church's experience of its faith in Christ, and description here needs to be understood as the verbal articulation of the feeling of absolute dependence upon Christ. He does so by placing Christianity alongside other forms of religious consciousness in order to demonstrate and describe what makes it distinct from other religions. Schleiermacher's notion of the feeling of absolute dependence is an abstraction from particular forms of religious consciousness. He does not hold that there is a religious consciousness in general, a general feeling of absolute dependence, but rather that we can artificially abstract similar features found in all human forms of religious consciousness. For Schleiermacher, all religions demonstrate some form of absolute dependence. The distinctive Christian form is the redemption accomplished in Jesus Christ. Schleiermacher's aim was not to determine the essence of human religiosity but rather to describe the essence of Christianity. In order to do so he found it necessary to inquire into the origins and subsequent development of the church's faith, i.e., to make clear its distinctiveness. This critical inquiry, along with the tools of historical consciousness developed by the modern sciences, makes possible a scientific description of the essence of the Christian faith, and in turn allows for the continual critical development of doctrine and judgment about appropriate and "diseased" developments of the church's faith. The church for Schleiermacher "is a being in becoming, in which the present must always be grasped as a product of the past and as a seed of the future."[25] Schleiermacher conceives of dogmatics as the theological science based on this concept of the church. It is the discipline that learns from exegesis and church history about the past dogma of the church and in this light informs Christian leaders of the current developed state of Christian doctrine, giving them tools to judge the appropriateness of such judgments and to continue along such paths, or to initiate reform in order to serve the future church. The church is a product of history; it has developed and will continue to do so. As it moves through time, the church must borrow language from the historical context in which it finds itself to proclaim the Good News of Jesus Christ. This is because its message, the gospel, like the God in Jesus Christ who proclaims it to the church and world, is not static but alive. The church for Schleiermacher is a being in becoming, a community that continues to be formed by the living God. Theology is scientific to the degree it functions as the community's critical self-reflection as it continues to develop in conformity to the living Word of God.

25. *BO* (1811) §33.

2. Barth

To begin, it should be noted that for Barth, as Thomas Schlegel has so concisely put it, "the question of the role of theology in the university . . . is not the central question."[26] Thus Barth does not approach the question of the scientificity of theology with the same concerns as Schleiermacher—he is not primarily concerned to secure its place in the university. The discussion of Barth's treatment of this issue is herein restricted to *Church Dogmatics* §1.1 and §7.2, leaving aside any questions of development in the later volumes.[27]

I take it to be uncontroversial that there is little formal disagreement between Barth and Schleiermacher that theology is a science that serves the church's task of proclamation. Indeed Barth begins with the *Leitsatz*: "As a theological discipline dogmatics is the scientific self-examination of the Christian Church with respect to the content of its distinctive talk about God."[28] The question is: Does Barth understand theology to be a science in the same sense (materially) as Schleiermacher?

For Barth, the scientificity of theology is directly related to the church's critical self-reflection and examination of its God-talk and the creation's relationship (and the church's as it is part of and contained within God's creation) with God: "Theology as a science . . . is a measure taken by the Church in consideration of the vulnerability and responsibility of its speech."[29] As we turn to Barth then, it appears at first glance that he shares Schleiermacher's conception of theology as a positive science, i.e., as a science motivated by a particular practical task.

Looking at §1.1 and §7.2, Barth gives several principles for the scientificity of theology, and dogmatics in particular; these are summarized below.

1. Theology is concerned with truth; with the designation "science" it recognizes that it shares this concern for the truth with other human disciplines that are classified by the designation "science." Consciousness of this similarity reminds theology that it too is a human discipline and that it is not superior to the other human spheres of inquiry just because of its subject matter. "Dogmatics is in fact an *ars* among *artes*."[30]

---

26. Schlegel, *Theologie*, 270.

27. Barth did take up the question of the scientificity of theology and its place in the university elsewhere (e.g. the debate with Heinrich Scholz), but constraints of space do not allow for discussion of these texts here. See Molendijk, *Aus dem Dunklen ins Helle*, 129–230, and the bibliographic materials.

28. *CD* 1.1:3. Translations from *CD* here are freely revised in reference to *KD*.

29. *CD* 1.1:4.

30. *CD* 1.1:284.

2. By not giving up the designation "science," theology protests against "a general concept of science that is admittedly pagan."[31] Theology's very presence unsettles the confidence of the modern scientists and fellows of the research university who are self-assured in their understanding of science. The self-conscious adoption of the designation "science" is then a bearing witness to the scientific world of the gospel.

3. By adopting the designation "science," theology demonstrates that it does not take the paganism of such an understanding (in point 2) seriously, but rather counts these persons as part of the church in spite of their refusal of the theological task and their adoption of a definition of science which excludes theology. Theology does so because it believes in God's justification of sinners.

4. Theology is scientific only if it is devoted to church proclamation, i.e., determined by the task or act of church proclamation and not ancillary issues that arise relative to proclamation. Inquiry into theology's realm of knowledge that is not motivated by the task of proclamation is unscientific. In short: "Dogmatics is preparation for Church proclamation; it formulates the statements to be pondered before Church proclamation formulates its statements. But it is by this relation that statements of dogmatics are to be tested."[32] In other words, theology informs the task of proclamation, but if its statements are unintelligible to the preparatory task of proclamation it is thus unscientific, because as such it is only concerned with pure knowledge separate from the practical task of proclamation.

5. Theology is scientific only if it is devoted to the development (in Barth's terms, "criticism and correction") of church proclamation rather than the mere repetition of some classical historical expression of the Christian faith. The scientific character of dogmatics "consists in unsettling rather than confirming Church proclamation" in either its past or contemporary forms. Historical and contemporary accounts of Christian dogma are only a means to an end. Barth terms a theology that simply conforms to some past or present understanding of the Christian faith as "comfortable [bequem]." A comfortable theology is an unscientific theology. The question put to dogmatics, writes Barth, is "whether dogmatics should be a part of Church history, or a part of current ecclesial affairs, or whether it is itself a part of Church action. Only in the final case is it a science in the sense of its assigned task."[33]

Barth is critical of Schleiermacher on this point: Barth ranks Schleiermacher's dogmatics as merely the "clarification and presentation of the faith as the dogmatician concerned personally thinks it should be

---

31. CD 1.1:11.
32. CD 1.1:280.
33. CD 1.1:282.

proclaimed."[34] Barth contends that Schleiermacher reduces theology to a concern with current ecclesial affairs and to this he writes: "one might ask whether here all the criticism and correction amounts to, and wants to amount to, a grandiose conformity."[35]

6. Decisively, and above all else, theology is scientific only when it asks whether or not the church's proclamation agrees with the revelation testified to in Holy Scripture. Scripture is the criterion of theology and must not be usurped by or confused with other subsidiary criteria. Theology stands or falls to the degree to which Scripture is made the standard of the church's proclamation. However, the theologian *must* have an education in and be familiar with other sciences, viz., philosophy, psychology, history, etc. "The dogmatician also," writes Barth, "must think and speak in a particular age and should thus be a person of his or her age, which also means a person of the past that constitutes his or her age, i.e. an educated person. But no element of his or her education makes a person a dogmatician besides the one that is not provided in all those disciplines, which consists in unsubstantiated and unassuming regard for the sign of Holy Scripture around which the Church gathers and becomes the Church again and again."[36]

Theology is more than a mere *ars* among other *artes*. Theology is autonomous, and this means that it is free from any definition of science set by other disciplines. Theology is the science of the Word of God testified to in Holy Scripture. It self-defines as a science to the degree that it pursues its own special path of knowledge defined by the object testified to in Scripture. When theology takes as its primary criterion something other than the self-revelation of God that God makes available in Scripture, it is rightly judged, by Barth's lights, to be unscientific.

3. Theses on the Similarities and Dissimilarities of Barth and Schleiermacher

Thesis I: Barth and Schleiermacher share a notion of theology as a "positive" science and, moreover, the material content of this science. For both, theology is not a science pursued for its own sake but rather is the science of church proclamation. It is the science that forms and continues to inform church leaders, enabling them to hear and proclaim the Word of God that continues to be revealed to the church.

---

34. *CD* 1.1:281.
35. *CD* 1.1:282.
36. *CD* 1.1:283.

Thesis II: Furthermore, both understand theology as a part of the whole, a particular realm of inquiry within an overall coherent discipline (Schleiermacher) or a science among the sciences (Barth). Theology is a human discipline and should not be exalted above the other sciences because of its subject matter. This also means then that the other sciences likewise have no basis to exalt themselves over theology.

There are discontinuities, however. For Barth, the other sciences have no basis to exclude theology from the scientific table because it does not conform to some *a priori* definition of what constitutes a science. For Schleiermacher, theology, as knowledge of the community's faith and of the being of God, is part of the general theory of science.

Thesis III: Barth's material criticism of Schleiermacher is inaccurate. Schleiermacher's conception of the scientificity of theology is not, as Barth claims, the particular theologian's concern for what should presently be proclaimed. Like Barth, Schleiermacher conceives of theology as the church's critical self-reflection upon its continual reception of the Word of God's revelation. Questions remain as to the location of the church's reception of revelation. For Barth this location is clearly the witness of Scripture whereas for Schleiermacher the location is in the church where the inherited tradition, including Scripture, is developed.[37] The role of Scripture in theology has often been put forward as a primary dividing line between Schleiermacher and Barth in the scholarly literature. However, when the role of the Spirit is taken into account, particularly in the case of Schleiermacher, it appears the two are far closer than one might expect. To put it simply, it cannot be denied that Barth developed the received tradition with just as much freedom as did Schleiermacher. The question of the Spirit and Scripture is a clear area for future scholarship to pursue in comparing Schleiermacher and Barth.

Thesis IV: Schleiermacher's understanding of science is rooted in the rapid social developments that led to the formation of the University of Berlin. More precisely, his conception of the scientificity of theology is, from a contemporary standpoint, unduly motivated by the concern to guarantee theology a place in the university. In order to secure a place for theology it must be defended as an essential element in the complete system of science. This requires a general theory of science, i.e., an overarching conception of science that organizes the "sciences" into a complete system with theology having a particular place within the system. Just what science is, its nature and task, is defined beforehand, i.e., prior to the actual practice of theology or any other of the individual sciences. For Barth, this will not do. On the

---

37. See Schleiermacher, *On the Glaubenslehre*, 66–67; Gerrish, "Friedrich Schleiermacher," 48.

contrary, a science is a human inquiry in which the norms that make it a science emerge only in practice; thus, the norms of theological science emerge only in the act of theologizing and not prior to its practice. As distinctly human disciplines, the standards of the various sciences are created *in the act* of the particular domain of inquiry: "No science holds the lease rights to the name 'science' and there is no scientific theory with the final authority to grant or withhold this title."[38] For Barth, the determination of what is a science cannot be defined prior to the actual practice of theology (or any other science). Thus for Barth, when it comes to judgments about the scientificity of theology—if I might borrow a phrase from Schleiermacher—"beginning in the middle is unavoidable."[39] Barth defends this view of science in order to not give one iota to the "pagan" sciences in regard to the scientificity of theology. This in part explains Barth's ultimately unsatisfactory treatment of the role of theology in the university. He would not allow it to be judged by anything but methods appropriate to its object. And it must be admitted that if God is the object of theology, then theology is unique in comparison to the other sciences and has a likewise unique and somewhat uncomfortable and even disruptive role in the university. And this is the very role in which Barth envisioned its continuing practice in the academy. It is up to the contemporary generation of theologians to continue to define theology's role in the university without forgetting that our primary task is to serve the church's proclamation that God is for us in Jesus Christ.

On the Critical Science of Theology

A Response to Matthew Bruce

—By Matthias Gockel

MATT BRUCE HAS OFFERED us a nuanced consideration of an important issue. His procedural method is exemplary in two respects. First, he rightly presupposes that Schleiermacher and Barth still have something important to say today. Theological reflection in our own time can only be enriched by listening to their voices. Second, he operates with the interpretive strategy

---

38. *CD* 1.1:10.
39. Schleiermacher, *Dialektik*, 1:353.

that Barth's reflections on Schleiermacher must be evaluated critically on a case-to-case basis and, as much as possible, independently from one's own allegiance to either author. Pointing out instances in Barth's writings where he attacks Schleiermacher and using them as the final word on the matter under discussion is insufficient and does not entail a serious understanding of Barth's relation to Schleiermacher.

My response consists of three points, which address considerations and suggestions made by Bruce. The overall goal is to clarify central issues and delineate trajectories for further debate.

1. Theology as a Science

Connections between Schelling and Schleiermacher have been noted before, especially their common philosophical roots in transcendental idealism: e.g., both thinkers assume an identity of "subject" and "object" as the precondition of human knowledge and action. Bruce suggests that they also share a view of science as organic unity and collective undertaking. When we add Barth as a third conversation partner, we have to bear in mind that he worked in a similar academic context but more than a century later. In order to arrive at a meaningful comparison, I suggest that one distinguishes between the definition of science and the practice of the sciences. In practical terms, Barth understands theology as playing a particular role in the concert of academic sciences. Theology is a science because, like other sciences, it has a specific object of knowledge and treads a specific path of knowledge (*Erkenntnisweg*), for which it can give account (*Rechenschaft*) to itself and to others.[40] In classical academic language, theology is an *ars* among *artes*. This view, which does not presuppose a generally accepted definition of science, is compatible with Schleiermacher's (and Schelling's) understanding of the university as a distinguished place for the collective human search for knowledge and truth. In regard to scientific practices, the university represents, albeit in a provisional form, the "unity of all human endeavors at knowledge."[41] Schleiermacher (and Schelling) certainly could have agreed with this view.

An agreement is also possible when it comes to the definition of science, although Barth does not explicitly endorse the idea of science as an organic unity. Moreover, he opposes the idea that theology should be subject to those standards that are valid in other sciences, or that theology has to set forth its own concept of science, in order to justify the "scientific"

---

40. Cf. *KD* 1.1:6; *CD* 1.1:7–8.
41. *KD* 1.1:291; *CD* 1.1:275. All translations from the German are my own.

character of its claims and propositions.[42] This opposition does not entail a lofty separation of theology from the other sciences, however. Barth claims that theology's peculiar existence at the university should not be regarded as necessary. In principle, every human science could be concerned with the truth of human words about God.[43] This is an astounding claim that even goes beyond Schleiermacher, who also rejected the separation of theology and science, but for different reasons.[44] For Barth, the fact that theology calls itself a science among other sciences is a sign of solidarity and shows that the theologian stands under the same verdict as every other scientist. It also challenges the "quasi-religious" absoluteness inherent in the (allegedly) objective interpretation of the concept of science. The presence of theologians at a "secular" university is a reminder of the relativity of human science, including theology. At the same time, it is a witness to the universality of the forgiveness of sins or, if we add Schleiermacher's voice here, of Christ's testimony to the general situation of humankind and the need of redemption.[45]

2. Theology as a Positive Science

Schleiermacher's famous definition of theology as a "positive science" (in both editions of *Brief Outline*) is not limited to dogmatic theology but relates to the entire field of theological reflection. The definition includes a functional and a historical aspect.

The first aspect concerns the "solution of a practical task" and the formal unity of theology.[46] According to Schleiermacher, theological edu-

---

42. Cf. *KD* 1.1:8; *CD* 1.1:10. Hence, the description of theology as a "scientific discipline" needs a qualifier. The English translation of the passage in von Balthasar, which Bruce has chosen as his opening, is not quite precise. The German text speaks of the unity, grandeur, and totality of "theological science" (not "theology as a scientific discipline"). Cf. Balthasar, *Karl Barth*, 210.

43. Cf. *KD* 1.1:3; *CD* 1.1:5. Barth lists specifically the disciplines of philosophy, history, sociology, psychology, and pedagogy. A few pages later, he says that "*all* sciences could ultimately be theology" (*KD* 1.1:5; *CD* 1.1:7; my emphasis), but he does not explain how the natural sciences would inquire into the truth of human discourse of God.

44. Schleiermacher's approach can be classified as "accommodation without adaptation"; cf. Gockel, "Mediating Theology," esp. 303–4. Dole also speaks of accommodation, as opposed to segregation. Cf. Dole, *Schleiermacher on Religion*, 144–47.

45. For Barth, cf. *KD* 1.1:9–10; *CD* 1.1:11. For Schleiermacher, this testimony was an essential part of Christ's "self-proclamation," not in the form of dogmatic propositions but rather as the "text" for the latter: cf. Schleiermacher, *Christian Faith*, §16.2. Citations of *The Christian Faith* and *Kurze Darstellung* are given by paragraph, so that readers can use the various versions available.

46. Schleiermacher, *Kurze Darstellung* (1830), §1.

cation provides the knowledge (*Kenntnisse*) and techniques (*Kunstregeln*) that are needed for good church governance (*Kirchenregiment*).[47] The last term should be understood in a broad sense. It refers not only to the highest ranks of ecclesial leadership but to every active member in the congregation who is involved in official decisions.[48] Schleiermacher, like Barth, regards theology as a function of the church. But his explanation follows a different path. For Barth, the task of theology consists primarily in the "self-examination" of the church regarding the latter's "genuine discourse of God,"[49] specifically the proclamation of the gospel through preaching and the sacrament.[50] Barth distinguishes between biblical theology, dogmatic theology, and practical theology. They deal respectively with the *foundation*, the *content*, and the *goal* of proclamation. The overarching criterion of truth—and truthful proclamation—is the correspondence to God's revealing and reconciling turning toward humankind in Jesus Christ.[51] Schleiermacher, on the other hand, does not define theology on the basis of the connection between theology and proclamation. He addresses the question of truth differently, according to his distinction of theological disciplines into philosophical, historical, and practical theology. Dogmatic theology belongs to the historical branch, but it is also related to philosophical theology, as we will see shortly.

Besides the functional aspect, theology as a "positive science" has a second feature: the common ground of all theological endeavors is a specific, historically existing religion or way of belief (*Glaubensweise*). In other words, every theology is characterized by a "particular formation of the God-consciousness,"[52] which provides its material unity as a positive science with a descriptive and a normative side. The descriptive side is related to dogmatic theology, the normative side to philosophical theology. The task of the former is the "coherent presentation of doctrine, as it is valid . . . at a given time."[53] The key word here is "valid," since it implies the distinction

---

47. Cf. ibid., §5.

48. Cf. Albrecht, *Schleiermachers Theorie der Frömmigkeit*, 99–103. This does not imply that only persons with a degree in theological studies should hold an ecclesial office. The point is that every activity of a church or congregation can and shall be a matter of theological reflection.

49. *KD* 1.1:1; *CD* 1.1:3.

50. Cf. *KD* 1.1:47; *CD* 1.1:47. In the later volumes of the *Church Dogmatics*, Barth avoids using the term in the traditional sense. For instance, he speaks of Baptism and the Lord's Supper as "so-called 'sacraments'" (*KD* 4.1:744; *CD* 4.1:667).

51. Cf. *KD* 1.1:2–3; *CD* 1.1:4–5.

52. Schleiermacher, *Kurze Darstellung* (1830), §1.

53. Ibid., §97. Cf. also Schleiermacher, *Christliche Glaube*, §19.

between valid and invalid propositions. According to Schleiermacher, dogmatic theology shall be able to view the historical development of Christianity in the light of a "constitutive principle" and to apply its knowledge about the present moment to the future, in order to exert the "right and appropriate influence on both the healthy and the diseased."[54] Dogmatic theology is descriptive not in an enumerative but in a critical sense. It strives for the right balance of fixed and flexible elements and is "orthodox in the central parts of its teaching," but it also considers heterodox propositions as long as they correspond to "the basic teachings of our faith."[55] In general, "corrections and new developments of Christian doctrine"[56] are possible.

It is necessary to define a normative core in order to be able to evaluate the claims of dogmatic propositions. This is the task of philosophical theology, which develops a critical understanding of both the history of Christianity and contemporary Christianity. In doing so, it presupposes the data provided by historical theology and makes possible their evaluation over against the "peculiar essence" of Christianity,[57] which is determined in comparison to other faith communities. The introduction of the *Glaubenslehre* offers such a comparison by using "borrowed propositions" from the field of ethics,[58] philosophy of religion,[59] and philosophical theology, and concludes: "Christianity is a monotheistic way of belief . . . and is essentially distinguished from other such beliefs by the fact that in it everything is related to the redemption accomplished through Jesus of Nazareth."[60] The

---

54. Schleiermacher, *Kurze Darstellung* (1830), §81. Schleiermacher suggests that the development of Christianity knows the distinction between the "pure expression" of "the idea of Christianity" and the "deviation" from this idea (§35). It is doubtful, however, that such a "pure expression" ever occurred after the appearance of Jesus of Nazareth: see the comprehensive and illuminating discussion of "ideal" and "actual" religion in Dole, *Schleiermacher and Religion*, 71–100.

55. Schleiermacher, *Kurze Darstellung* (1830), §206. In an unusually polemical manner, this paragraph rejects the "servile comfort" that accepts every teaching, as long as it is "edifying for many."

56. Schleiermacher, *Christliche Glaube*, §19.3.

57. Schleiermacher, *Kurze Darstellung* (1830), §32, 65.

58. For Schleiermacher, ethics as *Sittenlehre* is the "science of the principles of history," aimed at uncovering the laws of human actions that shape human history. The science of ethics studies "the always advancing but never completed organization of human nature by reason." Dole, *Schleiermacher on Religion*, 116.

59. Philosophy of religion "represents not a component of theology but a nontheological branch of ethics." Ibid., 195.

60. Schleiermacher, *Christliche Glaube*, §11.

exclusive way to receive a share in the "Christian community" is "the faith in Jesus as the redeemer."[61]

For Schleiermacher, dialectics and ethics can become important conversation partners of theology. Still, it is an exaggeration to claim that he defines the nature and task of theology "prior to the actual practice of theology" (Bruce's Thesis IV), in order to secure the place of theology in the family of sciences. Such an undertaking would equal the project of a rational theology, which also relates to "the God of our God-consciousness" but as a "speculative science" seeks to transcend the historical character of the Christian faith.[62] In contrast, Schleiermacher's definition of theology as a "positive science" already belongs to the practice of theology. To be sure, it precedes the practice of *dogmatic* theology, but the same is true for Barth, who first considers the role of theology, in relation to the church and to other sciences, then addresses the task of prolegomena to dogmatic theology, and only then begins his proper dogmatic reflection with the doctrine of the Word of God. Moreover, it is an exaggeration that Schleiermacher's position entails a "destructive handing over of theology to the general concept of science"[63] since his understanding of Christian theology as an academic science is tied to a normative core. The evaluation of Christian beliefs and propositions in the past and the present in the light of this core (the "essence of Christianity") is not given up to other sciences but remains the joint responsibility of dogmatic and philosophical theology.[64]

3. The Norm of Theology

For Schleiermacher, dogmatic theology consists in reflection on expressions of the Christian pious-self-consciousness.[65] It is a critical function of the church, to use Barth's terminology, since it considers all doctrines in the light of the essence of Christianity—that is, faith in Christ as the redeemer—which must be understood in a way that excludes the "natural heresies" of Docetism, Ebionitism, Manicheism, and Pelagianism.[66] The Christian

---

61. Ibid., §14.

62. Schleiermacher, *Kurze Darstellung* (1830), §1. Cf. Fischer, *Friedrich Schleiermacher*, 73.

63. KD 1.1:9; CD 1.1:10.

64. Here I differ from Fischer, who relates historical theology, and thus dogmatic theology, only to the "empirical discipline of history." Fischer, *Friedrich Schleiermacher*, 79.

65. Cf. Schleiermacher, *Christliche Glaube*, §§16–17.

66. Ibid., §22.

character of dogmatic propositions is determined by their agreement with the New Testament, which is both the "first link" in the historical series of presentations of the Christian faith and the "sufficient norm of Christian doctrine."[67] Dogmatic propositions are proven valid when their content can be traced back to the New Testament and when their "scientific expression" fosters the coherence among related propositions.[68]

According to Barth, the task of dogmatic theology is a normative one: the critical examination of the agreement of the proclamation of the gospel, which always occurs in human words, with God's revelation in Jesus Christ attested by Scripture. Such agreement he calls the "dogma."[69] It is crucial to recognize that, for Barth, "Christian discourse is reality-depicting without claiming to be directly descriptive."[70] The church must carefully distinguish between the Word of God and its own word. Scripture is authoritative in an indirect sense. Both Scripture and proclamation are dependent on revelation, not vice versa. The theologian cannot claim for himself or herself "a viewpoint above proclamation and the Bible."[71] At this point, an important issue for further consideration is the priority of Christ (Schleiermacher) or revelation (Barth) over Scripture, which also has some bearing on the question of the Spirit and Scripture (Bruce's Thesis III),

In conclusion, Barth and Schleiermacher agree that theology is not a function of the state to promote a particular religion, but serves the needs of a particular church in a critical way and, if necessary, may act as a corrective. The differences between the two theologians can hardly be grasped by binary oppositions like objectivism vs. subjectivism. Both reflect the internal and external perspectives on the Christian faith, but they do so differently. For Schleiermacher, Christianity offers a comprehensive view of reality (internal perspective), while it is also one historical religion among others in which the human capacity for piety is manifest (external perspective). His theory of piety and his doctrinal exposition of the Christian faith are two sides of the same coin.[72] Barth, on the other hand, reflects on the internal and external perspectives once more from an internal standpoint. He does not only co-ordinate the two universal perspectives of theology and philosophy, as Schleiermacher did, but he seeks "to integrate this co-ordination itself

67. Ibid., §129 and 131, respectively.
68. Schleiermacher, *Kurze Darstellung* (1830), §209.
69. Cf. *KD* 1.1:280; *CD* 1.1:265.
70. Dalferth, *Theology and Philosophy*, 116.
71. *KD* 1.1:273; *CD* 1.1:259

72. Cf. Dalferth, *Theology and Philosophy*, 101: "'[P]iety' marks an essential capacity of human existence which all religions manifest; 'Christian faith' is a particular manifestation of this capacity under the impact of Jesus Christ."

once more *theologically*."⁷³ For example, he revises Schleiermacher's view of religion and its distinction between faith and piety without reversing it: in the internal perspective of faith, religion and atheism are two sides of the same unbelief, that is, human rebellion against God's grace; in the external perspective of reason, religion is a general phenomenon of human existence; and in the theological meta-perspective, religion "is seen as a human mode of existence which, because of God's eschatological co-presence with us, may *become* a more or less adequate expression of faith."⁷⁴

Similarly, Barth's understanding of theology as a science in the service⁷⁵ of the truth of God's Word can be seen as a meta-theological reconstruction of Schleiermacher's view of theology as a positive science with a functional and a material (descriptive as well as normative) side. Moreover, Barth's doctrine of reconciliation affirms not only the existence of the living Jesus Christ as the "true witness," as the heading of *Church Dogmatics* 4.3 says, but also the possibility of true human words *extra muros ecclesiae*.⁷⁶ Such an appreciation of the "secular" realm encourages us to envision a legitimate place of academic theology at the university.⁷⁷

---

73. Ibid., 122.

74. Ibid., 125.

75. Barth develops the idea of the service (*Dienst*) of theology, as one aspect of the service of the congregation in the world, in *KD* 4.3:1007–11; *CD* 4.3:879–82.

76. Cf. *KD* 4.3:122–53; *CD* 4.3:110–35. Cf. Thompson, "Salvation."

77. The presupposition here is that the university is a place where different academic disciplines are publicly engaged in the search for truth. This is different from Schleiermacher's and Schelling's argument, which points to the social role of the person who undergoes a theological education: a pastor has learned to be a "good citizen" and will teach "good citizenship" to others. In many ways, theological education in the U.S. is more diverse than in Europe. It reflects the denominational pluralism characteristic of countries without "state churches." Thus, it is unthinkable that "positive" theological faculties that serve particular denominations or confessions exist at a public university. Nevertheless, theology and the study of religion (at departments of Religious Studies, for instance) have many similarities and "might find themselves in agreement regarding the extent to which particular historical episodes count as faithful expressions of a religion's 'distinctive force.'" Dole, *Schleiermacher on Religion*, 196. To be sure, only theology has the task of inquiring into the alignment of a religious tradition with the essence of the religion in question. Nevertheless, why should not theology lend its distinctive voice to the concert of sciences in a country, where only Christian politicians may claim their religious affiliation if they want to be elected to a public office? This situation is indeed peculiar, and theology could provide a remedy by helping people to realize that God does not belong to one nation, even if it were "my country."

3

Dietrich Bonhoeffer in the Theology of Karl Barth

—By Matthew Puffer

LITTLE SPECULATION IS REQUIRED to discern what "Karl Barth in conversation with Dietrich Bonhoeffer" might look like. Their numerous interactions during the tumultuous years from 1931 to 1942 are both preserved in personal correspondence and noted extensively, particularly in Bonhoeffer scholarship. The significant indebtedness of Bonhoeffer's theology to Barth's is widely recognized. It is apparent during his student years in Tübingen and Berlin, in the final extant chapters for his *Ethics* foreshortened by his arrest, as well as in Bonhoeffer's prison theology where dependence and divergence are simultaneously evident. Comparisons of Eberhard Bethge's and Eberhard Busch's respective biographies of Bonhoeffer and Barth—or of almost any work on Barth's theology and nearly any on Bonhoeffer's—bears out that Barth was of tremendous import to Bonhoeffer's theology.[1] A significant void remains, however, in that little consideration has been given to the opposite trajectory—that is, to the influence of the younger theologian upon his esteemed mentor.

The suggestion that Bonhoeffer influenced Barth will strike some as implausible. Certainly Barth appreciated Bonhoeffer's ecumenism and opposition to National Socialism, but it is widely recognized that Barth was unimpressed by the "fragmentary" prison writings, confounded by the suggestions of a "positivism of revelation," and found the discussion of

---

1. Pangritz's work offers the most detailed examination of Barth's influence upon Bonhoeffer to date. He assesses their relationship in response to interpretations of Bonhoeffer's charge that Barth's theology exhibits a "positivism of revelation": cf. Pangritz, *Karl Barth*, and Pangritz, "Dietrich Bonhoeffer."

"mandates" in *Ethics* as "arbitrary," "inadequate," and suggestive of "a North German patriarchalism."[2] In a letter to Bethge—not only Bonhoeffer's biographer, but editor of his posthumous publications, closest friend, and nephew—Barth offers a seemingly devastating assessment of Bonhoeffer's theology: "very softly I venture to doubt whether theological systematics (I include his *Ethics*) was his real strength." Given such critical evaluations from Barth's own pen, skepticism toward claims regarding substantive contributions from Bonhoeffer is surely appropriate.

Of course Barth can be as generous in praise as adamant in opposition. His engagement with interlocutors often becomes more critical, rather than less, when he holds them in high regard. Thus, it is not entirely inexplicable that Barth appraises Bonhoeffer's *Sanctorum Communio* as a "theological miracle," his *Discipleship* as "the best that has been written" on *imitatio Christi*, and *Ethics* as "brilliant."[3] Understood within the context of their relationship and respective theologies Barth's critical assessments, negative and positive, illumine rather than discredit a reciprocal indebtedness between Barth and Bonhoeffer.

Still, Barth's critical assessment of Bonhoeffer presents a challenge to understanding his importance to Barth's theology. And numerous complicating factors contribute to a dearth of attention given to the young theologian's contributions. For one, their writings have often been appropriated for apparently distinct and sometimes divergent purposes in academic, theological, and popular discourses—the Death of God theology, universalism, pietism, liberalism, socialism, conservatism, dogmatics, social ethics, pacifism, justification of assassination, etc.[4] Not only can secondary discourse lead to diverse reductive oppositions, a textual study attentive solely to Barth and Bonhoeffer's publications tells an equally distortive and distinctly counterintuitive story about their mutual influence. For in Bonhoeffer's publications, one finds only highly critical explicit engagement with Barth in *Sanctorum Communio* and *Act and Being*, and the elder theologian goes unmentioned in Bonhoeffer's last four books—*Creation and Fall, Life Together, Discipleship*, and *Ethics*. In *Church Dogmatics* 3 and 4 alone, on the

2. CD 3.4:22.

3. Godsey, *Theology*, 21n6; Barth, CD 4.2:533, and 3.4:4.

4. Jüngel offers another explanation shared by numerous scholars when he observes that Bonhoeffer's compelling biography has inhibited criticism of his thought. Jüngel recalls, "Heinrich Vogel was the only teacher in the course of my studies whom I heard express critical words and reservations with respect to Bonhoeffer. It does not say much for the state of Protestant theology that he was the only one. Probably because of Bonhoeffer's life and its violent end, an aura of theological unassailability has come to rest around his work, which has done a great disservice to this work itself. For Bonhoeffer's sake, the aura needs to be destroyed" (Jüngel, "Mystery of Substitution," 153).

other hand, Barth makes explicit reference to four of Bonhoeffer's books, offering extensive positive critical assessments, even where he disagrees, quoting from Bonhoeffer at length in numerous instances.

Appreciating Bonhoeffer's contributions to Barth's theological project, then, requires that one attend to Barth's appraisals and appropriations both in his correspondence and in his dogmatics. A reconsideration of Bonhoeffer's importance to Barth's theology not only holds promise for a greater appreciation of Bonhoeffer and better understanding of Barth, but more importantly, it discloses places where constructive conversations might advance the theological and ethical insights to which Barth and Bonhoeffer gave considerable attention.

1. Barth and Bonhoeffer: Life Together

Bonhoeffer imbibed Barth's early writings during his student years in Tübingen and Berlin (1924–27). Studying under Barth's former professor and recent sparring partner, Adolf von Harnack, Bonhoeffer experienced Barth as a "liberation" through the lecture notes he collected from family members and friends who were Barth's students in Göttingen and Münster. Still, Bonhoeffer's dissertations, *Sanctorum Communio* and *Act and Being*, voice critical assessments of the seemingly exclusive emphasis upon God's transcendence in Barth's early theology.[5] In 1931, as a young Berlin University theology lecturer, Bonhoeffer spent three weeks in Bonn where the two theologians became acquainted. Barth was "delighted" when his visitor quoted one of Luther's witticisms in a seminar, launching a friendship that would last until Bonhoeffer's death.[6] Bonhoeffer wrote of these weeks in Bonn, "I don't think I have ever regretted anything I have failed to do in my theological past so much as the fact that I did not come here earlier... I have

---

5. Cf. Bonhoeffer, *Sanctorum Communio*, 169–70n28; Bonhoeffer, *Act and Being*, 83–87, 98–100, 124–26.

6. Bonhoeffer is said to have interjected, "The curses of the godless sometimes sound better to God's ear than the hallelujahs of the pious" (Bethge, *Dietrich Bonhoeffer: A Biography*, 176). Luther's text reads "*cum tales blasphemie, quia sunt violenter a diabolo hominibus invitis extorte, aliquando gratiores sonent in aure dei quam ipsum Alleluja vel quecunque laudis iubilatio*" (Luther, *Vorlesung über den Römerbrief*, 2:227, quoted in Bonhoeffer, *Act and Being*, 160n31). According to Bethge, the lectures by Barth that Bonhoeffer attended in July of 1931 were on ethics: cf. Bethge, *Dietrich Bonhoeffer: A Biography*, 181. However, Barth's ethics seminars were held the previous two semesters. Barth's 1931 summer seminar read Schleiermacher's *Glaubenslehre* and his lectures were on "Prolegomena to Dogmatics," i.e., *CD* 1.1. Barth also gave a seminar on natural theology in the winter semester for which Erich Przywara was a guest lecturer. Cf. *CRDT*, 415–16.

been even more impressed by my discussions with him than by his writings and his lectures. For he is really all there. I have never seen anything like it before and wouldn't have believed it possible."[7] The two discussed ethics and natural theology, and—in all likelihood—their assessments of Przywara's *analogia entis*, about which both had previously written.[8]

In the years of the *Kirchenkampf* Barth and Bonhoeffer labored together and exchanged notes about developments, until Bonhoeffer—exasperated with the Confessional Church's cautiousness, the watered-down Bethel Confession, and Barth's reticence to proclaim a *status confessionis*—took up a pastorate in London. Barth responded to a letter of explanation from Bonhoeffer with words neither would soon forget:

> Get back to your post in Berlin straightaway! . . . you need to be here with all guns blazing! . . . standing up to these brethren along with me . . . Why weren't you there pulling on the rope that I, virtually alone, could hardly budge? Why aren't you here all the time? . . . Just be glad I do not have you here in front of me, because then I would find an entirely different way of putting it to you . . . that you are a German, that your church's house is on fire, that you know enough, and know well enough how to say what you know, to be able to help, and in fact you ought to return to your post by the next ship! . . . If you did not matter so much to me, I would not have taken you by the collar in this fashion.[9]

When Bonhoeffer returned to direct a non-sanctioned seminary in the spring of 1935, Barth had already been forced to resign both his professorship and his leadership role in the Confessing Church. With Barth's return to Basel the two corresponded less frequently, though they remained important to each other, personally and intellectually.[10]

---

7. Bonhoeffer, *Testament to Freedom*, 383.

8. Given Barth's polemics against the *analogia entis* during this period, it is little surprise to find Bonhoeffer's 1933 lectures—published as *Creation and Fall*—positing an *analogia relationis* and renewing the opposition to Przywara already present in *Act and Being*: cf. Bonhoeffer, *Creation and Fall*, 62–65; *Act and Being*, 27, 73–76, 138.

9. Bonhoeffer, *London*, 39–41.

10. Numerous fascinating aspects of their relationship are revealed in their subsequent correspondence—discussions about justification and sanctification, Barth's skepticism about the monastic tendencies of Bonhoeffer's seminary and anxieties about Bonhoeffer's conspiratorial activities, as well as Bonhoeffer's procurement of the proofs for *CD* 2.2. On one occasion in 1941, the Swiss border police refused to let Bonhoeffer cross, since he was a civilian employee of the German Military Intelligence Agency. Bonhoeffer had them phone Barth, who agreed to vouch for his old friend.

2. Bonhoeffer's *analogia relationis* and Barth's Doctrine of Creation

As Bonhoeffer was reading *Church Dogmatics* 2.2 and writing letters from prison, Barth was working through Bonhoeffer's 1933 lectures, published as *Creation and Fall*, and developing his theological anthropology. Published shortly after Bonhoeffer's death, Barth's exegesis of Gen 1:26-27 in *Church Dogmatics* 3.1 inaugurates Barth's public engagement with Bonhoeffer's theology. He appropriates Bonhoeffer's *analogia relationis* as the manner in which human persons bear the *imago Dei*, reaffirming his opposition to the *analogia entis*.[11] Barth's reflections on the *analogia relationis* prove generative for the exposition of his christological-trinitarian anthropology in the first three part-volumes of his *Doctrine of Creation*.

In *Creation and Fall* Bonhoeffer argues that human persons bear the Creator's likeness in their freedom, not as an inherent quality, but as "a relation between two persons."[12] "The 'image that is like God' is therefore no *analogia entis* in which human beings, in their existence in-and-of-themselves, in their being, could be said to be like God's being."[13] No person exists alone, divine or human, and to perceive God or a human being is to perceive a person in relation.[14] In place of the *analogia entis*, Bonhoeffer argues that an *analogia relationis* is a preferable rendering of Gen 1:26-27. The human person's created likeness to God entails two relations that image God's relations. First, in her freedom *for* [*für*] God and other human persons she reflects God's freedom for her and for others. Second, in her freedom *from* [*von*] the creation, in dominion, she reflects the divine aseity, God's freedom from the creation.

Rejecting numerous alternative interpretations of the *imago Dei*, Barth affirms Bonhoeffer's analogy of freedom for God and for one-another. Barth

---

11. It is curious that Barth does not specifically comment on Bonhoeffer's *Act and Being* here or elsewhere. Barth's copy has an inscription: "In great gratitude and admiration, Dietrich Bonhoeffer." Balthasar employs Bonhoeffer's critiques of Barth and Przywara in his analysis: cf. Balthasar, *Theology of Karl Barth*, 365.

12. Bonhoeffer, *Creation and Fall*, 63.

13. Ibid., 64-65.

14. Bonhoeffer identifies God's freedom only in relation to human persons and creation, explicitly denying this freedom in the relations between the persons of the Trinity: "[I]t is the message of the gospel itself that God's freedom has bound itself to us, that God's free grace becomes real with us alone, that God wills not to be free for God's self but for humankind." Barth will say God is free *not only* for God's self, but truly for God's self *and also* for humankind. For Bonhoeffer, like Barth, freedom is never autonomous, but always in relation to another: "Because God in Christ is free for humankind, because God does not keep God's freedom for God's self, we can think of freedom only as 'being free for'" (ibid., 63).

writes, "Dietrich Bonhoeffer offers us important help in this respect... In this relationship which is absolutely given and posited there is revealed freedom and therefore the divine likeness. As God is free for man, so man is free for man; but only inasmuch as God is for him, so that the *analogia relationis* as the meaning of the divine likeness cannot be equated with an *analogia entis*."[15] Following Bonhoeffer, all else that might be said to comprise the *imago Dei* of the human person—dominion, intellect, reason, morality, conscience, structures, dispositions, or any other attributes or capacities—is either excluded, denied, or a consequence of God's determination to relate to humanity in repetition of God's self-relation.[16] "The image of God is such that, as the *analogia relationis*, it can never cease to be God's work and gift or become a human possession."[17] A "solitary" person, one not in relation to God and others, would be incapable of expressing God's image.[18] Barth does not merely affirm this analogy of relation as he finds it, however, but develops several christological-trinitarian dimensions.

First, Barth's exposition proposes that God's own freedom for Godself occurs in the trinitarian "loving co-existence and co-operation, the I and Thou, which first take place in God Himself."[19] For Barth, the original relation or prototype to which the *imago Dei* corresponds is not God's relation

---

15. *CD* 3.1:195. Barth makes fairly clear in this part-volume that he borrows the term *analogia relationis* from Bonhoeffer. However, the indexes for 3.1 and the *Church Dogmatics* as a whole do not list the occurrences of *analogia relationis* in 3.1 or 3.3, but only those in 3.2. Because Bonhoeffer is not mentioned in 3.2 or 3.3, but only 3.1, scholars have at times overlooked Bonhoeffer's relevance to Barth's discussions of the *imago Dei*. For example, Price gives careful attention to the discussion of the *analogia relationis* in 3.2, arguing that this concept "may one day prove to be his most lasting contribution to modern theology." Price, *Karl Barth's Anthropology*, 132. Focusing as he does on the anthropology of 3.2, Price does not consider the development of the *analogia relationis* from 3.1 and does not mention that the term is drawn from Bonhoeffer.

16. Hunsinger makes much the same point, drawing explicitly from Barth and Bonhoeffer: "When Christians appeal to the image of God... they are pointing to the ultimate meaning of human life. From Bonhoeffer through Barth to recent Catholic theology, the doctrine of the *imago Dei* has been reconceived in terms of relationality instead of the traditional rationality. It is human relationality as such that stands in analogy to the Holy Trinity, and therefore to the ultimacy of community. For the Trinity is itself a holy communion of love and freedom, joy and peace" (Hunsinger, "Torture," 68).

17. *CD* 3.1:201.

18. Cf. *CD* 3.1:290.

19. *CD* 3.1, 196. "Not without genuine astonishment at the diversity of man's inventive genius," Barth considers and then rejects proposals from Late Antiquity (Ambrose, Athanasius, Augustine, Philo), the Reformation (Luther and Calvin), and his Modern interlocutors (Hegel, Seeberg, Troeltsch, Delitzsch, Jacob, von Rad, G. Kittel). Cf. *CD* 3.1:192–94.

to humankind *ad extra*, but "the relationship and differentiation between the I and the Thou in God Himself."[20] It is this original triune relation that is imaged in God's relation to the human Jesus, Jesus Christ's relation to humanity in general, and human persons' relations to one-another.[21]

Second, to Bonhoeffer's concept of human existence in freedom for God and human persons, Barth adds that the real human person exists in a threefold by-for-with [*von-zu-mit*] orientation and dynamic relation precisely in her freedom for [*für*] God and others. Jesus Christ reveals the true human person as one who is determined "*by* God *for* life *with* God."[22] He is the true human person who serves as God's covenant-partner in his humanity and, also, as humanity's covenanting-partner in his divinity. Jesus' *humanity* consists in his existence as the human person for [*für*] his fellow human persons. His *divinity* consists in his existence as sent by God for this purpose, to be this human person for [*für*] God. Jesus Christ actualizes God's twofold triune-*ad intra*-relating and triune-*ad extra*-relating, as well as the corresponding faithful human action for God and for his fellow human persons.

Third, Barth adds, not only does the humanity of Jesus evidence life in relationship with humanity—by, for, and with others—and not only does his history constitute God's actualization of the covenant-relationship—from, to, and with humanity—but his humanity reveals, indirectly, God's own inner divine essence. "If 'God for man' is the eternal covenant revealed and effective in time in the humanity of Jesus, in this decision of the Creator for the creature there arises a relationship which is not alien to the Creator, to God as God, but we might almost say appropriate and natural to Him. God repeats in this relationship *ad extra* a relationship proper to Himself in His inner divine essence."[23] Jesus' human existence for [*für*] humanity—his determination by humanity, his living for humanity, and his solidarity with humanity—corresponds to his existence for [*für*] God—his determination by [*von*] God for [*zu*] life with [*mit*] God. These two relationships, equally true of Jesus' humanity, are repetitions, images, or analogues of the relations

---

20. *CD* 3.1:198.

21. Cf. Jüngel, "Möglichkeit theologischer Anthropologie, 541–42.

22. *CD* 3.2:203. By "orientation and dynamic relation" I mean to collect two aspects of Barth's *von-zu-mit* prepositional collocation that are difficult to render consistently in English. *Von-zu-mit* is translated variously as by-for-with and from-to-with in §45.1. The latter formulation better captures Barth's actualistic conception of divine and human existence in dynamic relation. Unfortunately, rendering *von-zu-mit* as from-to-with generates rather awkward English constructions capturing even less of Barth's meaning than by-for-with—e.g., "determination from God to life with God."

23. *CD* 3.2:218.

in God's eternal existence. In God's essence, in the inner being of God, God is not alone but exists in active relation from, to, and with Godself.

With these modifications, Barth thoroughly reconfigures Bonhoeffer's *analogia relationis*. In Jesus' humanity the relationship of free and loving interaction recur between God and humanity. It is this pattern of relating—*for* God and humanity in one's *by-for-with* determination—as opposed to a correspondence of being, to which the image of God refers.

> This is the positive sense of the term 'image'—there is a correspondence and similarity between the two relationships. This is no correspondence and similarity of being, no *analogia entis* ... Between these two relationships as such there is—and in this sense the second is the image of the first—correspondence and similarity. There is an *analogia relationis* ... The Father and Son are reflected in the man Jesus and his fellow-humanity. There could not be a clearer reference to the *analogia relationis* and therefore to the *imago Dei* in the most central, namely, the christological, sense of the term.[24]

The *analogia relationis*, the active relating by human persons in correspondence to God's own active-relating (to Godself and all that is not God), is the *imago Dei*. To image God is to relate as God relates. Jesus' human history is the specific time, place, and event in which God's eternal inner divine relating is revealed. It is through Jesus' activity, the history in which he interacts with God and humanity as the God-human, that human beings learn not only what humanity is, but who God is.

For Bonhoeffer, the analogy reflects a twofold relation: first, in freedom for God and human persons—a freedom of service—and, second, in freedom from the creation—a freedom of dominion. The structure and dynamics of Barth's *analogia relationis* image the hypostatic union and processions and missions of Chalcedon and Nicaea. For both theologians, the *analogia relationis* invalidates any *analogia entis* and, for both, it bears directly upon ethics.

Barth writes, "When God and man meet as revealed in the Word of God, then definite spheres and relationships may be seen in which this encounter takes place ... The one will of God and his one command embrace his work as Creator, Reconciler and Redeemer ... Similarly, the action of the one man is his action on the three corresponding planes"[25] For Barth, "all

---

24. *CD* 3.2:220–21, rev. Cf. *KD* 3.2:262.

25. *CD* 3.4:29. Barth allows that the different elements might be called spheres, relationships, planes, fields, even orders or ordinances, so long as they are understood as the different forms of the relation between God and humanity wherein the ethical event

ethical activity consists in discerning the will of God and bearing witness to it" as it is encountered by human persons within the framed reference of these three relations through which God relates to human persons.[26]

Like Barth, Bonhoeffer maintains that discerning the relationship in which one stands vis-à-vis God and neighbor is essential to faithfully responding to God's will. He affirms that God relates to human persons as Creator, Reconciler, and Redeemer. But, emphasizing concrete social institutions, Bonhoeffer adds that the church, Christ existing as community, relates to worldly institutions through christological-eschatological realities given concrete expression in the divine mission here and now. Criticizing the historical justifications given for the orders of creation, Bonhoeffer's representation of Luther's estates finds its basis in Scripture's witness to Christ's eschatological relations: Marriage and Family witness the relations of Christ to the church-community, of God the Father to the Son of God and Son of Man, and of Jesus Christ as brother to humankind; Work manifests "the creative service of God and Christ toward the world and of human beings toward God"; Government points to Christ's lordship over the heavenly city.[27] In, with, and under these three mandates, the Church, a fourth mandate, presences Christ in the concrete social form of the church community. The worldly mandates bear witness to the promised heavenly kingdom precisely in their concrete encounters with the church-community. Bonhoeffer's Lutheran commitments are evident in his appropriation of the estates and implicit *genus majesticaticum* seen in the church's role as the present body of Christ in relation to the worldly mandates. These encounters give provisional and temporal expression to eternal divine-human relations, foreshadowing and indicating here and now, the original and prototype existing in eternity.

Bonhoeffer's divine mandates, like Barth's "spheres and relationships," reflect eternal dimensions of the divine-human relating revealed through Scripture's witness to Jesus Christ. Favoring Bonhoeffer's approach to the ethics of Althaus, Brunner, and Søe, Barth writes, "It is along these lines that we certainly have to think, and we may gratefully acknowledge that Bonhoeffer does this, even though it may be asked whether the working out of his view does not still contain some arbitrary elements . . . The God who works and is revealed in His Word, in Jesus Christ, characterizes Himself

---

occurs—that is, human obedience or disobedience. They are not laws, prescriptions, or imperatives, but "the reality of the event in which [divine command and human action] meet" (*CD* 3.4:31). Knowledge of these spheres makes possible "ethics as a formed reference to the ethical event," that is, "well-founded and legitimate witness" (32).

26. *CRDT*, 278.

27. Cf. Bonhoeffer, *Conspiracy and Imprisonment*, 549–50.

(in accordance with His inner trinitarian being) as Creator, Reconciler and Redeemer."[28] Here, again, Barth offers critical modification to Bonhoeffer's insights on divine-human relationships through reflection upon God's trinitarian existence. Throughout *Church Dogmatics* 3 the reader finds Barth critically appropriating Bonhoeffer's insights with significant implications for his own theological anthropology and special ethics.[29]

3. "Seeing Around Corners" in Barth's Doctrine of Reconciliation

While publicly opposing "cheap grace" in *Church Dogmatics* 4.1, Barth privately writes to P. W. Herrenbrück responding to questions about Bonhoeffer's theology and the enigmatic prison writings. Although the letters from prison leave him "disturbed . . . embarrassed . . . confused," and "a lessening of the offence he has provided us is the last thing I should wish," Barth nevertheless notes reservations. "As always with Bonhoeffer one is faced by a peculiar difficulty. He was—how shall I put it?—an impulsive, visionary thinker who was suddenly seized by an idea to which he gave lively form, and then after a time he called a halt (one never knew whether it was final or temporary) with some provisional last point or other. Was this not the case with *Discipleship*? Did he not also for a time have liturgical impulses—And how was it with the 'Mandates' of his *Ethics*, with which I tussled when I wrote III/4?" On the theme of imitation in *Discipleship*, Barth indicates "it has long been clear to me that I will have to devote a lot of room to this matter in the *Church Dogmatics*." And, again, "I always read his early writings, especially those which apparently or in reality said things which were not at once clear to me, with the thought that—when they were seen round some corner or other—he might be right."[30] Barth seems to have seen around additional corners during his supervision of John Godsey's dissertation on Bonhoeffer's theology as he was working out his doctrine of sanctification in *Church Dogmatics* 4.2.[31]

---

28. *CD* 3.4:22, 25.

29. In this volume Barth singles out Bonhoeffer's theological and ethical proposals as superior to the alternatives in discussions of the *imago Dei* (*CD* 3.1:195), ethical method (*CD* 3.4:23), and the borderline case of suicide (*CD* 3.4:404). The analogy of relation recurs in various contexts throughout *Church Dogmatics* 3 and 4: cf. *CD* 3.2:222–23, 243, 324, 341, 438; *CD* 3.3:51, 102, 419; *CD* 4.4, 78.

30. Barth, "From a Letter," 89–92.

31. This dissertation was published as Godsey, *Theology*.

Barth expresses his appreciation for *Discipleship* in §66 on "The Sanctification of Man." Barth describes the book's opening chapters with effusive commendation.

> Easily the best that has been written on [*imitatio Christi*] . . . the matter is handled with such depth and precision that I am almost tempted simply to reproduce them in an extended quotation. For I cannot hope to say anything better on the subject than what is said here by a man who, having written on discipleship, was ready to achieve it in his own life, and did in his own way achieve it even to the point of death. In following my own course, I am happy that on this occasion I can lean as heavily as I do upon another.[32]

Barth proceeds to propose four main points: grace takes the form of a command that requires the particular action of following as the only proper response; the call to discipleship binds the disciples not to a principle but to the person who calls others to follow, obey, and believe; the call requires a first step of obedience in faith; and the call entails a break that is achieved not by the individual's decision but by the calling, the divine action which demands a corresponding human act of faith. In expositing each of these points Barth develops the central claims from *Discipleship*'s first five chapters.

In the next paragraph, §67 on "The Holy Spirit and the Upbuilding of the Christian Community," Barth offers another high commendation, this time in reference to Bonhoeffer's *Sanctorum Communio*—the work he referred to as a "theological miracle."[33]

> If there can be any possible vindication of Reinhold Seeberg, it is to be sought in the fact that his school could give rise to this man and this dissertation, which . . . makes far more instructive and stimulating and illuminating and genuinely edifying reading today than many of the more famous works which have since been written on the problem of the Church . . . [M]any things would not have been written if Bonhoeffer's exposition had been taken into account. I openly confess that I have misgivings whether I can even maintain the high level reached by Bonhoeffer, saying

---

32. *CD* 4.2:533–34.

33. Godsey, *Theology*, 21n6. Barth's comment was made in a private conversation. It appears on the dust jacket of the 1963 English translation of *Sanctorum Communio*, titled *Communion of Saints*.

no less in my own words and context, and saying it no less forcefully, than did this young man so many years ago.[34]

As with the *analogia relationis* and *imitatio Christi*, Barth proceeds to incorporate Bonhoeffer's exposition of the creedal *communio sanctorum*, this time expanding upon the concept of "upbuilding" as essential to the church's being in action.

From *Church Dogmatics* 3.1 to 4.2 Barth draws inspiration from Bonhoeffer's *Creation and Fall*, *Discipleship*, *Sanctorum Communio*, and *Ethics*. By the time he delivers the lectures that would become 4.3 and 4.4, even the prison writings he had described as a "particular thorn" in 1952 may have grown less objectionable. In their respective readings of §69 on "The Glory of the Mediator," Andreas Pangritz and Kevin Hart point to passages where *Letters and Papers from Prison* appears to provide inspiration for Barth's discussions of "secular parables" of the kingdom and his "doctrine of lights" in other religions.[35] Barth's exposition of lying and un-truth in §70 on "The Falsehood and Condemnation of Man" offers yet another instance with its striking parallels to the younger theologian's phenomenological representation of truth-telling as a disclosive practice in "What is Meant by Telling the Truth?"[36]

The prison writings continue to echo in the questions taken up in the posthumous publication of Barth's ethics of reconciliation lecture fragments, *The Christian Life*. "Had the world first to become mature in order that in its own way the Church should become mature in a positive sense?"[37] It comes as little surprise to find congruence with Bonhoeffer in Barth's conclusion: the church is "free for the secular world." Barth reiterates this point where an extended quote could easily have been taken from Bonhoeffer's "Outline for a Book": "[The Christian's] job, then, is to usher in a kind of Christian secularism or secular Christianity . . . thinking, speaking, and acting in the expectation that he can most fittingly serve the gospel of God among children and citizens of the world by the closest possible approximation and assimilation to their attitude and language and even their thought forms, so that in his own person he will set before them the fact of God's love . . . Christians have the freedom . . . to take seriously their solidarity with those outside."[38] At this point Barth acknowledges, "Dietrich Bonhoeffer possibly

---

34. CD 4.2:641.
35. Cf. Pangritz, *Karl Barth*, 134; K. Hart, "Bonhoeffer's 'Religious Clothes,'" 190.
36. These reflections were written after Bonhoeffer had read and embraced Barth's ethics in CD 2.2.
37. ChL, 21.
38. ChL, 200.

had something of this view in his last years when he made certain rather cryptic statements."[39] As Barth's dogmatics lectures come to a close, Barth affirms even those aspects of Bonhoeffer's writings that trouble Barth most as overlapping with his own conceptions of secular Christian possibilities.

4. Bonhoeffer's Lasting Impression

Bonhoeffer remained important to Barth long after aspirations of completing the *Church Dogmatics* had been set aside. In 1967 Barth wrote Bethge regarding his "masterpiece" on Bonhoeffer, "I have learned many things about Bonhoeffer for the first time," including "the fact that in 1933 and the years following, Bonhoeffer was the first and almost the only one to face and tackle the Jewish question so centrally and energetically. I have long since regarded it as a fault on my part that I did not make this question a decisive issue, at least publicly in the church conflict. Only from your book have I become aware that Bonhoeffer did so from the very first. Perhaps this is why he was not at Barmen nor later at Dahlem."[40] Bethge's biography reminds Barth that Bonhoeffer's opinions on the Aryan Clause and his isolation on these matters were, in part, what brought tension to the relationship between Bonhoeffer and the nascent Confessing Church movement, leading to his departure for London in 1933. He sees in Bonhoeffer one who shared the convictions he held at the time "when I left theological Liberalism," including the trajectory "from Christian faith to political action."[41] In the years of their acquaintance, "there was a genuine need in the direction which I now silently took for granted or emphasized only in passing ... and the need to fill [this gap], Bonhoeffer obviously saw very keenly from the first ... [H]e became a martyr, too, for this specific cause."[42] This apprecia-

---

39. Although Barth likely refers to *Letters and Papers from Prison*, his observations regarding Christ's relation to the secular or worldly are similarly apparent in *Ethics*: cf. Bonhoeffer, *Ethics*, 168–70, 339–51.

40. Barth, *Letters 1961–1968*, 250. In the decades since Barth made these comments to Bethge, Bonhoeffer scholarship has become increasingly ambivalent regarding his legacy of resistance, his participation in the *Abwehr*, and the motivations for his opposition to National Socialism. Cf. Holmes, *Bonhoeffer Legacy*; and Dramm, *Dietrich Bonhoeffer*. On other hand, in conversations and in *Unter dem Bogen*, Busch conveys that Barth's recollection of his own engagements downplay the extent of his early opposition to National Socialism. According to Bethge, it was not primarily Barth's reticence to pronounce a *status confessionis* but more so his experience drafting the Bethel Confession that so frustrated Bonhoeffer in 1933 and led to his departure for England.

41. Barth, *Letters 1961–1968*, 251.

42. Ibid. Barth expresses distaste for the diverse ways the prison fragments have been used to lay claim to Bonhoeffer's legacy—by middle-class Liberalism, East

tive and somewhat self-deprecating letter also expresses the "doubt" that systematic theology was Bonhoeffer's "real strength"—a point to which we will return. First, however, a last reference to Bonhoeffer among the final correspondences we have from Barth merits mention.

In a letter dated October 1, 1968, two months before his death, Barth declines Hendrikus Berkhof's request that he advise their mutual friend, J. Boulon. He writes, "To direct him to remain in Beirut—which, purely theoretically, would be best—I could not take responsibility: I already have in my memory the advice that I once gave Bonhoeffer to return from London to Germany, upon the execution of which he wound up in Flossenbürg."[43] In this personal aside we discern the residual regret lingering thirty-five years after Barth's scathing letter exhorting Bonhoeffer's return, "you need to be here with all guns blazing!"[44] Barth's own final letters and papers suggest Bonhoeffer's impact upon the elder was no less personal than it was theological.

5. Barth and Bonhoeffer in Differentiation and Relationship

While Barth was wrestling intensely with the epistemological and ontological conditions of possibility for Christian theology and witness in *Church Dogmatics* 1 and 2, Bonhoeffer was writing and acting upon conclusions to which *Church Dogmatics* would not give expression until volumes 3 and 4—creation and cosmology, theological anthropology, special ethics, justification and sanctification, discipleship, the communion of saints, and secular Christianity—namely, the lived experience of Christian discipleship in the church-community. As Paul Lehmann rightly points out, Barth's "specific attention to these concerns did not emerge until . . . it was too late for further exchange on these matters," at least not in person.[45]

German ideologues, and High Lutheranism. Barth is well aware of "all the things, or most of the things, that the experts have made of [the 'positivism of revelation'] right up to Heinrich Ott," and conveys more puzzlement than offense. He appreciates that Bonhoeffer was capable of "the most astonishing evolutions" analogous to his own theological development, and he sympathizes, "I hate to think of what people might have made of me if I had suffered a natural or violent death after the first or second *Romans* or after the first volume of my *Christian Dogmatics* in 1927. What I would not have wanted in such a case I would rather not see inflicted on Bonhoeffer, least of all in the way it has been done most recently by H. Ott" (252).

43. Barth, *Briefe 1961–1968*, 505; author's translation.
44. Bonhoeffer, *London*, 39.
45. Lehmann, "Concreteness of Theology," 68.

If Bonhoeffer is passed over as an important interlocutor for Barth's mature theology, it is in spite of, not because of, Barth's engagement with Bonhoeffer's thought. Barth develops Bonhoeffer's contributions in each part-volume of *Church Dogmatics* 3 and 4 and in *The Christian Life*. Given the widely recognized trajectory of influence from Barth to Bonhoeffer, closer attention to the historically overlooked influence in the other direction is overdue. If we take Barth at his word in *Church Dogmatics*, significant elements of his theology and ethics in volumes 3 and 4 would have gone missing had Bonhoeffer's influence not exerted itself. Theologians constructively engaging Barth's later theology should expect to find additional insights productive for their own reflection in Bonhoeffer's writings that were not available to Barth.

It yet remains to reconcile Barth's extensive use of Bonhoeffer's thought in *Church Dogmatics* 3 and 4 with the "doubt" Barth expressed to Bethge, "whether theological systematics (I include his *Ethics*)" was Bonhoeffer's strength. Barth himself may provide the greatest help on this question. In *Church Dogmatics* 1.1 Barth draws a distinction between regular and irregular dogmatics that pivots on the completeness and consistency with which one attends to constellations of theological loci. Regular dogmatics aim at completeness (e.g., Origen, Thomas, Calvin, Dorner). However, Barth notes that the early church, Athanasius, Luther, and Kutter performed irregular dogmatics, theological reflection which "will be, and will mean to be, a fragment."[46] Barth himself aims to engage in regular dogmatics without demeaning the irregular approach, "a little of which all of us secretly do and which we ought to do boldly."[47] For Barth, "the ultimate question cannot be whether we are doing regular or irregular dogmatics." Rather, "what finally counts is whether a dogmatics is scriptural."[48] On this basic commitment, Barth and Bonhoeffer are of a like mind.

This distinction between regular and irregular dogmatics, consistent versus fragmentary (yet equally provisional), helpfully illuminates Barth's seemingly devastating appraisal of Bonhoeffer in an otherwise effusive letter to Bethge.[49] Barth's assessment differentiates his own self-consciously regu-

---

46. *CD* 1.1:277.

47. Barth, *Göttingen*, 38.

48. *CD* 1.1:287.

49. That Bonhoeffer works erratically in relation to Barth bears on this point as well—beginning his theological writings with *Sanctorum Communio*, a treatise on the church; jumping to prolegomenal matters of epistemology and ontology in *Act and Being*; to *Creation and Fall*; followed by *Discipleship*, a book on works, grace, the Sermon on the Mount, justification, and sanctification; then his "special" *Ethics*; and a theological critique of religion in *Letters and Papers*. The disparity between the organized flow

lar dogmatics from Bonhoeffer's theological writings, which he gives high praise in *Church Dogmatics* as elsewhere. It explains how Barth is able to laud Bonhoeffer's insights while submitting them to extensive revision—*Ethics* is "brilliant" even as it is "fragmentary and provisional."[50] For him, the form of Bonhoeffer's *Ethics* had to do not only with its unfinished state (Barth's *Church Dogmatics* had been in a similar unfinished and non-progressing state for some years when he made this comment of Bonhoeffer's *magnum opus*), but specifically with the lack of systematic perspective from which Bonhoeffer had approached his *Ethics* which left a disorganized, unpolished result.[51]

Barth's appraisal and incorporation of Bonhoeffer's irregular and often fragmentary writings evidence that he found in them not only nascent indicators but seminal insights he could develop in ways productive for his own distinctive theology. Barth's reformulation of the *analogia relationis* for his theological anthropology extends far beyond Bonhoeffer's original concept. Similarly, Barth's insistence that the Creator, Reconciler, Redeemer relations constitute the threefold form of God's active-relating as "Commander" critically opposes and embraces aspects of Bonhoeffer's divine mandates that serve as the relational form, or "framed reference," in which the encounter with God's command always takes place.[52] It is not only theological anthropology and the relational domains of ethical frameworks, nor only *imitatio Christi* and the *communio sanctorum*, that warrant further consideration as possibilities for conversation between Barth and Bonhoeffer. Attention to their respective conceptions of vicarious representative action as accordance and obedience as correspondence, re-presenting the truth and giving witness, borderline cases of euthanasia and suicide, and the difference election makes to ethical discernment, are but a few potential convergences where their theological-ethical visions might be brought into constructive dialogue.[53]

Barth and Bonhoeffer shared the conviction that analogy entails both differentiation and relationship, correspondence of the unlike, and so it proves fitting to close noting a central shared commitment. As both

---

of the *Church Dogmatics* and Bonhoeffer's writings could hardly be more pronounced.

50. *CD* 3.4:4.

51. Three editions of *Ethics* include different manuscripts, chapter titles and headings, and orderings of the various manuscripts included: cf. Bonhoeffer, *Ethics*, 477.

52. Cf. *CD* 3.4:22.

53. Greggs and Ziegler are among a growing number of scholars who, in the spirit of Jüngel's *God as the Mystery of the World*, are constructively dialoguing with Barth and Bonhoeffer's theological criticisms of religion: cf. Greggs, *Theology against Religion*; Ziegler, *Doing Theology*. Also indebted to Jüngel, Webster finds harmony in the reading of Scripture as basic to Barth and Bonhoeffer's theological commitments: cf. Webster, "Reading the Bible." Ellis offers an excellent comparison of Barth and Bonhoeffer's divine command ethics: cf. Ellis, "Moral Action."

theologians came to know the loneliness of forging new paths, resisting cultural norms of their day, seeking for themselves not popular appeal but faithful witness to the Word of God, they took seriously the Baptist's saying, "He must become greater, I must become less."[54] And at least one specific practice resulted from and informed their often shared and uncommon vision, sustaining them in the midst of busyness, solitude, and crisis. Bonhoeffer wrote after seven months in prison, "in addition to daily Bible study, I have read the Old Testament two and a half times through and have learned a great deal."[55] The result was his essay, "What Does It Mean to Tell the Truth?" in which new insights on relational truth-telling and guilt redress his account of lying in *Ethics*.[56] Similarly, in the midst of exegetical preparations for his ethics of reconciliation in *Church Dogmatics* 4.4 Barth wrote to his son Markus, the New Testament scholar, that he had again read "the New Testament from A to Z and word by word."[57] His sacramentology followed. Those who travel with or beyond these two theologians may discover that analogous disciplines prove necessary for sustaining their corresponding vocations.[58]

Response to Matthew Puffer on Dietrich Bonhoeffer's Influence on Karl Barth

—By Andy Rowell

First, I would like to affirm Matthew Puffer's attempt to trace the ways Bonhoeffer influenced Barth. Though it is a difficult task, it has the potential to yield significant theological dividends. Second, I would like to briefly identify six types of evidence that Puffer explores. Third, I would like to underline the severe strain placed on both Barth and Bonhoeffer under the

54. John 3:30 (NIV).
55. Bonhoeffer, *Letters and Papers*, 181.
56. Cf. Bonhoeffer, "What Does It Mean to Tell the Truth?," 601–8; *Ethics*, 279–80.
57. *ChL*, xv.
58. I wish to thank the Karl Barth Blog Conference organizers for their invitation, the participants for their helpful comments, and Andy Rowell in particular for his thoughtful response. I am also grateful to Daryl Ellis, Tim Hartman, Keith Johnson, and Chad Wellmon for their corrections, contributions, and criticisms.

Nazi regime which engendered doubt in Barth about Bonhoeffer's trustworthiness, which inhibited Bonhoeffer's influence on Barth until 1967.

The significance and difficulty of commenting on Bonhoeffer's influence on Barth

Much of the secondary literature on Dietrich Bonhoeffer notes the influence Karl Barth had on Bonhoeffer. But the secondary literature on Karl Barth only rarely explores how Barth was influenced by Bonhoeffer. Puffer aims to remedy this in his essay. Admittedly, Puffer has given himself a difficult task. Unless a theologian explicitly states what he has learned from another theologian, trying to discern and reconstruct how one influenced the other is difficult, because such influences on a given theologian are so varied and numerous. Conclusions about possible sources of ideas almost invariably involve a certain degree of conjecture. In the case of Barth and Bonhoeffer, in their most formal theological work—for Barth the *Church Dogmatics*, and for Bonhoeffer *Sanctorum Communio* and *Act and Being*—they both explicitly acknowledge that they are reflecting on the work of the other, thus validating the historian's suspicion that there is insight to be gained here. Therefore, even though Puffer's descriptive work (raising into relief the connections between the two theologians) cannot render definitive conclusions about Bonhoeffer's influence on Barth, it is useful not only for historical curiosity but also for theological clarity. The net effect of Puffer's analysis is that the evidence indicates Bonhoeffer stimulated, prodded, and goaded Barth to clarify issues related to the divine-human relationship, including the *analogia relationis*, discipleship, *sanctorum communio*, and ethics.

Approaches to analyzing the evidence that Bonhoeffer influenced Barth

If one wants to find out how one theologian has influenced another, there are a number of levels to that analysis. Puffer analyses six types of evidence to explore how Bonhoeffer may have influenced Barth.

First, *instances of explicit acknowledgement*: Puffer notes the instances when Barth cites Bonhoeffer. Because much of Barth's corpus is now digitized, it is fairly straightforward to note the thirty-three instances of "Bonhoeffer" in the 8,000 pages of the *Church Dogmatics*. Barth interacted extensively with the *analogia relationis* from Bonhoeffer's *Creation and Fall* in *CD* 3.1 (7 mentions in §41), which was published in 1945. Barth also drew from Bonhoeffer's *Ethics* in *CD* 3.4 (11 mentions in §52; 3 in §55; 2 in §56; 1 in §57), which was published in 1951. Finally, he effusively praises Bonhoeffer's *Discipleship* (7 mentions in §66) and *Sanctorum Communio* (two mentions in §67) in *CD* 4.2, which was published in 1958.

Second, *instances of explicit assessment*: Puffer summarizes Barth's explicit comments that assess Bonhoeffer's theology. Barth's letter to Bonhoeffer's biographer, Eberhard Bethge, is the most important of these texts because of its extensive, substantive reflection on various parts of Bonhoeffer's legacy.[59]

Third, *probing for implicit dependence*: Puffer notes the claims by some scholars that Barth draws on Bonhoeffer at a number of points even when he does not explicitly say so, such as in his treatments of secular parables, the doctrine of the lights, and truth-telling. The sentiment expressed by Paul Lehmann and cited by Puffer is important to reiterate in this regard: Barth took up many of the issues Bonhoeffer wrote about after Bonhoeffer's death. Therefore, it is difficult to precisely determine whether Barth's treatments of ethics, politics, witness, and the church-community are the inevitable logical outworking of his own trajectory or whether he was provoked to address them with more clarity because of Bonhoeffer's influence.

Fourth, *modification of a concept*: Puffer sometimes analyzes the degree to which Barth maintains or modifies a concept introduced by Bonhoeffer. Puffer pays particular attention to the ways Barth elaborates the concept of *analogia relationis* that he takes from Bonhoeffer.

Fifth, *comparative study*: Puffer at times compares the theologies of Barth and Bonhoeffer without speculating on whether one influenced the other. For example, Puffer ends his essay commenting on the practice of Bible reading as a resource utilized by both for inspiring their theologizing. He does not argue that Barth picked this habit up from Bonhoeffer or *vice versa* but rather is content to assert that it may be an important similarity. There is more literature than mentioned by Puffer that compares Barth and Bonhoeffer's theology more generally. For example, John Godsey, who wrote his dissertation on Bonhoeffer with Barth, has a very interesting article in which he probes their backgrounds, relationship, and theological inclinations. He argues that the basic difference between Bonhoeffer and Barth is that "Barth's theology tends toward a *theologia gloriae* in order to ensure the graciousness of God's action in Christ. In contrast, Bonhoeffer's theology is a *theologia crucis* in order to ensure the costliness of God's grace in Christ."[60] Charles Marsh disagrees with Godsey's analysis. Marsh argues that the basic

---

59. Barth, *Letters 1961–1968*, 251.
60. Godsey, "Barth and Bonhoeffer," 25.

difference can be found in what Barth calls "the primary and secondary objectivity of God."[61] In a review, Godsey praises Marsh's analysis while maintaining Marsh's position is compatible with his own analysis.[62] Again, however, this literature has more to do with direct theological comparison rather than probing the historical connection for ways that Bonhoeffer may have influenced Barth.

Sixth, *description of personal relationship*: Puffer notes that Barth was initially delighted by Bonhoeffer's quotation from Luther when they first met and years later was dismayed by Bonhoeffer critical remarks of him published posthumously in *Letters and Papers from Prison*. It is this evidence that I would like to expand upon in the remaining part of my response.

Bonhoeffer's influence on Barth hampered by a lack of trust

Bonhoeffer and Barth met for the first time in July 1931. Bonhoeffer was 25 and Barth was 45. Bonhoeffer had interacted extensively with Barth in his dissertation *Sanctorum Communio* and habilitation *Act and Being*, while Barth had read nothing by Bonhoeffer.

Barth was indisputably Bonhoeffer's most influential contemporary theological mentor. In 1927, Bonhoeffer's dissertation advisor Reinhold Seeberg noted about *Sanctorum Communio*, "here and there one finds references to Barth."[63] Writing in the English introduction to the critical edition, Clifford Green writes that Seeberg had no idea how influential Barth was on Bonhoeffer and would continue to be.[64] Eberhard Bethge, Bonhoeffer's close friend and biographer, emphasizes that despite the criticisms Bonhoeffer lodged against Barth's theology, Bonhoeffer was fundamentally loyal to Barth. "Whatever the implications of Bonhoeffer's criticisms of Barth . . . Bonhoeffer viewed these criticisms as coming from within, not without, the Barthian movement."[65]

It is not only Bonhoeffer interpreters who acknowledge the massive influence of Barth on Bonhoeffer; it is also clear from Bonhoeffer's own writing that he treasured the time he spent with Barth and longed for Barth's

---

61. Marsh, *Reclaiming Dietrich Bonhoeffer*, 29–33.
62. Godsey, Review of *Reclaiming Dietrich Bonhoeffer*; see also Pangritz, *Karl Barth*, 11–13.
63. Bonhoeffer, *Sanctorum Communio*, 8.
64. Ibid., 2–3.
65. Bethge, *Dietrich Bonhoeffer: Theologian*, 178.

feedback and approval. For example, in a letter to Barth on December 24, 1932, Bonhoeffer writes:

> I should like you to know that I know no one else who can free me from these persistent questions as you can, and therefore you are the one with whom I feel I must talk like this. It's hard to say why, but with you I just have this very distinct feeling that the way you see things is somehow the right way. It's just that when I am talking with you, I am brought right to the heart of the matter, whereas before I only kept circling around it at a distance. That for me is the very unmistakable sign that here is where I am right on target. And since nowhere else is this awareness with anything like this intensity, I shall have to keep asking you now and then for the gift of some of your time; at such times, please forgive me.[66]

In prison, he wrote to Barth—"there are only a few who have remained as loyal to you in countless conversations over these years as I have attempted to do."[67]

But Barth did not share the same trust of Bonhoeffer. Barth did not interact with Bonhoeffer's theological work until 1945, when Bonhoeffer was in a concentration camp and then executed. In their correspondence during the Third Reich years, four times Bonhoeffer earnestly sought Barth's advice on practical issues and each time Barth responded skeptically about Bonhoeffer's judgments. Thirty years later, Barth acknowledged that Bonhoeffer was prescient on all these concrete issues and that his mistrust of Bonhoeffer was misplaced. However, this is not to say that Barth was lacking in his response to Nazism—rather he was arguably Bonhoeffer's most powerful influence to act—but that the fog of the crucible of Nazism clouded their relationship.

First, on September 9, 1933, Bonhoeffer inquired of Barth whether he supported their leaving the national church because it had adopted the Aryan paragraph which removed Christian pastors with Jewish backgrounds from their positions. Barth wrote back two days later urging him to take up a posture of "waiting."[68] In his letter to Bethge in 1967 Barth notes his regret about this. "Especially new to me was the fact that in 1933 and the years following, Bonhoeffer was the first and almost the only one to face and tackle

---

66. Bonhoeffer, *Berlin*, 81–82.
67. Bonhoeffer, *Conspiracy and Imprisonment*, 278.
68. Bonhoeffer, *Berlin*, 164–69.

the Jewish question so centrally and energetically. I have long since regarded it as a fault on my part that I did not make this question a decisive issue."[69]

Second, on October 24, 1933, Bonhoeffer wrote to Barth of his decision to protest the adoption of the Aryan paragraph by taking a post in London.[70] On November 20, 1933, Barth wrote back a sharp letter urging Bonhoeffer to return to Germany.[71] In a 1968 letter, Barth regrets "the advice he had once given Bonhoeffer to return from London to Germany . . . a return which had finally led to his execution."[72]

Third, in the fall of 1936, Bonhoeffer wrote another letter to Barth explaining his practices in the seminary at Finkenwalde.[73] Barth wrote back on October 14, 1936, stating that "an almost indefinable odor of a monastic eros and pathos about your description disturbs me."[74] In 1968, Barth wrote to Bethge that he appreciated that Bonhoeffer was seeking "the renewal of personal and public worship . . . I sense what was in his mind here and might perhaps sum it up in the term 'discipline' [*Disziplin*]. If this is right, then I can only endorse his intention as such."[75]

Fourth, in May 1942, Bonhoeffer went to visit Barth in Basel for the third time. Before he arrives, Bonhoeffer writes that he is disappointed to hear from a number of people that Barth is "unsettled as to the objectives" of Bonhoeffer's visit. Barth's assistant Charlotte von Kirschbaum writes back that indeed Barth is unsettled about any effort to "rescue Germany," which Bonhoeffer is in some sense doing by seeking to plan for a post-Nazi regime.[76] Bonhoeffer concludes in prison that Barth's "ethical observations, so far as they exist, are as important as his dogmatic ones—but in the nonreligious interpretation of theological concepts he gave no concrete guidance, either in dogmatics or ethics." In 1967, Barth acknowledges that Bonhoeffer was right about this. He was slow to engage politics while Bonhoeffer rightly saw the need to do so. "In Germany . . . burdened with the problems of its Lutheran tradition, there was a genuine need in the direction which I now silently took for granted or emphasized only in passing: ethics, fellow-humanity, a serving church, discipleship, socialism, the peace movement,

---

69. Barth, *Letters 1961–1968*, 250.

70. Bonhoeffer, *London*, 263.

71. Ibid., 39–41.

72. Editor's summary of a letter from Barth to Hendrikus Berkhof; see Barth, *Letters 1961–1968*, 316.

73. Bonhoeffer, *Testament to Freedom*, 430–33.

74. Bonhoeffer, *Way to Freedom*, 121.

75. Barth, *Letters 1961–1968*, 251–52.

76. Bonhoeffer, *Conspiracy and Imprisonment*, 274–82.

and in and with all these things, politics. This gap, and the need to fill it, Bonhoeffer obviously saw keenly from the very first, and he felt it with increasing intensity and expressed it on a broad front."[77] There are warm aspects to each of these letters from Barth on and to Bonhoeffer, but in each case Barth was hesitant to affirm the concrete moves that Bonhoeffer was making.

Letters and Papers from Prison was published in 1951. This brought significant new attention to Bonhoeffer's writings. While Barth grew to appreciate Bonhoeffer's *Sanctorum Communio*, *Discipleship*, and *Ethics*, critics seized on Bonhoeffer's oblique references to Barth in *Letters and Papers* to cast doubt on Bonhoeffer's affection for Barth. Once again, the fog of war caused by the Nazis shrouded their relationship. Eberhard Bethge writes, "When one was tired of Barth, one could go to Bonhoeffer's 'revelation positivism' for one's ammunition."[78]

It was not until 1967, just a year before Barth's death in 1968, that Barth read Bethge's 800-page biography of Bonhoeffer and realized how important he was to Bonhoeffer. Barth writes to Bethge, "it was new to me that with Bishop Bell I myself was always so important a figure to him . . . Until now I have always thought of myself as one of the pawns, not the knights or castles, on his chessboard."[79] If the various misunderstandings between the two had somehow been clarified earlier than 1967, it seems probable that Barth would have interacted earlier, more extensively, more explicitly, and less suspiciously with Bonhoeffer's work. The harsh environment under the third Reich forced stark repugnant choices regarding: the Aryan clause, fleeing Germany, secretive theological education, undesirable alliances such as Bonhoeffer's with the *Abwehr*, and secret communication with the Allies. Barth initially objected to all of this but later came to view it as not inconsistent—given the desperate circumstances—with his own theological positions. Furthermore, communication was so severely limited that only smuggled letters survived. It is possible that this crucible then exacerbated their other differences: Barth not having read Bonhoeffer earlier, differences in age (20 years), nationality (Swiss vs. German), differences in class (son of a Swiss pastor vs. son of Berlin psychiatrist), ecclesial pressures (Reformed vs. Lutheran), vocational journey (pastor turned academic vs. academic turned pastor), and styles of writing (regular vs. irregular dogmatics).

Matthew Puffer rightly points out the evidence for Bonhoeffer's work being a catalyst to Barth on issues related to the *analogia relationis*,

---

77. Barth, *Letters 1961–1968*, 251.
78. Bethge, *Dietrich Bonhoeffer: Theologian*, 794.
79. Barth, *Letters 1961–1968*, 250–51.

ethics, discipleship, and *sanctorum communio*. However, the crisis of Nazi Germany forced horrible choices that made it difficult for Barth to discern friend from foe. It was only thirty years later that Barth came to see what a friend he had in Bonhoeffer. Until then, his willingness to be influenced by Bonhoeffer was mixed with a strong sense of caution—another of the sad consequences of Hitlerism.

4

Pauline Apocalyptic and Political Nihilism

Jacob Taubes and Karl Barth

—By Benjamin Myers

> "Here is a Messiah who is condemned according to the law.
> Tant pis, so much the worse for law."
>
> —JACOB TAUBES

1.

THE JEWISH INTELLECTUAL JACOB Taubes (1923–87) is one of the most eccentric figures of twentieth-century philosophy. A political thinker of the far left, Taubes's greatest intellectual debt was to the arch-conservative German jurist Carl Schmitt. An ordained rabbi, his work was driven by a lifelong engagement with Christian theology in an attempt to lay bare the roots of modern political power. With Schmitt, Taubes believed that in today's world everything is theological—except perhaps the chatter of theologians.[1] He began his career with a doctoral dissertation on the secularization of Christian apocalyptic, a response to Hans Urs von Balthasar's work on the same theme,[2] and ended his career—just weeks before his death—with lectures on the explosive political impact of Paul's Epistle to the Romans.

At the center of Taubes's work is an attempt to rehabilitate radical Paulinism in the interests of a Jewish messianic politics. Taubes returns again

---

1. Taubes, *Ad Carl Schmitt*, 34.
2. Balthasar, *Apokalypse*.

and again to Karl Barth in this connection, and he develops a highly idiosyncratic appropriation of Barth's theology. In his view, Barth's interpretation of Paul is "perhaps the most significant contribution to the general consciousness of our age";[3] Barth's *Römerbrief* "gave voice to man's self-estrangement long before philosophy had taken notice of it."[4] For Taubes, Barth's political theology plunges us back into the world of Paul's Jewish apocalypticism. Every worldly power is set under the enormous shadow of the impending judgment of God. The existing political order is not so much critiqued as utterly relativized. One's hope lies not in any alternative political system, but in the fact that time is coming to an end. The new messianic age sets itself against the totality of this world. Thus the believer accepts neither the legitimation of worldly powers nor their need for replacement through revolution. By refusing to take the powers seriously, believers bear witness to the judgment of God. In Barth's interpretation of Paul, Taubes finds a recovery of the powerful "nihilistic" impulse of Jewish apocalyptic politics. It is a politics generated by an abyssal vision of the absolute gulf between time and eternity, divine action and all worldly action. It is the politics of a new community founded on the vision of time's ending, and thus on the dissolution of politics as such. Taubes therefore follows Walter Benjamin in describing nihilism as "the task of world politics."[5] It is a politics of "militant pessimism."[6]

Taubes is not a Christian. He reads Paul as a Jewish messianic thinker and describes himself as "a Paulinist."[7] That Paul's letters could be turned into the basis of formal doctrines of political authority, or the justification of human projects to stabilize or overturn the status quo—this Taubes sees as an astonishing betrayal of Paul's apocalyptic vision. In contrast, Barth's theology brings the ghost of Paul back into the world of modern politics. Barth reverses the trend by which Paul's "nihilistic" impulse was translated into doctrines of positive social or political engagement.[8] In other words, what the early Barth was widely criticized for—his apparent negation of everything human before the inexorable majesty of an alien God—Taubes sees as exactly the point at which Barth's theology reveals its political potential. Barth's devastating repudiation of *Kulturprotestantismus* should now be repeated as a repudiation of modern political order. By articulating

3. Taubes, "Theodicy," 177.
4. Taubes, "On The Nature," 198.
5. Benjamin, "Theological-Political Fragment," 306.
6. Gould, "Jacob Taubes," 146.
7. Taubes, *Political Theology*, 88.
8. Taubes, "Christian Nihilism," 270.

"the apolitical premise of all Christian theology,"[9] Barth lays bare the nation state's pretensions to political legitimation while also dissolving the justification of any revolutionary response. In this way—in the critique of politics as such—Barth's interpretation of Paul clears the space for a renewed messianic politics. For the Christian church, the problem with Paul's letters is simply that they are too familiar: "sixteen hundred years of Christianization in Europe have made them understandable."[10] Against this, and with Barth, Taubes wants to recover the "totally illiberal" Paul of the first century, the "fanatical" Paul, the alien and offensive figure who speaks not so much *to* our political concerns as *against* them.[11]

For Taubes, it is above all Barth who retrieves this nihilistic Paul, a figure who cares nothing for human progress or social stability, who has no political doctrine simply because such considerations are eclipsed by the righteousness of God. This is a strange, unsettling, yet intellectually vigorous appropriation of the early Barth. In what follows, I will explore Taubes's relation to Barth by considering the way both thinkers strategically mobilize Romans 13 as an apocalyptic-political text, and the way their exegetical strategies lead to divergent conclusions about law, authority, and the possibility of theological reasoning.

2.

While entire ecclesial traditions have assumed that Romans 13 propounds a positive doctrine of political authority, Barth's *Römerbrief* immediately dismantles this assumption by arguing that Paul's discussion of worldly rulers there is an extension of the passage on enemies in chapter 12. Paul's fundamental attitude toward rulers is altogether negative: the rulers are a subset of the wider class of "evil" and "enemies" (12:20–21). This is the crux of Barth's interpretation of Romans 13. As soon as Paul's view of rulers is viewed under this dark aspect, much of Barth's reading ineluctably follows. For a start, any interpretation that claims a positive legitimation of authority cannot be admissible; it would contradict the whole message of Romans. Worldly powers are ordained by God, Barth argues, only in the sense that they "bear involuntary witness" to the true order of God, an order which stands over them in absolute judgment.[12] In relation to worldly authorities, the Christian is someone who "has so much to say against them that he no

---

9. Taubes, "Christian Nihilism," 272.
10. Taubes, *Political Theology*, 4.
11. Ibid., 24.
12. Barth, *Epistle*, 485.

longer complains of them"; his behavior as a good citizen "means 'only' the judgment of God."[13]

To be constantly preoccupied with the problems and inadequacies of an existing political order is therefore no longer possible for the believer, who sees not merely the specific imperfections of all human endeavors but "their pure and complete negativity." Even at its best, worldly power serves a strictly negative role: it sets up an absolute contrast to the righteousness of God. In this contrast between God's order and worldly order—a distinction much more fundamental than the more familiar contrasts between good/evil and justice/injustice—the powers are affirmed as "good" only in the negative sense that they reluctantly and accidentally become the shadows that preserve the lineaments of God's righteousness.[14]

In a nutshell, Barth's position consists in a dual negation: both "Nicht-Revolution!" and "Nicht-Legitimität!"[15] Barth admits that his commentary has little to say against the politically conservative notion of legitimation; after all, Barth's readers will hardly be tempted to draw conclusions about the legitimacy of the political status quo! The real danger, he thinks, is that his "emphatic insistence" on negation will be taken as a call to some "positive method of human behavior," a means of self-justification through "the Titanism of revolt and upheaval and renovation."[16]

Revolutionaries rightly perceive that the real political problem is not the particular flaws in government but the legitimacy of government as such, "the right of governments to *exist* at all."[17] They rightly see that the existence of government is itself an evil, a power devoid of any ultimate legitimacy. However, revolutionaries fall under Paul's judgment in Romans 12:21: "Do not be overcome by evil." They are enslaved by resentment against the power of the existing order, and their struggle to bring forth a new order is always a tragic exploit, since it necessarily participates in the state's own logic of power. The legality of revolutionaries will always be illegal, just as their authority always ultimately devolves into another tyranny, another earthly *nomos*.[18]

In contrast, Barth says, Paul's injunction to "overcome evil with good" demands a refusal of *all* action in relation to worldly power. The overcoming of evil takes the form of a complete cessation of human power. "And how

---

13. Ibid., 488.
14. Ibid.
15. Ibid., 477.
16. Ibid., 478.
17. Ibid., 479.
18. Ibid., 480.

can this be represented except by some strange not-doing [*Nicht-Handeln*] precisely at the point where human beings feel most powerfully called to action?"[19] The real vocation of political subjects is to bear witness to the action of God. Such witness is a self-effacing act, a penitent turning-away from their own "justifiable action." It is in "not-doing" that the human turns back to the apocalypse of divine action; in not-doing, one makes way for the righteousness of God, refusing to grasp at any worldly righteousness. God alone can overcome evil with good. Revolutionary conflict with the world's powers will always be a conflict between evil and evil. It will not bring about the necessary antithesis between the divine righteousness and the existing order as a whole. In Barth's mathematical metaphor, where the existing order as a whole is *(a b c d)*, the total dissolution of this order is represented by a minus sign outside the bracket: $-(+a+b+c+d)$. God is this minus sign, this absolute negativity. No revolution, no human agency, can ever amount to this "divine minus" by which "the totality of human ordinances is dissolved." Indeed, any negative within the bracket, any revolutionary negation, results inevitably in another positive, restoring false legitimacy to an order that has already been negated by the action of God.[20]

Subjection to the ruling powers (Rom 13:1), therefore, is a "purely negative" act: "It means to withdraw and make way; it means to have no resentment, and not to overthrow."[21] This refusal to act on God's behalf is itself the most devastating criticism of the social order. It is a sheer refusal to entertain the worldly powers' pretensions to an immanent legitimacy, and it likewise neutralizes the "pathos" by which these powers perpetually nourish their own sense of importance. Even revolutionary zeal is merely "fresh fodder" for their fundamental claim to legitimacy. Revolution proves, for example, that the state ought to be taken with complete seriousness. But in Barth's view, "*Nicht-Revolution* is the best preparation for the true revolution." To be in subjection to the rulers is an act "void of purpose," springing solely from obedience to God as human beings leave room for God's own righteous judgment.[22]

Where the first *Römerbrief* had insisted that Christians should find themselves on "the extreme left" of the political spectrum,[23] by the second edition Barth is thus able to accept—though still himself a socialist—that it is largely irrelevant whether believers lean toward the political left or right,

19. Ibid., 481.
20. Ibid., 482–83.
21. Ibid., 481.
22. Ibid., 483–84.
23. Barth, *Römerbrief*, 508.

as long as neither position is taken with any final seriousness, and as long as both are understood as having nothing to do with the righteousness of God. Christian radicalism and Christian conservatism are alike resolved into the single posture of "the not-doing of our relationship to God."[24]

3.

Taubes seeks to follow the broad lines of Barth's "ingenious"[25] interpretation of Romans 13. The problem with most readings of the passage, Taubes notes, is that they fixate on the topic of obedience to worldly authority instead of grasping the text's underlying apocalyptic logic. "If you stare at the topic of authority as if it were a predator, then it's hard to see how to get out of there."[26] The real point of Romans 13 is to raise the question, "In what epoch are we living, what sort of present time is this?"[27] Paul's answer is stark and arresting: "It is now the moment for you to wake from sleep. For salvation is nearer to us now than when we became believers" (Rom 13:11).

For Taubes, then, Romans 13 functions in the same way as Paul's injunction to the Corinthians: "from now on, let those who have wives be as though [ὡς μὴ] they had none . . . , and those who deal with the world as though they had no dealings with it. For the present form of this world is passing away" (1 Cor 7:29–31). Now that God has acted, all natural and social ties are relativized. Paul still speaks of ethics and politics, but in a purely negative way: one continues to live in the world's present form only because it no longer matters; one obeys the authorities only because they have become obsolete, because they are not worth worrying about. The essential point is that time is rushing to an end. The present time is a time of crisis, a momentary preface to the messianic age. In Taubes's words: "Under this time pressure, if tomorrow the whole palaver, the entire swindle were going to be over—in that case there's no point in any revolution! That's absolutely right, I would give the same advice. Demonstrate obedience to state authority, pay taxes, don't do anything bad, don't get involved in conflicts, because otherwise it'll get confused with some revolutionary movement."[28]

Walter Benjamin's proposal that the task of politics is to strive nihilistically for the world's "total passing away" is, for Taubes, a profound insight

---

24. Barth, *Epistle*, 489.
25. Taubes, *Political Theology*, 52.
26. Ibid.
27. Ibid., 53.
28. Taubes, *Political Theology*, 54.

into Paul's political vision.[29] Paul is "nihilistic" because he has seen the reality of God. "This is why you can't make Lutheran deals with Romans 13, unless you give up the entire frame . . . Here we have a nihilistic view of the world, and concretely of the Roman Empire."[30]

Taubes recognizes of course that such apocalypticism is not "political" in the usual sense of the term. Apocalyptic expectation "does not refer in the first instance, or exclusively, to the existing social order." It is "at first not concerned with changing the structure of society," nor is it revolutionary since it knows nothing of "replacing an existing society with a better one."[31] The Pauline community represents a new form of "pneumatic" collective. All members of this community "have severed . . . their natural, organic allegiances" so that they are bound together solely by the "inorganic" life of the spirit.[32] Such a collective thus represents not an alternative form of society, but an alternative to society as such. It is the instantiation of a "new creation" (Gal 6:15) in which the present order as a totality is set aside by the action of God. The Pauline community might be described as "revolutionary" then, but only if revolution means "opposing the totality of this world with a new totality that comprehensively founds anew in the way that it negates, namely, in terms of the basic foundations." God's apocalypse in Christ is both a "form-destroying [gestalt-zerstörend]" and a "forming [gestaltend]" occurrence.[33] It is equally nihilism and hope. The Pauline "as though not" arises from an assurance of the imminent end of time. On the site of this "as though not" there appears a new community which, in its own form of life, opposes the totality of the world and shows that it has been rendered obsolete.

4.

This stark apocalyptic vision underlies Taubes's criticism of law. There was something like a latent apocalyptic logic already in the political life of ancient Israel: "Theocracy is built upon the anarchical elements in Israel's soul. It expresses the human desire to be free from all human, earthly ties and to be in covenant with God. The first tremors of eschatology can be traced to this dispute over divine or earthly rule."[34] If western politics springs

29. Benjamin, "Theological-Political Fragment," 306.
30. Taubes, *Political Theology*, 72.
31. Taubes, *Occidental Eschatology*, 9.
32. Ibid., 64.
33. Ibid., 9–10.
34. Ibid., 19.

from the seed of ancient Israel's political theology—as Oliver O'Donovan has more recently argued, albeit with very different conclusions[35]—then Taubes's claim is that all politics is founded on anarchy, and on the sharpest possible repudiation of the idea of earthly power. If one submits oneself to earthly rulers, it is only because one recognizes their illegitimate status, the emptiness of their claims to right.

In the same way, Taubes's reading of Paul stresses that the continuing submission of believers to the law is a sign not of the significance of the law, but of its redundancy and ultimate powerlessness. Jewish Christians are to keep the law only because it is part of the fashion of this world which is passing away. Submission to law shows that the believer relies solely on the apocalypse of God in Christ. "As it is the task of Christ on his return finally to dispose of this world, a world which is already passing away, the believer should not act on his own authority to bring about [*vorgreifen*] the eschatological events and suspend the old order of things."[36] Paul's injunction for each to "remain in the condition in which you were called" (1 Cor 7:20) reflects this apocalyptic logic. At the same time, Gentile believers must resist law-observance at all costs. For them, submission to the law would be a rejection of Christ. Thus law-observance by Jewish Christians and non-observance by Gentile Christians spring from the same conviction: that the old world, founded on *nomos*, is passing away. Neither observance nor non-observance counts for anything: what counts is a new creation.

Like Carl Schmitt, Taubes wants to probe what lies beneath the modern state's claims to legality and legitimacy.[37] But Taubes's conclusions could not be further from Schmitt's. The apocalyptic political vision is, for Taubes, a way of undertaking "a critique of the principle of power itself," a "theological delegitimation of all political power."[38] This critique dissolves the logic of the nation state, and indeed of an entire world founded on *nomos*. Taubes recognizes, as much as Schmitt does, that "law and fate are the foundations of the cosmos," but Taubes pursues the first-century claim that "*for just this reason . . . the cosmos is an abundance of that which is bad.*"[39] Law belongs to the old world that is passing away.

In Taubes's reading, Paul turns the law on its head, producing a "transvaluation" of all worldly values. Christ's death is the dissolution of law—or rather, the total relativization of law under the light of God's advent. "It

---

35. O'Donovan, *Desire*.
36. Taubes, *Occidental Eschatology*, 68.
37. See Schmitt, *Political Theology*; Schmitt, *Legality*.
38. Taubes, "Theology," 232; Terpstra and de Wit, "No Spiritual Investment," 324.
39. Taubes, *Occidental Eschatology*, 9–10.

wasn't *nomos* but rather the one who was nailed to the cross by *nomos* who is the imperator!" Compared to this insight, Taubes remarks, "all the little revolutionaries are *nothing*."[40] The crucified messiah is "a total and monstrous inversion of the values of Roman and Jewish thought," and this inversion represents "the inner logic of the messianic."[41] It is for this reason that Taubes regards Paul as the quintessentially Jewish thinker, the great architect of messianic politics. The point here is not that the messianic community embodies lawlessness: after all, Paul still commends observance to Jews just as he commends non-observance to Gentile believers. The messianic community is founded on a different principle altogether. It is generated negatively, one might say, by its lack of any worldly legitimation. It is sustained not by anything in this world, since it lives from the other side of the end of time.

It is true that this militant critique of *nomos* owes more to Walter Benjamin than to Barth. And it is true that Barth's explicit considerations of law are often governed by the classical (if, perhaps, rather trivial) Protestant dialectic of "law and gospel." But none of this should conceal the deep continuities between Taubes's interpretation of Paul and the apocalyptic vision of Barth's *Römerbrief*. Law represents demarcation and division; it draws lines between communities, nations, states, and peoples. It forms and orders the world according to a system of antitheses—most fundamentally, the antithesis between Jew and Gentile. The problem with such divisions is not that they have been drawn in the wrong place (so that one could simply redraw the lines), but that they are rendered meaningless by reference to the *real* antithesis between this world and the world to come. Where the righteousness of God looms over the world, the entire structuring logic of *nomos* is obliterated—not because it is inherently evil, but because its time has passed. To cling to the law while standing under the righteousness of God is like trying to retain your shadow in a solar eclipse. God's righteousness dissolves the law not because it is *against* law but because it is infinitely *more than* law: an annihilating fulfillment.

5.

For all his indebtedness to Barth, Taubes nevertheless subjects Barth's theology to a Pauline critique. His target is not so much the content of Barth's thought as the bare fact that it is *theology*. Even though Barth wants to recover Paul's apocalypticism, Taubes argues that a theological "abyss"

40. Taubes, *Political Theology*, 24.
41. Ibid., 10.

separates Barth from Paul.[42] For Paul, the old age has already passed away, the time of the messiah is already upon us. Barth's theology, by contrast, "unwittingly reveals the crisis of Christian theology in a world that does not pass away."[43]

The Christian movement was founded by an event believed to be cosmic and apocalyptic in scope: the death of Christ destroys the present evil age and brings about a new creation. The mere fact of writing a theology testifies to the disappearance of this apocalyptic imagination. The world did not end as expected. The church resolved this problem by assuming its own institutional legitimacy, its position as one of the powers of the current age. Theology's entire history is thus tragic, Taubes argues, since the Christian tradition necessarily erases the footprints of its own apocalyptic origins. In such a situation, where the church has resigned itself to existence in this world, theology will inevitably "fall back again into the ontological pattern of a theodicy."[44] Taubes views Barth's dogmatics as a particularly impressive symptom of this malaise. Having deftly sidestepped the history of theology in order to glimpse the world-negating vision of Paul, Barth later retreats back into the safety of the Christian tradition:

> No religion can have the luxury of theology without paying a price for it. Secularization is the price the Christian community had to pay for its development from an adventistic sect to a universal church, and the history of theology is the spiritual account of this price. The history of the development of Christian theology is a tragic history because there is no "solution" to the conflict between eschatological symbols and the brute fact of a continuing history. One may admire the achievement of theology but at the same time be aware of the price involved in such an achievement.[45]

Merely by undertaking the task of writing church dogmatics, Barth shows that he can no longer bracket out the church's pretensions to legitimacy within the present world. The church is presupposed; its existence is no longer seen as inherently problematic. In sum, it is precisely the immense scale of Barth's dogmatics that makes it so poignantly tragic. In order to write *Church Dogmatics*, one must first give up the apocalypticism of the *Römerbrief*; this, as Taubes sees it, is the spiritual price of theology.

---

42. Taubes, "Christian Nihilism," 270.
43. Ibid., 272.
44. Taubes, "Theodicy," 194.
45. Taubes, "On the Nature," 196–97.

In a remarkable text of 1954, Taubes predicts that the Christian tradition will eventually domesticate even the wild apocalyptic energies of Barth's *Römerbrief*. In order to assume a place among the powers of this world, the church produces its own self-justifying and self-legitimating tradition. More than anyone else, Barth has exposed the fact that the church denies its own proclamation when it becomes "part of the powers and principalities that rule the world here and now."[46] But theology is no match for the church. Barth's fate, Taubes predicts, will be his ultimate absorption into the self-justifying apparatus of the Christian tradition; he is doomed to become a "classic" figure of that very tradition whose legitimacy he strove so hard to undermine. Taubes thus compares the fate of Barth's political theology to that of Augustine's *City of God*, where the power and virtue of the Roman empire is pitted against the righteousness of the heavenly city. Augustine was "the 'nihilistic' critic of Roman virtue,"[47] but his thought was soon absorbed into the machinery of churchly tradition, becoming a theoretical underpinning for the ideal of a Christian civilization. His "nihilistic" criticism of Rome was translated into an invincible legitimation not only of empire but of a *holy* Roman empire, a worldly power directly authorized by God. And so Taubes asks: "Is it too bold to imagine that Barth's theologico-political tracts might have a similar destiny, finding their place on the shelf of 'Great Books' of a Western civilization that Barth has constantly rejected?" Might Barth in the end share "the tragi-comical fate" of Augustine's *City of God*?[48]

6.

Whatever one might think of these critical questions, one can scarcely deny that Taubes's remarks have proved to be uncannily prescient. Barth's work is widely read today as a theological classic, a particularly impressive achievement within the larger trajectory of a Christian intellectual tradition whose basic legitimacy is taken for granted. Indeed, Taubes's half-joking prediction that Barth would become one of the Great Books of western civilization has been fulfilled in the most remarkably literal way: in 1990, Barth was included in a new volume of Encyclopedia Britannica's series of the *Great Books of the Western World*. And it was precisely the early apocalyptic Barth who was included in this series: his startling early addresses, collected in *Das Wort Gottes und die Theologie*, appeared alongside John Dewey, Wittgenstein, Heidegger, and other "classic" twentieth-century figures. Barth's

---

46. Taubes, "Christian Nihilism," 272.
47. Ibid., 270.
48. Ibid., 272.

apocalypticism is thus celebrated as a cherished contribution to the ongoing project of western intellectual culture. From our privileged position of progress and maturity, we can look back fondly on the early Barth, just as affluent baby boomers look back wistfully on Bob Dylan's idealistic protest songs of the 1960s. Things are not much better in the current discipline of theology, where Barth's thought is routinely invoked as a self-legitimating standard of orthodoxy and academic respectability. Taubes challenges us, then, to consider whether Barth's theology—including his criticism of worldly power—might not itself be undergoing a hideous metamorphosis into one of those very principalities and powers by which the interests of the status quo are shored up against the righteousness of God.

But even if there is good cause for reserve about the contemporary use of Barth's theology, I think it's also true that his work retains the seeds by which its own cultural legacy might yet be subverted. After all, Barth's theology strikes continually at the church's pretensions to institutional self-justification, what Donald MacKinnon has called the "ecclesiological fundamentalism" by which the mere existence of the church is equated with its divine authorization.[49] Barth reminds the Christian community that it is always suspended in a precarious moment "between the times," poised over an unfathomable abyss. Just as Taubes's messianic vision issues in a nihilistic politics, so Barth testifies to what might be described as ecclesiological nihilism—a refusal to see the church as one of the powers of the world, or to view the church apart from its relationship to the coming kingdom of God. For Taubes, politics should always be grounded in a recognition of its own illegitimacy; similarly for Barth, the church is paradoxically sustained by the awareness that it has no foundations, nothing to secure its place in the world. At the heart of the church's life gapes this void, this ontological devastation, this resolve to live only by an eschatological Word of hope and judgment.

The apocalypticism of the early Barth continues to animate the *Church Dogmatics*, not least in the insistence that the church lives solely by witness.[50] The church's vocation is to witness to a divine act that remains absolutely distinct from the church itself. One of the most remarkable features of Barth's prolegomena to *Church Dogmatics*—though it tends to attract little attention—is the denunciation of both Catholicism on the right hand and Protestantism on the left. Far from looking to the self-validating practices and beliefs of any specific Christian community, Barth begins by insisting that the church as such—in *both* its great western traditions—is part of the

---

49. MacKinnon, "Kenosis," 23.
50. I have tried to demonstrate this elsewhere: Myers, "From Faithfulness," 291–308.

world's rejection of revelation. The problem, Barth argues, is that these traditions have succumbed to the arrogant illusion that the church stands "in an immediate relationship to the direct, absolute and material authority of God." Both the Catholic and the liberal Protestant are always "on the way to a pantheistic identification of Church and revelation," and their assumed legitimacy is a flight from the righteousness of God. In this way the church itself becomes another demonic principality, "a representative, like all other worldly constructs, of the darkness in which the world will necessarily lie if God has not been revealed."[51] To live by the righteousness of God is to live solely by the vocation of witness. The church brings charges against itself whenever it bears witness to God. Its testimony to divine action is simultaneously an acknowledgment of its own poverty and devastation.

For Barth, therefore, the church possesses no security in the world. It has no proper work in the world, only that "peculiar not-doing"[52] which is encapsulated in the concept of witness. It exists "between the times," a refugee with no place in the world. It is poised precariously on the edge of nonbeing. Nothing sustains it except the Word of revelation by which it is continually judged and forgiven. Its existence is altogether contingent, unnecessary, gratuitous—upheld by anarchic, unprincipled grace.

7.

According to Taubes's political stance, we are to ignore the powers of the world and instead to "engage with all the questions and afflictions which are *left* by the established order of the world," thus taking the side of "those who are cast out and despised."[53] The triumphant march of the principalities and powers through world history leaves behind an unsightly trail of refuse. It is this useless remainder that forms the site of a messianic politics. In the same way for Barth, the church's peculiar existence stems from the fact that it is "left over" in the world. It has no proper place or work in the world, no *nomos* that could bind it to the world, nothing except the hopelessly vulnerable and superfluous gesture of witness.

If Christian theology is to be undertaken at all—Taubes is, I think, right about this—it can only be as an expression of this appalling superfluity. The genius of Karl Barth was to perceive this clearly, yet to go on writing church dogmatics all the same—not to make the church stronger, but to

---

51. *CD* 1.2:544–45.
52. Barth, *Epistle*, 481.
53. Taubes, *Occidental Eschatology*, 39.

show that the church has nothing in the world except the promise of the coming righteousness of God.

The Missing Enemy & A Missed Opportunity

A Response to Myers's Pacification of Political Theology in Taubes and Barth

—By Derek Alan Woodard-Lehman

TAUBES'S BARTH IS THE theologian of *krisis* who sets off the bomb on the theological playground of his liberal fellows. For Taubes, the Barth of the *Römerbrief* is nothing less than the Paul of Romans *redivivus*. Taubes reads *Romans* as the apocalyptic return of messianic politics. *Romans* thus becomes the megaphone through which Taubes amplifies his own Paulinist "*Nein!*" to modern Judaism and Christianity. On his view, modern Jews and Christians alike too easily accept a comfortable cultural synthesis (*Kirchentum-Deutschtum-Judentum*). Taubes marshals Barth's radical rereading of Romans 13 against such *bürgerlich* ethical monotheism. Barth reads chapter 13 as an extension of Romans 12, rather than as an exception to it. As Myers notes, Barth thinks these rulers belong to the wider class of "evil" and "enemies" mentioned in 12:20–21. Romans 13, therefore, cannot be read as a programmatic summary of political obeisance as in the Lutheran doctrine of the two kingdoms. "Subjection" to the lawful rulers now becomes subversion of the law's rule. Subjection subverts by no longer taking the present political order with any final seriousness. Such subversion *via* subjection takes the form of a double negation: "*Nicht-Legitimität*" and "*Nicht-Revolution.*"[54] And this double-not issues in a third: "*Nicht-Handeln.*"[55] The Christian's proper political action is neither legitimization nor revolution. Rather, it is non-action. This threefold-not is what Taubes calls Barth's "political nihilism," the *Römerbrief*'s "Great Negative Possibility" of "not-doing."[56]

---

54. Barth, *Epistle*, 477.
55. Ibid., 481.
56. Ibid., 477. Neither Myers nor Taubes mentions the *Römerbrief*'s subsequent discussion of the correlative "Great Positive Possibility" that immediately follows discussion of the "Great Negative Possibility" (see 492–502).

Myers endorses Taubes's account of Barth's political nihilism, qualifying it only by saying that Taubes's own critical messianism draws more from Walter Benjamin than from Barth. Following Taubes, Myers claims that Barth's reading of the Pauline injunction to overcome evil with good demands a refusal of *any* action whatsoever in relation to worldly power. Yet where Barth worries over political activism, Myers is anxious about ecclesial fundamentalism. He marvels at Taubes's uncanny prescience in predicting that Barth would be domesticated as a classic of the Christian tradition and a great book of Western civilization. Taubes's nihilistic reading of Barth thus provides Myers with a cautionary tale against orthodoxy and virtue as insidious forms of cultural respectability and worldly power. These, for Myers, are the real danger. Orthodoxy and virtue are the contemporary temptations to Promethean titanism. He therefore commends a further "ecclesiological nihilism." Doctrine and congregation can only be a placeless remainder, a superfluous witness. He wistfully surmises that Barth's real genius lies in clearly perceiving the superfluity of witness, yet nonetheless writing thousands of pages of dogmatics. The author of Barmen thus becomes a theological Bartleby, the scrivener of Basel who sits in his study blithely penning theology while the children of Israel are firing the furnaces of Auschwitz. But nothing could be further from the truth! As Eberhard Busch has shown, from the earliest pre-Barmen days to the last days of the Final Solution, Barth busied himself resisting the Nazis and rescuing Jews.[57] Myers's radically nihilistic conclusions, therefore, are untenable. They can account for neither the not-doing discussed by Paul nor that done by Barth. The great negative possibility of not-doing must be understood otherwise.

Myers fails to take notice of just what counts as the "not-doing" of Romans 12–13. Romans 12 reprises the Sermon on the Mount and reiterates its command to love the enemy. This is a particular theopolitical not-doing: not harming enemies and not doing evil in order to do good. This new commandment suspends the primordial *nomos* of natural sociability: help friends, harm enemies. As Taubes realizes, Jesus of Nazareth is *Christos Kurios* and his *nomos* of love for enemies is nothing short of a declaration of war against the imperium of Rome and the sovereignty of every Kaiser

---

57. See Busch, *Unter dem Bogen*. Myers, no doubt, would account this as what Taubes calls siding with those cast out and despised. And surely it is that. Moreover, Myers likely would hasten to add that Barth did not identify his human actions with divine action, the justness of his cause with the justice of God. Surely he did not. Nevertheless, it is hard to read Barth's own reflections on the *Kirchenkampf* and the wider struggle against Nazism and think that he thought these had absolutely nothing to do with the righteousness of God.

or Führer who follows.[58] The theological suspension of the law's rule necessarily is a political subversion of lawful rulers, a point not lost on Carl Schmitt. For Schmitt, as for Taubes, the friend-enemy distinction thus defines "the political" itself and determines the course of politics.[59] Political sovereignty is the power to consolidate the nation-state (*Volkstaat*) through the friend-enemy distinction and the state of exception. As the first sentence of Schmitt's own *Political Theology* announces, "Sovereign is he who decides the state of exception."[60] Sovereignty not only is the power to promulgate but also to suspend the law, *in extremis* to declare war. War, then, is the *ultima ratio* of the political. As the grim remark associated with Charles Tilly puts it, "War makes the state and the state makes war." Sovereignty is nothing other than the state's decisionist power to declare the exception, "to demand from its own members the readiness to die and unhesitatingly to kill enemies."[61] This, as Schmitt emphasizes, precludes the Christian command to love the enemy from any application within the realm of the political. Christians can love their personal *inimicus*, but not their political *hostis*. There can be no love for enemies of the state.[62]

Despite this, Myers neither considers the friend-enemy distinction nor confronts the state of exception, even where they appear in Barth's *Church Dogmatics*. In fact, Myers mentions Schmitt only twice, and in passing. Barth's own treatment of enmity and emergency is not addressed at all. In other words, Myers altogether ignores the political. The enemy goes missing from his argument, and he thus misses the opportunity to engage Barth's own political theology as elaborated in "The Protection of Life."[63] Barth there considers the permissibility of killing. He makes a case for so-called presumptive pacifism, which "has almost infinite arguments in its favor and is almost overpoweringly strong."[64] But in this same section Barth also makes explicit concessions in circumstances of emergency, first for high treason and tyrannicide, and then for war itself. The environing conditions within which Barth considers these three types of killing to be permissible are those of the Schmittian exception. In the case of treason and tyrannicide, Barth writes, "What must be at stake in these cases is not the state in its stable and peaceful form, but the state convulsed and at-

---

58. Taubes, *Political Theology*, 13.
59. See Schmitt, *Concept*, 7.
60. Schmitt, *Political Theology*, 5.
61. Schmitt, *Concept*, 46.
62. See ibid., 28–29.
63. *CD* 3.4, §55.2.
64. *CD* 3.4:455.

tacked and therefore in serious difficulties. It must be a question of absolute emergency when not just the *bene esse* but the very *esse* of the state and its members is at issue."[65] In the case of war, Barth continues, "[The possibility of Christian support] rests on the assumption that the conduct of one state or nation can throw another into the wholly abnormal situation of emergency in which not merely its greater or lesser prosperity but its very existence and autonomy are menaced and attacked."[66] By invoking the exception in order to preserve the state's existence, Barth is doing nothing if not taking the present political order with final seriousness. Despite the strength of presumptive nonviolence, Barth makes a general allowance for the state of exception, albeit under the stricture of divine command. He further argues that it would apply specifically to "any attack on the independence, neutrality and territorial integrity of the Swiss Confederation."[67] While Barth refuses any freestanding *Volksrecht* of blood or soil, he does not reject the exception or the friend-enemy distinction absolutely. In fact, in the case of his own nation-state he accepts them unhesitatingly, and prior to any divine command.

What matters most in Taubes's reading of Barth is not his caution against the self-legitimization of theological orthodoxy or ecclesial virtue, no matter how prescient or pressing that criticism may seem. Far more important is that Taubes raises the issue of the political itself as a theological problem. Taubes's political theology challenges Barth's view that the exercise of lethal power is an *opus alienum* of the state. Following Schmitt, Taubes reveals that the modern state-form institutionalizes violence and is an institution of violence. He reopens the possibility and necessity of political theology. But in missing the enemy, Myers misses the opportunity occasioned by the conversation between Barth and Taubes. Theological existence today is politico-theological existence. Christological counter-sovereignty is neither political nor ecclesiological nihilism, at least not in Myers's overstated sense. Apocalyptic rejection of political radicalism and violent revolution is not messianic quietism. Rather it is what John Howard Yoder calls God's "original revolution."[68] The originally revolutionary not-doing of Paul is the refusal to return evil for evil. It is antinomian love, even, and perhaps especially for the enemy of the state. The refusal to take the powers and principalities of the total state with any final seriousness does not issue in inaction. Barth's not-doing is not non-doing. Not-doing is un-doing. Para-

---

65. *CD* 3.4:446–47.
66. *CD* 3.4:461.
67. *CD* 3.4:462.
68. See Yoder, *Original Revolution*.

digmatically it is the not-doing of the Messiah himself, whose crucifixion according to the law is the un-doing of the law itself—even the law of sin and death that cannot but culminate in the state's god-like command to die and to kill.

Section 2

Present Conversations

5

"You Wonder Where the Spirit Went"

Barth and Jenson on the Hiddenness of God

—By Peter Kline

> "Your life is hidden with Christ in God."
>
> —COLOSSIANS 3:3

1.

I ENTER HERE INTO a conversation that Jenson has already begun with Barth. In a constructive essay on the hiddenness of God,[1] Jenson considers Barth's position on the matter only to find it lacking. I want to explore why Jenson has problems with Barth on this issue and think critically about his constructive alternative. My suggestion is that Jenson is only partly right in his treatment of Barth; in fact, he overlooks the heart of Barth's teaching on divine hiddenness. Jenson does this because he looks in the wrong place for Barth's pneumatology. In an earlier essay, Jenson wonders "where the Spirit went"[2] in Barth's pages, claiming that the Spirit's agency is continually usurped by Christ's agency. But this fails to understand how the Spirit works within Barth's theological discourse. Jenson can't find the Spirit in Barth not because the Spirit isn't there, but because the Spirit is *hidden*. These

---

1. Jenson, "Hidden and Triune."
2. Jenson, "You Wonder."

considerations will open out into a comparison of Barth and Jenson on the issue of revelation. In the end, I want to suggest—beyond both Jenson and Barth—that the "logic" of God's revelation in Christ that we ourselves enact in the Spirit is a *doxa*-logic. *Doxology*, rather than analogy, ontology, or epistemology, is the shape of our participation in God. God is hidden in the revelation of God's *doxa*, God's glory.[3]

2.

Jenson focuses his analysis of Barth's doctrine of divine hiddenness on the doctrine of the Trinity in *Church Dogmatics* 1.1. Before turning to Jenson's analysis, therefore, allow me to trace out a few of Barth's central theological moves with regard to the Trinity.

Barth makes the dialectic of hiddenness and revealedness or veiling and unveiling the very root of his doctrine of the Trinity. He writes, "Revelation means in the Bible the self-unveiling to humanity of the God who essentially cannot be unveiled to humanity."[4] The doctrine of the Trinity is the engine of this dialectic since it supports the affirmation that the event of revelation is itself the event of God's utterly free and lordly essence. That is, only the doctrine of the Trinity allows us to say: this human Jesus is God's revelation, God's Son in the flesh, God speaking in person ("the self-unveiling to humanity of . . . God"), but the source (Father) and effect (Spirit) of this human Jesus is utterly transcendent, beyond our ability to produce or control ("the God who essentially cannot be unveiled to humanity"). Without the doctrine of the Trinity, either one side or the other of this christological dialectic is lost. Either we posit a gap between the events of revelation and God's essence, which would make the validity of revelation dependent on our religious efforts to close the gap, or we make revelation a static given, something we have come to produce or control, which would violate God's freedom and lordship. Either way, we will not have truly encountered *God*.

In Barth's hands, then, the doctrine of the Trinity is simply the theological guarantee of human participation in God,[5] which is to say that it

---

3. This essay's argument is the inverse of Malysz's in "Divine Sovereignty." Reading Ables's dissertation, "Pneumatology," was immensely helpful in crystalizing my thoughts for this essay.

4. *CD* 1.1:315.

5. "The doctrine of the Trinity tells us . . . how far the One who reveals Himself according to the witness of Scripture can in fact be our *God* and how far He can in fact be *our* God. He can be our God because in all His modes of being He is equal to himself, one and the same Lord" (*CD* 1.1:383).

is simply commentary on the an/enhypostatic dialectic of revelation that constitutes Christ's person. Just as the human action of Jesus is wholly the act of the Son understood as the self-speaking of the Father in the veil of Jesus' flesh, so our human knowledge of God is wholly the act of the Spirit understood as the self-speaking of the Father in the Son reaching out to incorporate us into the humanity of Jesus. We know God not as those given an object for conceptual mastery but as those who have been freed, by the Spirit, to enact the act that God is in Christ—which is Jesus' human action. Such liberation involves a transfiguration of human subjectivity as it is opened beyond itself and empowered to enact the unique objectivity of God.[6] In other words, God is an object of knowledge unlike any other object of knowledge because our act of knowing God is God's own act in us—the Spirit. Knowing God is not simply a matter of gathering knowledge off the data of revelation, be it the Bible, the church, even Jesus' humanity. This would make revelation simply the actualizing of possibilities residing immanently in creation, which is a reduction of revelation to the "peace of the *analogia entis*."[7] Knowledge of God happens only as we ourselves *perform* God's eschatological act in Christ with the power of God's own agency, as we are brought into that act as secondary agents who correspond to Jesus in lived movement of faith, hope, and love. But this is impossible for creatures, much less sinful creatures. It is possible for God, however, and this possibility is the Spirit.

This inscrutable work of the Spirit, transforming sinful creatures into those who enact the act that God is, is the heart of Barth's *analogia fidei*. The site of analogy is "not a being which the creature has in common with the Creator for all their dissimilarity, but, an act that is inaccessible to any mere theory, i.e., human decision, is in faith similar to the decision of God's grace for all its dissimilarity."[8] The analogy between God and creatures is not a state of Being, not even a state of Being actualized by Christ. The analogy is an *ana-Logos*, an "action in response to that Word" that is Jesus.[9] It happens only as creatures are given to act ever anew beyond their creaturely

---

6. "In the Bible faith means the opening-up of human subjectivity by and for the objectivity of the divine He, and in this opening-up the re-establishment and re-determination of human subjectivity" (*CD* 2.1:14). "Knowledge of God is thus not the relationship of an already existing subject to an object that enters into his sphere and is therefore obedient to the laws of this sphere. On the contrary, this knowledge first of all creates the subject of its knowledge by coming into the picture" (*CD* 2.1:21).

7. The phrase is from Barth's letter to Thurneysen concerning Przywara's visit to Münster in 1929; as quoted in *CRDT*, 383.

8. *CD* 1.1:239.

9. Barth, *Evangelical Theology*, 17.

capacities—that is, beyond Being as such—as secondary agents enclosed within (and therefore empowered by) God's own eschatological agency. Barth writes: "Man acts as he believes, but the fact that he believes as he acts is God's act. Man is the subject of faith. Man believes, not God. But the fact that man is this subject in faith is bracketed as a predicate of the subject God, bracketed in the way that the Creator encloses the creature and the merciful God sinful man, i.e., in such a way that man remains subject, and yet man's I as such derives only from the Thou of the subject God."[10]

Bruce McCormack has argued that Barth's *analogia fidei* is really an *analogia entis* if understood in its full implications. Rightly noting that Barth's mature *analogia fidei* is grounded in his doctrine of election, McCormack wants to articulate the "ontological implications"[11] of such grounding in the form of a theological "actualism,"[12] that is, an ontology. If divine and human Being are always already given together in the act of God's pre-temporal election, then created Being as such is already christologically determined and so in analogy to God.[13]

The question that needs to be raised against this construction is whether developing the "ontological implications" of Barth's doctrine of election in this way remains faithful to Barth's dialectic of revelation, or what is the same, Barth's theology of grace. This gets to the heart of the reality of divine hiddenness, a central feature of which is that God's revelation is "inaccessible to any mere theory," an "inexhaustible reality that cannot be established, deduced or explained."[14] God's revelation is the giving of Godself in *grace*. It is therefore known truly only in our *living* it, in our enacting God's eschatological act in Christ by the Spirit. Such action is always singular, always performed inscrutably under the mysterious blowing of the Spirit, and therefore irreducible to any theory of Being.[15] This is

---

10. *CD* 1.1:245.

11. McCormack, *Orthodox*, 310.

12. See the essays in Part 3 of McCormack, *Orthodox*, titled "Karl Barth's Theological Ontology."

13. To be sure, we have no independent access to this Being apart from revelation because its reality is grounded in God's protological and eschatological relation to us, which is not something we possess or control: "If this analogy is already effective in some way even before God addresses any particular individual, it is not because a gift of creation is somehow still effective even after the fall but because divine election is already effective on the ontological plane of the reality of the covenant of grace even before it has an effect on the phenomenal human" (McCormack, *Orthodox*, 176).

14. Respectively *CD* 1.1:239 and *CD* 2.1:198.

15. This is not to condemn the unavoidable practice of using the language of "being," that is, speaking in terms of predication or the sheer facticity of things. Ontology in the strict sense goes beyond this mundane practice in accounting for the reality of

Barth's christological dialectic of veiling / unveiling. It is not a theory of Being but a gesture toward what is finally unthinkable and unrepresentable, namely, our gracious inclusion in God's act.[16] Ontology proper, however, is precisely the attempt to construct a theory of Being, an account of the many by way of their participation in the One—the Being of beings. To attempt to account for the divine / human relation within an ontological "actualism," accounting for the many ontologically by referring them to the One that is God's act of election, is to be in danger of falling prey to the "peace of the *analogia entis*," a deceptive peace that not even christological analogy is immune from. Such actualism in the end cannot help but evade the living and unrepresentable reality of revelation by freezing the dialectic in a stable order of actualized Being that is comprehended under the concept of election.[17] The Spirit then becomes what Barth's critics fear—not the lively and hidden overflow of God's act in Christ, but a mere echo in us of what is frozen in eternity.[18]

Barth's doctrine of the Trinity is not an ontology. It does not answer the question, "What kind of being does God have that would make God's economic action possible?"—as if God's act were grounded in anything other than its own actuality. The doctrine is rather a way of affirming that the act of God's self-knowing, God's "primary objectivity," is the prevenient or antecedent reality of the act of God's self-giving in the humanity of Jesus,

---

any particular by way of a *concept* of Being, i.e., the Being of beings.

16. "The kingdom of God is inconceivable and incomprehensible to us, or, as we must freely say, it is an unthinkable thought" (*ChL*, 237).

17. McCormack writes, "In putting it this way, I am also suggesting that there is a sense in which the relation between God and the human is 'fixed and stable.' But this is a truth that remains 'hidden with Christ in God' (Col. 3:3), in the divine election" (McCormack, *Orthodox*, 178). Herein lies the error—to equate our hiddenness in Christ (which is God's hiddenness to us) with a "fixed and stable" ontological reality outside of time is precisely to misunderstand the nature of divine hiddenness, which is the mystery of our transformation by grace *in time*, the inscrutability of our enactment of God's act by the Spirit.

18. This is not to say that McCormack is not developing real possibilities within Barth's thought. He is. Barth does at times slip into thinking ontologically across the *Church Dogmatics*, reifying God's act and its human response within an order of Being. These ontological tendencies work to undo Barth's central insight concerning the christological dialectic of revelation. In his *Karl Barth*, Johnson speaks of an "analogy of being-in-action" (225) as the mature form of analogy in Barth. Everything hinges on the sense in which "being" is meant here. If the emphasis falls on *action*, where "being" is used in its more mundane sense as the ontic facticity of the human subject, then we have the christological dialectic of the *analogia fidei*. If the emphasis falls on *being*, as I think it does in McCormack, such that God's act in Christ produces a stable order of actualized Being, then we have the freezing of the dialectic. Again, Barth equivocates on this point. Johnson's construction nicely captures this equivocation.

God's "secondary objectivity."[19] Our knowledge of God is therefore *objective* because rooted in God's immediate self-knowledge, as well as *wholly miraculous or gratuitous* (i.e., hidden) because God's self-knowledge simply *is* a self-giving that is received only as the human subject is radically transformed by grace to correspond to the humanity of Jesus. God just is self-giving love, the Father speaking himself freely and without reserve in the veil of the Son's flesh. This speaking in its boundless excess in the Spirit is the very freedom of creatures as they are made to follow Jesus. Revelation *is* reconciliation. Knowledge of God the Trinity is knowledge of the man Jesus insofar as this "knowledge" means trust, obedience, and praise to his Father in his Spirit. To say "Trinity" is therefore to say "grace," and to say "grace" is *not* to articulate a concept or theory of Being but the lived reality of our eschatological transformation by the action of God.

The crux of the dialectic here is pneumatology, i.e., that moment when we acknowledge the inscrutable reality of the Spirit transforming us into those who enact God's act in Jesus. Pneumatology, then, is not a discourse about a *second work* of God running parallel to that of the Son, but rather that theological moment when we recognize that the Father's *single work* in the Son, which corresponds to the singularity of God's essence, has an intensity or excess that overflows to include human subjects in its reality. Barth's refusal to accord the Spirit an independent work alongside the Son is not a downplaying of the Spirit's role but an affirmation of the Spirit's role in all its centrality. Because God's self-giving in Christ *is* God's self-knowing, *our* knowing of God by the Spirit is this same self-giving of God in Christ insofar as it reaches beyond itself to include us by transforming us into those who enact Jesus' human life. If we think of the Spirit otherwise, as an *additional* work of God alongside of Christ, we fracture the essence of God and so compromise the integrity of our participation in God.

This is the logic of Barth's mapping Revealer, Revelation, and Revealedness onto God's three modes of being.[20] Barth operates here with an Augustinian understanding of divine simplicity according to which the personal distinctions between Father, Son, and Spirit are the formal structure of a materially simple essence by which we understand that essence as one in act. Because God's essence has reality only in movement as the begetting

---

19. CD 2.1:16–25. God's primary objectivity is not the ontological condition for the possibility of the act, but that act in its self-sufficient integrity and internal momentum. Barth's distinction between primary and secondary objectivity is not an ontological distinction in God, as if God's primary objectivity were some hidden reserve outside of time. It is merely an analytic distinction that guarantees that God always maintains the initiative in our participation in God.

20. CD 1.1:295–99.

of the Son by the Father and the breathing of the Spirit by the Father and the Son, its unity and simplicity is that of an act of self-giving love. God's essence is only ever the doing of one thing—love—as the operation of one mind and will. The formal character of this simple love is sheer outgoing or self-giving—begetting and breathing—by which we are made participants and enactors of that love. By transposing this Augustinian logic into the idiom of revelation, Barth names the Father "Revealer," the Son "Revelation," and the Spirit "Revealedness." This understanding of each mode of God's being as a "repetition"[21] of God's simple essence is meant to signify that God's essence is one in act—that there is no reality of God other than God's singular act of self-giving and the relations by which that act is actual. For Barth, God is only ever the doing of one thing—self-giving in the veil of Jesus' flesh.[22] "Father" names the antecedent source of this act, while "Spirit" names the intensity or excess of this act that incorporates us into its movement.

2.

Jenson, however, points to an instability in Barth's doctrine of the Trinity in *CD* 1.1.[23] For Barth, trinitarian doctrine is fundamentally about the *christological* dialectic of revelation. There are moments, though, when Barth allows this christological dialectic to slip into a *trinitarian* dialectic. The seminal insight that grounds Barth's theology from 1924 on, namely, that the time / eternity dialectic is inscribed in Christ's person, that the Son enacts *both* the veiling and unveiling proper to God by hiding in the an/enhypostatic flesh of Jesus, is at times in tension with a trinitarian dialectic of revelation in which the Father and Son, rather than Christ's two natures, are the two sides of the dialectic. For instance, in *CD* 1.1 Barth uses the doctrine of the Trinity to say that there is in God the ontological *possibility* of revelation that is distinct from its christological *actuality*. The possibility

---

21. *CD* 1.1:350–53. "Repetition" here should be understood in contrast to "mediation" as the principle of the movement of God's essence. God's being is in becoming not because the Father is an abstract subject who needs to mediate a concrete identity to himself through the history of the Son in the space of the Spirit, but because in its strict identity with the begetting of the Son and the breathing of the Spirit, God's essence is sheer outgoing action. It is when Barth feels tempted to understand God's self-relation as a self-mediation rather than a self-repetition, i.e., to indulge in "Hegeling," that he begins to think ontologically and therefore against his own best insights.

22. The full force of this "only ever" is articulated in Barth's doctrine of election in *CD* 2.2.

23. Jenson, "Hidden and Triune," 8.

of self-giving or unveiling is the eternal Son,[24] the possibility of remaining utterly free or veiled in this self-giving is the eternal Father,[25] and the possibility of these two possibilities meeting us in the event of revelation as the single possibility of the one God is the eternal Spirit.[26]

Jenson criticizes this account of divine revealedness / hiddenness for tending toward a subtle form of subordinationism. That is, God's essential nature or deity, the inability to be "unveiled to humanity," is here appropriated uniquely to the Father. God remains hidden—and therefore *God*—in revelation because there is an infinite reserve in God identical to the Father. This means that the Son and Spirit, although the same Subject as the Father, are not directly identified with that which separates God from all that is not God, namely, hiddenness. The subjectivity or essence of God is therefore fractured. Jenson acknowledges that this criticism is somewhat ironic, since by far the most common complaint against Barth's doctrine of the Trinity is that it tends toward modalism precisely because, it is claimed, he is so set *against* subordinationism.

I think Jenson is right to raise a complaint against Barth here. What this means is that Barth's doctrine of the Trinity in *CD* 1.1 is not fully stabilized with his christology. Rather than being simply and totally in service of explicating the *actuality* of the christological dialectic of revelation, his doctrine of the Trinity functions here—even if only for a moment—to ground the *possibility* of revelation by positing a moment in eternity in which God "produces" God's identity as open to participation by creatures. Despite explicit protests to the contrary,[27] Barth operates here with a kind of Hegelian logic. The moment of self-reflexive othering in eternity, what Barth calls the moment in which God is God's own "*alter ego*,"[28] is the ontological condition for the possibility of including creatures in the divine act. Yet this introduces a split into God's essence, between the moment of God's self-knowing in which God "prepares" Godself for revelation, and the event of God's self-giving in which God actualizes that revelation. This supposes that God's act in time is not its own possibility but grounded in a more primal being of God in eternity. This in turn prevents Barth's doctrine of the Trinity from doing the very thing he intends it to do—guarantee that there is no God behind the actuality of revelation.[29]

24. *CD* 1.1:320.
25. *CD* 1.1:324.
26. *CD* 1.1:332.
27. *CD* 1.1:330.
28. *CD* 1.1:316.
29. This onto-logic returns with remarkable clarity in *CD* 4.1 when Barth maps the

The sub-section in *CD* 2.1 titled "The Hiddenness of God" corrects this error of appropriating hiddenness uniquely to the Father. Barth writes, "the hiddenness of God is the inconceivability of the Father, the Son and the Holy Spirit."[30] Here Barth speaks of hiddenness not in terms of an ontological reserve in God outside of time, but in terms of the quality of God's act in time—its intensity or excess as unbounded grace. "It is because the fellowship between God and us is established and continues by grace that God is hidden from us."[31] God cannot be known as a static object because what encounters us in Jesus is a "bestowal which utterly transcends all our capacity, being and existence as such."[32] God can only be praised as a living Subject whose objectivity is the utter singularity of a Jewish peasant whose life we ourselves are given to enact in the Spirit. This is what gives God's hiddenness what I want to call its "doxological" determination. "Our confession of God's hiddenness . . . becomes a worship of God and therefore the beginning of our knowledge of God."[33] Worship here is not the analogical ascription of words and concepts to the divine being. It is a lived abandonment to the action of God. "God's revelation demands our trust and its command our obedience."[34] Crucially for Barth, the concepts and words that we use to think and speak of God—grace, holiness, mercy, righteousness, patience, wisdom, etc.—do not operate according to an *onto*-logic but according to a *doxa*-logic. "It . . . lies in the nature of this revelation that we can meet it only with the praise of thanksgiving."[35] We speak of God truly not because a correspondence obtains on the level of Being between God and creatures—which would, at best, enable us to speak *about* God (statically, that is). We truly speak *of* God only as our words and concepts are borne along by "the exuberance of the worship of God in the heart and mouth of the sinful creature,"[36] only as our thinking and speaking is the overflow of a lived movement of love of God and neighbor. Faith, therefore, "is not a

---

difference between "command" and "obedience" onto the difference between the Father and the Son (196–210). The reality of a command and obedience in God's immanent life becomes the ontological ground for God's economic action. That McCormack has pointed to this ontological moment in Barth as the culmination of Barth's trinitarian thinking confirms his tendency to read Barth in terms of ontology: see McCormack, "Election."

30. *CD* 2.1:197.
31. *CD* 2.1:188.
32. *CD* 2.1:197.
33. *CD* 2.1:198.
34. *CD* 2.1:201.
35. *CD* 2.1:198.
36. *CD* 2.1:219.

viewing and conceiving but consists in our being apprehended by the invisible God,"[37] that is, taken up into God's action. "Our knowledge of God is always compelled to be a prayer of thanksgiving, penitence and intercession. It is only in this way that there is knowledge of God in participation in the veracity of the revelation of God."[38]

This doxological determination of God's hiddenness is where we ought to look for the richness of Barth's pneumatology. The Spirit is the repetition of Jesus' lived history insofar as that history becomes the determination and momentum of our own praise and action, work and prayer. The Spirit is not a separate ontological moment in God that we can pick out and uniquely identify, but simply the hidden excess of Jesus' singular life.

But Barth again here in *CD* 2.1 has moments when he fudges this *doxa*-logic, when he turns his back on or doesn't follow through with the full implications of thinking our relation to God doxologically.[39] Even when Barth speaks in terms of doxology, the desire to find an epistemological—and therefore ontological—foundation for our "apprehension" of God is not far from the surface. Doxology, even in the passages just quoted, threatens to be instrumentalized for the sake of "knowledge" understood as "authentic information about God."[40] The problem is that the "indirection" of Barth's theology, its emphasis on the dialectic of veiling and unveiling, at times turns out to be simply a *method* for obtaining objective knowledge. Although God hides or veils Godself in human flesh, this veiling is for the sake of authorizing an objective content of revelation that can be grasped as knowledge. Barth therefore condemns as "blasphemy" the attempt to speak of the human response to revelation as one of unknowing rather than knowing.[41] Rather than the uncertainties of passion, yearning, or ever-increasing desire, Barth in this section prefers the satisfactions of "giving thanks," "acknowledgment," "joy," and "wondering awe."[42]

Knowledge of God, however much it is "actualized" or "doxologized" in Barth's hands, is still tied at various moments to a certain onto-logic of analogical correspondence. The veil of Jesus' human form is in ontological correspondence to what it veils—the divine essence—and so authorizes

37. *CD* 2.1:201.

38. *CD* 2.1:223.

39. See *CD* 2.1:58, where Barth repeats the mistake he make in *CD* 1.1 of appropriating hiddenness uniquely to the Father: God relates to us "in such a way that, by His being revealed to us as He and as Thou, He remains hidden from us as I and therefore in the being and essence of His Godhead."

40. *CD* 2.1:210.

41. *CD* 2.1:201.

42. *CD* 2.1:216–20. I owe this last point to Hughes, "Subversive Revelation."

objective knowledge of what it hides. It is the very structure of analogical knowledge, however, that doxology problematizes. Speaking of "praise" in terms of "knowledge" of our "correspondence" to God threatens to reduce praise to an epistemological act. Praise, at least biblically, is a lived abandonment to the resurrecting action of God,[43] and "resurrection" cannot be "known" by way of its analogical correspondence to anything—"for who hopes for what he sees" (Rom 8:24; ESV)? Resurrection is the irruption of utter newness.[44]

Barth's best moments happen when he stabilizes his doctrine of the Trinity with his christology. This occurs when the doctrine of the Trinity is used not to ground the *possibility* of revelation—epistemological, ontological, or otherwise—but rather to refuse the very question of possibility by riveting our attention on the always-prior *actuality* of revelation. This is the heart of Barth's teaching in *CD* 2.2 that Jesus Christ is the Subject of election. It is not a claim that in the act of election God "gives to himself his own being,"[45] which would be to introduce into God's essence a split between self-knowing and self-giving. Rather, it is an attempt to think through the implications of divine simplicity more thoroughly and more radically. To say that Jesus Christ is the Subject of election means that there is such a unity between God's being and act, between God's essence and existence, that—inexplicably—God's self-giving in Jesus Christ *just is* God's essence. Barth couches this thought in the idealist language of "self-determination" that opens him to the onto-logic of identity production, according to which concrete identity is explained as the mediated result of a prior moment of self-objectifying. But I think he resists this temptation in his best moments. The language of "self-determination" functions for Barth more in an ethical than in an ontological register, not to explain the "how" of God's eternal identity (its ontological possibility) but simply to gesture toward the mystery of a love that is pleased to give itself totally in the disfigured face of a Jesus Christ. Barth's doctrine of election is meant to close off not only the possibility of there being a God behind Jesus Christ but, in so doing, to close off also the possibility of asking *how* there could be no God behind Jesus

---

43. Cf. Psalm 13:3–6: "Consider and answer me, O Lord my God; light up my eyes, lest I sleep the sleep of death, lest my enemy say, 'I have prevailed over him,' lest my foes rejoice because I am shaken. But I have trusted in your steadfast love; my heart shall rejoice in your salvation. I will sing to the Lord, because he has dealt bountifully with me" (ESV).

44. Barth does, at times, express this: "All errors at this point have their source in the idea that we are able by analogy to get some picture and concept of the kingdom of God, understanding, or thinking we understand, what is meant by the terms, 'God' and 'kingdom' and 'coming.' The kingdom of God defies expression" (*ChL*, 237).

45. McCormack, *Orthodox*, 266.

Christ—which would ironically be to question behind Jesus Christ! "The will of God in His grace knows no Wherefore. God's decision is grounded in His good-pleasure, and for that reason it is inexplicable to us."[46] "Where we see what has actually happened in His Son, there can be no question of understanding how the condescension of God acts. We can only know and worship its actuality."[47] This is a doxological refusal of ontology.

To say that Jesus Christ is the Subject of election is to say that in *this man* we are confronted with the divine "I," the divine essence in total, without reserve. Jesus Christ is not simply the divine "Thou" or "He" behind which stands the divine "I" of the Father. Jesus is the hiddenness of God in his own person, in his own action and work. "Whoever has seen me has seen the Father" (John 14:8). Saying also that Jesus Christ is the *Object* of election brings into striking clarity the christological dialectic of revelation. In this one person, we have the Subject God and the Object humanity, this Subject/essence veiling and unveiling itself by enacting the objectivity of Jesus of Nazareth's human life. The divine Subject is veiled in this enactment not because the divine essence stands "behind" Jesus—as the spatial metaphor of "veiling" might suggest—but because the divine Subject's enactment of Jesus' life is done for the sake of our participation in it. It is done with an eschatological direction, with such intensity that it overflows itself to include us in its movement.[48] This intensity and excess simply is the Spirit.

4.

I want to claim that Barth's pneumatology—which is simply his christology in a different key—*is* his theology of divine hiddenness. This explains why so many critics have failed to notice his pneumatology. The Spirit, precisely by virtue of the Spirit's unique "role" in the Trinity, is hidden in Barth's pages. Pneumatology is not an isolatable discourse that identifies another agency in God alongside the single agency of the Father that gives itself without reserve in the Son. This would be to fracture God's essence. Rather, pneumatology is an apophatic moment in Barth. It is the place where his theological discourse is broken apart by that which exceeds it, namely, the lived reality of our transformation by the risen Jesus. To give due witness to the Spirit is simply to turn the reader ever again to Jesus Christ as a present reality claiming her for radical and free action. This is why Barth admits toward the end of his doctrine of election in *CD* 2.2, for example, that his

46. *CD* 2.2:30.
47. *CD* 1.2:34.
48. Hence in *CD* 4.2, Barth will speak of the "direction of the Son" (see §64.4).

theological discourse needs "a final intensification . . . which can be given only as we abandon not merely the language and style but also the intention and attitude of definitive exposition, and pass over directly to . . . the *genre* of preaching and pastoral admonition."[49] Barth then suddenly begins to address his reader directly with the gospel. Merely talking *about* the election of Jesus Christ fails to understand it and handle it faithfully. Election is an "act of the divine life in the Spirit,"[50] and therefore it has to be spoken *of*, proclaimed, enacted. Barth *performs* his pneumatology here.

We can turn here to Jenson's criticism of Barth's pneumatology in his essay, "You Wonder Where the Spirit Went." Jenson's misreading of Barth in this essay can be traced to a single inappropriate gesture: his attempt to read Barth ontologically. What he looks for in Barth's doctrine of the Trinity is the ground in God of a communion ontology.[51] He doesn't find this, of course, which is why he complains that the Spirit is absent in much of Barth's theological discourse—absent, that is, as a unique "*party* in the triune actuality."[52] But this assumption that the goal of trinitarian doctrine is to arrive at a correct balance between unique divine parties or agencies is one that Barth simply rejects. Barth's locating the objectivity of revelation always in the human Jesus does not somehow rob the Spirit of the Spirit's share in objectivity, as if the Son and Spirit were in competition with each other over who does what in the production of God's essence. God's essence is singular, one simple act of self-giving. Father, Son, and Spirit simply name the different modes of God's essence by which this act is actual.[53]

Jenson's constructive alternative to Barth in fact employs the same logic as the faulty doctrine of divine hiddenness that he criticizes in Barth— he locates divine hiddenness within a *trinitarian* dialectic. "God is hidden precisely by his triunity, by the mutual life of Father, Son, and Holy Spirit."[54] By "mutual life," Jenson means the "plot lines of the narrative constituted

---

49. *CD* 2.2:323.

50. *CD* 2.2:184.

51. "When the specific role of the Spirit . . . is grasped, an ecclesiology of *communion* ensues . . . If the Community between the Father and the Son were himself an *agent* of their love, immanently and economically, then the church, as the community inspirited by this Agent, would be the active *mediatrix* of faith" (Jenson, "You Wonder," 302–3).

52. Ibid., 301.

53. Jenson is correct to note that Barth does have moments when he posits a two-sided ontological ground in God as the condition for the possibility of revelation—the I-Thou relation between Father and Son (ibid., 302). Jenson's criticism is that this ontological ground is not three-sided. I have argued that the move to posit *any* ontological ground in God undoes the nerve center of Barth's theology.

54. Jenson, "Hidden and Triune," 9.

between [the triune persons] and with us."[55] In other words, God *is* a story. An idealist logic is at work here, similar to the one that allowed Barth to slip into subordinationism. This logic is operative whenever theology attempts to *explain* revelation by interpreting it as the necessary unfolding of a concept, one rooted in a prior moment of identity production. For Jenson, the concept is that of story or narrative. God has a concrete identity only insofar as God's essence unfolds dialectically as a narrative. Therefore, God *must* enact Godself as a story in order to be God.[56] God is hidden according to this logic because every good story must have a crisis and an unpredictable resolution. Inhabiting God as creatures, we inhabit this story and therefore also the crisis of the Son's abandonment by the Father and the unpredictable resolution to this crisis in the Son's resurrection by the Spirit. This crisis of God with Godself is the hiddenness of God. This results in the same tilt toward subordinationism that occurs in *CD* 1.1, just flipped toward the Spirit. The deity of the Son is not *identical* to the Son's action but is located at a level removed from Jesus' lived history—in Jesus' *rescue* from the crisis of time and creaturehood by the Spirit that produces the "communion" that is the true location of God's deity.[57] God is hidden from creatures, it follows, because the Spirit has yet to rescue us from time and creaturehood in the same fashion—we have yet to be deified. Which is to say that God is not yet "all he ever could be."[58] Divine hiddenness is the fact that God's Being is not yet fully produced, that God will surprise Godself (and us) in the timing and manner of our eschatological inclusion into the divine Being.

What occurs here is the "'Jesus Christ pit' of the Lutherans" that Barth warned about in an early letter to Thurneysen.[59] By identifying divine revelation directly with the metaphysical import of Jesus' humanity, directly, that is, with the crisis that Jesus confronts as a finite human being situated over-against his infinite Father, Jenson is forced to locate divine hiddenness elsewhere than in the an/enhypostatic constitution of Jesus' singular *person*. It is located instead in the finite/infinite dialectic that constitutes Jesus' two natures.[60] But as Barth perceptively saw in his later christology, this leaves

---

55. Ibid.

56. "As it is, God's story is committed as a story with creatures. And so he too, as it is, can have no identity except as he meets the temporal end toward which creatures live" (Jenson, *Systematic Theology*, 1:65).

57. This is what he means in claiming that "the resurrection is God's *ousia*" (Jenson, *Triune Identity*, 168).

58. Jenson, *Systematic Theology*, 1:66.

59. As quoted in *CRDT*, 351.

60. When Barth speaks of the dialectic of Jesus' two natures as the dialectic of revelation, he speaks not in terms of the metaphysical relation between the finite and the

a door wide open to "wander right away from christology."[61] Without the enhypostatic performance of Jesus' humanity by the eternal Son, the priority of divine agency and the gratuity of God's act at the heart of christology is lost. Jesus' humanity then becomes the occasion to affirm other creaturely realities as themselves divine revelation, since revelation has become a matter of the human agency of Jesus determining the divine agency rather than the reverse.[62] Our attention is allowed to wander away from the personal singularity of Jesus that is his lived history. Jesus becomes a mediating moment (even if the central one) in an ontological or metaphysical scheme. The form this takes in Jenson is an ecclesiology that equates divine revelation with a directly apprehensible ecclesial culture.[63] Jesus is simply the central mediating moment in God's quest to become "all he ever could be,"[64] which, as it turns out, is the high culture of western christendom.[65]

---

infinite that is central to the *communicatio idiomatum*, but in terms of the an/enhypostatic constitution of the *unio hypostatica*. By prioritizing the *unio hypostatica* over the *communicatio idiomatum*, the Reformed Barth focuses on the actuality of Jesus' lived history and its overflow or repetition in the Spirit rather than on the metaphysical ground or result of that history. The Lutheran Jenson, by contrast, who thinks of theology as metaphysics, thinks the incarnation primarily in terms of a *communicatio idiomatum* and therefore as the actualization of a certain metaphysical reality—the infinite Father mediating his own identity to himself by positing a finite Son. See Jenson, *Systematic Theology*, 1:228–29. McCormack also thinks the incarnation in terms of a *communicatio idiomatum*, albeit a revised one in the form of a *genus tapeinoticum*. He also very subtly abstracts from the lived history of Jesus to articulate the ontological ground and result of that history. See McCormack, "Karl Barth's Christology"; McCormack, *Orthodox*, 201–33.

61. CD 4.2:81.

62. See CD 4.2:20–154, where Barth articulates the conceptual heart of his christology. He speaks of the mutual participation of divine and human essences as follows: "The determination of His divine essence is *to* His human, and the determination of His human essence *from* His divine . . . The word mutual cannot be understood in the sense of interchangeable. The relationship between the two is not reversible" (70–71). "This means that the two elements in the history . . . are not in simple correspondence" (71). "For all their reciprocity the two elements in this happening have a different character. The one, as the essence of the Son of God, is wholly that which gives. The other, exalted to existence and actuality only in and by Him, is wholly that which receives" (72). McCormack's "kenotic" Christology reverses exactly what Barth says is not reversible. The divine essence, for McCormack, is given its existence and actuality by way of a kenotic "receptivity" to the human essence. See McCormack, "Karl Barth's Christology."

63. See Kline, "Participation."

64. Jenson, *Systematic Theology*, 1:66.

65. See Jenson, "Christian Civilization."

5.

What we have here are two very different logics of revelation. When Barth is most consistent with himself, he interprets revelation according to the logic of a *christological* dialectic that centers on God's encounter with *humanity* in the an/enhypostatic constitution of Christ's person. The doctrine of the Trinity functions to articulate the theological intelligibility of this actualistic encounter. Jenson, by contrast, interprets revelation according to the logic of a *trinitarian* dialectic that centers on God's encounter with *Godself* in the narrative crisis of Jesus' death and resurrection. The doctrine of the Trinity functions as the metaphysical structure of this crisis and its resolution. It provides the guarantee that reality works like a story, with a beginning, middle, and end that serve to "bracket" time.[66]

Appeal to revelation performs very different work for these two theologians. For Jenson, revelation authorizes a particular language with which to tell the story that is itself what God is. In telling this story with its three primary actors—Father, Son, and Spirit—we know God without "any attenuated sense of knowing."[67] There is no God behind this story or its language. God *is* the sacramental language of the church. Knowledge of God is therefore primarily an act of interpretation.[68] It involves taking up the language of the Bible and the tradition and recasting it in language that is intelligible in whatever context the church finds itself. To say that God is hidden in this revealedness is to say that *what* we have to interpret is the crisis and unpredictable resolution to Jesus' story, of which we are characters. It is the *strangeness* and sheer *contingency* of this story that is God's hiddenness: "[Divine hiddenness] means . . . that we are stuck with the names and descriptions the biblical narrative contingently enforces, which seem designed always to offend somebody. It means that their *syntax* is hidden from us, so that we cannot identify synonyms or make translations. It means that we have no standpoint from which to relativize them and project more soothing visions."[69]

For Barth, on the other hand, the question of revelation to which the doctrine of the Trinity is the answer is a "Who" question, not a "What" question. Who encounters us in this man Jesus? To answer "the triune God" does not legitimize constructing an elaborate trinitarian ontology in which everything has its place within an order of Being. Rather, it is to be given the

---

66. Jenson, *Systematic Theology*, 1:222.
67. Ibid., 2:303.
68. Ibid., 1:14.
69. Jenson, "Hidden and Triune," 6–7.

startling realization that the manner in which we know the particular God spoken of by the church includes the renunciation of all "ontologizing." The "Who" we encounter in Jesus is One whose self-knowing is identical to an uncontrollable self-giving, which means that *our* knowing of this God cannot be knowledge of a metaphysical or ontological structure in God—even if that structure is named "Jesus Christ." What we know when we know this God is the event of our conversion by and to a boundless love. This is what it means to say that the revealed God is the hidden God. It means that we know God only in a movement of obedience that is possible only as God's love is poured into our hearts by the Holy Spirit. It means that we know God only in the face of our needy neighbor that we are given to serve. It means that we know God only as we are *sent* into the world as Jesus Christ's witnesses. Knowledge of God is not possessed in the church; it is performed in the world. It is not an act of thought that apprehends Being; it is an act of praise that abandons itself in love. All of this, of course, requires a severe qualification of what we mean by "knowledge."[70]

The key to both of these logics is once again pneumatology. More specifically, it is pneumatology as the enactment of *witness*. For both Jenson and Barth, revelation is a referential event, one in which the Spirit directs us to participation in God's reality in the world. Barth understands the Spirit's witness as witness *to Jesus*, whose identity, whose very person, is his self-giving to the world as its reconciliation to God. Therefore, the Spirit gives us to live the life of God only as we are sent into the world to witness to Jesus as the one who is himself the world's reconciliation to God. This is what Barth means by the "very special visibility" of the church,[71] which is the ecclesiological correspondence to the hiddenness of God. The church and its participation in God is an event of the world's transfiguration, a movement of reconciliation in which the church is the church only as it identifies with God's would-be enemies in order to call them God's friends. The church is never a stable gathering of those who have conversion behind them. Jenson, on the other hand, because he lacks the enhypostatic performance of Jesus' humanity by the eternal Son, cannot think of the Spirit's witness as witness to Jesus in his singularity—that is, as the one in whom reconciliation is an achieved reality. Rather, the Spirit witnesses to Jesus only insofar as, by the Spirit, Jesus is "risen into the church and its sacraments."[72] The Spirit witnesses to *itself* as the ecclesiological sublation of the dialectic between the finite Jesus and his infinite Father. This creates a church whose participation

---

70. It is, we might say, our being known by God (Gal 4:9).
71. *CD* 4.1:645.
72. Jenson, *Systematic Theology*, 1:229.

in God consists not in its sending into the world but in its self-maintenance over against the world.

6.

I have highlighted what I take to be Barth's doxological determination of divine hiddenness over against Jenson's metaphysical or ontological determination of the same. Let me conclude by pressing this point against both Barth and Jenson.

One finally has to move beyond Barth to affirm fully the doxological shape of participation in God. Barth's great gain is to show us that God's life in Jesus and our participation in it occur in the irreducibility of action. Yet there is a constant undercurrent in Barth pulling him into thinking action ontologically.[73] It is perhaps the very structure of analogy that is always reducible to ontology. Analogy is always the attempt to coordinate two objects within some shared space of meaning abstracted from those very objects.[74] Even Barth's *analogia fidei* that tries to think analogy as action still slides toward ontology. What needs saying is that our participation in God cannot finally be thought—it can only be lived in the work of praise. Of course, praise will involve a very mundane use of analogy and metaphor, such as when we speak to God in human words and concepts. But the key is to recognize that these analogies and metaphors do not operate analogically but doxologically. Their veracity does not lie in the ontological structure of analogy but in the inscrutable way in which the work of love we are given to enact in Jesus is borne along by the hidden blowing of the Spirit. Only as the shape of our very lives becomes a lived abandonment to God and neighbor do our words and concepts begin in any way to point to God.[75]

This is to speak of the Christian life not as the possession of objective knowledge but as a yearning for God's glory, for the transfiguration of creation, for "the freedom of the glory of the children of God" (Rom 8:21; ESV). This means thinking revelation not in terms of God's being but rather in terms of the shining forth of "the glory of God in the face of Jesus Christ" (2 Cor 4:6; ESV). To speak of the disfigured face of this man as the glory of

---

73. This is the central claim in Kerr's critique of Barth, with which I am in agreement. See Kerr, *Christ*, 63–92.

74. This is not to indict all theological uses of analogy. While analogy is perhaps always reducible to ontology, it is not always so reduced.

75. This kind of hiddenness or inscrutability is what Kierkegaard means when he speaks of "love's hidden life" in *Works of Love*, 23–25. "That which in its vast abundance is *essentially* inexhaustible is also *essentially* indescribable in its smallest act" (xxvii).

God is to say that God is hidden in the entirely singular life of a first-century peasant whose life is nothing but a constant doxological abandonment of himself to the poor and forgotten of this world. This life resists every ontology, every metaphysic, every analogy, and every logic that would seek to comprehend it, precisely because it is so singular and so determined by the pressure of God's *doxa*—the coming reign of God. Jesus gives himself not to be thought in the abstraction of an ontology, but to be lived in the concreteness our own self-giving to the poor and forgotten of this world. This self-giving is borne along in the Spirit by the momentum of praise—praise that because of Jesus the places of death in this world have been promised the new life of resurrection.

The Spirit Is in the Details

A Response to Peter Kline

—By William Barnett

> "Do not be conformed to this world, but be transformed by the renewing of your minds, so that you may discern what is the will of God—what is good and acceptable and perfect."
>
> —ROMANS 12:2

RATHER THAN A CONVERSATION, Peter Kline provides a constructive doctrine of the Spirit inspired by Karl Barth but conceived under the impress of Kierkegaard and Nathan Kerr's recent work. Nearly the whole of Robert Jenson's thought and all the apparent counter-strands in Barth are casualties. Like his mentor Barth, Jenson would not so much mind being theologically "dismembered"[76] so long as it occurs within its proper context: the church's ongoing critical and constructive conversation regarding the truth of God

---

[76]. Jenson did famously quip that it "is the fate of every theological system to be dismembered and have its fragments bandied about in an ongoing debate." Jenson, *Systematic Theology*, 1:18.

revealed in Jesus Christ.[77] This response focuses on the necessity of conversation about the reality of God for the ethical performance of the gospel.

Kline seeks to honor Barth's conviction that revelation is not the giving of fixed propositions, but an ethical encounter, the actualization of a covenant between God (Lord) and humanity (servant) in Jesus Christ characterized by command and obedience, grace and gratitude. Within this encounter, the Spirit is the power by which our lives are brought into correspondence with the humanity of Christ through the gifts of faith, hope, and love. The question regards the role of intellectual judgment and the conceptual description of reality (i.e., ontology) in the Spirit's inspiring of human agents unto obedience.

The fact that Barth engages in lengthy description of the being of God, humanity, and so on in light of the history of Jesus Christ is indisputable. According to Nathan Kerr, whom Kline follows here, this is "clearly in line with the Hegelian concern to objectify Christ as representative of the 'concrete universal.'"[78] Barth is said to suffer from "a certain obsession with the perennial idealist concern to establish 'history' as the mediating link between the particular and universal."[79] Why is identifying Jesus Christ with universal concepts problematic? Similar to Emmanuel Levinas, tarrying with ontology—i.e., reflectively placing things under conceptual description—inevitably abstracts and excuses us from the immediacy of the ethical relation, the summons issued by the face of the other.[80] This is a dressed-up version of Jesus' parable of the good Samaritan (Luke 10:25–37): "Don't spend your time in abstract reflection over the identity of your neighbor as she lies there in need; go and be merciful!" Accordingly, Kline summons us beyond Barth by rejecting all remnants of self-reflective Hegelian idealism in favor of Kierkegaardian existential engagement.

But can Barth's persistence in ontological reflection simply be attributed to idealist obsession with grasping, fixing, and totalizing reality? Does

---

77. In the sub-section on "The Hiddenness of God" that Kline builds on, Barth writes: "The attempt may and must be made, within the limits of human cognition, to ask about the truth, to distinguish the true from the false, and continually to carry the 'approximation' further . . . This means, to seek after better human views and concepts in closer correspondence to their object, and therefore, so far as we are able, to make the witness to the reality of God more complete and clear" (*CD* 2.1:203).

78. Kerr, *Christ*, 86–87. Kerr follows Rowan Williams here. See Williams, "Barth," 188.

79. Kerr, *Christ*, 87.

80. Cf. Levinas, *Totality and Infinity*. For Kerr's approximation to such an argument, consider claims such as: "For it is the peculiar work of the Spirit to witness always to another—*as other* (that is, not merely to himself-as-other, as in the Hegelian *Geist*)" (Kerr, *Christ*, 176–77).

such reflection abstract from the ethical? Barth gives us reasons to disagree. The primary reason is his intellectualist account of ethical agency where transformation by the Spirit comes through the renewing of the mind. On the way to action, the Spirit enjoins the human agent in explicit ethical discernment—of which ontology is a necessary ingredient.

In *Church Dogmatics* 2.2, Barth claims that God has graciously elected us for a life of grateful obedience to God in Jesus Christ. Not only "the sum of the gospel,"[81] this determining election confronts us as law in the form of God's command. How do we come to correspond to this law and so participate *de facto* in this election? Gerald McKenny argues that Barth endorses "a Christologically corrected Kantian form of morality."[82] The morally praiseworthy agent, for Kant, is one whose will is obligated by imperatives that take the form of universal law. If we ought to follow a course of action only because it is contingent to achieving some other desired end, we act selfishly. This is Barth's chief anxiety—human action that is self-grounded, self-directed, and ultimately self-justifying. Barth endorses Kant's distinction between categorical and hypothetical imperatives. As McKenny summarizes, the command of God itself is "rational in form, addressing its hearer as a categorical imperative which possesses the formal property of universality even in its singularity."[83] The history of Jesus Christ is a singular event, but the work of the renewed mind is to cast this history in its proper universal form as the norm that always and everywhere constrains our action. An agent who claims to be moved by pure desire, a hidden blowing of the Spirit, would raise Barth's suspicions. All kinds of selfish inclinations could be hidden under the guise of such holy desire.[84] Just as Kant proposed that reason must test all courses of action we are inclined to obey against the universality of the categorical imperative, so Barth intends the renewed mind to test all immediate inclinations against the universal standard of the divine command. Barth highlights the crucial role of discernment in Romans 12:2 as a form of human accountability before God.[85] Explicit ethical inquiry that examines, tests, and seeks God's judgment regarding

---

81. CD 2.2, §32.

82. McKenny, *Analogy*, 91.

83. Ibid., 115.

84. Selfish inclination is not the only problem: "Quite apart from the inclinations of our own fleshly nature, the existing situation as such is always ruled by all sorts of demons, and sensitiveness to it can have very little to do with sensitiveness to the will of God" (*CD* 2.2:639).

85. Since Christians have received the Holy Spirit and God's command "is not unknown to them . . . they can therefore ask themselves in what relation [God's will] stands to their future conduct and their future conduct to it" (*CD* 2.2:639).

the relation of our actions to God's universal will for us in Jesus Christ is instrumental to the Spirit's work of transformation. For Barth, the "operation [of the Holy Spirit] is neither anonymous, amorphous, nor . . . irrational."[86]

For Barth, the categorical imperative is not mere principle; rather, it is rooted in the indicative. Because the "obligation revealed and grounded in the person and work and lordship of Jesus Christ . . . is a categorical imperative, not merely in name, but in fact," Barth concludes that "to obey it is not merely the highest duty but also the highest good."[87] Here Barth repairs the broken link in modernity between ethics and teleology as Jesus is revealed as the *summum bonum*, the determinate end to which all human existence and actions are ordered. In his recent book, Matthew Rose concludes that "for Barth, as for the natural law tradition, a fundamental logos holds sway in creation that bears witness to God's intentions for human life. The world is order, not chance or chaos, and has a distinctly teleological character providing the deep structure of the moral life."[88] Where Kline suggests that Christ operates as the somehow hidden or implicit inner principle of our actions, Barth envisions Christ as the *telos* that must be explicitly acknowledged and confirmed in our existence.[89]

Order is a significant theological value for Barth. In his earlier *Ethics*, Barth writes:

> As we bow to the will of God, we do not bow to the power of caprice, whim, or chance; we bow to the power of order . . . We speak of order where reality is not only posited, but is posited as regular reality in a determined constancy of its reality. To subject oneself is to place oneself under an order and rule, in a series. To subject oneself to God is place oneself under *the* order and *the* rule, and in *the* series, outside which reality has neither necessity nor unity and is therefore no reality.[90]

Reflection on the true order of things—i.e., the "being" of God, creation, and humanity—in the light of Christ is for the sake of ethical action. To forsake such order is to bow to the false god of caprice, of pure voluntarism. This is the great temptation of modernity.

What does it mean to talk of the history of Jesus Christ as the order, *telos*, or good that structures our being? There is no general principle we

---

86. *CD* 4.2:361; as cited in McKenny, *Analogy*, 214.

87. *CD* 2.2:652.

88. Rose, *Ethics*, 59.

89. The teleological character of humanity's eternal determination in Christ is well maintained in Neder, *Participation*.

90. Barth, *Ethics*, 213.

can abstract from the history of Jesus Christ, yet that history constantly expresses a distinct ethos. Barth's preferred concept is *fellowship*: "fellowship as the inner connexion of all that God wills and requires yesterday, today, and tomorrow, from this or that man, in this or that situation."[91] Whatever diverse expressions discerning the will of God might take, Christian moral reasoning must always uphold and express the goodness of fellowship. While wary of Brunner's language of "orders" of creation, Barth cautiously endorses Bonhoeffer's notion of "mandates" that lend the divine command moral constancy, the sort he unpacks in CD 3.4, §54 when he treats male-female, parent-child, and neighborly relations. There are no traces here of an unreflective ethical movement toward some unspecified "other." Rather, we are responsible for the "other" precisely because she is conceived as the one to whom I am ontologically bound in "fellow-humanity."[92]

Such ontological reflection provides the *necessary* background but is not finally sufficient for the specification of concrete ethical acts. The encounter between the command of God and the human agent is finally consummated in prayer.[93] Here there is no exact predictability or precise knowing what will irrupt from the listening agent rapt by the Spirit of God. Yet the unknowing is really quite modest, simply the specification of proper means to an end. As McKenny finely summarizes: "The command of God always actualizes the covenant of grace, and ethical inquiry can know a great deal about the covenant of grace, and thus about what God commands, from the Word of God."[94] Recognizing any singular act as a performance requires certain constant conditions such as a mutually recognized authoritative script, a stage, and determinate roles. An ethical performance absent these conditions, absent the context of ontological reflection on the indicative, casts a veil over what truly moves the will, and so threatens to become the self-assertive voluntarism Barth opposes.

McKenny also identifies a dilemma in Barth's ethics. Prayerful discernment of action is the ultimate responsibility of the individual. Revelation can never become the possession of moral traditions as this threatens to make the command of God abstract and generic. On the other hand, the individual's responsibility must necessarily be exercised within the context of a "prophetic *ethos*"[95] where the Word of God is regularly declared

---

91. CD 2.2:711.
92. CD 3.4:116.
93. "The name for this practice of testing and waiting for which ethical inquiry prepares us and to which it directs us is prayer" (McKenny, *Analogy*, 265).
94. Ibid., 268.
95. CD 3.4:9.

as summons and space is made for the prayerful acknowledgment and discernment of faith. Pursuing revelation outside of this ethos results in arbitrary willing. The result is ambivalence about "ecclesial moral authority."[96] The Spirit works in and through a dynamic, intersubjective context, yet Barth is worried about an over-identification between the Spirit and the church's normative claims and practices.

Jenson gives his own reading of this dilemma. In Barth's theology the Spirit's work is not so singular and immanent in action that it becomes transparent, incapable of representation. In *CD* 4.3, §69.4 on "The Promise of the Spirit," the outpouring of the Spirit is treated as the distinct, middle form of three perichoretically related historical forms of the single event of God's self-declaration. So Barth makes conceptual space for the Spirit! Jenson's complaint is simply that Barth does not fill in the details. God's prophetic declaration becomes an extended meditation on the resurrection itself. Ignored are the Spirit's gifts to the congregation, precisely where Scripture registers prophecy as essential to the building up of Christ's body. Barth desires a prophetic ethos, but not one identical to our actual traditions and offices. Hence, Jenson's striking judgment: "One moment Barth's entire theology seems to be the first wholly existential theology; the next moment the whole thing seems a dream having nothing to do with us."[97]

Part of why Jenson finds it necessary to move forward and add formal texture to Barth's prophetic ethos is because he assumes the context of *late modernity*. Where Barth's major anxiety was modernity's unbridled self-assertion, Jenson writes in the wake of modernity's self-criticism. Modernity's critical pathos has become pitted against its own self-asserting totalizing tendencies. For example, Michel Foucault argues that faithfulness to the Enlightenment spirit now involves the constant criticizing and surpassing of the formal structures that constitute our identity.[98] Jenson is worried about the dissolution of the self, that all talk of personal integrity, constancy, and order—all values for Barth—are inevitably deemed hegemonic and so rejected in our late modern context.[99] The Protestant principle has outrun Catholic substance. If ethical agents are to be capable of proper ethical discernment and meaningful action, a concrete ethos is now required. Here the prophetic summons of the gospel finds constancy in the pastoral office, as practiced within the norms of canon, creed, and the episcopate. Here

---

96. McKenny, *Analogy*, 275.

97. Jenson, *God after God*, 92.

98. Foucault, "What is Enlightenment?"

99. This complaint and the suggested remedy are detailed in Jenson, "How the World."

the goodness of the gospel finds constancy in the "dramatic density, sensual actuality, and brutal realism" of the sacramental liturgy.[100]

For all of his traditionalism, Jenson never endorses the language of possession. The church does not *possess* the gospel and its command upon us, so that life in the Spirit is drained of existential risk, engagement, and prayerful deliberation. Jenson championed Bultmann's Word-event notion. He simply holds that Bultmann, like much of late modernity, fails to give that event any normative content. Barth provided the needed christological content, but the summoning force of that event remained transparent in its non-identity with any formal prophetic structures. Jenson's goal is to *localize* Barth's prophetic ethos, providing a visible link between the members of the body and their head. For Jenson, the church is the "active *mediatrix* of faith"[101] but only as it facilitates "anticipation" of who we are in Christ, our promised end.[102] The church is not the triumphalist realization of God's kingdom, only its concrete signpost in a culture where hope has become so apocalyptic that it threatens to become hope for nothingness.[103]

Jenson's thought requires more consideration than space permits. At the very least, he should not be cast as Barth's foil. Indeed, perhaps his attempt to make Barth's theology of the Spirit explicit and concrete takes one step toward a fulfillment of the possibility, even dream, of Barth for "a theology of the third article, a theology where the Holy Spirit would dominate and be decisive."[104]

---

100. Jenson, "How the World," 22.
101. Jenson, "You Wonder," 303.
102. Jenson, *Systematic Theology*, 2:171–73.
103. Ibid., 1:ix.
104. Barth, *Theology of Schleiermacher*, 278.

6

Dueling Ecclesiologies

Barth and Hauerwas in Con-verse

—By Halden Doerge

The topic with which I am concerned is what it might mean to bring Karl Barth into conversation with Stanley Hauerwas. As such I will try to avoid simply contrasting the two figures, or lodging a criticism of one's thought based on the other's. Instead, I want to investigate what it might mean to place these two figures in conversation with one another, and most specifically, my central concern will be with determining how we ought to read and appropriate the theology of Karl Barth in light of Stanley Hauerwas's work. In short, my concern is to discern what impact or opportunities Hauerwas makes for our reception of Barth.

Toward this end I will pursue two lines of inquiry. First, I will examine Hauerwas's own articulation of his theological relation to Barth, showing how Hauerwas seeks to "place" himself and Barth in relation to one another theologically. As any reading of Hauerwas's Gifford Lectures, *With the Grain of the Universe*, makes clear, Hauerwas clearly understands Barth to be a vital theological witness to the mission of the church in the world, even as he seeks to—in his view—move *beyond* Barth toward an ecclesiology "sufficient to sustain the witness that he thought was intrinsic to Christianity."[1] As such, Hauerwas understands his own work to exist along the trajectory of Barth's own work in some significant sense, carrying it *forward* in a way that exceeds Barth's own limitations. It is this self-perception of Hauerwas's own project as a further development or extension of Barth's project that must be laid to rest before we can see these two figures in their proper re-

---

1. Hauerwas, *With the Grain*, 39.

lation, a prerequisite for any sustained and fruitful conversation between their particular perspectives.

Secondly, having gestured toward a more accurate understanding of the relationship between Barth and Hauerwas, I will move toward an investigation of what truly reading Barth in conversation with Hauerwas might mean. In doing so I will show—or at least begin to show—the degree to which Hauerwas's particular departures from Barth help us to see and hear anew the particular challenge that Barth's theology poses for the task of theology and the faithfulness of the church to its mission in the world.

1. The Hauerwasian Quest for a Barthian Anchor

In his earliest book, *Character and the Christian Life*, Stanley Hauerwas engages Karl Barth's work on the topic of growth in the Christian life. Hauerwas discerns a vital contribution to this theme in Barth's work, namely Barth's "attempt to describe the Christian life in terms of the fundamental relationship of the self to God."[2] Barth falls short for Hauerwas in his failure to "exploit the language of growth and character."[3] Hauerwas is critical of the fact that Barth "treats the Christian life primarily in terms of events and acts which, while repeatable, cannot contribute in a theologically significant way to the development of ourselves as men of character."[4] In other words, although Hauerwas appreciates Barth's centering the ethical question on God's own agency and action, he is troubled by Barth's refusal to find a point of ethical concreteness in the language of character and growth.

While it is important to note that Hauerwas has moved away from the language of character and growth in favor of emphasizing the church as a configuration of social practices which form its members in virtue as his work developed,[5] this initial criticism of Barth remains fundamentally unchanged. Barth's insistence that "the relation between God and man is not that of parallelism and harmony of the divine and human wills, but of an explosive encounter, contradiction and reconciliation, in which it is the part of the divine will to precede and the human to follow"[6] remains problematic for Hauerwas in that such an insistence on the asymmetry of divine and

---

2. Hauerwas, *Character*, 176.
3. Ibid., 177.
4. Ibid., 173.
5. See Hauerwas, *Community*, 129–52.
6. CD 2.2: 644.

human action is unable to adequately express the "growth characteristic" of God's work of sanctification.[7]

In summary, Hauerwas's central dissatisfaction with Barth is that—in his view—Barth does not leave enough room for human and, specifically, ecclesial action to contribute to the formation of the good. Barth's insistence on the radical verticality of grace seems to occlude the notion that the church as a community of virtue can form its members in the way of Jesus. Indeed, for Hauerwas "Jesus" names not so much a historical figure to be reconstructed, or a divine inbreaking into history, but rather the communal story of the church which forms it into a peaceable community over-against the societies of the world: "Jesus is the story that forms the church. This means that the church first serves the world by helping the world to know what it means to be the world. For without a 'contrast model' the world has no way to know or feel the oddness of its dependence on power for survival."[8]

For Hauerwas, the problem with Barth is that his transcendental Christology, which insists that Christ is a sovereignly free actor who breaks into history and alone is the agent of the world's salvation, does not allow for what he deems to be a "sufficient" ecclesiology.[9] For Hauerwas, Barth's depiction of Christ as the sole effective agent of the divine work threatens to eliminate any necessary place for the church in the economy of salvation.[10]

This fundamental dissatisfaction with Barth is expressed in its mature form in Hauerwas's *With the Grain of the Universe*. While the title of this work is taken from John Howard Yoder, Yoder interestingly makes only a minor showing in the argument. Rather, Hauerwas calls upon Barth in the attempt to rehabilitate a (christological) natural theology. For the purposes of this essay I have left aside the issue of whether it is viable to read Barth in a manner amenable to any sort of refurbished natural theology in order to concentrate on the way in which Hauerwas positions himself relative to Barth in theologically describing the nature of the church's witness.

What is crucial for Hauerwas in *With the Grain of the Universe* is Barth's insistence that witness to the triune God revealed in Jesus Christ is the proper form of Christian discourse.[11] Indeed, Hauerwas posits throughout *With the Grain of the Universe* that the whole project of Barth's *Church Dogmatics* is in fact to offer "a manual designed to train Christians that the

---

7. Hauerwas, *Character*, 176.
8. Hauerwas, *Community*, 50.
9. Hauerwas, *With the Grain*, 39.
10. See ibid., 192, 203.
11. Ibid., 174–76.

habits of our speech must be disciplined by the God found in Jesus Christ."[12] Thus Hauerwas finds Barth to be a major ally against Protestant liberalism in that he insists on the particularity of Christian theology as witness to the God revealed in Jesus Christ. But he fears that Barth's constant emphasis on the radical completeness of God's act in Christ eliminates the church's *necessity* for the world's salvation.

This point is crucial. It is absolutely vital for Hauerwas that the church, as a community of moral practice which forms its members in virtue, be necessary for the world's salvation. In contrast to Barth's argument that the world would not necessarily be lost if there was no church—since "Jesus Christ, his Word and his work" alone actualize the world's salvation[13]—Hauerwas insists that "if the world is not necessarily lost without the church, then it is by no means clear what difference the church makes for how we understand the way the world is and, given the way the world is, how we must live."[14] Here we come to the crux of the matter: for Hauerwas the church provides an anchor, a fundamental point of theological, ethical, epistemological, and indeed, soteriological concreteness. Were the church not *necessary* in this fundamental sense we would literally have no place to stand, no way to get our bearings or even to recognize the revelation of God in Christ if such thing had occurred at all.[15]

Hauerwas finds in Barth the truly praiseworthy virtue of breaking with liberal Protestantism's individualism and social fragmentation.[16] Hauerwas wants to assert with Barth theology's particularity as a specifically ecclesial witness to the God revealed in Jesus Christ. However, Hauerwas is dissatisfied with Barth precisely at the point where Barth is most forceful about the fundamental shape of Christian witness itself. For Barth it is axiomatic that the church, as a witness, points to an entirely complete, utterly singular reality outside itself, Christ's work of reconciliation to which the church witnesses but does not complete, add to, or extend:

> In Jesus Christ the alteration of the human situation did take place, and does take place to-day, the situation of Christians and of all men, the reconciliation of the world with God in Him who is the living Mediator between God and man in the power of His resurrection. What remains for them is high and appropriate

---

12. Ibid., 182–83.
13. CD 4.3:826.
14. Hauerwas, *With the Grain*, 193.
15. See Hauerwas, *Peaceable Kingdom*, 99–102; Hauerwas, *Community*, 89–94; Hauerwas, *Christian Existence*, 59–62.
16. See Hauerwas, *With the Grain*, 147–59.

and joyful and stringent enough—to welcome the divine verdict, to take it seriously with full responsibility, not to keep their knowledge of it to themselves, but by the witness of their existence and proclamation to make known to the world which is still blind and deaf to this verdict the alteration which has in fact taken place by it. Their existence in the world depends on the fact that this alone is their particular gift and task. They have not to assist or add to the being and work of their living Saviour who is the Lord of the world, let alone replace it by their own work. The community is not a prolongation of His incarnation, His death and resurrection, the acts of God and their revelation. It has not to do these things. It has to witness to them. It is its consolation that it can do this. Its marching-orders are to do it.[17]

For Hauerwas this insistence on the utter gratuity and completion of the divine work of reconciliation leaves no space for the church. Rather the church's witness, if it is not to be rendered superfluous and unnecessary, must be *constitutive* of salvation's reality. Hauerwas insists that "the truth of Christian convictions requires witnesses."[18] But unlike Barth, the performance of Christian witness for Hauerwas does not point to something beyond itself; rather, it is—at least in some sense—reflexive. It is precisely in the church's own faithful act of witness that the Gospel is rendered true: "Does the truth of Christian convictions depend on the faithfulness of the church and, if so, how do we determine what would constitute faithfulness? Am I suggesting that the ability of the church to be or not to be nonviolent is constitutive for understanding what it might mean to claim that Christian convictions are true? Do I think the truthfulness of Christian witness is compromised when Christians accept the practices of the 'culture of death'—abortion, suicide, capital punishment, and war? Yes! On every count the answer is 'Yes.'"[19]

Here we see the zenith of Hauerwas's mature position about the nature of Christian witness *vis-à-vis* Barth. While Hauerwas seeks to break company with liberal Protestantism's faith in humanity as an immanent field through which God's will is achieved in the world, he has regurgitated a vision that is structurally identical to it by simply replacing an immanent faith in humanity with an immanent faith in the church. For Hauerwas it is no longer Christ himself but the church that is "the subject of the narrative as well as the agent of the narrative."[20] Or more precisely, Hauerwas's logic

---

17. *CD* 4.1:317–18.
18. Hauerwas, *With the Grain*, 211.
19. Ibid., 231.
20. Hauerwas, *Christian Existence*, 59.

means that Christ has become so utterly appended to the church that *any* meaningful distinction between them seems impossible. At the very least it is not apparent how any admitted distinction between Christ and the church matters to or plays any role in Hauerwas's theological vision. The church is no longer a witness in any ordinary understanding of the term. After all, witnesses are—by definition—those who point away from themselves to a reality beyond them. This is fundamental to Barth's understanding of the church as witness. Hauerwas, in his zeal to make the church's witness "necessary" rather than a superfluous overflow of grace[21] has actually constructed a notion of witness diametrically opposed to Barth, whose very project he claims to be carrying forward. Far from taking up Barth's impetus and seeking to extend his thought, Hauerwas loops back *behind* Barth's critique of liberal Protestantism and recasts it in ecclesiastical form. Hauerwas's quest to find in the church a conceptual anchor from which to go beyond Barth has yielded something entirely opposite: a retroactive bypassing of the very challenge that Barth poses for theology and the mission of the church.

2. Barth's Witness to Hauerwas

Where are we left if the above exposition of Barth and Hauerwas above has merit? If Hauerwas's theology is a calculated reversal of Barth's thought rather than its extension, what might it mean for us to put these two theologians into conversation? What would it mean to read Barth in light of and in contrast to Hauerwas's rejection of Barth's theology of witness? There are, I believe, two important consequences that would follow from such an attempt at conversation between the theologies of Barth and Hauerwas which I will gesture toward, albeit briefly and incompletely.

First, reading Barth in light of Hauerwas's turn to an ecclesiocentric rather than christocentric notion of witness offers us an opportunity to hear anew Barth's criticism of liberal Protestantism and Roman Catholicism. Indeed, and as I have argued previously,[22] Barth's criticism of liberal Protestantism and Roman Catholicism are two sides of the same coin.[23] For Barth both of these ecclesiastical modes were problematic insofar as they reduced God to an object within the immanent frame of either humanity or the historical process (Protestant liberalism), or the hierarchical church as the extension of the incarnation (Roman Catholicism). In both cases the

---

21. See *CD* 4.3:608.
22. See my response to Congdon, "No-God."
23. See especially Barth, *Word of God*, 112–15.

diastasis between God and the world is lost and we are left with the gospel's ideological captivity to humanity's social and political constructions.

In an interesting way Hauerwas's move toward an ecclesiocentric notion of witness actually brings together both the Roman Catholic and the liberal Protestant tendencies which were the very objects of Barth's parallel criticisms. Highly suggestive of this is that Hauerwas's couches his own criticism of Barth in the assertion that Barth is not "sufficiently catholic," by which Hauerwas means that "his critique and rejection of Protestant liberalism make it difficult for him to acknowledge that, through the work of the Holy Spirit, we are made part of God's care of the world through the church." Hauerwas further specifies this lack of catholicity as consisting in the fact that Barth "cannot acknowledge that the community called church is constitutive of the gospel proclamation."[24]

Hauerwas is quite correct that Barth cannot acknowledge the church as constitutive of gospel proclamation precisely because Barth rejects liberal Protestantism's commitment to immanence and Pelagianism. Indeed, insofar as Hauerwas seeks any sort of "catholicity" that finds its constitutive source in the church rather than solely in the death and resurrection of Christ, Hauerwas forsakes Barth at the most fundamental level possible. Hauerwas's mature statement of an ecclesiocentric vision of salvation and the church provides the most perfect crystallization imaginable of the object of the early Barth's multifaceted critique of religion:

> Religious righteousness! There seems to be no surer means of rescuing us from the alarm cry of conscience than religion and Christianity. Religion gives us the chance, beside and above the vexations of business, politics, and private and social life, to celebrate solemn hours of devotion—to take flight to Christianity as to an eternally green island in the gray sea of the everyday. There comes over us a wonderful sense of safety and security from the unrighteousness whose might we everywhere feel. It is a wonderful illusion, if we can comfort ourselves with it, that in our Europe—in the midst of capitalism, prostitution, the housing problem, alcoholism, tax evasion, and militarism—the church's preaching, the church's morality, and the "religious life" go on their uninterrupted way . . . A wonderful illusion, but an illusion, a self-deception! We should above all be honest and ask ourselves far more frankly what we really gain from religion. *Cui bono?* What is the use of all the preaching, baptizing, confirming, bell-ringing, and organ-playing, of all the religious moods and modes . . . the efforts to enliven church singing, the unspeakably

---

24. Hauerwas, *With the Grain*, 145.

tame and stupid monthly church papers, and whatever else may belong to the equipment of modern ecclesiasticism? Will something different eventuate from all this in our relation to the righteousness of God? Are we even expecting something different from it? Are not we hoping by our very activity to conceal in the most subtle way the fact that the critical event that ought to happen has not yet done so and probably never will? Are we not, with our religious righteousness, acting "as if"—in order not to have to deal with reality? Is not our religious righteousness a product of our pride and our despair, a tower of Babel, at which the devil laughs more loudly than at all the others?[25]

Secondly and finally, reading Barth in light of Hauerwas provides us with the opportunity to appropriate anew Barth's explicitly missionary vision of the church. While Hauerwas thinks that the first task of the church is "to be the church,"[26] for Barth the fundamental meaning of "church" is to be called and sent out into the world as witnesses to Christ's death and resurrection. Indeed, one cannot put too fine a point on this difference: for Hauerwas the mission of the church is to *be*, while for Barth the being of the church is *mission*. For Hauerwas the reality of the church is fundamentally oppositional. It exists as a "contrast model" for the world.[27] This oppositional definition of the church gives rise to a fundamentally centripetal notion of mission in which the church's (reflexive) witness is primarily to its liturgical practices which are then asserted to be its "effective social work."[28] Thusly the church's central task in the world is to "find a way to sustain its existence generation after generation."[29] The Hauerwasian notion of mission establishes that the church's primary task is to preserve, defend, and prolong itself.

Barth, by contrast, understands the being of the church fundamentally in terms of Christ's sending of the church into the world as the community that witnesses to the resurrection. From beginning to end the church exists as a community sent into the world, for the sake of the world, bearing witness before the world in word and deed that in Christ all creation has been reconciled to God:

> As an apostolic Church the Church can never in any respect be an end in itself, but, following the existence of the apostles, it

25. Barth, *Word of God*, 19–20.
26. See, e.g., *Peaceable Kingdom*, 100.
27. Hauerwas, *Community*, 50.
28. Hauerwas, *Peaceable Kingdom*, 108.
29. Ibid., 107.

exists only as it exercises the ministry of a herald. It builds up itself and its members in the common hearing of the Word of God which is always new, in common prayer, in baptism and the Lord's Supper, in the practice of its inner fellowship, in theology. But it cannot forget that it cannot do these things simply for its own sake, but only in the course of its commission—only in an implicit and explicitly outward movement to the world with which Jesus Christ and in His person God accepted solidarity, for which he died, and in which He rose again in indication of the great revelation of the inversion accomplished in Him. For this reason the Church can never be satisfied with what it can be and do as such. As His community it points beyond itself. At bottom it can never consider its own security, let alone its appearance. As His community it is always free from itself. In its deepest and most proper tendency it is not churchly, but worldly—the Church with open doors and great windows, behind which it does better not to close itself in upon itself again by putting in pious stained-glass windows. It is holy in its openness to the street and even the alley, in its turning to the profanity of all human life—the holiness which, according to Rom. 12:5, does not scorn to rejoice with them that do rejoice and to weep with them that weep. Its mission is not additional to its being. It is, as it is sent and active in its mission. It builds up itself for the sake of its mission and in relation to it. It does it seriously and actively as it is aware of its mission and in the freedom from itself which this gives. If it is the apostolic Church determined by Scripture and therefore by the direction of the apostles, it cannot fail to exist in this freedom and therefore in a strict realism more especially in relation to itself. And when it does this it cannot fail to be recognisable and recognised as apostolic and therefore as the true Church.[30]

In the thought of Barth and Hauerwas we are confronted, despite certain affinities and even Hauerwas's own self-presentation, with two decidedly divergent understandings of the gospel, the church, and the world. From what has been said up to this point it should be abundantly clear that I believe that Barth offers a decidedly necessary corrective to the views exposited by Hauerwas. Whatever else it may mean to place Hauerwas and Barth in conversation, it cannot mean less than clearly presenting the radically different theological visions at work in their respective proposals. In so doing we are given the opportunity to see how deeply Barth's vision of the gospel stands in variance to that of Hauerwas. At the very least such analysis will

---

30. *CD* 4.1:724–25.

serve to exemplify the important differences between these two thinkers. At its best, we can hope that such an exercise will spur us on to ever and again fix our eyes on Jesus, the author and finisher of our faith (Heb 12:2).

A Response to Doerge on Barth and Hauerwas

—By Ry O. Siggelkow

"We are not saints because we make ourselves such. We are saints and sanctified because we are already sanctified, already saints, in this One."

—CD 4.2:516.

IN THIS RESPONSE I will seek only to build on Halden Doerge's analysis of the relationship between Karl Barth and Stanley Hauerwas. Doerge has properly set the terms of this discussion within the theme of "Karl Barth in Conversation." To the extent that Hauerwas's work has come to be associated with a form of "Barthianism" in America, Doerge has performed the invaluable service of highlighting significant differences between the two thinkers. In this response I simply want to further press the point—already made forcefully in Doerge's piece—that Hauerwas's dissatisfaction with Barth should be viewed as a rejection of central elements of Barth's theology.[31] To this end, I will briefly touch on three interrelated doctrinal loci that I think are particularly at stake in this "conversation" between Barth and Hauerwas: (1) the question of where to properly locate the church's "concreteness," specifically with regard to the doctrine of sanctification; (2) the question of the nature of the church's "visibility"; (3) and the question of the church's role and function in the economy of salvation. All three issues raise important questions about how to construe the relation between divine and human agency, the nature and mission of the church in the world, and the extent to which the church plays a "mediating" role in the economy of salvation.

---

31. Hauerwas, in significant respects, is dependent upon the recent criticisms of Barth's doctrine of the Holy Spirit in relation to his ecclesiology. See, especially, Hütter, "Karl Barth's 'Dialectical Catholicism'"; and Mangina, "Bearing the Marks."

The doctrine of sanctification has occupied a central place in Hauerwas's thought as early as his doctoral dissertation.[32] Following the lead of Barth and others, Hauerwas has sought to resituate the work of Christian ethics within a properly dogmatic and ecclesial framework. As a Wesleyan, the doctrine of sanctification seemed to provide a fertile ground for Hauerwas to treat the themes of character, community, and growth within a specifically theological context. Indeed, Hauerwas's theological ethics may be best understood as the outworking of a particular construal of the doctrine of sanctification. Hauerwas's later interest in the retrieval of the Aristotelian-Thomistic virtue tradition makes sense in light of his concern to think about sanctification in terms of the development of character through the concrete practices of the church community.[33]

Especially important to highlight here is Hauerwas's conception of the doctrine of sanctification is, in significant ways, deeply at odds with Barth's. For Hauerwas, the point of concrete contact between God's act of justification in Christ and the Holy Spirit's work of sanctification is *unequivocally* the empirical church defined by its core practices, habits, and liturgical traditions. The church as a culture and a *polis* forms its members into a distinctive people through practices of worship and other aspects of its life together. This ethico-political formation just is, for Hauerwas, the work of the Spirit to sanctify a people of witness. In fact, if the concreteness of the Spirit's work of sanctification is *not* directly located in the empirical life of the church itself, then, Hauerwas worries, the truth of the Christian gospel risks not only losing its visibility and distinctiveness but also its salvific efficacy. Indeed, such a loss would affect the destiny of the world precisely because the empirical church is an "ontological necessity,"[34] the "condition of possibility" for grasping the message and truth of the gospel, and "constitutive of the gospel proclamation" itself.[35] The truth of the gospel is thus inextricably bound up with the church's ongoing ethical life and witness.[36]

Attempting to locate the "concreteness" of the Spirit's work of sanctification in the empirical life of the church is precisely what Barth's actualist doctrine of reconciliation forbids. For Barth, the sanctification of the church (and the whole world) receives its concreteness not from *within* the immanent life of the empirically visible church *in abstracto*, but from *without*—in the concreteness of the Spirit's work which is a form of the *singular*

---

32. Hauerwas, *Character*.
33. Hauerwas, *Vision*.
34. Hauerwas, *Hauerwas Reader*, 161.
35. Hauerwas, *With the Grain*, 145.
36. For a reading of Hauerwas along these lines, see Kerr, *Christ*, 93–126.

redemptive action of God in Jesus Christ.[37] Sanctification does not await completion in a second movement of concretion in the church, nor does it become a stable predicate of the church's immanent life, providing it with continuity through history.[38] Instead, sanctification is only properly understood as an operation of God's transcendence. Sanctification does, indeed, "take place" in an earthly-historical form, but it only happens as an *event* of God's action in the Spirit and *for the world*. Certainly, the Christian community is "marked off from all others" as "a special people" "set aside by God," but precisely as such it exists in order that it may "make a 'provisional offering' of the thankfulness for which the whole world is ordained by the act of the love of God."[39] That concreteness is only properly located in the Spirit as the active subject of sanctification means, ironically, that Hauerwas's search for concreteness in the empirical church finally ends in *abstraction*.[40]

In the same manner, the true "visibility" of the church—what Barth calls its "very special visibility" or its "third dimension"—is not directly or immediately perceivable in its empirical institutions, moral life, or liturgical tradition, as Hauerwas maintains, but is *hidden* and can be seen only in relation and correspondence to the *event* of the world's transfiguration in God's act in Christ, which is the church's only "living basis."[41] While Hauerwas thinks he has found an ally in Barth especially at points where he positions his work against Schleiermacher and other so-called "liberal Protestants," it is ironic that Barth's most pointed criticisms of the *Glaubenslehre* are directed precisely at Schleiermacher's identification of the church with its empirically visible form. According to Barth, if the *Glaubenslehre* in some way marks "a fall of Christianity, or the canonization of it," this is precisely because of the way in which Schleiermacher's ethical conception of the church as a "pious society," distinguished from all other societies by the fact that "everything in it is connected with the redemption accomplished in Jesus Christ." The problem with this definition of the church, Barth observes, is "that the third dimension, in which the church is what it is, is completely absent."[42]

Locating the concreteness of sanctification and the visibility of the church in the *event* of God's redemptive action in Christ occludes any

---

37. CD 4.2:514–18, 615–16.
38. CD 4.2:507.
39. CD 4.2:511.
40. See also Healy's criticisms of Hauerwas's ecclesiology and, more generally, his cautionary remarks about what he calls the "new ecclesiology" in Healy, "Practices."
41. CD 4.1:654–58; CD 4.2:616–19.
42. CD 4.1:656.

attempt to ground or directly identify sanctification, much less the world's salvation, with the church's empirical reality (e.g., its practices, habits, culture, or liturgical traditions). Contrary to Hauerwas, Barth's account of the truth and efficacy of God's act in Christ does *not* finally depend on the church's "mediation" of it or on its ability to form or produce a "community of character." Instead, the truth and efficacy of the gospel are grounded solely in God's redemptive act in Christ. The church is visible precisely as a *provisional* witness to what God has done in Jesus Christ and continues to do, in the Spirit, for the sake of the world's transfiguration.

Insofar as the church exists and is borne by the revelation of God in Christ, and insofar as that revelation is the world reconciled to God in Christ, the church is borne and exists by way of the world's transfiguration in Christ. This is never something the church possesses in and for itself—never something the church ontologically bears within itself. Instead, the church's visibility is always understood only in correspondence to the action of the Spirit which is not an immanent property of the church's ongoing life. What Barth insists on—over against Hauerwas—is that God's relationship to the church must always be understood unilaterally, as apocalyptically coming from beyond. The church does not become the "subject" or "agent" or "continuation" of Christ in the world, but a witness to what God has done and is doing for the sake of the world. The church's visibility is thus not "necessary" to the transfiguration of the world, as Hauerwas would have it, precisely because the church receives itself in the Spirit's ongoing work to transfigure the world. The church lives as the visible witness to that reality, and this is what renders the church properly "three-dimensional" and "special" for Barth. What one sees when one sees the church's hidden reality in faith is precisely *not* the church as a distinct empirical or cultural form, but rather the world itself transfigured. Such visibility is not a possession but a gift, and as gift it is to be received ever-anew in prayer and thanksgiving. The church must be ever open to the action of the Spirit to live into what the church is called to be: a gate and signpost to the eschatological reality of the world reconciled to God in Christ, the *new creation*.

7

Christ vs. Mammon

Tanner and Barth on Economics and Theological Method

—By J. Scott Jackson

1. Can There Be a Christian Theology of Economics?

IN WHAT CRITICAL AND constructive ways might systematic theology address real-world problems of the twenty-first century, such as questions of economic justice? This contentious question excites contemporary theologians in schools of thought ranging from liberation theology to radical orthodoxy. Through more than twenty years of published work, Kathryn Tanner has made substantial contributions to clarifying how traditional Christian claims about God, Christ, and the world might be fruitfully integrated with progressive proposals for social justice. She has accomplished this by rigorously engaging such diverse resources as analytic philosophy, critical social theory, and postmodern cultural theory to mobilize classic theological motifs—centering, especially, upon divine transcendence and the doctrine of the incarnation—in novel and striking ways. Taken as a whole, this work amounts to a thorough reconstruction of theological method to take account of and empower liberating practices in everyday life, which include ethical actions to reform society. In pursuing this constructive project, Tanner draws widely from the history of Christian thought, engaging such diverse thinkers as Irenaeus, Maximus the Confessor, Aquinas, and Schleiermacher. One of her most significant theological interlocutors is Karl Barth, though Tanner is best understood as a constructive thinker in her own right and would not label herself, strictly speaking, as a "Barthian."[1]

---

1. See Tanner, "Barth," 187.

Much of Tanner's recent work seeks to reframe contemporary discussions of economic theory and practice in light of a theological account of God as the beneficent donor of free gifts and, concomitantly, of creation as a realm of sheer grace.[2] Barth's explicit reflections on economics, at least in his post-Safenwil period, are not developed thoroughly or systematically. But Tanner discerns resources for such a systematic treatment in Barth's mature dogmatic writings, especially in their consistent christological focus. Her criticism of Barth stems neither from his theological claims per se, nor from his reticence to reify any socio-political agenda as *the* normative expression of the gospel in the world. Rather, she argues that Barth has not clarified the concrete implications of his doctrinal claims—that the material connection between theological theory and ethical practice needs to be drawn out more explicitly. A major impetus for reading Barth today (though not the only one) is to retrieve the potential contributions of his thought for contemporary constructive theology and ethics, and this would certainly include theological proposals oriented to social change. Thus, to take a classic case in point, if James Cone can construct a black liberation theology by appropriating elements of Barth's doctrine of reconciliation, then perhaps Tanner might help us discern a link between economies of creation and incarnation with liberating possibilities for reconfiguring market economies and the sharing of vital resources.[3]

As the questions stemming from these issues are complex, it will be helpful to prescind from three concerns. First, I will not offer a critique of Tanner's economic proposals, either in terms of theory or practice. Second, I will not evaluate the relationship of Tanner's work as a whole to Barth's thought, for example, in his doctrines of creation and reconciliation. Third, and above all, I will not try to assess Barth's political theology as a whole in general or, more specifically, his writings on capitalism and socialism. Rather, what interests me is how Tanner's reading of Barth on economics exemplifies a commitment to tie specific proposals from the sphere of social ethics into a theological account of reality with deep roots in the theological tradition. But if Barth in his later years demurred from vigorously defending any particular economic system on the basis of Christian dogmatics, might he have had good reasons for doing so? Christopher Holmes argues this position in a response to Tanner's criticism of Barth's economic writings. According to Holmes, Barth was rightly reticent to endorse specific social programs and principles on theological grounds. Barth famously

---

2. Tanner's ideas in this vein are developed systematically in her work *Economy*. Her essay on Barth's economic views ("Barth") offers a more concise version of the proposals developed in this book.

3. See Cone, *God*, esp. chapter 10.

eschewed a "systematic" theology derived from abstract principles and instead viewed theology as an open-ended description of the free movement of God. Similarly, God's sovereign rule, enacted in Jesus Christ, transcends the dichotomies of human social ethics (capitalism vs. communism, for example). Thus, in support of this reading, Holmes cites Barth's treatment of Jesus Christ as the "Royal Man" (in *CD* 4.2) who rises above the power plays of the socio-political factions of his day.[4] The main burden of Holmes' argument, however, is to show not that Barth advocates a divorce of social ethics from the gospel that safeguards the spiritual purity of the later; on the contrary, according to this reading, the concrete ethical force of God's kingdom is so strong and efficacious in itself that any attempt to yoke theology to concrete social programs and principles would be superfluous, if not even inappropriate. If I might paraphrase Holmes in this way, if the theologian seeks first the reign of *God* and *God's* righteousness, the practical import of the gospel will be self-evident. Put another way, in his view God's rule in Christ *just is* the divine agenda for society and this dynamic and liberating power cannot be captured in any particular program, no matter how beneficent or high-minded.

Certainly Tanner, defender of a radical notion of divine transcendence, would not object to Holmes's basic Barthian argument that no agenda for social ethics can be simply equated with the divine will. Holmes marshals an impressive array of Barth citations to support his argument, and he shows facility with the Swiss theologian's overarching theological project. Tanner herself concedes Barth's point that all human ethical programs are contingent and subject to constant revision in light of God's righteousness as perfectly manifest in Christ. But is there not more to be said here? Of course, Christians need to retain some humility and reserve when they engage the ambiguous realm of politics and social ethics; still, such modesty should not excuse the systematic theologian from wrestling with the concrete *implications* of her doctrinal claims. Since Holmes misses this key point from Tanner's essay, he fails to take the challenge of her proposal with due seriousness. Christian theologians—whether they are speaking to the church, the academy, or the broader public—have a responsibility to consider the potential practical consequences of their intellectual moves, and they need to be open to criticism and challenge on that score.[5] In line with numerous liberationists and other praxis-oriented thinkers, Tanner illustrates at least one set of possibilities for constructively engaging resources from the his-

---

4. Holmes, "Karl Barth," 207.

5. For a discussion of the theologian's vocation in terms of these three "publics," see Tracy, *Analogical Imagination*.

tory of Christian thought to promote human flourishing—in this case, in the sphere of economic relations.

One must grasp the common ground the Yale theologian shares with the Swiss dogmatician to understand Tanner's disagreement with Barth on the possibility of a theologically grounded economic program. To that end, the points I develop below are as follows: First, Tanner and Barth agree on the propriety of relating Christian theological claims to concrete questions of social justice (even today, the theologian cannot presume such a connection but must argue for it). Thus, both thinkers find Christian grounds, though somewhat differently, for criticizing capitalist notions of private property. Second, Tanner and Barth agree on the proper theological basis for this relationship, namely the transcendent Creator's free gift of grace perfected in Jesus Christ. Third, nonetheless, Tanner seeks to go beyond Barth in articulating the implications of theology for socio-political ethics more explicitly.

2. Theology as Inherently Political

Tanner and Barth would agree on the propriety—perhaps even the necessity—of linking theology to socio-political concerns; but they would also recognize the inherent dangers and ambiguities in this effort. As Tanner has noted, Barth himself suggests in his 1932 preface to *Church Dogmatics* 1.1, written at a time of dire crisis in Europe, that clarity about theological first principles is essential to responsible Christian engagement with politics.[6] If we take Barth's words at face value, we might understand the *Dogmatics* on the whole as a sustained attempt at political theology or,[7] more plausibly, as an effort to construct an adequate doctrinal basis for engaging politics in sound ways. Of course, Helmut Gollwitzer and others have argued that Barth as an academic theologian was less than entirely successful in his endeavor to keep theology politically relevant, radical, and real.[8]

Barth's critical stance toward capitalism, especially its ideological conception of private property, was never more explicit than in his early days as a left-leaning pastor and labor organizer in Safenwil. In a famous 1911 lecture, he rejects the common claim that the aims of Christianity and of modern social democracy are mutually exclusive because the former promotes an otherworldly piety that shortchanges the practical agenda

---

6. See Tanner, "Barth," 181.

7. For example, to advance a socialist agenda, as Marquardt has argued. See Marquardt, "Socialism."

8. See Gollwitzer, "Kingdom."

of the latter. On the contrary, Barth argues, Jesus himself taught a coming kingdom of God that would establish radical social and economic justice in *this* world. What stands in the way of this transformed world is capitalism itself, especially what one might call a model of private property based on scarcity ("What's mine is mine!"). This system pits the capitalists, who own the means of production, against the workers, who must sell their labor at a cost far below its actual value. Barth is a fairly straightforward socialist here: "This system of production must therefore *fall*, especially its underlying principle: *private property*—not private property in general, but private property as a means of production."[9] Only state ownership of the means of production will neutralize the competitive class struggle that afflicts capitalist society. Barth quotes with approval a secular socialist who named self-seeking as the "original sin" of humanity. Barth appeals straightforwardly to Jesus' critique of mammon in various Synoptic sayings, but he does so without any clear reference to the broader sort of theological or christological bases he would later seek to explicate in the *Dogmatics*.

Still, in our day and context, answering the question "What does Wall Street have to do with Jerusalem?" is more complicated, perhaps, than the early Barth would seem to suggest. As invigorating as his rhetoric is, even a century later, the pertinence of classical Christian theology for complex contemporary socio-economic issues is far from self-evident. Would Barth in his later work continue to argue for a strong and explicit connection between doctrinal claims and concrete positions on economic issues? What would be the proper shape of the relationship between the doctrines of creation and Christology on the one hand, and particular questions of social ethics that are inevitably situation specific on the other? As Tanner and Holmes both show, Barth was dissatisfied with the dominant political and economic alternatives and refused, as a theologian of the church, to give a blanket endorsement of any system. If at the height of the Cold War, however, Barth sought a "third way" alternative to Soviet-style state socialism and Western laissez-faire capitalism, I do not think this entails eschewing altogether a political theology that promotes a certain shape for economic relations. Tanner argues that the potential for a theology of economics remains undeveloped in Barth, though such a proposal would not contradict his theological claims and methodology; Holmes, on the other hand, counters that Barth would eschew such a program as a matter of theological principle.

Integrating the spheres of doctrinal theology and economic ethics requires careful elucidation within a constructive argument. It is not a matter

---

9. Barth, "Jesus Christ," 29.

of simply "applying" abstract theological principles to concrete questions of praxis. Tanner wrestles with such questions in her book *Economy of Grace*, in which she offers an alternative proposal for a noncompetitive economics grounded in a theology of divine gift-giving and human sharing. Since the practical economic import of the gospel is so often contested, she seeks to demonstrate explicitly "how every Christian idea about God and the world is directly and from the first an economic doctrine."[10] This means that the economic dimension of theology may not be reduced to the realm of individual, personal morality.[11]

In an earlier work on political theology, Tanner similarly demonstrated the potential relevance of classical theism, and especially claims about divine transcendence, for Christian engagement with progressive social causes.[12] In particular, she showed how a theology that clearly distinguishes God from creation, and that posits a non-contrastive relationship between universal divine sovereignty and contingent human freedom, can serve as a basis for criticizing oppression and fostering tolerance, a respect for difference, and other progressive social values within a stance of engaged commitment. Still, she admits, the liberating power of such doctrines is not self-evident. Tanner notes that, historically, Christians in power have often used notions of a transcendent God to legitimate oppressive hierarchies—for example, by using notions of divine sovereignty to promote absolute monarchy. Tanner's point is that abstract theological principles, in and of themselves, are neither *inherently* oppressive nor liberating. Moreover, radically different theological standpoints may provide a foundation for the same political and ethical commitments. If I may suggest an example of my own: both an ecofeminist conceiving of the world as God's body and a Thomist asserting a clear distinction between God and creation could support the same proposal to slow climate change, and both could do so on theological grounds even if the trajectory of arguments would differ.[13] The process of linking theological theory to Christian practice is a matter of careful argument within specific contextual limitations. Yet, Tanner suggests, this task of engagement is one

10. Tanner, *Economy*, 1.
11. Ibid., 2–4.
12. See Tanner, *Politics*.

13. While Tanner argues cogently for the liberating potential of a radical notion of divine transcendence, she also admits that competing conceptions of the Creator-creature relationship might have similar potential waiting to be appropriated by constructive theology. The articulation of Christian doctrine is not static or fixed but is intrinsically a work of ongoing conversation and debate. Thus, Tanner notes, contemporary theology might also appropriate Hegelian notions of God and the world or panentheist notions of the world as God's body and marshal this material for a critique of Christian theology and ethical practice. See ibid., 252–53.

that theology should not shirk. Christian communities are inevitably implicated in a complex web of social practices from a variety of cultural influences; in this environment, theologians should carefully explore ways to promote cultural changes that are consonant with central Christian claims and practices.[14]

3. The Economy of God in Creation and Incarnation

A second and even more significant parallel between Tanner and Barth consists in a striking agreement about some key first principles; both theologians share formal theological commitments to views about God and creation, and about the normative impetus for Christology to shape theology as a whole—a view which logically also means that claims about Christ should govern the way theology's import ramifies in practical applications. In her first book, Tanner articulates and defends the coherence of traditional claims that God is the transcendent Creator who exercises universal providence without detriment to the contingent freedom of finite human agents.[15] This noncontrastive account of Creator-creature relations, she argues, was a commonplace in Christian philosophical theology from the time of the second-century apologists through the medieval Scholastics, until it began to break down in early modernity (e.g., in Nominalism). In making her case, Tanner draws extensively from Thomas Aquinas and Karl Barth. This noncontrastive paradigm became and continues to be a linchpin in Tanner's subsequent work. For example, her concern to defend divine transcendence recently has taken the form of an apophatic theology that resists any direct correspondence between human beings, whether as individuals or as communities, and a God who remains ineffable. Humanity bears the *imago dei* not by virtue of its created nature per se but only through the mediation of Jesus' incarnate humanity.[16] Consequently, and contrary to recent social trinitarian accounts, she argues that it is improper to model human social relations directly upon the unique inter-communion of persons within the Trinity; again, an absolute ontological distinction between God and the world is being upheld.[17]

As I noted above, Tanner draws heavily on Barth in articulating a noncontrastive notion of the God-world relationship—a conception which affirms radical divine transcendence and the utter contingency of all created

14. See Tanner, *Theories*, chapter 7.
15. See Tanner, *God*.
16. See Tanner, *Christ*, chapter 1.
17. See ibid., chapter 5.

life while also upholding the dignity of finite human freedom. In an essay explicating Barth's accounts of creation and providence, Tanner draws a parallel between the Thomistic notion of divine concursus and Barth's account of how divine action accompanies the actions of free creatures, a theme developed in *Church Dogmatics* 3.3.[18] For Barth, she writes, "the creature's action is always only a response to what God has already done for it. This sequence, or order of call and response, is irreversible, and in that sense one must say that God's action is never conditioned by the creature's action. The creature is, moreover, most itself and properly free only when its actions so follow God's primary action for it."[19] Thus, the radical transcendence of God as Creator does not mitigate the freedom of the finite creature but grounds and empowers genuine human agency.

For neither Tanner nor Barth does the doctrine of creation hang speculatively in the air. Both agree that Christ is the measure of all God's ways and works in the world and, consequently, Christology should give the decisive shape and impetus to all aspects of theology. Arguably, the most salient feature of Barth's doctrine of creation, as of all other loci of the *Dogmatics*, is that it is framed by the reality of Jesus Christ, the formal and material norm of theology as a whole. Drawing on Barth—and many other thinkers, from the church fathers to Karl Rahner—Tanner frames her own systematic theology within an account of the incarnation. Both Barth and Tanner construct Christology "from above," in dialogue with the patristic framework that culminated at Chalcedon. In Jesus, the eternal Son assumes, heals, and redeems human nature because in Jesus, divine and human natures are joined in perfect unity without mixture or confusion.[20]

Although both theologians emphasize the formal and material significance of the incarnation for theology as a whole, Tanner does not follow Barth strictly in constructing her Christology. On the one hand, in his doctrine of reconciliation Barth frames his Christology within such reinterpreted Reformed doctrinal rubrics as election, covenant, exaltation and humiliation, and the threefold office. Tanner, on the other hand, tends to focus more consistently on the classic incarnational framework as developed by Irenaeus, the Cappadocians, Athanasius, Cyril, Maximus, and others. Material drawn from Barth, Rahner, and other modern thinkers is appropriated from within this perspective. Thus, for example, whereas Barth conceives the incarnation of the Son in *CD* 4.1 as the culmination of the one covenant

---

18. Tanner, "Creation," 123–25.

19. Ibid., 123.

20. See Tanner, *Jesus*, chapter 1. For an account of Barth as a Chalcedonian christologian, see Hunsinger, "Karl Barth's Christology."

of grace, Tanner criticizes Barth for assimilating incarnation into a covenantal schema. She argues, rather, that "the incarnation is a higher form of unity than fellowship with God, and thereby the closest approximation to the triune life that is possible for a creature."[21] I suggest, without exploring the point in depth here, that incarnational Christology is more of a fixed point systematically for Tanner than it is for Barth, who freely interweaves a wider variety of christological motifs from different sources in a more fluid fashion.[22] Thus, in one striking difference, Barth seeks to retrieve elements of a Western penal substitutionary atonement soteriology in his discussion of "The Judge Judged in our Place," whereas Tanner jettisons such a theory completely. For Tanner, atonement occurs not through a perfect human satisfaction for sins, but through the communication of divine blessedness to humanity in the hypostatic union.[23]

4. Toward a Theological Vision for Economics

Without delving into the complexities of the soteriological debate here, I suggest that this more rigorously incarnational focus gives Tanner an edge over Barth in terms of just how a christocentric theology might inform ethical and political positions. This point reveals the most notable way Tanner departs from Barth by establishing a more direct link between the loci of Christian theology and particular questions of politics and social justice; in this vein, her work shows the profound influence of the turn to praxis characteristic of so many contemporary North American theologians. Tanner's approach to theological ethics is developed most clearly and extensively in her recent work on economics, which seeks to deploy her systematic forays into the rich resources of the Christian theological tradition to fund a noncompetitive vision for economic relations. In *Economy of Grace*, Tanner seeks to reconstruct economic theory and practice on the basis of a theology of gift, a vision of an overflowing divine beneficence with the incarnation

---

21. Tanner, *Jesus*, 50.

22. So Tanner: "Systematic theology offers a vision of the whole, a sense of how to bring together all the elements of Christian involvement into unity around an organizing center or centers" (ibid., xiii); "This book sketches a systematic theology that centers on Jesus Christ and his meaning for life in the world" (ibid., 1). Barth, by contrast, has a more open-ended conception of the task of dogmatic theology. Webster writes in interpreting Barth's method: "If dogmatics is about the business of tracing the path which God's Word takes, then it must be oriented to the movement which it follows. No system, no organizing principle, no critical theory and certainly no methodological prescription can be allowed to have the upper hand" (Webster, *Barth*, 69).

23. See *CD* 4.1:244–56; Tanner, *Jesus*, 87–88; Tanner, *Christ*, chapter 6.

at its center. God, the gracious font of all free gifts, offers creatures a share of the divine bounty in creation, covenant, and—above all—the hypostatic union of the Son of God with humanity in Jesus Christ. In light of the sheer giftedness of our status as creatures before God, our common economic life should be characterized by sharing with others what God has freely given us. Because everything comes from the overflowing love of the creator and redeemer, I have no claim to hoard goods that could benefit others and that in no wise belong exclusively to me. Tanner's strategy, as she lays it out in the preface, is to bring economic and theological concerns together under a more generalized discourse on economy. The third part of the book relates a host of specific proposals (often quite technical) for economic exchange. What interests me here is her criticism of capitalism, a position that draws her into explicit conversation with Barth.

Tanner pointedly criticizes a zero-sum notion of exclusive property, which holds that competition drives the exchange of inevitably scarce resources regardless of whether that competitive struggle is adjudicated by the "free" markets of capitalist theory or the government agencies of state socialism.[24] From a Christian standpoint, the claim that God freely creates and sustains human beings and showers the riches of God's own being on us in Jesus Christ points to an alternative, noncompetitive vision for economics. "The history of God's relations with us as those have their beginning and end in Christ contain in themselves a critique of competitive relations."[25] If God in Christ has freely given us all we could ever need, we might imagine new ways of equitably sharing the goods all people need to survive and flourish. Giving becomes unconditional (based on need and not merit), universal, and mutually beneficial for all. Tanner's counterexample to exclusive property is a lighthouse, common property of the community that benefits all ships equally. There is no need to parse out its beams among ships, but all travelers may share its rays without draining it.[26]

Tanner's alternative to prevalent views of private property has some resonances with Barth's own reticence to enter the Cold War fray between East and West, and his groping to find a "third way" between free market capitalism and state socialism.[27] Barth was worried that taking one side or the other would compromise the freedom of theology to witness to the Kingdom of God as a transcendent reality that cannot be instantiated by

---

24. See Tanner, *Economy*, 34–40.

25. Tanner, "Barth," 187.

26. Ibid., 196–97.

27. Ibid., 176–79. Tanner highlights Barth's controversial decision not to engage the Western polemic against Communism during the early years of the Cold War. See Barth, "Church between East and West."

sinful human agents, but can only be brought about by free divine initiative. "Upholding 'a third way' in this sense simply signals the need to maintain a distinction between God's kingdom and any human claimant. God's kingdom, Barth reminds us, is found already complete in Christ, and therefore one needn't turn to the church or any trajectory of human history in search of it."[28] The third way, then, is more of a critical principle of judgment than a concrete proposal or agenda in its own right. Tanner notes, "Christian insistence on a third way becomes the constantly applicable rebuke to any power, human movement or trajectory in the world purporting to be lordless, hoping, that is, to exempt itself from judgment in light of that history of God's dealings with the world that has its beginning and end in Christ."[29] To be sure, Barth maintains that Christians are free to engage in concrete efforts at social, economic, and political justice on an *ad hoc* basis as situations demand. Efforts within and without the church to instantiate freedom, justice, and peace may serve as fallible yet real "parables" of God's coming kingdom. Nonetheless, Christian social ethics must remain grounded in the basic story of what God has done for us in Christ.

Tanner affirms Barth's basic standpoint here, both in his commitment to the integrity of a critical and distinctively Christian discourse on social matters and his intent to frame this discourse christologically. Indeed, her firm commitment to a theology that affirms radical divine transcendence and the contingency of all human actions is consonant with a critical stance vis-à-vis all economic systems. No human proposal or agenda can be identified univocally with the Kingdom of God. In her earlier work on political theology, Tanner shows how an anthropology that acknowledges human finitude and fallibility can serve to safeguard genuine activism from ideological extremism and demonization of political opponents.[30] All human proposals for social justice are limited, provisional, and subject to ongoing criticism and revision.

Nonetheless, a healthy dose of humility in the face of divine mystery and human brokenness does not absolve theologians from the responsibility of engaging real-world problems in light of the gospel. Barth himself was not reticent to speak out pointedly, as a theologian of the church, on controversial practical issues—for example, the question of the church exercising prophetic political resistance against the state. Tanner seeks to go beyond Barth in arguing that a Christ-centered theology should be able to speak more explicitly, more critically, and more constructively to economic issues

---

28. Tanner, "Barth," 177.
29. Ibid., 178.
30. Tanner, *Politics*, 246–50.

than Barth himself did. "The gospel message is of much more direct social and political consequence than the ethical portions of the *Church Dogmatics*, at least as far as we have them, imply."[31] The passages that speak most directly on the subject of capitalism occur in the ethical reflections tied to the doctrines of creation and reconciliation—in *CD* 3.4 and 4.4, respectively. In the section from the ethics of creation, Barth argues that the amassing of resources by the few within the capitalist system tends to dehumanize workers and diminish the value of their labor. The inherent inequality of this system presses many to embrace some sort of Marxist response, but this leads to its own kind of tyranny.[32] As Tanner notes, Barth perceives the problem of capitalism to stem from this competitive notion of private property, but he does not offer an alternate proposal based on his overall theological claims.

Moreover, Tanner articulates a criticism of capitalistic assumptions that is more pointed than what Barth offers in the unfinished lecture fragments of *Church Dogmatics* 4.4 (published in English translation as *The Christian Life*). In that work, Barth tackles problems of socio-political ethics under the general rubric of his doctrine of reconciliation developed in *CD* 4.1–3. According to Barth, the framework for Christian engagement in the political sphere is the second petition of the Lord's Prayer: "Thy kingdom come. Thy will be done in earth, as it is in heaven" (Matt 6:10, KJV). Barth's brief criticism of capitalism emerges in a discussion of mammon as one among the "lordless powers," those created-yet-fallen human capacities and forces that have turned against their human agents because of the fall.[33] Under the conditions of humanity's alienation from God, we have lost the freedom to govern our own desires and capacities, and these created powers have begun to exercise an almost independent and lawless agency in their own right. They have "become spirits with a life and activity of their own, lordless indwelling forces."[34] Just as humans have rebelled against God, so these disordered forces turn against human beings, spreading chaos throughout society. Among these powers, the New Testament mentions mammon, indicating "the material possessions, property, and resources that have become the idol of man, or rather his very mobile demon."[35] Material human resources needed to secure a livelihood and human well-being become twisted and disturbed under sinful human alienation. The Synoptic

---

31. Tanner, "Barth," 182.
32. See *CD* 3.4:531–34 and 542–45.
33. *ChL*, 222–24.
34. *ChL*, 214.
35. *ChL*, 222.

Gospels depict mammon as a second lord competing with Christ for human servitude.

Within a modern context, Barth identifies mammon as money, which does not directly support human need but rather serves as an effective symbol and agent of distributing material resources and negotiating social status. Barth's insight here suggests an interesting analogy: Just as mammon is a natural human power that has become abstracted from its salutary function under human freedom, to secure material human well-being, money itself has become abstracted from the actual material goods it is intended to mobilize—food, housing, clothing, etc. Money becomes something people crave in and of itself quite apart from the concrete good it can do. As such, mammon—like its cousin, Leviathan (the state)—becomes a prime candidate for idolatry.

Tanner finds this Barthian criticism pertinent for the contemporary context. As state socialism seems to be waning today, she writes, "capitalism has become the lordless power par excellence in our day, by seemingly exhausting the field of economic possibility and by conformity to the neoliberal ideal of markets completely unconstrained by any governmental or social regulation that might subordinate their workings to the ends of human well being."[36]

Nonetheless, she charges Barth's criticism of capitalism with a lack of specificity, as being almost strictly "formal." What specifically about capitalism, Tanner asks, tends to foster this distortion from a Christian standpoint? And what would the alternative look like in a human nature redeemed and governed by Christ? According to Tanner, Barth does not draw out the specific implications of his christological doctrine of reconciliation for a criticism of economic practice. Her assessment at this point is correct, in my view, and she is much better positioned than Barth was to articulate a real criticism of private property on christological grounds. She argues that the incarnational fulcrum of the doctrine of reconciliation provides the theological paradigm that speaks directly to economic relations. If God has given Godself freely to humanity in Jesus Christ—fully, without reserve, but also without any diminishment of the plenitude within the divine life—then the zero-sum ideology of scarcity that underpins both classic capitalist and socialist theories is unmasked as deceptive and distorted. If God accomplishes reconciliation with humanity without abrogating the distinction between Creator and creature—as Chalcedonian Christology has always held—we have no theological grounds for pitting the fulfillment of individual needs and capacities against the common good. If God in Christ has established

---

36. Tanner, "Barth," 183.

and perfected the noncompetitive relationship between Creator and creator, this relationship may serve as a model for economic relations within the world, wherein public resources may be equitably shared. If everything we have, including our very lives, comes as a free gift of God, how can we be justified in parsing out the essential goods of life under the constraining notion of "private property"?

5. Conclusion

I will not parse out the specific proposals that Tanner offers for reconstructing economic relations. Such proposals would need to be evaluated on pragmatic grounds with her overarching theological vision of life in view. Rather, more modestly, I have sought to explicate and defend the potential ethical relevance of a contemporary constructive theology that draws nourishment from some of Barth's best theological insights. But I want to suggest one way Barth's suggestive view might broaden and enrich Tanner's. A theology of the powers that seeks to relate New Testament insights to a criticism of socio-political realities has become a major theme in contemporary theology, thanks to the work of such thinkers as William Stringfellow and, more recently, Walter Wink. Barth's own work anticipated, to some degree, this powers theology, as was evident in his fascinating interchange with Stringfellow in Chicago in 1962.[37] In brief remarks—which echo the discussion in *The Christian Life*—Barth presents the principalities and powers as possibilities that inhere in humanity's created nature as such but have become intractable and disordered under the conditions of the fall. Yet human servitude to these powers has been destroyed in the cross and resurrection of Christ. "We pray, 'Thy Kingdom come,' and the Kingdom is Jesus Christ, because in him, as the Lord, man as a sinning man is replaced by a new man; what binds him in these powers is driven away and in the coming of the Kingdom he becomes free over against these powers."[38] Such a freedom looks back in faith to the first coming of Christ, to the fulfillment of his vocation. But it also looks forward in hope to Christ's second coming.

I wonder how such an understanding of the powers might be integrated with Tanner's own incarnational framework by, let's say, a more explicit retrieval of what a dialectical theology might say about the problem of idolatry (a theme well developed in Tanner's earlier political theology). I wonder, in short, whether an exclusively incarnational framework, while undeniably crucial for Christian thought, is by itself adequate to convey the

37. See Kellerman, *Keeper*, 187–91.
38. Kellerman, *Keeper*, 191.

fullness of what the New Testament has to say about Christian engagement with economic forces in a fallen world. If one were to follow this line, one would need to say much more about what the principalities and powers are and wherein their power consists. If mammon is just such a power, an intractable force that afflicts the socio-economic well-being of a fallen humanity, I question whether it is adequately named merely as a human capacity run amok, as Barth does in the passages I cited. Is there something about the experience of mammon and its power to wreck human life that might point to some sort of cosmic disorder that transcends mere human agency?

Following the Deacon Jesus in the Prophetic Diaconate

Toward an Apocalyptic "Third Way" Beyond Barth and Tanner

—By David W. Congdon

SCOTT JACKSON'S LUCID ANALYSIS of Tanner's theology in relation to Barth points out the way each theologian criticizes free market capitalism as an idolatrous worship of mammon. While both ground their criticisms in christology, Tanner goes beyond Barth in using her noncompetitive-incarnational model of divine and human agency as the basis for her economic counterproposal to the competitive economics that currently rules the day. Where Barth's criticism of capitalism remains formal and abstract—revealed, as she points out, by the fact that his criticisms in *KD* 3.3 and *KD* 4.4 are essentially identical despite their location in different theological loci[39]—Tanner's is quite concrete and specific. Her christologically grounded ethics is thus a positive supplement to the christocentric dogmatic revolution that Barth began. This view is reinforced by Tanner herself in the paper she gave at the 2008 Karl Barth Conference at Princeton Theological Seminary.

---

39. Tanner, "Barth," 183–85. Tanner makes the point even more strongly by including Barth's pre-dialectical 1911 article, "Jesus Christ and the Movement for Social Justice." She claims that "the earlier article more clearly bases its judgments directly on the gospel—ironically enough" (186).

Tanner begins her essay on Barth by referring to his famous proposal for a "third way" beyond East and West. In what follows I wish to respond to Jackson by proposing a "third way" beyond Tanner and Barth. I will do so in two parts. First, I will examine an alternative synthesis beyond Tanner's noncompetitive soteriology of incarnation and Barth's competitive soteriology of crucifixion. Second, I will explore what this alternative might look like by appropriating insights from Barth's development of the prophetic office of Christ. In his conclusion Jackson says, "I wonder how such an understanding of the powers [in Barth] might be integrated with Tanner's own incarnational framework by, let's say, a more explicit retrieval of what a dialectical theology might say about the problem of idolatry." This essay constitutes my brief attempt to provide an answer.

1. Via Tertia: Apocalyptic Noncompetitiveness

Jackson rightly points out that Barth views mammon as a "lordless power," an aspect of the sinful and fallen creation that enslaves humanity in systems of oppression, and which God has decisively judged and nullified in Jesus Christ. What this means, crucially, is that Barth's "solution" to the problem of mammon is essentially *competitive*, rather than noncompetitive. Barth locates the source of an anti-capitalistic Christian ethic in the competitive arena of Christ's *crucifixion*, where God combats the lordless powers and emerges the victor in the light of the resurrection. By contrast, Tanner locates the source of her ethic in the noncontrastive, gift-giving union of divinity and humanity in the Son's *incarnation*.[40] The difference this makes becomes evident in her doctrine of the atonement. Tanner thoroughly rejects the substitutionary and satisfaction models favored by the reformers and appropriated by Barth, and opts instead for the Greek patristic (especially Athanasian-Gregorian-Cyrilline) view wherein the locus of redemption is found in the deifying assumption of human flesh. Her view is thus an ontological, rather than forensic, version of the "happy exchange."[41] Tanner's view is attractive because it frees atonement from the legal, penitential, and violent logic that severely hampers most reformational accounts of salvation.

I take it for granted that both Tanner and Barth's emphases are worth retaining: Tanner rightly focuses on the noncompetitive relation between God and the world, while Barth rightly focuses on God's competitive (and victorious) confrontation with both personal and systemic human sin.

---

40. Tanner, *Economy*, 64–5.
41. Tanner, "Incarnation," 41.

Tanner highlights the way God's advent in Son and Spirit is a nonviolent presence in which creaturely life comes to its proper perfection; Barth highlights the fact that God's advent confronts our sinful disobedience as a radical disruption. To put it another way, in Barth we hear God's No against the power of mammon, whereas in Tanner we hear God's Yes toward a gift-giving economy of grace. If there's anything that dialectical theology has taught us, it is that we need both the No and the Yes. In this case, we need both Barth and Tanner, though that will require finding a "third way" between and beyond them.

I suggest here that this "third way" will require thinking creatively about an *apocalyptic noncompetitiveness*—that is, a noncompetitive theology of God's apocalyptic interruption in Jesus Christ. This is obviously a paradoxical manner of speaking, but only in this way can we bear faithful witness to the God who is present with us *as* the crucified one. With Tanner (*contra* Barth), we need to replace the penal conceptions of the atonement with the notion of a superabundant divine self-donation in Jesus Christ which exposes and subverts the fallen logic of debt and redemptive violence. But notions of assumption and deification—which Tanner admits trade "on a Platonic reification of universal terms such as 'humanity'"—need to be jettisoned.[42] I agree with Barth here in seeking to overcome the abstract metaphysical language of *natura* or *physis*, though I suggest we need to go still further than Barth was able or willing to go.

In my "third way," God's self-donation is not an ontological *communicatio idiomatum*, but rather a kerygmatic event in which the "word of the cross" (1 Cor 1:18) confronts us with a judgment on our sin that simultaneously grants us unconditional forgiveness. The gift of God is the gift of an apocalyptic interruption by Christ through his Spirit that frees us for a subversive counterpolitics. It is noncompetitive in that this interruption is not a miraculous intervention but paradoxically coincides with and occurs within our social historicity. In the modality of faith, we encounter the word of Christ in the word of our neighbor. "Jesus Christ is *the* neighbor!" as Barth declared to a crowd gathered at Princeton Seminary in 1962.[43] Christ's gracious judgment confronts us in our contingent historical situation, disrupting our bondage to systemic patterns of idolatry and opening us up to a new future of freedom from mammon. In short, I suggest that we unite Tanner's gift-giving focus with a thoroughly nonmetaphysical, apocalyptic-kerygmatic *theologia crucis*. The gift is not an abstract ontological exchange,

---

42. Ibid., 45.
43. Barth, *Gespräche 1959–1962*, 515.

but rather a contemporary encounter with God that funds a subversive theopolitics in every new *hic et nunc*.

2. The Deacon Jesus and the Prophetic Diaconate

As we have seen, Tanner focuses on Christ as the incarnate Son of God—with an emphasis on the ontological relation between deity and humanity—as the basis for her theopolitical insights. In his critical engagement with Tanner, Christopher Holmes focuses on Barth's image of Christ as the "royal man." Holmes rightly and helpfully points out how Barth's deployment of this notion is economically provocative (since Barth connects Christ's kingly office to his role as a revolutionary partisan of the poor), while absolutely free from all ideology and partisan politics (since Christ the king transcends all this-worldly conflicts with a royal freedom).[44] On both counts Holmes is on solid ground in Barth, but the recourse to divine freedom on its own is insufficient. If Tanner's focus on the noncompetitive presence of divinity can be correlated with *KD* 4.1, and if Holmes develops his proposal on the basis of *KD* 4.2, then I would like to offer my own "third way" on the basis of Barth's christology in *KD* 4.3.

To develop an apocalyptic account of the economy in light of Barth I suggest we take up the insights in the third part-volume of his doctrine of reconciliation, where he develops his understanding of Christ's prophetic office as the true witness. The implications of this section for a theology of the economy are more indirect than other sections—especially compared to his early socialist writings and his final *KD* 4.4 fragment on the "lordless powers" (§78.2)—but they are possibly more profound. To see why this is so, we first need to understand what Barth is doing in this part-volume. In *KD* 4.1 he develops his doctrine of Christ's divinity in relation to the priestly office; in *KD* 4.2 he develops his doctrine of Christ's humanity in relation to the kingly office; here in *KD* 4.3 he develops his doctrine of the unity of Christ's divinity and humanity in relation to the missionary vocation of Christ within the world as the prophetic bearer of the good news. To use an old metaphor, the relation is not "vertical" (as it was in *KD* 4.1–2), but rather "horizontal." The divine action is neither incarnation nor exaltation, but rather now mission. The community called into existence by this prophetic witness thus corresponds to Christ through its own life of missionary witness.[45] It is no accident that *KD* 4.3 includes Barth's potent notion of

---

44. Holmes, "Karl Barth," 198–215, esp. 207–12.

45. Here I wholly concur with Holmes's point that "the fight Barth encourages is of a very particular kind: it is a fight rooted in witness; indeed, the fight of the Christian

"secular parables of the kingdom" (§69.2) and his powerful exposition of the church as the "community for the world" (§72.2).

What makes this material distinctively *apocalyptic* is how Barth unfolds the worldly significance of Christ in terms of his *victory* over the powers of death and oppression (§69.3). Jesus Christ comes to the world as the disruptive event of God's prophetic word, not as the giver of a gift of ontological participation. "The prophetic word of Jesus Christ declares positively," Barth states, "that in the midst of the present there is the *future*—or more precisely: the arrival, advent, appearance, and incursion . . . of a new humanity."[46] This irruptive appearance of new humanity in Christ retains the competitive dimension, insofar as Christ's prophetic word addresses us in a way we cannot anticipate and that unsettles our existence. But it is equally noncompetitive in the sense that "all that lives and moves and stirs . . . lies in the realm of [Christ's] power" (130/116) and for this reason "there is no secularity [*Profanität*] abandoned by [Christ] or withdrawn from his control" (133/119). Jesus is the victor, as Barth argues in §69.3, precisely in such a way that he is present to us in the neighbor. It is precisely this idea that Barth raises in his remarkable discussion of the church's service in the form of the diaconate in §72.4.

The diaconate is the tenth of twelve forms of the community's service—not "ministry," as the English mistranslates the German *Dienst*. Barth begins by giving a fairly formal definition of this task, but he quickly decides to describe more concretely "the form of the action of the community in which . . . it aids and helps the physically and materially *needy* both within and outside their circle" (1021/890). After a brief paragraph describing the need for deacons who uniquely manifest the community's calling to service, he goes on to discuss the christological basis for the diaconate. He does so through a very creative combination of the parable of the sheep and goats from Matthew 25 and the parable of the Good Samaritan from Luke 10:

> Now we come to the *material point*: in the diaconate, the community solidarizes itself with the *least of these*, with the ἐλάχιστοι (Matt 25.40, 45), with those who are in obscurity and are not seen, with those who are pushed to the margin and perhaps the very outer margin of the life of human society, with fellow-creatures who temporarily at least, and perhaps permanently, are useless and insignificant and perhaps even burdensome and destructive. In the diaconate these human beings are recognized

---

community over and against the lordless powers takes shape as witness." Ibid., 210.

46. *KD* 4.3:282/245–46. Future citations from vol. 4.3 will be parenthetical, with the German page first followed by the English. All translations are my own.

> to be brothers and sisters of Jesus Christ according to the significant tenor of the parable of the Last Judgment (Matt 25.31f.), and therefore the community confesses Jesus Christ himself as finally the hungry, thirsty, homeless, naked, sick, imprisoned human being, and the royal human being as such. In the diaconate the community makes plain its witness to Christ, just as he commanded, by fulfilling the service of the Samaritan in fellowship with the one who has fallen into the hands of thieves—a service fulfilled with him who was the Neighbor of this lost human being. In the diaconate it goes and does likewise (Luke 10.29f.). And woe to it if it does not, if its witness is not service in this elementary sense! (1021/891)

Barth's creative interweaving of these two parables results in the remarkable conclusion that Jesus Christ is both the one who has fallen among thieves (by virtue of his self-identification with the poor, naked, and homeless) *and* the true Neighbor who cares for this person. This is not simply the "royal man" here, even though Barth makes reference to that notion in this passage. This is Jesus as the paradigmatic deacon of the world, such that the diaconate is called into existence in order to "follow the deacon Jesus," as J. C. Hoekendijk puts it.[47]

Barth does not leave it there. The christological point becomes the basis for the corresponding action of the community. The "cosmic character" of Christ's reconciling work translates into the sociopolitical work of Christ's obedient witnesses (1022/891). The community attends to people "in the totality of their human existence," which means that the need of individuals is "grounded in certain disorders of the *whole* of human social life [*Zusammenleben*]" (1023/892). The diaconate is distinguished by the fact that its eyes are open to these disorders and it takes responsibility for them. The community's task is to declare its recognition of these disorders for the purpose of altering the society for the good of others: "with its proclamation of the gospel [the community] calls the world back to its senses regarding social injustice and its consequences in order to change those conditions and relations" (1023/892). He then concludes by stating, "The open *word* of Christian social criticism will need to intervene in this situation in order that Christian action can be given a new space and a new meaning" (1023/892).

In themselves, these statements are not a revolutionary theology of the economy. But when read in light of Barth's larger argument they contain the seeds of a possible way forward beyond Tanner and Barth. First, it is

---

47. Hoekendijk, *Church*, 143.

important to recognize that Barth's refusal to endorse any particular economic ideology is grounded in his conviction that theology is a thoroughly contextual and missionary enterprise. Theology does not trade in universal worldviews but only in contingent, contextual reflections on the gospel within a particular historical situation. For this reason, a theologian cannot declare in advance and in the abstract what a community must proclaim in its "open word of Christian social criticism," nor for that matter can she state where parables of the kingdom will appear. This is a correction to both Tanner and Holmes. Tanner is right to question why Barth's criticism of capitalism is basically identical in different doctrinal loci, but Holmes is right to point out that Barth's apparent formalism is due to a theological conviction regarding the dialectical relation between God's word and human words. That being said, we can affirm Barth's point regarding the nonideological nature of the community's prophetic witness while still affirming Tanner's point that the community can and must make concrete claims. Barth's discussion of the gospel's sociopolitical implications is in some sense formal by design, so that others (in certain cases Barth himself) can concretize the dogmatic claims in relation to specific situations. Tanner thus has every right to do precisely this within the context of the current regime of credit-capitalism in the United States. Her attempt to connect dogmatic theological claims to a specific political situation by making concrete suggestions for reforming the society is the proper extension of Barth's project, *pace* Holmes. Against Tanner, however, we ground this concretization not in the *being* of Christ as the noncompetitive unity of divinity and humanity, but rather in the prophetic *action* of Christ in his apocalyptic inbreaking into each new situation.

Moreover, if we read Barth's discussion of the diaconate in light of his broader understanding of the covenant-creation relation (*KD* 3.1) and his discussion of secular parables, we can tease out a dogmatic basis for making precisely the kind of positive economic proposals that Tanner is developing. Here we must be brief. As is well-known, Barth understands creation as the external basis of the covenant; the covenant ontologically determines the entire created order. It is this ontological grounding of the creation in the covenant of grace that makes possible the unanticipatable manifestation of secular parables of Christ's kingdom. On this basis Barth orders Christ, the community, and the state in ever-wider concentric circles. Each circle comes to correspond (i.e., actively exist in an analogous relation) to the inner circle. So the church community corresponds to Christ, while the state is called to correspond to the church community and thus to Christ.[48]

48. Barth develops these ideas in his essays "Justification and Justice" ("Church and

The actualization of the latter is the grace of God made concrete through the work and witness of the community as it calls out social injustice and declares new ways in which the secular economy might bear witness to the economy of Christ's reign.

If we add to this cosmic order the discussion of the "deacon Jesus" and the prophetic diaconate, we come up with something like the following. The Christian community's primary calling is to a life of faithful and self-giving service in obedient discipleship (*Nachfolge*, literally "following-after") to the deacon Jesus. Jesus goes ahead of the community as the true prophetic witness and the agent of God's inbreaking apocalypse. His ever-new advent involves both his paradoxical identification with the materially poor and his caring for the poor through the active mobilization of others to be neighbors in correspondence to him as the true Neighbor for all. God's neighborliness attends to the totality of our existence in the world, and this entails an active revolution of the socioeconomic systems that keep people in material bondage. The church—not at all to be identified with the institutional religion of Christianity!—comes into existence when and where people's eyes are opened to this divine revolution and are empowered by the Spirit to participate in it. The community of faith is thus called to engage in a process of prayerful discernment regarding both social criticism and prophetic proclamation in relation to its concrete historical situation.

By attending to the kerygmatic word of God's economy of grace, the community freely speaks out against the systemic injustices that maintain a demonic disorder of society. But its word of negation is always included within a more expansive and embracing word of affirmation—not an affirmation of the status quo but of a new socioeconomic order. This prophetic proclamation will necessarily involve recognizing where "secular parables" of God's economy appear within the world and, if possible, participating in this parabolic moment. A current example today of such a parable is the Occupy Wall Street movement.[49] This movement is by no means a direct manifestation of the divine economy, but it can be and often is a parabolic or indirect witness to God's revolutionary order. In addition to discerning where such parables are present in the world, the community will also necessarily engage in creative efforts when the current parables are absent or insufficient. This might involve mobilizing local social and economic initiatives where none exist, petitioning state leaders with proposals for economic action (e.g., Tanner's proposal for more public spaces), and even engaging

---

State" in the standard English translation) and "The Christian Community and Civil Community," both collected in Barth, *Community*, 101–89.

49. Cf. McMaken, "Why I Support." This article grew out of a talk given the previous year, a month and a day after the Occupy movement began: See McMaken, "Religion."

in mass protests against injustice and on behalf of societal changes. The community of faithful witnesses to Jesus Christ must see its life of discipleship as taking place in and through these concrete and prophetic practices of sociopolitical engagement. In this way it will be an apocalyptic community corresponding to the apocalypse of God's reign in Christ. That is to say, it will be the prophetic diaconate living for the world in faithful obedience to the revolutionary mission of the deacon Jesus.

8

Beauty, Glory, and Trinity in Karl Barth and David Bentley Hart

—By Keith Starkenburg

KENNETH OAKES RECENTLY PRESENTED an argument which shows that Barth was able to affirm human capacities for grace as long as those capacities are derived from the history of Jesus Christ.[1] One of Oakes's primary interlocutors is John Betz, who claims that Barth's refusal of the *analogia entis* entails Barth's refusal of a natural desire for the supernatural. Among other things, Oakes points to Barth's admission in 1962 at Princeton Seminary that if the *analogia entis* is a form of an *analogia relationis* or *analogia fidei*, then Barth had no objection to its use. However, interestingly, Oakes does not take up the question of beauty and the sublime—the heart of the issue for Betz. According to Betz, Barth's difficulty with the *analogia entis* comes from "an aesthetic prejudice for the sublime against the beautiful."[2] David Bentley Hart, who is a close collaborator of Betz, makes similar claims in *The Beauty of the Infinite*.[3] If aesthetics has to do strictly with the escapability of the known from the knower, then the *analogia entis* will be difficult to maintain. Conversely, for Hart, the *analogia entis* is a way to maintain properly both the beauty of the triune God and the creation. As Hart makes this claim, he positions himself against Barth. In this essay, I approach this question indirectly. Instead of analyzing Barth's concepts of the *analogia entis* and the *analogia fidei*, I argue that Barth's doctrine of glory achieves

---

1. Oakes, "Question," 601.
2. Betz, "Beyond the Sublime," 370.
3. D. B. Hart, *Beauty*, 229–30. Betz and Hart probably derive this thesis from Hans Urs von Balthasar, although they do not directly mention this. See Wigley, *Karl Barth*.

the same purposes that Hart sets out for his own theology of beauty. Consequently, Hart's (and Betz's) claims about Barth's analogical mechanics are misleading or incomplete.

1. Hart, Beauty, and the Trinity

Hart claims that the question he answers in *The Beauty of the Infinite* is this: "Is the beauty to whose persuasive power the Christian rhetoric of evangelism inevitably appeals, and upon which it depends, theologically defensible?" Beauty is "theologically defensible" if it allows the Christian tradition to provide a bulwark for the claim that the evangel is "a gospel of peace."[4] Thus, Hart's thesis is that "beauty belongs continuously to the Christian story (as, indeed, a chief element of its continuity), and that it appears there as peace . . . [and] that for theology beauty is the measure and proportion of peace, and peace the truth of beauty."[5] With Nietzsche, is the Christian proclamation of reconciliation in Christ simply a power grab for the sake of one's own aesthetic vision of order? Or is this proclamation really a proclamation that does not oppose peace and the beautiful?

There are two large moves in Hart's argument. First, Hart claims that "the most elementary statement of theological aesthetics is that God is beautiful: not only that God is beauty or the essence and archetype of beauty . . . God is beauty and also beautiful."[6] The trinitarian life of God fuels Hart's argument, despite the book's title. He writes, "The Father's entire being, which he possesses in his paternal depth, is always both filial—manifest, known, imparted—and spiritual—loved, enjoyed, perfected—and this event of God's knowledge and joy is the divine essence—exteriority, happiness, communion—in its infinite unity." Since God is Father and Son, God's life has mutuality and reciprocity. Since God is Spirit, God's mutuality has an exteriority and that mutuality can be "differently inflected . . . as plenitude."[7] This allows Hart to say that the Christian God is "infinitely *formosus*, the supereminent fullness of all form . . . always possessed of his Logos" and is "delight, the whole rapture of the divine essence." God is beauty since beauty is "the distinction of the different, the otherness of the other, the true form of distance."[8] God is beautiful in that God enjoys God's own beauty without lack.

4. D. B. Hart, *Beauty*, 1.
5. Ibid., 33.
6. Ibid., 177.
7. Ibid., 176.
8. Ibid., 177.

How is this connected to peace? Given God's triune life, to be God is to move, to enact difference in unity and unity in difference. Thus, God is peace, since Christian language is able "to place difference at the origin."[9] The triune God "is not that which negates—or is unveiled through negating—difference; he has no dialectical relation to the world nor any metaphysical 'function' in maintaining the totality of being . . . He shows that difference is . . . peace and joy."[10] Against modern ontologies of difference, such as Hegel's or Deleuze's, Hart aims to show that the Christian story declares a triune God who creates difference without self-alienation or a merciful self-recession. As a result, it is only the Christian, trinitarian God who is peace, and thus elicits a peaceful ontology in which differences on the surface of created being do not compete with one another or with an infinite which establishes that created order.

This brings us to Hart's other central claim. The Christian gospel is peaceful because it announces that the creation participates in the divine infinity, beauty, and peace. While the most elementary statement of theological aesthetics is that God is beautiful, according to Hart, the "cardinal axiom of any Christian theological aesthetics" is that "creation is without necessity." Creation is without necessity because "God is Trinity, who explicates himself, utters himself, and responds eternally, and has all fellowship, exposition, and beauty in perfect sufficiency." On the other hand, of course, the act of creation is "from eternity fitting to God's goodness."[11] Creation is not necessary, but its existence befits God's triune life.

These are common Christian theological motifs, but what Hart does is convert them into aesthetic claims that are distinctly expressed in an *analogia entis*. Just as Hart makes a trinitarian maneuver around conceiving God as the externally negating or self-negating force, trinitarian theology also leads Hart to affirm the *analogia entis*. This happens in two steps. In the first step, Hart affirms that an analogy obtains "between the entire act of my being and the transcendent act of being in which it participates."[12] Since God is "one perfect act of self-manifesting love" as God is Father, Son, and Holy Spirit, for God "to be is to be manifest."[13] The creation manifests the Creator because it participates in the self-manifesting love of the triune Creator. The creature and the Creator have the Creator in common, not some third entity called being.

9. Ibid., 180.
10. Ibid., 181.
11. Ibid., 256.
12. Ibid., 245.
13. Ibid., 245, 243.

At times in this first step, Hart might seem to indulge in an ontology that naively compares the creaturely and the Creator. For instance, he writes, "'greater unlikeness' in the proportion of the analogy means that the 'likeness' in the analogy is ever greater the more fully anything is what it is, the more it grows into the measure of its difference, the more profoundly it drinks from the transcendent moments that compose it."[14] This would undercut his point about the nonviolence of a Christian gospel, since he would be open to the charge that the divine life has become an ideal that the immanent seeks to hew out of itself. But the unfolding of a creature's particularity—its particular difference from God and from other creatures—does not function in this way. It is simply proof that God is free. Hart writes, "God . . . is always the God who wants for nothing . . . Creation, *as* creation, is free, unforced, apportioned, elected, known, and loved by God, and so is most originally an aesthetic moment to the divine, and a moment of peace . . . [W]hereas Hegel sought to discover in worldly being the dignity of divine necessity, Christian theology ascribes to creation the still higher dignity of delight."[15] In other words, given that God is triune, the growth of creatures into their own identity or essence simply provides an even deeper sense of their gratuity. As their power and definition take shape, God continues to provide creatures with God's own life, unencumbered and unthreatened by their needs and powers. In other words, God does not need their existence and does not need their distinctive way of filling time, and this nonnecessity bears witness to God's delight in creation.

This brings us to the second step, which brings these layers of the second claim together around the *analogia entis*. For Hart it is too simple to say that the difference or distance between creaturely being and divine being results from the fact that God exists necessarily and creatures exist contingently. Instead, the creation bears an analogy to God *precisely because of* its greater unlikeness to the triune God, not despite its unlikeness. Hart's claim becomes clear and precise when he says that "the analogy is a disjunction and a difference, while also being the interval of creation's participation in the being that God gives as his gift: creation tells of God's glory precisely because it is needless, an expression of a love always directed toward another."[16] In other words, the shape of creaturely being—its form—is one of "absolute contingency."[17] Creation is marked by its fragility or needlessness, and that shape or form bears witness to God's life. The creation's needless-

---

14. Ibid., 246.
15. Ibid., 257.
16. Ibid., 251; see also 158, 180.
17. Ibid., 250.

ness provides for its "analogy" to the divine life. The analogy is an analogy of act because it is an analogy of expression. The triune God expresses God's self and thus contains God's own *analogia entis* apart from the creation.[18] Creation is analogous to God precisely as it expresses, in its nonnecessity in relation to the triune God, God's ever-sufficient self-expressiveness. It is infinitely different from the triune life insofar as it is unneeded by triune life. If creation were not infinitely different, the triune God would need it in order to act with love. However, because it is infinitely different—more concretely, it is absolutely unnecessary for God—it can bear witness to the triune God. Only an unnecessary creation can bear witness to the triune God. But it is also the case that an unnecessary creation, insofar as it is unnecessary, does indeed bear witness to the triune God. Thus, it is the gratuitous shape of creaturely existence, as that gratuitous form arises from its source in the triune life, which ensures the peacefulness of the Christian gospel.

Hart is quite dismissive of Barth's claim that the *analogia entis* is the invention of the antichrist. Perhaps that is *apropos*, given that Barth himself drops this polemic after considering the work of Gottlieb Söhngen and Hans Urs von Balthasar—a fact that Keith Johnson has argued with great force.[19] According to Hart, this is "inane (and cruel) invective" and Barth's later *analogia relationis* "reduces God to the status of a mere being, in some sense on a level with us."[20] It is difficult to respond to these claims because Hart does not interact with Barth's multiple deployments of analogy within the *Church Dogmatics*. It would have been useful for Hart to admit that Barth thought that the dominant form of the *analogia entis* within Roman Catholic theology still posited a concept which transcended and delimited both divine and human being.[21] Hart agrees that that is a virulent form of the *analogia entis* and, as we saw above, he was careful to avoid it, at least formally.[22] However, as Johnson has recently made clear, Barth never withdrew his criticisms of certain versions of the *analogia entis*—even those versions of the *analogia entis* which led him to drop his polemic. I will not adjudicate these claims directly, but I think we can see why Hart dismisses Barth on this score. Hart handily connects a version of the *analogia entis* to the Christian doctrine of the Trinity and to the peacefulness of the gospel. If Barth is right that the *analogia entis* is not a Christian doctrine, then that

18. Ibid., 248.
19. Johnson, *Karl Barth*, esp. chapter 6.
20. D. B. Hart, *Beauty*, 241.
21. CD 2.1:240–41.
22. D. B. Hart, *Beauty*, 240–41. *Pace* Hart and in accord with Johnson, the implication is not that Barth misunderstood Söhngen, but that Barth judged that Söhngen had not successfully maneuvered around this problem despite his attempts.

undercuts Hart's case for a nonviolent Christian theological ontology. However, given Hart's material moves summarized above, we can test Barth's doctrine of glory to see if it is capable of similar purposes.

2. Barth's Doctrine of Glory

Barth's first major presentation of glory appears in §31 of *CD* 2.1, the first half of Barth's doctrine of God. God's glory "is God Himself in the truth and capacity and act in which He makes himself known as God."[23] God's glory is "the fullness of God's deity" because it is "the emerging, self-expressing, and self-manifesting reality of all that God is."[24] For Barth, glory is God's self-expressiveness, that which makes God accessible. Barth's purpose is to absolutely affirm God's "freedom to love" in relationship to the creation: "in the fact that He is glorious He loves." Due to God's glory, God is able to be described as one who truly and successfully "seeks and finds fellowship, creating and maintaining and controlling it."[25] If God's life in the creation can be accessed by the creature, then God's freedom to love the creature would be conditioned by the creature's capacity to recognize God's life. God is graceful, holy, unified, and omnipresent and thus has *de jure* fellowship with creatures. But if *de facto* fellowship with God is to be achieved, then that gracefulness, holiness, unity, and omnipresence within the creation must be declared by God alone. God's glory accounts for his lordship over God's own transition to creatures.

Barth develops this thesis in three parts. First, he delineates the subjects and objects of glory. God is glorious because he excels all other beings absolutely.[26] However, God in God's self is given to the creation and creatures are induced to participate in God's own glory and mediate God's glory to other creatures, especially as creatures worship. At this point, Barth will define glory as "the indwelling joy of his divine being which as such shines out from Him, which overflows in its richness, which in its superabundance is not satisfied with itself but communicates itself."[27] Second, Barth queries the mode of God's glory and how it is that God is joyful and thus desirable for creatures. Barth's answer is that God is beautiful; God is "the perfect form." He clarifies, "the form of the perfect being of God is . . . the wonderful, constantly mysterious and no less constantly evident unity of identity and

23. *CD* 2.1:641.
24. *CD* 2.1:643.
25. *CD* 2.1:641.
26. *CD* 2.1:646.
27. *CD* 2.1:647.

non-identity, simplicity and multiplicity, inward and outward, God Himself and the fullness of that which He is as God."[28] Since God's life is beautiful in that it is a life of unified distinction and of distinguished unity, God's life is characterized by "movement" and "peace."[29] Barth mentions three examples of unity and identity in God's life which demonstrate and embody this unity of identity and nonidentity: the perfections of God, the triunity of God, and the incarnation. It is this movement and peace which God enjoys, which satisfies God, and which overflows into the life of creatures. Lastly, Barth unfolds in more depth what it means for creatures to be glorified.

How does Barth's doctrine of glory achieve the same purposes that Hart sets out for his theology of beauty? The primary purpose of Barth's treatment of divine glory is to establish that God makes God's own life accessible to creatures. Barth also has a subsidiary purpose: to delineate a nonviolent relationship between divine and human activity. God's glory is a presence "which opens them[,] . . . which also looses at once tongues that were bound."[30] More precisely, God's glory draws out creaturely glorification of God, or worship. Since God is glorious, God has "the power of attraction." Beauty names the persuasive character of God's life and act: "If we can and must say that God is beautiful, to say this is to say how He enlightens and convinces and persuades." God is not lord of the transition to creatures simply by "ruling, mastering and subduing with the utterly superior force." This way of presenting the matter would not be "worthy of the knowledge . . . of the God who is the truth."[31] For Barth, just as we saw for Hart, God's life is irresistible *and* attractive, powerful *and* persuasive, overwhelming *and* nonviolent. Another way to put it this same point is that God's beauty accounts for creaturely joy. It is God's beauty which "attracts us to joy in Him." Creatures are joyful because they are persuaded by the form of God's life, God's beauty. Thus, just as Hart opened his book with the question of the persuasiveness of the gospel, Barth states quite directly: "where this element is not appreciated—and this is why the question of the form is so important—what becomes of the evangelical element in the evangel?"[32]

Second, does Barth actually achieve a peaceful ontology and how does he do this? Barth formulates a peaceful theo-ontology with the same trinitarian strategy that Hart employs. For Barth, "the triunity of God is the

---

28. CD 2.1:657.
29. CD 2.1:658.
30. CD 2.1:647.
31. CD 2.1:650.
32. CD 2.1:655.

secret of His beauty."[33] Why? He writes, "Here first and in final truth we have to do with a unity of identity and non-identity . . . [I]t certainly follows from God's triunity that the one whole divine being, as the Father, the Son and the Holy Spirit whose being it is, must be at the same time identical with itself and non-identical, simple and multiple, a life both in movement and at peace." God's triunity has no "disparity or dissolution or contradiction."[34] In other words, the triunity of God is beyond negation for Barth, as it is for Hart. God does not achieve God's identity through self-negation or self-recession in order to make room for creatures. God's self-achievement is peaceful since God is triune. For Barth, as for Hart, peace is at the origins.

Barth is also careful to mention both that God's triunity makes the creation unnecessary and that the creation expresses God's life. Just as with Hart, God's self-satisfaction underlines that both the creation and the divine coexistence with the creation are gifts. When Barth dives into his exploration of the glorification of creatures in Jesus Christ, he opens by saying "God stands in need of nothing else. He has full satisfaction in Himself. Nothing else can even remotely satisfy Him. Yet He satisfies Himself by showing and manifesting and communicating Himself as the One who He is . . . He is what He is in irresistible truth and power and act even for that which is not God, which is something else, which exists only through him."[35] What is the implication of this claim? As Barth says, "God gives Himself to the creature. This is His glory revealed in Jesus Christ . . . What can ability and obligation and necessity mean when everything depends on the gift of the divine love?"[36] Since God has no need of the creation, the creation's existence and the self-giving of God to the creation are gratuitous. The nonnecessity of the creation exhibits God's self-giving as grace and marks the creation as a gift.

Following this line of thought, as with Hart, Barth makes it clear that it is the "utter creatureliness" of creation that is "the echo of God's voice."[37] Given what happens in Jesus Christ, creatures correspond to the divine life by giving themselves entirely, just as God gives God's self entirely in Jesus Christ.[38] As God's self-giving in Christ is grace, creatures give themselves entirely to the triune God with gratitude. Gratitude participates in the divine glory because it "becomes as such the confirmation of the divine

33. CD 2.1:661.
34. CD 2.1:660.
35. CD 2.1:666–67.
36. CD 2.1:671–72.
37. CD 2.1:668.
38. CD 2.1:671, 674.

existence."[39] For as Barth claims within an ontology that refuses to reduce act to being or being to act, "gratitude is to be understood not only as a quality and an activity but as the very being and essence of this creature."[40] Grateful creaturely existence, in the face of its gratuitous participation in the divine glory, expresses the divine life insofar as it expresses its difference from that life. The history of Jesus Christ happens because God invests the fullness of God's glory in the man Jesus. That divine self-investment in Jesus Christ forms the creation in gratitude. Due to the glory of Jesus Christ, the creation just *is* gratitude. Thus, creaturely unlikeness to God makes for creaturely likeness to God, for Barth as well as Hart.

3. Differences between Barth and Hart

There are, of course, many differences between Hart and Barth. First, unsurprisingly, for Barth the glory of creation is actuated because of the history of Jesus Christ.[41] The creation, apart from Jesus Christ, does not express God's life. It is only the incarnation and the outpouring of the Holy Spirit upon the creation which makes that possible. As in the example we saw above, only Jesus Christ shapes the creation's being into gratitude. Hart, however, thinks of Jesus Christ's work as one of restoration and perfection, not initial establishment.[42] The differences here are over natural theology, or at least the reliability of natural theology. Hart affirms the practice of natural theology—not a "naïve 'natural theology'"—but a natural theology nonetheless.[43] In his doctrine of glory in CD 4.3, §69 ("The Light of Life"), Barth does affirm that the creation expresses itself and that all of creation shares in the history of God's revelation in Christ. That may be a kind of natural theology. But more likely it is a way to say that creation expresses the triune God, but only because of the history of Jesus Christ.

---

39. *CD* 2.1:673.

40. *CD* 2.1:669.

41. *CD* 2.1:668: "It is only in the light of . . . Jesus Christ . . . that we can be bold to say that there does exist this echo to be given by creation . . . We cannot possibly escape confessing the unlikeness, indeed the opposition to God, at least of our own voice, and our inability to glorify God . . . Since our ears are just as creaturely and sinfully impotent as our tongues we cannot even perceive this echo in the chorus of all other creaturely voices."

42. D. B. Hart, *Beauty*, 317–18: "As Bonaventure insists, the soul could never, in its condition of sin, reason its way from the things of the world to the beauty of God . . . In the time of sin, God himself, who imparts the theme of creation, must give the theme again."

43. Ibid., 242.

Second, Hart cannot countenance Barth's claim that, due to God's election, "apart from this man and apart from this people God would be a different, an alien God . . . He would not be God at all."[44] Against this, Hart writes that if "history is the theater within which God . . . finds or determines himself as God, there can be no way of convincingly avoiding the conclusion . . . that God depends upon creation to be God and that creation exists by necessity[,] . . . so that God is robbed of his true transcendence and creation of its true gratuity."[45] Hart's argument is that creation offers nothing to God that God does not already possess—God is needless because God is triune.[46] Yet Barth agrees with Hart's reasoning while disagreeing with the conclusion. The creation does not offer anything to God. God does not need the creation. The triune God is entirely self-sufficient. God does not change. But Barth argues that *God has eternally moved God's self* to be God in and for the creation in Jesus Christ.[47] The bond that God has elected to have with creation—out of the freedom of God's glorious love—is a "bond with which He has bound Himself" and is "the fact of His nature for the sake of which we are bound to Him."[48] For Barth, unlike Hart, it is not simply the needlessness of creation which depicts it as a gift. The creation exists as gift, in gratitude, because it exists as the recipient of God's electing, of God's inalterable choice to be in relationship to the creation in Jesus Christ. For Barth, God is inalterably Creator, Reconciler, and Redeemer due to God's inalterable choice to invest God's triune life in Jesus Christ.[49] For Hart, the incarnation is not a new act for God because God is triune.[50] For Barth, the incarnation is a new act for God because God is "eternally new" and God has invested that newness in the creation in and through Jesus Christ.[51]

Third, and in close relation to our last point, God's peace in Barth's work is not uniquely expressible in terms of beauty. In other words, God's

---

44. CD 2.2, 7.

45. D. B. Hart, *Beauty*, 157.

46. Ibid., 158. Hart repeats this same principle throughout his book.

47. The bibliography surrounding this question in Barth grows steadily. For details, see Dempsey, *Trinity*.

48. CD 2.1:514. Keen students of the debate surrounding election and the immanent life of God will wonder whether I have not paid sufficient attention to the difference between CD 2.2 and previous volumes of the *Church Dogmatics*. However, statements like this make it clear that 2.2 solidifies and makes conspicuous moves that are made throughout the *Church Dogmatics*. That is why Jüngel can make the case he does from CD 1.1. See Jüngel, *God's Being*, 27–53.

49. CD 2.1:495.

50. D. B. Hart, *Beauty*, 358.

51. CD 2.1:500.

transcendence of negation and creation, God's restoration and perfection of creational difference, and the gratuity of those divine acts are established not by an appeal to God's beauty. Instead, the peace of God is established by an appeal to God's triunity. What Barth writes about all of the divine perfections applies to all subsidiary concepts: "Since God is Father, Son, and Holy Ghost, i.e. loves in freedom, every perfection exists essentially in him."[52] For Barth, beauty is not the measure and proportion of peace, as Hart has it. The triune God, who "has that which He seeks and creates between Himself and us,"[53] is the measure and proportion of peace. God is, of course, also beautiful. But both peace and beauty are simply formal ways of describing the Father, Son, and Holy Spirit, a life that eternally (and in relation to the creation) seeks and finds fellowship. One can easily link peace to other perfections that Barth discusses, such as eternity, constancy, or omnipotence. Barth's work forces us to ask whether Hart's own work testifies to this, despite the claims at the beginning of his study.

Fourth, on a related point, for Barth, beauty is a "subordinate and auxiliary idea which enables us to achieve a specific clarification and emphasis." It is an "essential" term which clarifies how it is that God is glorious, but the wider term is glory.[54] Hart's brief explanations on this point seem to indicate a similar way of organizing his terms.[55] However, even though Barth considered beauty to be an essential term, it is rarely used in the rest of the *Church Dogmatics*. For instance, the term "beauty" never appears when Barth uses the term "glory" in other parts of the *Dogmatics*—for instance, in *CD* 4.3. Is Hart correct in the end? Is Barth's version of the *analogia entis* incapable of sustaining a theology of beauty? Barth probably lets beauty drop out of his discourse so that he can rid himself of the danger of treating beauty as "the ultimate cause which produces and moves all things," which is how it often appears in various kinds of Neoplatonism. Beauty could quite easily be "the ideal for all human striving,"[56] a cause that human beings construct to order their world in their likeness; it could be what Feuerbach thought all theology projected for itself. Yet something in the linguistic domain of beauty is always readily at hand for Barth. Thus "joy," "form," "splendor," and "shine" appear consistently, but rarely "beauty." Those other terms are readily at hand for Barth because they express God's glory. Glory is not an optional term because of its biblical resonance, but beauty becomes an optional term

---

52. *CD* 2.1:323.
53. *CD* 2.1:273.
54. *CD* 2.1:653.
55. D. B. Hart, *Beauty*, 17–18, 251–52.
56. *CD* 2.1:651.

because it is reducible to other terms. Indeed, the question is, given the way that Hart uses trinitarian theology to unpack God's life as form and delight, whether beauty is more optional than he makes it to be. The term beauty has its advantages, since it allows for conversation with philosophical aesthetics, but theology simply does not need the term. Both Barth and Hart (despite their respective claims) show this to be the case.

4. Conclusion

If Hart and Barth agree that trinitarian theology is the heart of a peaceful ontology and a workable *analogia,* then it is unclear whether Barth's trinitarian theology can achieve what he sets out to achieve. This has to do with how Barth's trinitarianism often dissolves into a binitarianism by virtue of a deficient form of the *vinculum amoris.* As Barth often does, in *CD* 2.1 he describes the unity of the triune God simply in terms of the Holy Spirit. For example, he writes, "in its form, what is repeated and revealed in the whole divine being as such, and in each divine perfection in particular, is the relationship and form of being of the Father and the Son in the unity of the Spirit."[57] Barth also exhibits this model when he claims that the Son "forms the centre of the Trinity" and that the Son as the "perfect image of the Father" displays the beauty of God in "a special way."[58] The unity of identity and non-identity to which this model refers is the unity of the *Father* and the *Son* in their shared divinity and distinctive modes of being. Thus, while Barth does not say it, the Spirit would be identified as the beauty which the Father reveals through Son. This corresponds to Barth's earlier claim in *CD* 1.1 that the three modes of being are specifiable as the Revealer, the Revelation, and the Revealing.[59] The relationship between the Father and the Son is revealed by the Father in the Son.

This sort of trinitarian theology, however, does not work well for the triune glory because glory is God's self-illumination or self-declaration. Who is it that receives God's self-illumination? Barth specifies that creatures receive God's self-illumination, as they participate in God's self-glorification. But if God is to be free to self-illuminate and is to be able to share that freedom in grace, then God would need to be God's own audience. As Barth says, God is inwardly what God is outwardly.[60] The immanent God must be fully externalized, fully shining outward, and fully receiving that shin-

57. *CD* 2.1:660.
58. *CD* 2.1:661.
59. *CD* 1.1:314.
60. *CD* 2.1:667.

ing. But Barth does not clearly specify the receiver of this shine in terms of the divine ways of being. Barth seems to vacillate between claims that God externalizes only in relation to a creation and that God has an outward life without a creation: "God stands in need of nothing else. He has full satisfaction in Himself... Yet He satisfies Himself by showing and manifesting and communicating Himself as the One who He is. He is completely Himself and complete in Himself. But He comes forth and has an outer as well as an inner side. He is not only immanent in Himself but He moves over to others."[61] Instead of showing that God is external to Himself even as God, he says that "the Son in His relation to the Father is the eternal archetype and prototype of God's glory in His externalization."[62] In other words, God does not have an externalization in God's life; God is merely the prototype for God's own externalization in relation to creation. While Barth does vacillate between this model of the Trinity and other models that seem to depict the Spirit's full agency, this model is dominant within the *Church Dogmatics*.[63]

Barth does not clearly specify the receiver of this shine in terms of the divine ways of being, because he cannot do so. The Holy Spirit is the relationship between the Father and Son: the Holy Spirit is their unity; the Holy Spirit does not exhibit an agency within the triune life. But if God is to be God's own audience, then the Holy Spirit's agency will need to be described with as much verve as Barth describes the agency of the Father and the Son. If he had been able to maintain the Holy Spirit's immanent agency, his theology would have enunciated a God who loves in freedom more successfully. Barth is able to say that the Son particularly reveals the divine beauty as the perfect image of the Trinity. Yet he does not say anywhere in his description of the divine delight that any particular divine way of being specially displays the divine joy, even though that is another way he specifies God's glory. The Gospel of John refers to the Holy Spirit as an advocate and as the living water which springs from Jesus Christ. Perhaps the joy of the triune God occurs because the Spirit advocates for the unity of the Father and Son. This may be where Hart offers Barth an important corrective, given the similarity of their work.[64]

---

61. *CD* 2.1:666–67.

62. *CD* 2.1:667.

63. For hints at a model that does seem to use the agency of the Spirit as a mode of externalization within the immanent Trinity, see *CD* 2.1:659, 661, 667. See also *CD* 4.2:341–49 for similar pneumatological patterns.

64. This essay was made possible by an Interim Research Grant provided by Trinity Christian College in January 2011.

Beauty, Glory, and Trinity in Karl Barth or in David Bentley Hart?

A Response to Keith Starkenburg

—By Han-luen Kantzer Komline

Keith Starkenburg's essay makes a cartographical contribution. Through the landscape of Barth's Reformed theology he maps an alternative route leading to the fulfillment of the same objectives that Hart sets out for his theology of beauty. Hart constructs his defense of the beauty of God, the beauty of creation, and their compatibility *via* the *analogia entis*. In Barth's theology, Starkenburg argues, the doctrine of glory leads to these aesthetic desiderata.

Starkenburg's essay thus offers a succinct variation on the type of argument Ken Oakes advances. In the face of John Betz's charges that Barth's rejection of the *analogia entis* led to a number of undesirable consequences in and surrounding Barth's understanding of the relationship of nature and grace, Oakes enjoins that "sympathy for one's subjects requires considering the possibility that Barth might have used other doctrinal resources to express something similar" to a natural desire for the supernatural.[65] Oakes shows how Barth's understanding of humanity, as both creature and covenant-partner, in analogy to Christ as both human and divine, constitutes a doctrinal alternative to the *analogia entis* that at once performatively exemplifies Barth's capability of analogical modes of thought and affirms something like a natural human openness to God. Like Oakes, Starkenburg aims to uncover a hidden path in Barth's theology to an endpoint with which an advocate of the *analogia entis*—Hart in Starkenburg's case, though Starkenburg notes Betz's critique of Barth as well—might be satisfied.

I have some questions about this kind of methodological or formal approach in general, as well as about its instantiation in Starkenburg's defense of Barth. Neither Oakes nor Starkenburg wants to say simply that theological ends are all that really matter in the final calculus, or that all theological roads lead to Rome. To dismiss these kinds of apologies for Barth as relying on methodological presuppositions reminiscent of Jeremy Bentham, or even of John Hick, would be to overstate the point. Certainly different

---

65. Oakes, "Question," 597.

theologies offer different strategies for resolving the same perennial puzzles, in this case, the puzzle of how to affirm God's utter transcendence without falling into either nihilism, dualism, or immanentism. Starkenburg, like Oakes, points to this phenomenon in a case where it has been overlooked. He has the flexibility and charity to make room for more than just one answer to a theological difficulty. I wonder, though, if the accent of such approaches on ultimate doctrinal destinations incurs—though by no means inevitably succumbs to!—the risk of obscuring the irreducible particularity of the peculiar paths chosen by each theologian. Is it legitimate to leave that irreducible particularity behind when pronouncing two theologians to be in agreement? If not, to what extent does this particularity of theological *means* always demand a qualification of any agreement of theological *ends*? I wonder, in other words, if two different paths actually can lead to the same place in the realm of theology, or if different theological journeys necessarily lead to different theological destinations.

Applied to Starkenburg's thesis, for example: What, if any, are the implications of the fact that Hart's affirmation of creation's beauty rests on the *analogia entis* while for Barth "we must keep strictly to Jesus Christ. It is indeed only of Him that we can speak when we dare to say such extravagant things about ourselves and the rest of creation"?[66] Does this difference in the basis of creaturely beauty in Barth and Hart entail a concomitant difference in each theologian's understanding of what creaturely beauty actually is? I believe it does. For Barth, a kind of participation that could be described as *koinonia* supplies the form and content of creaturely beauty whereas for Hart this beauty lies in a kind of participation closely akin to platonic *methexis*. There could be a way of constructively synthesizing two such accounts, as I have argued elsewhere,[67] but such a synthesis presupposes an acknowledgment of their differences.

Though the bulk of his argument is dedicated to highlighting continuities in the thinking of Barth and Hart, Starkenburg does focus at the conclusion of the essay on what he thinks sets the two thinkers apart with respect to trinitarian aesthetics. The issues toward which Starkenburg gestures here are foundational: the scope of Christ's work and its relation to the doctrine of creation, the conditions securing the gratuity and gratitude of creation, and the theological basis and criteria for peace and beauty. In each of these cases Starkenburg highlights how Hart and Barth use similar terms in disparate ways in light of differing background assumptions. Might these contrasts signal fundamental differences between the theological aesthetics

---

66. *CD* 2.1:668.
67. Kantzer Komline, "Finitude."

developed by each thinker, rather than accidental exceptions to a pattern of overarching compatibility?

In the final analysis Starkenburg himself seems to acknowledge that the unique features of Barth's doctrine of the Trinity could ultimately demand a reconsideration of the thesis he stated at the beginning of the paper, that "Barth's doctrine of glory achieves the same purposes that Hart sets out for his own theology of beauty." In the end Starkenburg's paper suggestively qualifies its identification of a sameness between the theologies of Barth and Hart, implicitly raising the question of whether it would not be better to see any *analogia theologiarum* that might relate the two as a matter of similarity amid greater dissimilarity.

Section 3

Expanding Conversations

9

On *The Monstrosity of Christ*
Karl Barth in Conversation with Slavoj Žižek and John Milbank

—By Paul Dafydd Jones

FOR A WHILE, I hoped to frame this conversation in terms of a dramatic interchange—something along the lines of "A Slovenian philosopher, a British theologian, and a Swiss dogmatician walk into a bar . . ." Alongside an eye-wateringly hip assemblage of cinematic references, literary allusions, and comedic scenes—my early favorites being when Barth imagines a young adult novel entitled *Are you there God? It's me, Žižek*, and when Milbank waxes poetic about the *Twilight* movies—I wanted to engage some topics that would likely receive attention, were the authors to meet for drinks. Primarily, I envisioned an intense discussion of the *logos asarkos* and the *logos ensarkos*, with Milbank talking up the former category, Barth emphasizing the latter, and Žižek asking whether recent debates are but symptoms of a secret puzzle, embedded in the *Church Dogmatics*—a puzzle that later generations were tasked to solve, with only Barth knowing that it is by definition unsolvable, a symptom of the Real.[1] There would then follow remarks on the orthodoxy/heresy binary as it relates to theology and contemporary Marxism; comments on materialism, new forms of transnational religious militancy, and globalization; an animated discussion of the church, in which Barth and Žižek would speak up for a politicized ecclesiology and Milbank

---

1. A statement from Lacan's "Seminar on 'The Purloined Letter'" is relevant here: "[T]he real, whatever upheaval we subject it to, is always and in every case in its place; it carries its place stuck to the sole of its shoe, there being nothing that can exile it from it" (see Lacan, *Écrits*, 17).

would ask Barth some difficult questions about the Eucharist; and, finally, a cameo for a discerning bartender who, having challenged each thinker to speak frankly about sexism and heterosexism, finds herself appalled by their awkward responses. No doubt, my fictional interchange would not provoke much laughter. While Žižek's and Barth's prose has genuinely humorous moments, and while Milbank's hyper-seriousness would provide an amusing contrast, there is little chance of *this* writer viably impersonating the thinkers, and no prospect of his penning a winsome script. Still, a contribution of this sort might usefully signal what a profitable academic exchange should involve: a frank exchange of views, with each thinker refining his or her best insights, appreciating the legitimacy and cogency of others' ideas, and recognizing that the truth can only be approximated, by the grace of God, in provisional and halting ways.

Given my inferior skills as a dramatist, then, as well as a lack of expertise with Žižek's various works and an inability to inhabit a "radically orthodox" outlook, I am reduced to offering a more prosaic—and rather less evenhanded—contribution. Using *The Monstrosity of Christ* as the principal text, my goal is to imagine what Barth might add to the conversation currently underway between Žižek and Milbank. My suggestion, in brief, is that Barth would urge both authors to take the monstrosity of Christ rather more seriously than they seem to do. On one level, he would criticize the christological positions that Žižek and Milbank favor. Granted their disagreements, both authors err insofar as they fit Christ into preexisting theological or philosophical schemes, as opposed to considering him as the concrete, particular, and personal reality who determines theological reflection as such. On another level, the description of God, Christ, and the atonement in the later volumes of the *Church Dogmatics* supplies us with a more theologically vital perspective—that is, a perspective that is more intellectually compelling, more attuned to the scriptural witness, and more pertinent to the political moment in which we find ourselves—than either Žižek's materialist Hegelianism or Milbank's "radically orthodox" celebration of plenitude, paradox, and participation. Certainly the contemporary authors contribute to theological reflection in valuable ways, and their willingness to admit frank disagreement across disciplinary lines is particularly salutary for those looking to escape the persistent syndrome of "neo-orthodoxy." But neither Milbank nor Žižek, I think, proffers an account of Christ that has the theological richness or political suggestiveness that distinguishes Barth's later work.

Before elucidating this rather partisan thesis, three caveats are in order. First, I must ask readers' indulgence for sidestepping a number of important issues—particularly Milbank's assessment of medieval theology and its legacy in the modern West; Žižek's synthesis of Lacanian, Hegelian, and Marxist insights, as well as his forays into popular culture; both authors' treatment of Chesterton, Kant, Schelling, Kierkegaard, and others; and both authors' views on Scripture, tradition, faith, reason, and providence. Since a short essay cannot offer anything close to a comprehensive analysis, I have opted to address only those dogmatic matters that strike me as especially important. Second, in what follows I do my best to avoid polemics, despite the contemporary authors' fondness for brash overstatements, dubious generalizations, and idiosyncratic modes of argumentation. For sure, Milbank (to some degree) and Žižek (to an impressive degree) would defend their employment of hyperbole, just as Barth would defend the explosive language of the second edition of *Der Römerbrief* (1922).[2] Strong words, in fact, are probably unavoidable when two authors engage in "the intellectual equivalent of Ultimate Fighting"[3]—although I'll refrain from wondering overlong as to why Creston Davis, who edited *The Monstrosity of Christ*, believes that *this* academic exchange is comparable to testosterone-fuelled displays of violence, staged to entertain teenage boys. Still, in this context I do not want to spend time worrying about rhetorical excesses. My goal is otherwise: to take both authors as seriously as possible, and to imagine how Barth might respond to each. Third, I would note that this essay is somewhat hampered by the absence of a counter-counter-response: space constraints mean that I cannot turn the tables once again, and imagine what Žižek and Milbank would make of Barth's *sed contra*. I would grant, too, that this is a serious failing. It forestalls a substantive and critical consideration of Barth's distinctive christological concentration (is it a live option for Žižek or Milbank, given their respective ecclesiologies?); it risks stymieing discussion about Barth's importance for constructive and political theology in the present; and it deflects attention away from the benefits that accrue when Barth is criticized from diverse theological, philosophical, and political positions. Still, I expect that others are better able to indicate how Žižek and Milbank might respond to my (post)"Barthian" perspective, so as to correct, refine, and perhaps improve it. As such, I leave this task for them.

1. Monstrosity Diminished

While Žižek claims to tender a "modest plea for the Hegelian reading of Christianity" in *The Monstrosity of Christ*, readers will be unsurprised to learn that there is nothing remotely modest about his petition. What he

2. See Jones, "Rhetoric of War"; and Webb, *Refiguring Theology*.
3. Žižek and Milbank, *Monstrosity*, 19. Hereafter cited as *MC*.

offers is a thoroughly materialist interpretation of Hegel: a perspective that twists Hegel from side-to-side, then turns him upside-down and downside-up, until all references to "transcendence" are utterly dialecticized and utterly de-substantialized. Any construal of *Geist* "as a kind of meta-Subject, a Mind," in fact, is deemed a bad-faith attempt to make Hegel "a ridiculous spiritualist obscurantist."[4] Žižek views such construals, common though they may be, as erroneously supposing that finitude can be treated as a passing stage in the career of *Geist*: a failure to think about Spirit, mind, and matter in terms of their elemental and permanent co-implication. "Obscurantism" of this kind, moreover, is adjudged existentially and politically debilitating. Only as we inhabit a genuinely materialist perspective, which accepts finitude in all of its agonistic and negative complexity, do we become vehicles of Spirit and catch sight of a new kind of politics. Why so? Well, when we stare into the "abyss of the Spirit's self-relating" and reckon seriously with nullity, we no longer aspire to "regain the lost innocence of Origins."[5] We abandon reliance on either a theological "big Other" (a transcendent deity who controls our destinies) or a political "big Other" (the Party which, dependent upon a conveniently self-accrediting philosophy of history, presumes to occupy the vanguard and represent the proletariat). More positively, we begin to consider truly emancipatory courses of action. Dispossessed of a false totality and invigorated by a belief in "the ontological incompleteness of reality,"[6] we move toward subject positions that recognize and, still more importantly, *hold open* the "void" that gapes before us. We discover new resources to contest, in genuine and presumably effective ways, the structures of global capitalism.[7]

What does this curious reading of Hegel have to do with Christianity? More than one might think.[8] Žižek's philosophy of history—which, in good Hegelian fashion, is also a philosophy of human subjectivity—identifies Christ's life and death as the decisive occasion for individual and collective maturation. Žižek believes, specifically, that the incarnation of the Son, un-

---

4. *MC*, 60.
5. *MC*, 72.
6. *MC*, 240.

7. As Nietzsche's Zarathustra says: "Hail to me! You are coming—I hear you! My abyss *speaks*, I have unfolded my ultimate depth to the light!" (Nietzsche, *Thus Spoke Zarathustra*, 174). Žižek's project might be construed as a politicized outworking of this clutch of exclamations: an insistence that a certain kind of nihilism, when mixed with idiosyncratic interpretations of Marx, Lacan, and Hegel, offers a promising opportunity for disrupting twenty-first-century capitalism.

8. In exploring Žižek's work in relation to Christian theology, I have learned much from Kotsko, *Žižek*; and Pound, *Žižek*. I have also profited from O'Regan, "Žižek."

derstood in terms of the Father's exhaustive kenotic finitization, negates the possibility of thinking about a transcendent deity who governs the course of history and controls our destinies. Because of Christ, we need no longer suppose that our relationship to God *qua* Father defines what we are (alienated) and what we may do (not much). We are emboldened to consider futures of our own devising. Indeed, following the negation of the Father, the crucifixion and resurrection of Christ give birth to the community of Spirit. With self-alienation set behind us, we are afforded the opportunity to seize the power that we had mistakenly ascribed to the Father. Thus it is that the "universal God *returns* as a Spirit of the community of believers"[9]—a community that recognizes materiality to be irreducible, but knows also that human life is neither deterministically defined nor insusceptible to revolutionary change. In brief, then: the incarnation of the Son means the death of the Father; the death of the Son means the advent of the Spirit; the advent of the Spirit means an existential and political condition primed to imagine and effect a post-capitalist future.

One finds here, then, a bold reconceptualization of the old adage, *O felix culpa!* The fall is no longer construed in terms of Adam and Eve sinning against God; it is conceived in terms of the Father translating himself, without remainder, into the concrete life of the Son, whose death—the negation of negation—inaugurates the community of the Spirit. Redemption, concomitantly, is no longer something done to and for us (or even with us); it is a possibility that awaits human realization. Still more audaciously, Žižek is proposing that his reading of the Christian tradition become an integral part of the theoretical world of the left. A radically historicized construal of the Trinity and an appeal to the basal fact of the incarnation is an indispensable provocation for thought. It reveals, in a unique way, a revolutionary freedom that lies beyond belief in the "big Other," whether that "big Other" is construed as a hyper-transcendent dictatorial Nobodaddy, faith in the inexorable march of history, or the disgraceful beauty of late modern capitalism.

The obvious question: what would Barth make of this? He would probably accept, first of all, that Žižek operates with some entrenched convictions, the likes of which cannot be broken down by frontal assault. That is to say, Barth would probably not open proceedings with an attack on Žižek's supposition that human beings can shape the course of history, denouncing this as an intellectual misstep brought about by a surfeit of proud titanism, nor would he spend time bemoaning Žižek's willful heterodoxy or his creative (mis)handling of the scriptural witness. In fact, Barth might even

---

9. *MC*, 61; my emphasis.

grant Žižek's avant-garde materialism a *prima facie* cogency. Materialism of this sort may not be theologically desirable, but it is not logically impossible, intellectually incoherent, or ethically insufferable, and it cannot be summarily dismissed.[10] Should Barth wish to challenge Žižek, then, he would perhaps begin with an immanent critique. He would pose a simple question, consonant with his own style of thought: Is Žižek sufficiently dialectical in his thinking?

The answer, to my mind, is: probably not. As Milbank points out, Žižek's frequent recourse to the category of "nullity" is reminiscent of a flat-footed natural theology: it ends up "deriving all subsequent rationality in an ordered series from pure nullity—as from pure divine simplicity—in such a way that all reality can be logically situated with respect to this *nihil*."[11] For sure, this is not *quite* correct. Milbank draws a too-hasty parallel between God *qua* "first cause" and a nullity that, for Žižek, is by definition not simple (or, for that matter, complex). But he is on to something, and Barth would press the point. Nullity *does* function as an irreducible "given" for Žižek. It marks the terminus beyond which an anti-reductionistic materialism may not go. But if that is the case, it is not clear that reductionism has really been avoided. Can Žižek imagine, one might ask, what it might mean to *continue* the dialectical process, and to negate the "negation of the negation" that is the unclosed materialism of the spiritual community? The question is a little cute, but certainly not unfair. While Žižek claims to propound a new kind of materialism, and while his appeal to Christ's life and death as that which holds open the possibility of the "void" is intriguing, the dialectical negation that he does not truly consider is one brought about by an unforeseeable act of God—that is, the intrusive workings of a deity who cannot be preemptively thought as the "Big Other," a God who *happens* outside of the stifling binary of negativity-*versus*-positivity, and who confronts, judges, and redeems humankind. Recognizing this subtle curtailment of the dialectical process, further, raises the prospect of setting Feuerbach to work. Barth would surely ask: is Žižek doing theology here, or is he actually promoting a problematic kind of "religiosity"?[12] Certainly, it *might* be the former—theologians do not speak *sub specie aeternitatis* and should beware of hasty denunciations. But it could well be the latter. Such religiosity may not be akin to that of the cultured Prussian, quick to support military ventures and

---

10. It might even be deemed a "secular parable of the truth": certainly it seems more philosophically interesting, and more politically vital, than anything that the so-called new atheists have offered for public discussion. For more on "secular parables," see the Epilogue to Hunsinger's pioneering text, *How to Read*, 234–80.

11. *MC*, 158.

12. For Barth's mature account of "religion," see *CD* 1.2, §17.

eager to extol the glories of nation, blood, and soil.[13] It may be a religiosity of a new kind: one that objectifies an internally felt hollowness, nurtured by frustrated revolutionary aspirations, the uncanny ebbs and flows of desire, and the baffling transience of life in privileged quarters of the "first world," in order to play—and *only* play—at radical politics. Indeed, is not such religiosity vividly expressed when Christ is figured as a clown—an image that surely tames the monstrosity that Žižek otherwise acclaims, suggesting that when this "abyss *speaks*" it is not in the tones of Nietzsche's Zarathustra, who anticipates a genuinely new world, but in the lonely voice of an enfeebled political bystander? Could the figure of the clown, in fact, reflect something of Žižek's own identity as an academic celebrity—an identity that, to some degree, has been foisted upon him by an academy that hankers after an alternative to mainstream "liberalism" but lacks the stomach for genuinely disruptive left-wing politics? After all, what else can we imagine but the slapstick mischief of the circus when the Real is consistently trapped in the interstices of an ascendant capitalist regime?[14]

---

13. As is well known, Barth was dismayed to discover many of his former teachers supporting Germany's efforts in the Great War. In 1914, writing to Martin Rade, he lamented how "love of the Fatherland, enjoyment of war, and Christian faith" could be thrown into "hopeless confusion." See Barth, *Offene Briefe*, 27.

14. A suitably Žižekian illustration of this point is one of the finest North American films of the late 1970s, scripted by Jerzy Kosinski and based on his own novella: *Being There* (directed by Hal Ashby, 1979). At the end of this film, the clueless star of the drama (played brilliantly by Peter Sellars) has been thoroughly transformed. He is no longer Chance the gardener, rendered destitute by the death of the "old man" whose property he helped to maintain. Through various twists of fate and luck, a political culture defined by abject superficiality, and the misguided patronage of a dying business magnate, he is now the sophisticated Chauncey Gardiner: Shirley MacClaine's *avant garde* lover, a respected intellectual force in Washington, D.C., the heir to a massive fortune, and likely the next president of the United States. Could it be, then, that an unwitting clown—someone who walks on water at the end of the film, which suggests something significant about the "old man" whose garden he tended—is poised to effect real change? Well, no. Chance/Chauncey will in fact have no political impact, not least because corporate plutocrats organize his ascension to the presidency in order to maintain the *status quo*. Might there follow some kind of moral transformation in those same plutocrats, though, given Chance/Chauncey's unwittingly profound/obviously banal remarks? Again, no. Were the narrative to continue, in fact, the only outcome would be for this "clown" to be exposed for what he is—a mentally limited man, obsessed with bad television—and then subjected to a political "crucifixion," unaccompanied by any resurrection. Put simply, then: I fear that a political theology that construes Christ in analogous terms might do more harm than good. It risks encouraging activism that lacks significance beyond the comedic. It supports forms of political theater that amuse those who recognize capitalism's faults, but do not anticipate substantive social, economic, or political change.

Milbank's response to Žižek is characteristically uncompromising, and continuous with the line of analysis elucidated in his *Theology and Social Theory*. He detects in his conversation partner a style of thought that gained currency in the late middle ages, and which continues to afflict theology today: a "univocalist, voluntarist, nominalistically equivocal, and arcanely Gnostic"[15] vision that distorts Christianity's best insights. As an alternative, Milbank commends a participatory metaphysics, anchored in the abundance of the Holy Trinity. Against dialectical conflict, he favors an acclamation of paradoxical harmony; against the givenness of materiality, an order saturated with transcendence; against Christ as a "vanishing mediator," a living Word who enlivens the sacramental life of the church; against Protestant atheism, an "authentic Middle Epoch" in which faith and reason unite, and "catholic" societies anticipate God's peaceable kingdom.[16]

The way Milbank elaborates this position is intriguing. On one level, he appeals to a "transgeneric vision" that discerns the underlying harmony of creation.[17] He argues, more specifically, that since our common experience is not a matter of "random and aporetic contingent finitude"[18] there is no warrant for Hegel's ontologization of contradiction. Žižek's identification of the Real, by extension, is wrongheaded (and, to repeat, a misplaced endorsement of a mode of reflection inaugurated by Duns Scotus *et al.*, sustained by the magisterial reformers, and ingredient to much German idealism). The world in which we live, while complex and dialectical in certain respects, invites a different assessment, for its "pleasing harmony"[19] adverts to a "framing transcendent reality."[20] One finds here, in other words, a reading of experience keyed to God's orderly creative work: an updating of the opening of the *Summa* and a philosophical commentary on Psalm 19 and Romans 1:20. On another level—and here Milbank indicates that while reason and faith are congruent, their relationship is of an asymmetrical sort: the former being suggestive but insufficient, the latter being authoritative and directive—Milbank argues that God's revealed triune identity enables us to know *who* sustains creation and moves it toward a glorious end. Moreover, since the Christian knows that the Father, Son, and Spirit enjoy a paradoxical relationship of unity-and-difference ("paradoxical" in the sense that this relationship *gloriously* exceeds anything that kenotic and/or dialectical

---

15. *MC*, 218.
16. *MC*, 218.
17. *MC*, 172.
18. *MC*, 115; emphasis removed.
19. *MC*, 164.
20. *MC*, 166.

rationality can conceive), she can avoid Hegel's mistakes and engage the world as it truly is: an "embodied plentitude,"[21] grounded in God's illimitable beneficence, that awaits our fitting responses.

The incarnation of the Son makes such engagement with the world a live option. Although sin disorders desire and warps perception, Christ graciously reveals the triune identity of the God who precedes and defines all things. Christ's saving work, more particularly, has both cosmic and moral dimensions, for "the entry of the infinite into the finite and the paradoxical identification of the infinite with the finite" enables clarity of sight and heals wills for the purpose of forgiveness and peacemaking.[22] What about the cross? Against Žižek, it neither discloses divine self-emptying nor provides the best point of departure for a new kind of political community. The cross is the glorious conclusion of Christ's revelation of harmony and the crowning moment in the life of the One who orients finitude toward the triune God, no doubt, but it must not be overvalued in dogmatic reflection. It is because of the *whole* of Christ's life—"one specific finite moment . . . of absolute infinite significance, beyond all human imaginings"[23]—that we know that God has committed himself to us and will bring about our salvation. We know, too, that a community's political labors are coextensive with that community's participation in God's work, the principal mediation of which is the Eucharist. For when the *Christus praesens* is truly acclaimed and celebrated, the divine order is made manifest, the giving of gifts has no end, and the church performatively anticipates an eschatological joy that the prophets of nihilism cannot possibly foresee.

No doubt, Barth could respond vigorously to various elements of this proposal. He would dispute many of Milbank's historical judgments and offer a strong defense of the magisterial reformers; he would ask probing questions about Scripture and the *analogia entis*; he would worry greatly about Milbank's endorsement of paternalism. However, I want to keep touch with the criticisms directed at Žižek, and pose only one question at this juncture. Specifically: Is Milbank's statement in *The Monstrosity of Christ* also susceptible to Feuerbachian critique?

I think it is. Although Barth, at least in his later years, would grant that a "catholic" attempt to correlate faith and reason is defensible in principle, he would surely deem Milbank's account of the "paradoxes" of experience a dubious resource for theological reflection. At certain moments, in fact, Milbank's remarks seem ready-made for a Barth-inspired version of

---

21. *MC*, 138.
22. *MC*, 212.
23. *MC*, 215.

ideology critique. It all seems a bit *too* religiously intoxicating. A Hopkins-esque description of a car journey by the River Trent, undertaken alone, in which "[e]verything is univocally bathed in a beautiful, faintly luminous vagueness, tinged at its heart with silver,"[24] in which the mysterious interplay of a river, roofs, spires, and a winding road delight author and reader alike . . . Well, it requires little effort to imagine Barth's likely response. Do we *really* want experiences of this kind to inform dogmatic inquiry, even propaedeutically? Do we not find here a rhapsodical universalization of a particular standpoint—a quintessentially "Anglo-Saxon" one, to boot, albeit of a romantic and decidedly middle-class sort—that distracts attention from the scriptural record that ought to direct theological inquiry?

Barth's concerns would compound were he to consider how Milbank's experiential reflections dovetail with his treatment of the incarnation and divine triunity. On one level, Barth would note, perhaps somewhat mischievously, certain points of connection between Milbank and the younger Schleiermacher.[25] Certainly the "founder" of modern Protestant theology did not see "Christ's human existence [as] entirely derived from the divine person of the *Logos* by which he is enhypostasized" in his early writings.[26] Yet much like Milbank, he supposed Jesus to be the one who reveals to us, and thereby makes thinkable and experience-able, the coincidence of finitude and infinity. Schleiermacher, too, was rather reluctant to construe Christ's death-in-abandonment as the all-important culmination of his identity, the decisive pivot around which salvation turns, preferring to view "the 'perfect suffering' of the Cross" as "*but one aspect* of an entire action whereby the finite is restored to full existence in time through its paradoxical conjunction with the infinite."[27] And Schleiermacher, too, thought primarily in terms of the exemplary life of Christ transforming our religious consciousness, invigorating our sense of creation's harmony, prompting the formation of intensely relational church communities, and spurring progressive political activity.

24. *MC*, 160.

25. See Schleiermacher, *On Religion*, especially 120–21.

26. *MC*, 210.

27. *MC*, 212; my emphasis. For sure, neither Milbank nor Schleiermacher make the incautious claims of Badiou—that "death cannot be the operation of salvation," and that "the Christ-event is nothing but resurrection" (Badiou, *Saint Paul*, 70 and 73). In addition to their respective emphases on resurrection and a shared sense of the *Christus praesens* as a person- and community-forming power, both Milbank and Schleiermacher take seriously Christ's entire life and grant *some* significance to his death. Yet neither Schleiermacher nor Milbank dwell overlong on the saving effects of Christ's death, and in both authors one finds an intriguing anticipation of Badiou's creative misreading of Paul.

On another level, Barth would ask: what vision of the Trinity is invoked here? Milbank's account of the divine life—a "realm of fantastic pure play"[28] in which love circulates ceaselessly and dialectical agonism has no place—is certainly a dogmatic *tour de force*. This reworking of insights drawn from Gregory of Nyssa, Augustine of Hippo, Thomas Aquinas, and (to a lesser extent) Meister Eckhart and Nicholas of Cusa, sketches a doctrine of God that fits snugly with an understanding of creation organized around the categories of harmony, relationality, plenitude, and gift. It shows how a richly textured experiential faith might dovetail with doctrinal insights drawn from patristic and medieval theologians. Could it be, however, that just as Žižek cannot look beyond nullity, Milbank is stuck with an understanding of God that is controlled by easy presumptions about impassibility and transcendence? Is it not possible that Milbank writes so lyrically about God's "infinite relating" because he projects what he perceives as the gentle harmony of creation *onto* a theological screen, as opposed to thinking about God in light of God's self-revelation? Further, could it be that this very instance of projection leads Milbank to hold the hard realities of Christ's life, suffering, and death at too much of a distance from God's immanent being? This last question is perhaps the most important of all, and provides a fitting bridge to the final section of this essay. While Milbank's God participates in the world to a glorious degree, this God does not ever *open* himself to the ambiguity, sinfulness, and suffering of the creation of which he is Lord. At every point, God remains serene and untroubled: the infinite is "in" the finite, but in no way does any portion of finitude affect God's infinite triune relating. Consequently, God's solidarity with us, realized through the life and death of Jesus Christ, is downplayed to a worrying degree. Milbank will not allow even the slightest "*particula veri* in the teaching of the early Patripassians."[29] He does not imagine a doctrine of the Trinity that, in a radical way, takes it bearings from the incarnation. He does not think in terms of God freely *determining* himself, as Son, as one who suffers with us and on our behalf. As such, he cannot approach what Barth would adjudge to be truly "monstrous": the divine Son becoming and being flesh, submitting himself to the rejection that sinners deserve, electing himself to be Christ crucified.

2. Monstrosity Rethought

Thus far, Barth's imagined contribution to the Žižek/Milbank debate has been quite critical. With respect to Žižek, I have suggested that Barth might

28. *MC*, 186.
29. *CD* 4.2:357.

develop an immanent critique and ask whether "today's forms of radical scientific materialism" *really* "keep the spirit of infinity alive."[30] Žižek's own materialism, it seems, is less open than he would have us suppose: a fascination with nullity effectively rules out a dialectical negation of materialism and blocks any thought of the intrusive, liberative work of God as the "One who loves in freedom."[31] And this, in turn, raises a crucial question: Is Žižek's materialist Christology less a way to think novelly about the Real and more the projection of a subject allured and frustrated by the apparently unassailable ascendancy of global capitalism? With respect to Milbank, Barth would dispute the appeal to experience and worry about the grand metaphysical vision that accompanies it. Indeed, if Žižek fails to think beyond nullity, Milbank fails to imagine a theology that avoids an unhelpful binary: *either* an immanent Trinity of "pure play," wholly untouched by the world, *or* a completely historicized and materialized economic Trinity. He therefore never considers the possibility that God establishes some kind of "real relationship" between God and creation in the person of Christ; he never explores the idea, more specifically, that God sovereignly intends for the economic history of the Son to be constitutive of the Son's eternal being. And, perhaps not coincidentally, given his reluctance to dwell on the unlovely reality of Christ crucified, Milbank ends up with a fairly lackluster account of atonement. He focuses less on what P. T. Forsyth memorably styled the "cruciality of the cross,"[32] and more on Christ's restorative exhibition of the gloriously paradoxical relationship of creature and Creator.

Put bluntly, then: neither Žižek nor Milbank describe Christ in especially monstrous terms. Both fit their christologies into preexisting schemes of thought (a neo-Marxist reading of Hegel, on the one hand; a "radically orthodox" metaphysics, on the other). And these schemes of thought, beyond being susceptible to Feuerbachian critique, effectively *limit* what might be said about God, Christ, and radical politics.[33]

30. *MC*, 242.

31. See *CD* 2.1, §28.

32. See Forsyth, *Cruciality*.

33. I am of course not suggesting that Barth's theology is unaffected by philosophical influences, much less that it is the be-all-and-end-all of dogmatic work. All theological work bears the marks of its (sinful) context, and Barth's is no exception. Barth himself, in fact, was fully aware of this, thus his early remark that, "[o]f none of us is it true that we do not mix the gospel with philosophy" (Barth, *Göttingen*, 259), and his unwavering insistence that the truth of theological statements, if such there be, is a matter of God's gracious superintendence of our broken language—and *not* the talents of any given thinker, no matter how celebrated he or she might be. The question I want to press, rather, is this: In the final analysis, what *directs* the theological programs of Barth, Milbank, and Žižek? My answer, simply put, is that Barth's theology succeeds because

What would it mean, then, to take the monstrosity of Christ seriously in light of the Milbank/Žižek debate? Since Barth does not pose this question, we do now enter the realm of conjecture. It is also important to note straightaway that my account of Barth's theology—which, as will become clear, focuses on *Church Dogmatics* 2.2 and following—depends on some interpretative judgments that require a lengthier defense than can be provided in this context. However, since neither Milbank nor Žižek want shrinking violets for conversation partners, and since I have offered a fuller statement about Barth's theology elsewhere, there is no need for reticence.[34] Barth's positive account of Christ's monstrosity, I want to suggest, would likely involve three moves, which I will only sketch here: (a) a "post-metaphysical" account of the Trinity, developed in light of Christ's concrete history, that supports a flexible theological materialism; (b) a political theology that focuses on *human* "being in becoming" as well as divine "being in becoming"; and (c) an understanding of atonement that presents Christ's death as central to our salvation, and indicative of that which we often want to deny—the tragedy of sin and the victory of grace.

To consider the Trinity in light of Christ's concrete history, so far as Barth is concerned, requires that the theologian do more than draw connections between discrete dogmatic loci and thereby signal compatibility between her account of God and her description of Christ's person and work. At issue here is the conviction that the actual, concrete, and personal history of the relatively consistent way in which it derives theological claims from the utterly particular and concrete personal reality of Jesus Christ, the principal narrative witness to whom are the texts of the New Testament—and not abstract schemes of thought (generic "metaphysics," if you will). This does not mean, again, that Barth is rendered immune from criticism, given his conscious or unwitting acceptance of certain philosophical mores; nor does it mean that Milbank and Žižek should be deemed theological *personae non gratae*. The question of what it means to "derive theological claims" from a christological starting point must be held open, and I admit frankly that a christological concentration cannot be the *only* criterion for assessing a theological proposal, even if one considers it to be tremendously important. I would also grant that there might be christological dimensions to Milbank and Žižek's work that I have neglected, mis-described, or underplayed. But the overall point still holds. In my judgment, the distinction of Barth's theology is its unflagging determination to *follow*, to "think after" (*nachdenken*) Jesus of Nazareth, the Word incarnate. This theology is eccentric in the strict sense of the term: its principal "object" is the Subject named Jesus Christ, whose unique identity is mediated to us by way of the Old and New Testaments. In contrast, the work of Milbank and Žižek seems determined by "metaphysical" commitments that stand aloof from and prior to their descriptions of Christ's person and work. He is not the animating center of their respective viewpoints; he is an illustrative symptom of those viewpoints. He is not the "monster" in terms of whom they think; his monstrosity is a function of their general descriptions of reality.

34. See Jones, *Humanity*.

of Jesus Christ—that is, the life, death, and resurrection of the rabbi from Nazareth, narrated in the canonical gospels—should have a direct bearing on how one understands the being of God *qua* Son. This is what it means, in fact, to say that Jesus Christ is the "electing God" and the "elected human."[35] God has sovereignly decided upon an identity, as Son, that is irrevocably bound to, and in some way funded and constituted by, the lived history of Jesus of Nazareth.[36] Now this, I hurry to add, is not a decision that God is required to make. It is also not a decision that, à la Hegel and Žižek, "collapses" the immanent Trinity into the economic Trinity, with the result that God's being is now controlled by historical events. The point is rather that God assigns himself, as Son, an utterly specific identity. God is Lord over God's being to the point at which God's freely *deciding* to become the enfleshed Word coincides with the Word of God *being* enfleshed, being Jesus Christ, for all eternity. To think along these lines might be rather dizzying, but that is no reason for undue caution—dogmatics is not in the business of rendering God familiar, and it has made some of its greatest advances when thinking adventurously about the divine. There is here a starting point for a highly actualistic, "post-metaphysical" doctrine of God: an attempt to think Exodus 3:14, John 1:1–18, and Acts 2:33 simultaneously.[37]

Consider now what this means for the Žižek/Milbank debate. Generally, one need no longer treat the immanent Trinity/economic Trinity distinction as an unyielding binary. For sure, the distinction has utility. It identifies the priority of God's being; it signals that God's life is (infinitely) more than God's relating to humankind; it underscores that the incarnation has as its condition of possibility God's unlimited, transcendent sovereignty. But the distinction ought not to be reified to the point at which God's freedom to

---

35. See *CD* 2.2, §33.

36. In addition to the differences between the authors under discussion, it is worth noting that Barth and Badiou diverge dramatically. Badiou will say that "we need retain of Christ only what ordains this destiny [that of the 'new creature'], which is indifferent to the particularities of the living person: Jesus is resurrected; nothing else matters, so that Jesus becomes like an anonymous variable, a 'someone' devoid of predicative traits, entirely absorbed by his resurrection" (Badiou, *St. Paul*, 63). Barth takes the opposite position (albeit with Bultmann, not Badiou, as his conversation partner). Because it is *exactly* the "particularities of the living" person that God embraces as constitutive of the identity of the Son, the Christian theologian is effectively forbidden from viewing the resurrection in such a way that the cross is "absorbed" and rendered ontologically passé.

37. For more on these issues, see McCormack, *Orthodox*, 183–277. Among the challenges to McCormack's reading of Barth, the most valuable is the essay by Hunsinger, "Election." As is probably apparent to readers familiar with debates over Barth's view of election, my position has most in common with McCormack's, even granted certain differences.

define Godself is underrated or obscured. Indeed, if one disavows a crude disjunction between the immanent and economic Trinity, one is freed to posit an ontologically significant connection between the *history* enacted by the incarnate Son and the *being* of the Son. To draw on Eberhard Jüngel's phraseology: since, for all eternity, God sovereignly determines to become and be, as Son, the concrete person of Jesus Christ, *vere deus vere homo*, the *logos asarkos* is always becoming and being the *logos ensarkos*.[38]

More particularly, one now gains the foundation upon which a christologically defined theological materialism can be built. Because of a sovereign, elective decision, made "before the foundation of the world" (Eph 1:4), the embodied history of the man Jesus is now a permanent feature of the divine life. This is ultimately what Barth means when he writes that the "obedience of Jesus Christ as such, fulfilled in that astonishing form . . . is a matter of the mystery of the inner being of God as the being of the Son in relation to the Father"[39] and insists that Christians must "correct our notions of the being of God," even "reconstitute them."[40] In view of Christ's history, we begin to think beyond the "pure play" of the divine persons; we discover a divine perfection defined by God's *opening* Godself to the lived history of the Word. The fullness of divinity and the fullness of human physicality can be imagined to coincide in time and (divine) eternity; by the grace of God, these opposites, separated by an "infinite qualitative difference," are held together (although *not* confused). By extension, materiality as such, and more particularly the life of each human, might be said to receive a new kind of dignity. Because the "atonement is history,"[41] we know that God's openness to the concrete person of Christ is paired with Christ's openness to humanity. Christ accepts us as we are; he, the "firstborn of all creation" (Col 1:15) envelops the people whose head he is. Consequently, humanity as such—that is, humanity in all of its wondrous and awkward embodiment—is set before God the Father as a sanctified and redeemed creation. Christ's intercession on our behalf carries in its wake an affirmation of human (and perhaps nonhuman) materiality: an unsublatable dimension of the creation that God wills to save.

Some interesting ethical and political possibilities come into view when one begins to theologize in this way. Our point of departure, following Barth, is the fact that each human being is determined, now and forevermore, by his or her relation to Jesus Christ. On a general level, because

---

38. See Jüngel, *God's Being*.
39. *CD* 4.1:177.
40. *CD* 4.1:186.
41. *CD* 4.1:157.

Christ is God's definitive statement about the value of human life, and because we are charged to live as valued members of his body, it follows that Christian ethics includes a forthright affirmation of human rights. The rhetorical forms used by a theologian will perhaps differ from those employed by certain of her "secular" colleagues, but the content of her position will be welcomed: since God has affirmed the preciousness of human beings, we must do likewise. On a more particular level, because God reveals Godself as a "being in becoming" who is open to ontological difference (that is, the difference of the human Jesus), the Christian is emboldened to affirm various forms of *human* "being in becoming." Situated in and defined by a Word who becomes, the Christian is given a new kind of liberty, and begins to recognize and delight in difference and transformation—even in certain forms of individual and collective experimentation.

The theologian, then, discerns a key element of what Milbank and Žižek rightly identify as fundamental for radical politics today: a theological ontology that is also a theological anthropology, and that supports progressive political theory and praxis. True, a loose analogy is at work here. There is a huge difference between the self-constitution of the divine Son and the "opened" horizons that accommodate diverse forms of human flourishing. Yet there is no need for a strong analogy. My contention is simply that the obvious plasticity of human life, productive of an ever-expanding array of individual and collective identities, is comprehensible—or, even better, *affirmable*—when one accepts that we are made in the image of the God who, as Son, freely transforms himself, becoming and being what he need not be.[42] Moreover, while Barth sometimes fails to think radically about what it means to say that the human being is "set in motion from its very center by the act of the Subject who exists here,"[43] we have an opportunity to correct his mistakes. We can update the indirect but insistent democratic socialism of the *Church Dogmatics* with a fuller understanding of oppression—one that, among other things, complements Marx's insights with an analysis of sexism and heterosexism that brings Barth into conversation with those who struggle for women's rights and the rights of the queer community. Žižek's worries notwithstanding, the "politics of identity"—and is, mostly laudable attempts to expose and overturn an array of viciously discriminatory

---

42. This construal of human "plasticity" has various points of connection with certain claims in Tanner's recent work, *Christ*. Tanner and my/Barth's dogmatic frameworks differ at key points, but our theological anthropologies appear to end up in similar places.

43. *CD* 4.2:29.

conventions—can and should go hand-in-hand with criticism of economic injustice.[44]

Does this exhaust what might be said about the monstrosity of Christ? Not yet. Thus far, we have only what is "monstrous" for the doctrine of God (a God who determines himself, as Son, in terms of Christ's concrete history) and what is "monstrous" for a politically charged theological anthropology (an understanding of the human that recognizes that we, too, are "beings in becoming"). Barth presses us to take one more step, and to recognize Christ's monstrosity in terms of his burdening himself with the nearly unbearable weight of human sin.

God's love for humankind, Barth believes, means more than the Son becoming human. It means the Word becoming *flesh*, disposing himself as one who undergoes judgment. It means, even more dramatically, that Christ freely takes upon himself the wrongdoing of others, even as his own conduct proves irreproachable. As Christ sets his face toward Jerusalem, as his disciples forsake him and the elites of the day conspire against him, his solidarity with sinners becomes ever more intensive, ever more thoroughgoing—so much so that his being made "in the likeness of sinful flesh" (Rom 8:3) culminates in his being the one who "bore our sins in his body on the cross" (1 Pet 2:24) to the bitterest of ends.[45] His life is therefore *both* kenotic (as Žižek wishes it to be) *and* glorious (as Milbank wishes it to be). It is kenotic because Christ does not maintain his distance from his enemies, holding fast to an identity that stands aloof from their sinful machinations. Instead, he opens himself to the hateful schemes of those arrayed against him. He allows himself to be defined by others; he accepts their wrongdoing; he exposes our sinfulness for what it is—an attack on God and God's gracious ways and works—when he dies on Calvary.[46] Christ's life is glorious because, in the same moment that he is subjected to the wickedness of his

---

44. In a wonderful pair of sentences, Loughlin writes: "Queer seeks to outwit identity. It serves those who find themselves and others to be other than the characters prescribed by an identity" (Loughlin, "Introduction," 9). I am making a similar point to Loughlin, albeit from a different dogmatic position: my concern is to update, correct, and expand Barth's theological anthropology by way of his doctrine of election in order to ground a liberative theological ethics.

45. As such, while it is right to say that the cry of dereliction is "the uttermost cry of faith," it is not quite enough to say it is offered "at the edge of nothingness" (Niebuhr, *Faith*, 96). The situation is much more dire. Christ's words are spoken in *face* of nothingness, and express the condition of one who is encompassed and overwhelmed, if only for a moment, *by* nothingness.

46. He "did not regard equality with God as something to be exploited but emptied himself . . . and became obedient to the point of death—even death on a cross" (Phil 2:6, 8).

enemies, he endorses God's judgment upon sin and releases God's boundless love once more. Insofar as he disposes himself as the true representative of sinful humankind (one who takes our wrongdoing upon himself) and the sole substitute for sinful humankind (one who endures the punishment that we deserve), that which obstructs God's love is now *finished*. Indeed, precisely because he "made our sin His own,"[47] precisely because he offers what must *not* be to God, God is able to do "that which is 'satisfactory' or sufficient in the victorious fighting of sin." God brings about a "victory" that is both "radical and total": God *kills off* the sin that we commit and carries us, in the body of the *risen* Christ, toward a redeemed condition.[48] Granted that, by way of the cross, God says an unequivocal *no* to human wickedness and accepts the awful sacrifice of God's only-begotten Son—a sacrifice that is itself humanity's endorsement of God's rejection of sin—God's *yes* to humankind is spoken anew with unparalleled force and clarity when Christ is raised from the dead by the Father, in the Spirit.

The monstrosity of Christ crucified, then, cannot be thought apart from the monstrosity of sin. Our unfailing faithlessness, our petty and not so petty falseness, our abiding cruelty, our intolerable sloth and boundless stupidity: *this* is what we behold when Christ dies. And this, alongside a refashioned doctrine of God and an invigorated theological ethics, forms a crucial element in any "Barthian" response to the proposals advanced by Slavoj Žižek and John Milbank. As we look upon the figure of the crucified rabbi, we are brought face to face with sin. We learn about its deathly wage; we discover it to be that which God does not tolerate. *This* is what is truly monstrous. Or to frame the point in a way that Barth would surely approve: the outstretched finger of John the Baptist, powerfully depicted in Matthias Grünewald's Isenheim altarpiece, accuses *me* of monstrosity, just as it accuses *you*; it reveals God's rejection of our hate-filled efforts to impede a love that does not rest until all things are made well. Yet this disclosure of wrath is complemented by the mournful praise offered by Jesus' mother, by Mary Magdalene, and by the Beloved Disciple. These figures, positioned by Grünewald on the other side of the cross, bear witness to a grace that cancels sin, acquits us of guilt, and assures us of a joyous redemption. Jesus' mother, Mary Magdalene, and the Beloved Disciple subtly anticipate, in fact, Christ's resurrection—that mysterious public declaration of God's determination to go *beyond* forgiveness and to bring every human being into the closest possible union with God, in Christ, through the Spirit. Christ has "borne the

---

47. CD 4.1:241.
48. CD 4.1:254.

consequence of [our] separation" from God in order "to bear it away,"⁴⁹ and what follows is the ramifying of Christ's resurrection—a gradual and often imperceptible conforming of all human life to a future in which God's will on earth is truly done. It seems unbelievable, it seems politically impossible, it seems more unlikely with each passing moment, but it is a truth that Barth will not and cannot repress: monstrosity does not have the last word.

An Analysis and Diagnosis in Response to Paul Jones's "On *The Monstrosity of Christ*"

—By Sigurd Baark

IN HIS BRILLIANT SMALLER piece, *On the Difference between a Genius and an Apostle*,[50] Danish philosopher and theologian S. A. Kierkegaard—with his ever-present sense of irony and tragedy—provides a diagnosis of the prevailing embarrassment that his contemporaries feel with regard to the letters of Paul. The folly of priestly theology, which seems to know no bounds, suffers under the illusion that as long as one says something good about Paul—then it is all good. Paul is praised as a great stylist and a great ethicist, but as Kierkegaard notes, not only is Paul a poor writer and a mediocre moral theorist, but none of these particular qualities lead us to the core question, namely: Why can Paul's writings be said to have universal authority? But why worry? As long as one says something good about Paul—it is all good.

Paul Jones has provided us with a "Barthian" reply *in absentia* to the debate between Hegelian philosopher Slavoj Žižek and English theologian John Milbank. Both Žižek and Milbank are weighed and found wanting. Jones suggests a Barthian christological picture as a better, more suitable account. According to Jones, Barth takes the monstrosity of Christ more seriously than either of the two contemporary giants seems able to, especially in terms of theological richness and political suggestiveness. In short, Barth is better. But what is it that makes Barth a better and, perhaps, more authoritative voice than both Žižek and Milbank?

49. *CD* 4.1:247.
50. Kierkegaard, "Om Forskjellen."

Before turning to this question, we must make one quick observation: when dealing with the writings of Jacques Lacan, just as when one deals with the writings of Barth, terminology varies and the meaning of concepts change because what both authors seek to account for is a process or praxis more than a stable series of categories or first principles to be deployed always and everywhere. In terms of Lacan's work, a prime example of this is the elusive notion of the Real, and especially its relation to *jouissance* (Lacan's translation of Freud's *Genuss*, which has no equivalent in English—it is perhaps best translated as "enjoyment" or "lust"). To simplify significantly, the Real is the *virtual* existence of a "reality" prior to the advent of the signifier as it (the Real) makes its disruptive appearance within the Symbolic (linguistically mediated reality) and in the Imaginary (ideals, desired objects, and fantasy). That is, the Real manifests itself as pre-signified reality's effects in the Symbolic and the Imaginary after the irreversible advent of the signifier itself, which closes the realm of pre-signified reality off forever, sublating it through signifiers. The virtual realm of reality prior to the signifier does not exist (there is *nothing* that cannot be said), but it does insist (there *is* nothing that cannot be said). It thus manifests itself in the lack or loss of enjoyment (appearing as perverse *jouissance* or the death-drive) felt by the subject within symbolic representation; in the desire for a space or field of surplus enjoyment that the subject finds herself constantly barred from; or in the drive that turns the failure to satisfy desire into a source of obscene *jouissance* itself. The function of the Real in its symptomatic manifestations is difficult to pin down, since its appearance varies in the individuals analyzed. One thing is certain: this conceptual complexity is not well explained by Jones's enigmatic—and yet surprisingly casual—reference to the "Seminar on 'The Purloined Letter'" from *Ecrits*. A later reference to the Real is likewise perplexing: Jones, in his criticism of Žižek, posits a Real trapped in the Capitalist economy. How exactly, one might ask, is the Real supposed to be trapped in capital?

That aside, for Žižek, it is the Lacanian insight into the structure of reality in relation to the lack of *jouissance* and the economy of desire that is central to understanding his Hegelian account of Christianity. There is no divine realm of infinite *jouissance* of which we fail to partake. Christianity posits a God who is inherently incomplete as an abstract universal and requires actualization in the form of the human signifier Jesus to sustain Godself. The speculative insight is that the contingent multiplicity of material reality of the signifier has absolute priority—and the divine is abstract or, simply, impotent without its representation. Ultimately, the reality of the signifier is reality *tout court*, and it is material nature itself that needs the signifier to sustain it. This lack is primordial and is the basis of reality itself.

There is no unifying first principle; rather the position of such a unifying principle is the lack itself ("self-related negativity" in Hegel's terminology). This is what forms the core of Hegel's claim in the *Science of Logic* that essence must appear. Whether or not this is a correct account of Hegel is a different matter (I am inclined to say that it is). But it certainly doesn't appear to be an account that is familiar to Jones, who considers it "curious," and deems it an account that "twists Hegel from side-to-side." One might be justified in asking whether what Jones describes as the twisting of Hegel from side to side (supposedly more than Hegel's own texts twist themselves!) is Jones's slightly awkward term for (Hegelian) dialectics. The lack of clarity when it comes to the dialectic is also expressed in the unusual account of negating the negation of the negation, which Jones promotes as a reply to Žižek. Such thinking would appear "curious" to dialecticians, especially since—according to Jones's understanding of the tradition of dialectical thought—Žižek's left-wing Hegelian and materialist reading of Christianity is supposed to be susceptible to a Feuerbachian criticism. But what exactly is Feuerbachian criticism other than a left-Hegelian, materialist reading of the Christian religion? One could, perhaps, argue that Milbank would profit from the Feuerbach-treatment, but that seems to be precisely what Žižek is doing.

Leaving all this aside for the moment, *jouissance* as the insistence of a notion of surplus enjoyment is nevertheless a helpful tool in examining the ideas and desires present in Jones's paper. On the surface, Jones's final criteria for positing Barth as superior to Žižek and Milbank remain vague. The implied criteria seem to rely on a few assumptions that are never defended in the paper: (1) positing a dynamic account as opposed to a static account of being is "post-metaphysical," and this is a good in and of itself; (2) promoting an (unspecified) anthropology of "becoming" (abstractly conceived) is "post-metaphysical" and therefore a good in itself; and (3) measuring sin in relation to the death of Jesus as a mark of divine monstrosity is a good in itself.

According to Jones, Barth takes the monstrosity of Christ more seriously than the two contemporary thinkers. He does this in two ways. First, advancing from Jüngel's reading of Barth, Jones posits that in Christianity, God's freedom *qua* divine being is expressed in an "actualistic ontology"—which is posited as a post-metaphysical account of being that encompasses both the divine being of God and the concrete realm of material nature and biological organisms (foremost amongst these are humans), conceiving both as dynamic and malleable. Second, in becoming identical with the organism named Jesus, God encounters human sinfulness as an attack on God's will.

Much seems to hinge on Jones's claim that he is engaged in "post-metaphysical theology," but ultimately the post-metaphysical stance can be reduced to the claim that the abstract divinity immediately assumed as a universal first principle is subsequently positively identified with a particular sapient organism from Roman-occupied Palestine, as well as the requirement that one does not collapse the economic and the immanent Trinity. Yet we are never presented with a reason why, other than an unspecified appeal to 'utility'; so, as it stands, this simply reflects a subjective commitment. To this (unenlightened) reader it certainly looks like metaphysics, since it immediately posits, as an axiom, an infinite, intelligent and supersensible "One" that functions as the inherent unifying principle determining and expressing the totality of possible being. It might very well be "dizzying," but why is it not a metaphysical position—albeit a largely romantic and organic one? Is it not the zero-level metaphysical position to (1) immediately assume the existence of a first principle (infinite, transcendent Unity) and (2) to uncritically present this principle within the domain of the existing "world" as the universal domain of all domains (a naïve ontic monism)? Claiming that this transcendent unifying first principle is *actus purus* does not make this position any less metaphysical. Without a clear definition of metaphysics, it is unclear why the naïve positing of an immediate first principle that functions to reduce and represent the multiplicity of existent being within one single object domain, is not deeply metaphysical—even if it comes with organic and historicizing terminology.

That aside, the actual focus of Jones's paper is to understand Jesus' redeeming act as the measure of the monstrosity of human sinfulness. Here Jones's syllogism appears to be the following: that the first principle is positively identified with the organism Jesus determines the ultimate perspective on human existence and is therefore also the measure of human sin, and since this identification is posited as an act undertaken by the transcendent unifying principle of all possible existence, so the corresponding sinfulness must have been of universal and infinite dimensions—and thus it appears that the universality and infinity of human sin (its "sublimity") is what makes the figure of Christ monstrous. In short, the conceptual payoff seems to be that resentment toward an anthropomorphized, universal first principle is the most monstrous act imaginable, and the joyous moment is that Jesus (as the positive representation of the universal, first principle) remains kindly disposed nonetheless. (Notice that, according to this reading of Barth, it is not the act of immediately equating God with a universal first principle that is sinful; actual sin is opposing the unabashed anthropomorphism of this totalizing world-view.) Even in sin, Jesus invites the human organism to play along with God and posits the playful becoming of humanity alongside the playful becoming of the divine Trinity.

It is this latter moment that seems to be the key to understanding why Barth is superior to Milbank and Žižek. With Jones's Barth we get it all: recognition of human nature's desire for transgression, and a loving acceptance and sanction to playfully enjoy immersed in the knowledge of positive universal essence in eternal *jouissance* beyond the limits posed by an absolute gap between the human and the divine. To be precise, Barth's Christology is the locus of a surplus enjoyment denied us by Žižek and Milbank. While Zizek denies the reality of transcendent surplus *jouissance*, Milbank affirms it but denies us access to it.

For Jones, the good news seems to be the direct access to a reality of ever transforming and becoming divine pleasure without the cut of the signifier; that is, direct access, positive knowledge, and experience of the essential *jouissance* inherent to universal, absolute, self-identical being itself. Infinite suffering and sinfulness and divine *jouissance*, sublime pain and pleasure, overlap in Jesus and are directly available to a humanity that is ever becoming and ever enjoying without limits. This peculiar turn in Jones's paper appears to be confirmed by the (otherwise very perplexing) references to questions of sexual rights and the praxis of the queer community that appear quite abruptly—seemingly from out of nowhere. The good news is a positive answer to the question voiced by the imaginary female bartender, who suddenly materializes out of the blue in Jones's own fantasy-scenario at the very beginning of the paper. When it comes to concerns about heterosexism and play with identities found in the praxis of queerness, Christianity is no longer a barrier, but rather an invitation. Of course, heterosexism is a serious issue, and it should be fought actively. But are the insights and authority of dialectical theology over against the conceptual force of the a-theology of the (arguably) greatest living dialectician really reducible to a series of doctrinal postulates, a promise of greater enjoyment, and some remarks on accepting queerness?

The unhappy conclusion is either that dialectical theology is reducible to a series of pure postulates and promises, or the actual problem is that Jones has not fully understood Barth's dialectical theology and its resources. As it stands, this paper unfortunately reflects the implicit embarrassment that too many contemporary Barth scholars find themselves in. Locked in a unenlightening controversy over divine election and the value of the neologism "actualistic ontology"—a term completely absent from Barth's own writings—the actual possibility to dialectically penetrate into the core of Barth's work and rediscover the immanent structuring rationality (his insight concerning negativity) that governs the praxis of dialectical theology beyond appeals to variously construed first principles and axioms (be they "actualistic," "post-metaphysical," or otherwise) is passed by. The result is that in confronting the actual movements of current thought, Barthians are thrown back on the assumption that as long as one says something good about Barth—then it is all good. As Kierkegaard clearly saw, that gets us nowhere!

10

Karl Barth in Conversation with Pauline Apocalypticism

—By Shannon Nicole Smythe

AT FIRST BLUSH, IT might appear that putting Paul's apocalyptic theology in conversation with the work of systematic theologian Karl Barth would be a bit of a stretch—something cooked up to make Paul into a systematic theologian, or perhaps to make Barth Scripture's version of the "Everyman." What could there possibly be to discuss between these two seemingly odd conversation partners? According to New Testament scholar Douglas Harink—there is plenty. Harink notes that Barth's work in the second edition of his *Römerbrief* has a "powerful *apocalyptic* tone and message." Furthermore, between Barth's work in the second edition of his Romans commentary and that of *Church Dogmatics* 4.1, Harink finds that Barth actually anticipated the "discoveries" of recent Pauline scholarship regarding a more "genuine Pauline theology of justification," a theology which is quite antithetical to the "usual Protestant story of justification and faith."[1]

Following Harink, this essay builds upon the conviction that there is indeed a conversation to be had between Barth and Pauline apocalyptic theology. It will argue that while Barth's work in the second edition of the

---

1. Harink, *Paul*, 45–46. Harink is not the first to discern the apocalyptic tones in Barth's *Römerbrief*. Käsemann engages with Barth's *Römerbrief* throughout his own Romans commentary (see Käsemann, *Commentary*). Martyn, too, while referring occasionally in his scholarship to passages in Barth's *Church Dogmatics*, must have been familiar with the apocalypticism in Barth's reading of Paul in the second edition of his Romans commentary because he assigned it in his course on Romans at Union Seminary, NY. Gaventa relays this piece of information in her opening lecture for the Princeton Theological Seminary course, "Paul and Karl." As she narrates it, Martyn's course on Romans was her first introduction to Barth's commentary on Romans.

Romans commentary is quite compatible with Pauline cosmic apocalypticism, out of which Harink works, Barth's later theology of justification—in *Church Dogmatics* 4—is framed by forensic apocalypticism, thereby rendering it not only inherently Pauline but also deeply reformational. Barth's revision of forensicism, based on the historicized theological ontology of his mature Christology, is apocalyptic in nature. Just as Barth's mature Christology is apocalyptic in nature, Barth's later reading of Romans takes up some of the same concerns as the cosmic apocalyptic readings of Paul even if on different grounds. At the same time, Barth's revision of reformational forensicism according to Pauline apocalyptic means that his doctrine of justification is not susceptible to the criticisms commonly brought against forensicism even while his soteriology becomes more consistently forensic than that of the Reformation.

To argue my thesis, this essay will proceed in three parts. First, I will demonstrate that Barth's second edition of his Romans commentary is wholly commensurate with the cosmic apocalyptic reading of Paul as represented by the work of Ernst Käsemann.[2] Second, I will delineate the particular features of Barth's own theological development that occurred after his Romans commentary and pushed him from cosmic to forensic apocalypticism. Finally, I will highlight several features of Barth's forensic apocalyptic theology of justification in *CD* 4.1 and show how these features are at once both inherently Pauline and deeply reformational at their core.

A brief word of clarification is needed about cosmic and forensic apocalypticism. Martinus de Boer has argued that there are two different patterns of Jewish apocalyptic theology present in Paul's letters. The first pattern he names cosmic-apocalyptic. It is defined by the created world coming under the power of evil forces such that God's sovereignty is apparently overturned and the whole world is led into idolatry. The righteous remnant of God's people waits for the time when "God will invade the world

---

2. While Matlock has noted that the term "apocalyptic" itself can denote a variety of things, thus lending it an air of ambiguity with such frequent usage, it is important to state at the outset that the Pauline interpreters who undertake an apocalyptic interpretation of Paul's texts do so with a more focused agenda. See Matlock, *Unveiling*, 258–63. First, they define themselves in relation to different basic approaches to Paul. Second, they are most often influenced by the seminal work of Ernst Käsemann and, more recently, J. Louis Martyn. Third, Pauline apocalyptic scholarship can be characterized as emphasizing these four notions in Paul's work: (1) the sovereign, unconditional action of God in the world to set right what has gone wrong; (2) an emphasis on divine revelation which discloses a new reality and age; (3) a christological understanding that the old age was characterized by humanity's oppression by evil powers; and (4) an eschatological construal of the cosmic horizons of Christ's death and resurrection expressed in Paul's account of the gospel.

under the dominion of the evil powers and defeat them in a cosmic war."[3] The second pattern is a modified version of the cosmic-apocalyptic pattern. This is the forensic version of apocalyptic eschatology and, most notably, with this pattern the notion of evil cosmic powers does not play a role. Human free will and individual human decisions are stressed instead. Sin results from an individual choosing to reject God and death is the punishment. The Law is God's solution to humanity's sin, and the final judgment is not "a cosmic war but . . . a courtroom in which all humanity appears before the bar of the judge, God [who] will reward with eternal life those who have . . . chosen the law and observed its commandments (the righteous), while he will punish with eternal death those who have not (the wicked)."[4] Both of these patterns of Jewish apocalyptic eschatology are present in Paul's letters although "christologically adapted and modified,"[5] but de Boer goes on to suggest that—following the logic of Paul's progression in Romans 1–8—the cosmic-apocalyptic pattern circumscribes and overtakes the forensic motif.

While I will use de Boer's language of "forensic apocalypticism" to describe Barth's mature doctrine of justification, I will look to Barth rather than de Boer to supply the meaning of this phrase insofar as it describes Barth's work. Indeed, Barth's version of forensic apocalyptic eschatology looks considerably different from the description de Boer provides of the version found in Jewish inter-testamental literature. First of all, Barth follows Paul in thinking that the eschatological event by which God deals with sin and the sinner has already happened in the death and resurrection of Jesus Christ. Secondly, Barth follows Paul in noting that the most important relationship that God establishes is the one between an individual and Christ rather than stressing the importance of one's relationship to the Law.

Moreover, on a formal level, Barth's forensic apocalypticism is not set over-against cosmic apocalypticism. Rather, Barth revises the forensic approach to the doctrine of justification set by the Protestant reformers, thereby making it more christocentrically focused by way of his historicized theological ontology. This is how Barth's forensicism gains its apocalyptic thrust. Barth's later theology of justification integrates an adapted reformational forensicism with Pauline apocalyptic. This means that his version of forensic apocalypticism is not characterized by the same dimensions described by de Boer. Indeed, even as the second edition of Barth's Romans commentary is apocalyptic in tone and thrust, in a manner consonant with Pauline cosmic apocalypticism, it is Barth's engagement with the reformational reading of

3. De Boer, "Paul," 359.
4. Ibid.
5. Ibid., 362.

Paul that introduces the forensic framework into his theology and—coupled with his uniquely rendered doctrine of election—brings a new facet to his own apocalyptic theology of justification.

1. Barth and Käsemann

For Ernst Käsemann, Paul's message in Romans can be summed up under the phrase, "the self-revealing righteousness of God." For Käsemann, "the central problem of Pauline theology is concentrated in this theme."[6] Käsemann acknowledges the voices of the Reformation in interpreting Paul's genitive construction (*dikaiosunē theou*) as sometimes an objective genitive. However, he notices that a double eschatology is at work in Paul's talk of not only the righteousness bestowed on us but also God's own righteousness. Käsemann describes this as a Pauline dialectic. At times, God's righteousness is a gift that is already present; at other times, it is only possessed "by hope and its ultimate realization [is] lying still in the future."[7] Käsemann discerns that crucial to Paul's approach is an insistence on God's righteousness as power. "The key to this whole Pauline viewpoint is that power is always seeking to realize itself in action and must indeed do so."[8] Käsemann further articulates, "God's power becomes God's gift when it takes possession of us."[9] However, God always retains God's lordship in this giving, and the gift is never separated from God, its giver. Thus, Paul never makes power and gift to be irreconcilable opposites. This plays out in Romans 1:16–17 where "Paul designates the gospel which is revealed and given to a Christian simultaneously as the power of God."[10]

Käsemann's goal is to locate the center from which Paul unites both his present and future eschatology. While "the gospel is the power of God because in it the divine righteousness breaks into the world as eschatological revelation,"[11] Käsemann urges that it is only in Christ that Paul is able to maintain the dialectic of this double eschatology. "Δικαιοσύνη θεοῦ is for Paul God's sovereignty over the world revealing itself eschatologically in Jesus."[12] Käsemann avers that Paul articulates his Christology such that it is none other than Christ himself who is both the gift of God given for us and

6. Käsemann, "Righteousness," 168.
7. Ibid., 170.
8. Ibid., 175.
9. Ibid., 173.
10. Käsemann, *Commentary*, 28.
11. Ibid., 30.
12. Käsemann, "Righteousness," 180.

our Lord. For Paul, the righteousness of God is nothing less than the power of God invading our fallen world in the person of Jesus Christ. Furthermore, the salvation of the world depends upon the power of God recapturing it and making it right. "Because of his Christological connection and basis Paul must identify the righteousness of God with the righteousness of faith and let the stress fall on the conferred gift of salvation. On this account, however, standing in salvation is both here and everywhere standing in obedience, that is, in the presence and under the power of Christ."[13] Indeed, Käsemann insists that "we may summarize the whole message of the epistle in the brief and paradoxical statement that the Son of God is as our Kyrios the one eschatological gift of God to us and that herein is revealed simultaneously both God's legitimate claim on us and also our salvation."[14]

Turning to Barth's commentary on Romans 1:16–17, we hear a similar emphasis on the "not yet" aspect of Pauline eschatology. With vivid apocalyptic imagery, Barth writes that we are "imprisoned"[15] in this world and that even the "Resurrection, which is the place of exit, also bars us in, for it is both barrier and exit."[16] The reality of sin and death, the current state of the world—all of this presses in on us and remains the truth of our present existence. Nevertheless, the resurrection is a place of exit—"the barrier marks the frontier of a new country . . . We have therefore, in the power of God, a look-out, a door, a hope . . . The prisoner becomes a watchman. Bound to his post as firmly as a prisoner in his cell, he watches for the dawning of the day."[17] This is one of Barth's many articulations in the second edition of the Romans commentary of the infinite qualitative difference between God and humanity. As determined as Barth is at this point in his theology to guard the self-revelation of God from being co-opted in the event of its being given, he still acknowledges the other side of the Pauline dialectic brought out by Käsemann. In the resurrection of Christ from the dead there is a door, a hope—the prisoner watches for the dawning of a new day. Like Käsemann, Barth names Christ as the center from which to understand Paul's double eschatology. Indeed, it is because the "now" and the "not yet" cohere only in Christ that Barth sounds the note of future eschatology so insistently.

---

13. Käsemann, *Commentary*, 29.

14. Ibid.

15. Barth, *Epistle*, 37. Interestingly, Paul himself uses the language of imprisonment in Romans 11:32: "For God has imprisoned [the verb *sugkleiō*] all in disobedience so that he may be merciful to all."

16. Barth, *Epistle*, 38.

17. Ibid.

Barth, too, considers the Pauline understanding of the righteousness of God, calling it "the consistency of God with Himself"[18] in Christ. The righteousness of God means that God affirms himself "by denying us as we are and the world as it is" and then gives himself to be known "as the Redeemer of the prisoners . . . He guarantees our salvation by willing to be God and to be known as God—in Christ; He justifies us by justifying Himself."[19] In a corresponding manner, Käsemann remarks that "justification is the specifically Pauline understanding of Christology just as the latter is the basis of the former."[20] For both scholars, the righteousness of God is descriptive of the sovereign, high God. Contained within this phrase is a total and radical distinction between God and humanity. And yet at the same time, it is this sovereign, high God whom Paul proclaims has not left us to our own devices. In Christ, God is faithful in righteousness first to himself and, because to himself, so also to us. The gospel that Paul is at pains to communicate to the church in Rome proclaims the power of God not to abandon us, but to save us in righteousness. Such is the faithfulness of God that Barth says is revealed to faith. "To those who have abandoned direct communication, the communication is made . . . Those who take upon them the divine 'No' shall themselves be borne by the greater divine 'Yes.'"[21] Barth understands faith to be our acceptance of the judgment of God upon us, by which God righteously maintains consistency with himself, as revealed in the resurrection. We are righteous only insofar as we live by God's faithfulness to God's righteousness. "The righteous man is the prisoner become watchman . . . There is no other righteousness save that of the man who sets himself under judgment, of the man who is terrified and hopes. He shall live."[22] We are saved by the wholly otherness of God who shows forth the power of his righteousness in Jesus Christ and thus saves us by remaining true to himself. Therefore, for Barth as for Käsemann, the righteousness of God, revealed in Christ and by which we live, is the theme of Romans.

2. Apocalyptic and Barth's Development

As powerfully as the second edition of Barth's Romans commentary hones in on several defining aspects of Pauline apocalyptic, it contains only half the story. The second edition of the Romans commentary is one-sided in

18. Ibid., 40.
19. Ibid., 40–41.
20. Käsemann, *Commentary*, 24.
21. Barth, *Epistle*, 41.
22. Ibid.

its understanding of the relationship of God to humanity as Paul explains it. This is because Barth was singularly focused on the problem of revelation—on how God could reveal God's self to humanity in time and space without ceasing to be God. The solution, Barth argues, is that God must only be known *indirectly*, by way of an intermediary. More importantly, the revelation of God through the intermediary must always remain distinct from the intermediary itself. In Jesus Christ, God veils God's self completely in order that God may unveil God's self only to faith. Thus, in the second edition of the commentary, Jesus Christ is *not* the revelation of God but only the medium of God's self-revelation. While Jesus is the locus of revelation in the second edition, Barth's understanding of the incarnation and its place in Pauline theology is largely undeveloped. Revelation takes place in hiddenness. Barth has not yet developed his positive affirmation that the event of revelation is an event of divine-human union, which perfectly corresponds to the negative affirmation that revelation takes places in hiddenness. What changes in Barth's later theology is the idea that reconciliation is revelation full stop. "Revelation in fact does not differ from the person of Jesus Christ nor from the reconciliation accomplished in Him. To say revelation is to say, 'The Word became flesh.'"[23]

When Barth himself reflected retrospectively on the second edition of his Romans commentary, he pointed out three things that helpfully place the commentary within his genetic-historical development. First, he acknowledged that he had to speak the way he did at that particular time. Second, he insisted that he did not put something on Paul that was not inherently there in the letter to the church in Rome, but he did credit himself with being the first to draw out such threads.[24] Finally, Barth remarked that he had to move away from the *diastasis* of the Romans commentary and bring Jesus Christ to the center of his thoughts. "The sentences I then uttered were not hazardous (in the sense of precarious) on account of their content. They were hazardous because to be legitimate exposition of the Bible they needed others no less sharp and direct to compensate and therefore genuinely to substantiate their total claim. But these were lacking ... The result was that we could not speak about the post-temporality of God in such a way as to make it clear that we actually meant to speak of God and not of a general idea of limit and crisis."[25] Hence, even as Barth was faithfully listening to the radical message in Romans about the Godness of God, he was on the verge

---

23. *CD* 1.1:119.
24. Barth, "Brechen," 112.
25. *CD* 2.1:635.

of making Paul's witness to the living God into a generalized concept, which would only serve to diminish the apocalyptic thrust of the letter.

Moreover, when Barth composed the second edition of his Romans commentary he still possessed no real knowledge of the Reformation and its theology. All of that would change when he took up the post of honorary professor of Reformed theology in Göttingen—a post that he was awarded based upon the first edition of the commentary. His chair required that Barth teach courses on the Reformed confessions, doctrine, and church life. Barth felt unqualified for this task, remarking that he had not even read any of the Reformed confessional writings. He quickly set about to remedy this situation and was soon teaching various aspects of the Reformed theological tradition to his students. By the summer of 1922, Barth was giving a series of lectures on Calvin, whom he found to be "a waterfall, a primitive forest, a demonic power, something straight down from the Himalayas, absolutely Chinese, strange, mythological; I just don't have the organs, the suction cups, even to assimilate this phenomenon, let alone to describe it properly."[26] Barth lectured on Zwingli the following winter semester (1922–23). By the summer of 1923 he undertook to lecture on the Reformed confessional writings and, as an offspring of that, he spoke in the fall on "The Nature and Purpose of Reformed Doctrine." While Barth admitted previously to studying Calvin and Luther to some extent, in Safenwil he had yet to really unpack their theology and he admitted to not having access to them in the right way at this time. He attributed this to his formal, academic way of studying texts leftover from his student days. In Göttingen, however, this all changed. He reflected: "only now were my eyes properly open to the Reformers and their message of the justification and the sanctification of the sinner, of faith, of repentance and works, of the nature and the limits of the church, and so on. I had a great many new things to learn from them."[27] Yet for as much as Barth learned in these studies, he never attempted a simple replication of Reformation theology. Barth always approached these theological texts with imagination and critical judgment—remarking that he continually found them always to be both helpful and unhelpful. After having considered their historical context and meaning, Barth would decide for himself which classification to give to them.

While there were small shifts in Barth's thinking during his first two years at Göttingen, such as his more positive views on doctrine and the church, and his affirmation of "the Reformed Scripture-principle," "none of these modifications amounted to a shift away from the eschatological

---

26. Barth, *Revolutionary Theology*, 101.
27. As quoted in Busch, *Karl Barth*, 143.

perspective which governed *Romans II*."[28] Instead, the key shift that took place in Barth's thinking while at Göttingen came in May, 1924 when Barth first read two textbooks on Reformation theology by Heinrich Schmid and Heinrich Heppe. Specifically, Barth learned of the early church's anhypostatic and enhypostatic christological doctrines, which together affirm that the human nature of Jesus Christ had no independent existence alongside the Logos, but rather acquired its existence from God's own existence in the being of the eternal Son. The second person of the Trinity took on human nature completely and lived a human life in and through it. Outwardly, Jesus is a human just like any other; but inwardly, the subject of the human Jesus is the eternal Son of God. The outcome of this discovery allowed Barth to move away from the time-eternity dialectic that prevailed throughout the second edition of the Romans commentary, enabling Barth to maintain the Godness of God in the event of God's self-revelation. Now Barth saw a way to preserve the critical distance between God and humanity using christological means. Along with this christological grounding came a real space for the incarnation. Revelation was no longer limited to the single event of the cross but could now incorporate the whole incarnate life of Jesus Christ. Such christological grounding comes to expression in Barth's *Göttingen Dogmatics*. There Barth affirms that God not only exists above the contradiction of our lives but also freely enters into our contradiction and overcomes it from within. God's hiddenness really takes place in history because "the Subject in whom the humanity of Jesus is made real and exists is a Subject in history."[29] This does not mean that the radicalism of Barth's eschatological reservation disappeared, but only that this radicalism now found its ground in Christology rather than eschatology.

The second occurrence that helped further Barth's project came during the summer of 1936, when Barth heard a lecture given by Pierre Maury on the doctrine of election. Maury's lecture was given at a conference of Calvin scholars, and the effect of Maury's lecture on Barth's own thinking did not take long to sink in.[30] Barth subsequently gave a series of lectures in Debrecen, Hungary in September 1936 on "God's Gracious Election," which provided the basic structure of his full-length treatment of the doctrine of election in *CD* 2.2.[31] However, Barth's thinking in 1936 was still developing. Matthias Gockel has shown that in the Debrecen lectures it was the "*eternal*

28. *CRDT*, 305, 318–19.

29. *CRDT*, 363.

30. For a full narration and exploration of the significance of this discovery for Barth's theology, see *CRDT*, chapter 8. McCormack has since made a "modest correction" to his paradigm of Barth's development in "Seek God," 63–64.

31. *CRDT*, 458.

God and thus also the eternal Son of God [who] is the *electing* God"[32] for Barth, as it was for Maury. Not until *CD* 2.2, whose material Barth presented "prior to its publication in regular lecture-course at the University of Basel, . . . between the autumn of 1939 and the summer of 1941"[33] does Barth arrive at the new conclusion—which is his alone—that the person of Jesus Christ is both the object *and* the subject of election.

For Barth to hold that Jesus Christ, the God-human in his divine-human unity, is not only the elect human but also the electing God shows that he has done away with the classical theological distinction between the eternal Word and the incarnate Word. Consequently, the anti-metaphysical tendencies and actualism present in the second edition of the Romans commentary increase exponentially. Now "God *is* in himself, in eternity, the mode of his Self-revelation in time—God as Jesus Christ in eternity and God as Jesus Christ in time—thus guaranteeing that the immanent Trinity and the economic Trinity will be identical in content."[34] In other words, the primal decision of election is that event in God in which God differentiates God's self into three modes of being. Election is both the event of God constituting God's self as triune and the event in which God chooses to be God for us. The classical theological gap between the eternal Son and Jesus Christ is now gone and the distinction between the two is removed. "The eternal Son of God is Jesus Christ as he lived, died, and rose again in time *and he alone.*"[35] The being of God is already determined in eternity by what God reveals God's self to be in Jesus Christ—a God of grace who is radically for all humanity.

When Barth turns to set forth his Christology within his doctrine of reconciliation in *Church Dogmatics* 4, he replaces the classical ontological category of "nature" with the modern category of "history," thereby "integrating 'history' into his concept of 'person.'"[36] What results is a theological ontology that expresses both the reality that God has elected to take humanity into the event of God's being, and the reality that the human Jesus participates in the being and existence of God. God takes humanity into God's life in the incarnation. Thus, all that occurs in the human life of Jesus of Nazareth is taken into God's life and made to be God's own. God does not cease to be God in doing this, because God has elected to be God in this way. In the history of Jesus of Nazareth, God truly gives God's self over to

---

32. Gockel, *Barth*, 161n8.
33. Ibid., 164.
34. McCormack, "Karl Barth's Historicized Christology," 218.
35. Ibid., 222.
36. Ibid.

judgment, wrath, suffering, and death—the means "in and through which [God's] true being is realized."[37] In the history of Jesus Christ, the being of God the Son is constituted. In this way, Barth's new doctrine of election assumes a historicized theological ontology.

Furthermore, in an asymmetrical manner, the human Jesus has his being and existence in God by sharing in God's history through actively obeying the will of his Father. The human Jesus participates in God's being and existence indirectly "by freely willing to live in correspondence to the history of God inaugurated in the covenant of grace."[38] Again, election is the unifying factor in these two histories, which together constitute the unified person, Jesus Christ. God, from all eternity, freely chose to give—both to God's self and to humanity—essential being in relation to the same person, Jesus of Nazareth. "It is in and through the *one* history of the man Jesus that what is essential to both God and humanity is concretely realized."[39]

Barth's development of this historicized theological ontology is significant for this study because it changes the apocalyptic character of Barth's mature doctrine of justification. That both God's own being and humanity's are established through God's self-determination to be God for us in Jesus Christ means that God's justification of sinful humanity has a historical ontological ground. Barth comes to explain justification as an event between God and humanity. Even more, justification is a history that involves a movement from unrighteousness to righteousness. The history of Jesus Christ is the unfolding history of the movement and event of the justification between God and humanity. And because this justification of God and humanity in Jesus Christ is the result of the eternal decision of God—in which God elected that both our being and God's own being would be constituted in the history of the life, death, and resurrection of the God-man Jesus—Barth upholds the notion of God's in-breaking action to put the world aright that is central to Pauline apocalypticism. With this historicized theological ontology in place, the classically reformational emphasis on the forensic nature of justification and the atonement takes on new meaning.

Barth's new foundation of Jesus Christ as both the object and subject of election had an all-encompassing impact for the whole of his subsequent theology. It is the key to his mature theology. Furthermore, coupled with a new-found grounding in the key insights of the Reformation, it marks the difference between the earlier cosmic apocalyptic theology expressed in

---

37. Ibid., 225.
38. Ibid., 228.
39. Ibid.

the second edition of the Romans commentary and the forensic theology contained in Barth's mature theology of justification in *CD* 4.1.

3. Apocalyptic Justification

In this final section, we will see the way that Barth's theological development paved the way for a forensic apocalyptic theology of justification in *CD* 4.1. Barth's doctrine of justification cannot be classified as antithetical to its reformational roots, even as its fresh hearing of Paul's witness to the Gospel requires radically restating those roots at certain points.

It is clear from only a cursory glance at *CD* 4.1 that forensic language governs Barth's treatment of reconciliation. He begins by stating that the incarnation is the event that reveals the deity of Jesus Christ. He then poses Anselm's question: *Cur Deus homo?* Looking to the history of what God has done in Jesus Christ for an answer to this question, Barth concludes that God freely became human in order not only to save the world, but to magnify God's own glory. That which "God does for Himself is also done for us. Our answer can only be a repetition of the answer which God Himself has given in this fact [of the history of Jesus Christ], in which He Himself has pronounced concerning the end and scope and meaning of His activity."[40]

Barth's next question becomes, "How is God for us?" Once more, he looks to the history of the triune God's giving up of God's self in the person of the Son in order to be a human among all humans. He determines that God is for us in Jesus Christ by making our situation God's own, even to the point of taking our places as sinners and enemies before God. This leads Barth finally to ask: "What is it that takes place when the Son of God becomes flesh of our flesh"?[41] Here he finds Scripture speaking of two things: salvation ("the great positive answer") and judgment ("the grace of God is not a cheap grace"). These two themes are interconnected: "If He were not the Judge, He would not be the Savior."[42] It is the second theme of Christ as judge of all humanity, "and therefore . . . the judicial work of the Gospel concerning Him," for which he proffers, above all, Romans 1:18–3:20 as the "*locus classicus*."[43] Barth reminds us that Christ executes God's judgment. In light of Christ's work as judge, the true reality of the human situation is revealed. But even more than that, looking at what God has actually done in Jesus Christ reveals that the Son of God became human to judge the world

40. *CD* 4.1:214.
41. *CD* 4.1:216.
42. *CD* 4.1:217.
43. *CD* 4.1:219.

in grace. Romans 1:18 says that God's wrath is revealed from heaven in the fact that God gives God's self not only to encounter the sinner against whom God must direct God's wrath, but also to take the sinner's place. "In Jesus Christ we see who we are by being seen as those we are—being seen as God in Him acknowledges what we are, accepting solidarity with our state and being, making Himself responsible for our Sin."[44]

When Barth turns his attention in §60, "The Pride and Fall of Man," to examine the human situation in light of the events of the incarnation and crucifixion, he finds that God's verdict revealed in Jesus Christ's resurrection is the standpoint from which the human plight must be considered. In Barth's words, we are "going back a step behind the knowledge that we have already won of the salvation" made actual for all humanity in the death of Jesus Christ and revealed in the resurrection to "the negative presupposition of this event."[45] And yet this process of going back behind the event of salvation to its negative presupposition is not something that can be done in separation from the history of Jesus Christ for us: "only when we know Jesus Christ do we really know that man is the man of sin, and what sin is, and what it means for man."[46] J. Louis Martyn has observed that Barth's emphasis on this point, both in his exegesis and in his theology, is right in line with Paul. "It was from the event of Christ's crucifixion—perceived to be God's redeeming deed—that Paul came to know the true nature of the human plight."[47] Barth learned from Paul to work from solution to plight, and this is one point on which Barth is critical of the Protestant reformers. As Barth observes it, "the programme of Reformation theology did not allow for any radical consideration of the meaning, importance and function of Christology in relation to all Christian knowledge . . . This was the case in the doctrine of sin."[48] However, Barth still upholds Reformation theology for the very great care it gave to constructing a doctrine of sin "wholly or mainly out of biblical material" thereby ensuring that "the worst danger of this method [i.e., devising a doctrine of sin independent of Christology] will not be quite so acute."[49] Nevertheless, the reason Barth insists that we must ground our knowledge of sin only in the knowledge of Jesus Christ is because God has judged both sin and sinner in the death of Jesus Christ and in the resurrection revealed that our old selves have been done away

44. CD 4.1:240.
45. CD 4.1:359.
46. CD 4.1:389.
47. Martyn, *Galatians*, 95n43.
48. CD 4.1:366.
49. CD 4.1:365.

with once and for all. "In this verdict we learn what God knows about us, and therefore how it really is with us. For this reason its content is valid . . . The fact that man is a sinner, and what his sin is, is something that in the last resort we can measure properly and fully only by that which on the New Testament understanding is man's salvation, the redemptive grace which comes from God to man."[50]

Barth classifies Romans 1:18–3:20 as belonging to this New Testament message. Rather than being a digression, it is "the first and basic statement about the Gospel which Paul has made it his business to expound . . . The Gospel is God's condemnation of man, of all men and every man."[51] Taking his cues from 1:18, Barth suggests that the judgment revealed in the gospel is the judgment of God's wrath. Yet, because of the threefold *gar* in verses 16, 17, and 18, we see why Paul is not ashamed of this being a core part of the gospel message. The gospel is the power of God, effective for salvation (vs. 16). It is the revelation that God's righteousness is God's judicial decision on all humanity (vs. 17). And while God's righteous judgment aims at humanity's redemption, it is also (vs. 18) revealed as "burning and consuming wrath."[52]

In the first part of Romans, Barth argues that Paul is communicating that human sin is the disobedience that must be overcome by the obedience of faith (1:5). Barth calls this the "law of faith" by which human sin is revealed and known. This is the "truth" suppressed in the unrighteousness of humanity (1:18). Romans 1:19–23 demonstrates the progressive guilt of the world before God. However, the light of the gospel reveals all human sin against God in 1:24–32. In view of the corruption of humanity, God must say "No." History is concluded in disobedience in the threefold repetition of "God gave them up," yet we know that the "history of the world which God made in Jesus Christ, and with a view to Him, cannot cease to have its centre and goal in Him. But in the light of this goal and centre God cannot say Yes but only No to its corruption."[53]

Barth knows, however, that Paul is speaking of the No from the standpoint of the cross and resurrection and so he declares that "God says No in order to say Yes. His Word is the Word of the teleologically established unity of the death and resurrection of Christ."[54] In the same way that the purpose of the judges in the Old Testament was to be helpers and saviors for the

50. *CD* 4.1:391.
51. *CD* 4.1:392.
52. *CD* 4.1:393.
53. *CD* 4.1:506.
54. *CD* 4.1:347.

people of Israel, so too the New Testament's reference to Christ as the Judge "means basically the coming of the Redeemer and Savior."[55] Furthermore, the connection between God's salvation (the "Yes") and God's judgment (the "No") finds its coherence within the concept of the righteousness of God. God's wrath is revealed against the unrighteousness of humanity (1:18), yet the "righteousness of God means God's negating and overcoming and taking away and destroying wrong and man as the doer of it."[56] Barth sounds a similar note in his second edition of the Romans commentary, when he interprets the righteousness of God as the consistency of God with God's self in Christ as displayed in God's "maintaining the distance by which we are separated from Him."[57] Our sin is abominable to God, and it simply cannot exist in light of God's majesty. It must be destroyed. In the event of God's righteousness there takes place the "breaking of a catastrophe"[58] in which that sinner who provokes God's wrath must die. This is the "hidden grace of the righteousness of God" because it "demands this retribution."[59] Barth's decision to call God's vindicating righteousness, in Romans 1, a hidden grace is best understood in light of the way he reads, in *CD* 2.2, the negative divine "handing over" of 1:24, 26, and 28 in light of the positive divine "handing over" expressed in 4:25 and 8:32.[60] "The righteousness of God utterly crushes us. In it God asserts and vindicates His own worth over against the creature. Yet in the election of the creature even this righteousness reveals itself as the grace and loving kindness and favour of God directed towards it."[61] Barth identifies the apostle's greeting of "grace to you and peace from God the Father and the Lord Jesus Christ" (Rom 1:7) as that which is spelled out in the event of God's righteousness toward the enemies of grace.

4. Conclusion

In this short examination of Barth's treatment of Romans 1 in *CD* 4.1, we can see that Barth has not abandoned the forensic framework by which the reformational theologians understood justification. Yet the way in which

---

55. *CD* 4.1:217.
56. *CD* 4.1:535.
57. Barth, *Epistle*, 41.
58. *CD* 4.1:539.
59. *CD* 4.1:540.
60. I am following Gaventa's translation of the *paradidōmi* clauses here. See "God," 113–23.
61. *CD* 2.2:33.

Barth grapples with the form of God's judgment is through the lens of Paul's assertion of the power of the gospel in that chapter. Calvin explains "justification simply as the acceptance with which God receives us into his favor as righteous men. And we say that it consists in the remission of sins and the imputation of Christ's righteousness."[62] We see Barth's own argument mirrored in Calvin's first sentence. However, Barth uses the language of Paul in Romans 1 to speak of how we are justified as God justifies God's self and of how God's No serves the purpose of God's Yes. Barth does two things with reference to Calvin's second sentence. First, as regards the remission of sins, Barth speaks apocalyptically of the destruction of the sinner—the necessity of the in-breaking of a catastrophe in which we are freed by being imprisoned, saved by our destruction. Barth uses this language because he understands Paul's witness to the in-breaking action of God in the death and resurrection of Jesus Christ to reveal not only the solution, but also the nature of the plight of the whole world and all humanity.

Second, as regards the imputation of Christ's righteousness, Barth relocates the concept within God's own self-determination to be God for us in Jesus Christ. Christ's righteousness is not something applied to us in the first instance, but rather a decision God makes to be God for us in Jesus Christ. Justification takes place in the death and resurrection of Jesus Christ for both Barth and Paul, but Barth goes a step beyond Paul in arguing that God determined God's being for the incarnation. Reformation theology's emphasis on the "alien righteousness of Christ" as our justification is finally preserved in Barth's own radical re-centering of reformational forensicism upon the Pauline proclamation of the power of God's apocalypse: that in Jesus Christ's death and resurrection we see God's in-breaking, initiating action to rectify the world to God. In Barth's hands "forensic" does not refer to an external transaction that happens over our heads and has no real bearing on our lives. Rather, Barth's forensic ontology describes God's divine actions that constitute both God and us from within.

Apocalypse Ellipsis

A Response to Shannon Smythe

—By Andrew R. Guffey

---

62. Calvin, *Institutes*, 3.11.2.

The topic for this year's Karl Barth Blog Conference was deceptively simple: "Barth in conversation with . . ." The actual task of putting the great Swiss theologian in conversation with another thinker, especially with Paul the Apostle, is a complicated affair indeed. Shannon Nicole Smythe has offered us a valiant effort at introducing just such a conversation. The central claim of Smythe's paper is that Barth's theology was deeply indebted to Paul's apocalyptic thought throughout his career, but that his incorporation of Pauline apocalypticism developed in a specific direction—from the cosmic apocalypticism of the second edition of the Romans commentary to a forensically inflected apocalypticism in *Church Dogmatics* 4.1.[63] It is a worthy thesis to consider, and we should be thankful to Smythe for her interesting essay.

Theology—as I think the theological traditions of Christianity amply demonstrate, especially as enshrined in the Creeds—has a responsibility to be as precise as poetry (besides mathematics I know of no more precise use of language). It is in the spirit of that standard that I offer a few critical remarks. My criticism of Smythe is twofold. First, I think the essay needs to be more focused. No doubt, Barth's theology functions as a system such that no doctrine can really be examined in isolation from the others. Even so, the range of doctrinal *topoi* Smythe addresses in her discussion of Barth's relationship to Pauline apocalypticism unnecessarily occludes her conclusions. Second, the central category of apocalypticism remains vague, since Smythe neither constructs the category from the appropriate sources nor constructively and circumspectly draws on a useful model from the literature on Paul and/or apocalypticism.

Let me begin by commending Smythe's exposition of Barth. Following the important work of Bruce McCormack, Smythe deftly sketches the turn in Barth's theology toward a more informed reformational perspective, while at the same time highlighting Barth's continued interaction with Paul's letter to the Romans. This part of the essay is basically successful, documenting a shift—or perhaps a few shifts—in Barth's thought that produced an emphasis in Barth's later work that differed from his earlier theology.

---

63. It strikes me that Smythe is trying to do with Barth what Beker argued for Paul (see Beker, *Paul*). He argued that an apocalyptic core hid behind the contingency of Paul's letters. Smythe likewise claims that Paul's apocalyptic core constitutes the consistent element in Barth's theology. The only real difference between the two is that whereas for Beker the contingency of Paul's letters was situational and emphatically *not* due to development in Paul's thought, for Smythe the contingent element in Barth's thought is precisely due to a diachronic development in his theology.

Barth's discovery of the anhypostatic/enhypostatic account[64] of the relation between human and divine in Jesus Christ certainly enhanced Barth's christological focus, and there is little doubt that the Barth of *CD* 4.1 is more interested in a forensic view of justification than the Barth of *Romans* and that he appropriates Paul accordingly.[65]

The difficulty with this aspect of the paper that I wish to raise is Smythe's lack of precision with respect to the doctrinal context of Barth's apocalypticism. One is never quite sure what elements of Barth's thought correlate with Pauline apocalypticism since the doctrinal contexts for Smythe's exposition keep shifting. In the space of just a few pages Smythe roams from revelation and eschatology to christology, justification, election, and finally Barth's historicized theological ontology. Where does apocalypticism fit in this doctrinal web? Is Barth's apparent shift in his appropriation of Pauline apocalypticism merely due to the changing context of his theological discourse? Is forensic apocalyptic theology merely what one gets when Barth speaks of justification (*CD* 4.1) rather than revelation (*Romans*)? Smythe locates the heart of Pauline apocalypticism, at least in part, in Barth's historicized theological ontology—wherein God's being only obtains in the advent, life, death, and resurrection of Jesus. But as Smythe asserts, this particular ontology is characteristic only of the later Barth. The rest of Smythe's answer rests in her dependence on the work of Ernst Käsemann for what she considers to be the nature of Paul's apocalyptic thought.

This brings us to the very important question of what constitutes apocalypticism or, more specifically, *Pauline* apocalypticism, and it is this aspect of the paper that I found most wanting. Smythe identifies the work of Käsemann as representative of the cosmic apocalyptic perspective on Paul. Drawing on Käsemann's important article on the righteousness of God and his influential Romans commentary, Smythe traces Käsemann's solution to the eschatological dialectic he observed in Romans. In Christ future eschatology touches the present, as in Jesus the eschatological sovereignty of God is proleptically present. Smythe then traces the same theme—the location of God's eschatological sovereignty in Jesus Christ—in Barth's *Romans*. This part of the essay is intended to show the consonance between Paul's

---

64. The anhypostatic/enhypostatic formula, incidentally, does not go back to the early church, as Smythe suggests. Leontius of Byzantium (sixth century CE) is usually credited with the formula, though Shults follows Aloys Grillmeier and Brian Daley in questioning the attribution of "enhypostasis" as a philosophically precise concept in Leontius, arguing instead that the use of the formula in this way rests rather with the Protestant Scholastics of the sixteenth and seventeenth centuries. See Shults, "Dubious."

65. References to Barth's *Epistle* refer to the second edition of that work. The first edition has not been translated and is a significantly different work.

cosmic apocalyptic theology and *Romans*.⁶⁶ What it actually demonstrates is the consonance between Käsemann and Barth, a point to which we will return below. But there is a more important problem here: what in this is "apocalyptic," and why? Why should we not simply call this "eschatological," for instance?

If we seek clarity in the counterpart to Smythe's cosmic apocalypticism—namely, forensic apocalypticism—we will be disappointed. Dismissing the categories of cosmic and forensic apocalyptic eschatology patiently constructed by Martinus de Boer, Smythe insists that the category of forensic apocalypticism in Barth must be derived from Barth's own work.⁶⁷ Surely this is mistaken. Building a category of analysis *for* Barth's thought *from* Barth's work is entirely circular, and turns the dialogue between Barth and Paul into a monologue.

The fundamental problem here is that there is no underlying concept of apocalypticism, or a confused one.⁶⁸ Citing Barry Matlock's very useful analysis in a footnote, Smythe admits that "apocalyptic" is a fuzzy term but she then goes on to disregard Matlock's critique. Matlock does not merely claim that the meaning of "apocalyptic" is contested, and that one definition is therefore as good as another; rather, he claims that the confused state of defining apocalyptic makes it a problematic category to employ at all. Indeed, important work in biblical studies would identify "apocalyptic" more in terms of its mystical or visionary element rather than its eschatological element.⁶⁹ The problem is directly relevant, since the mystical/visionary interpretation of apocalypticism produces a different conversation partner for Barth than Käsemann's or J. Louis Martyn's Paul. According to this interpretation, the center of Paul's apocalypticism might be 2 Corinthians 12 rather than Galatians or Romans. Likewise, when Smythe claims that Barth followed Paul in asserting that God had already eschatologically dealt with

---

66. Following an observation by theologian Harink. See Harink, *Paul*, 45–55.

67. For de Boer's categories, see de Boer, "Paul," 357–66.

68. In a footnote Smythe does offer what she takes to be the main features of Pauline apocalypticism: God's sovereignty; divine revelation (especially of a new age); christologically motivated cosmic dualism and pessimism (the present age as evil and oppressive); and the cosmic eschatological view of Christ's death and resurrection. First, Smythe nowhere actually uses this definition as an analytic tool to correlate elements of Barth's and Paul's thought and thereby demonstrate that both are apocalyptic. Second, the definition is very broad, with significant (if not entire) overlap with the (Jewish and Christian) prophetic and wisdom traditions. Lacking is any discussion of *why* these features should be considered apocalyptic.

69. A development already noted in Matlock, *Unveiling*, 258–62. Especially important, for instance, is Rowland's excellent work: Rowland, *Open*; and Rowland and Morray-Jones, *Mystery*, 3–32 and 137–66.

sinner and sin in the death and resurrection of Jesus, we might ask if this is true for Paul in 1 Corinthians 5:5 when he orders the Corinthians to cast out the immoral man for the destruction of his flesh, so that his spirit might be saved *on the day of the Lord*. What does *this* eschatological perspective (no less apocalyptic, surely!) have to say in conversation with Barth?[70]

In fairness, Smythe has tried to correlate Barth's thought with what she takes as a standard apocalyptic interpretation of Paul (that of Käsemann). I do not know why the thematic similarity between Käsemann's Paul and Barth's Paul should surprise us, however, since Käsemann made use of Barth's commentary for his own work. It would be naïve to simply suppose both scholars were engaging in "pure" exegesis. More to the point, Käsemann's most basic definition of apocalyptic was imminent eschatology, but this is clearly not the definition Smythe has in mind.[71]

I take Smythe to be saying that Paul's apocalypticism is basically cosmic-eschatological, but that Barth created a theological *novum* by aligning Paul's apocalypticism with the Reformation's forensic doctrine of justification. This seems to bypass another methodological problem. Was it not Paul's forensicism that generated the Reformed doctrine in the first place? Does Barth really forensicize Paul's apocalypticism, or does he just emphasize the forensic aspect of Paul's apocalyptic thought in CD 4.1? I cannot help but feel that actually working within de Boer's categories would have helped Smythe's argument here. In brief, the argument suffers because Smythe's categories of cosmic and forensic apocalypticism should be drawn not from Barth, but from Paul's letters or a range of Pauline scholarship, or better—as in de Boer's work—from ancient apocalypses. Matlock also makes a plea for a definition of apocalypticism derived from close study of apocalyptic literature (not just Paul's letters!), concluding, "[A]n 'apocalyptic' which resists this methodological control suggests a notion perhaps retained more for its usefulness than its integrity."[72]

---

70. Another commentator on the original blog conference also noted that the argument of the essay was weakened by sticking too close to Romans, though I would suggest that even focusing on Romans *and* Galatians is far too narrow. A discussion between Barth's theology and the apocalypticism of Paul's Corinthian correspondence could be very interesting.

71. See Käsemann's two articles, "Beginnings" and "On the Topic," also conveniently collected along with articles by some of Käsemann's critics in Funk, *Apocalypticism*.

72. Matlock, *Unveiling*, 270. Matlock's criticism of Sturm (Sturm, "Defining"), and Martyn by implication, should be noted: "The assertion that, whatever problems may attach to the effort generally, Martyn hands us at least a means of clarifying *Paul's* 'apocalyptic' patently begs all the questions, forgetting, in the confidence that, after all, we really *do* know what we mean when we talk about 'apocalyptic' (and in the haste to do just that), that *it* is just the issue" (313). Matlock's concern arises in part from

Although I think Smythe is in the end overly anxious to impute Pauline apocalypticism to Barth's later work on justification, I do think the argument points toward an interesting conclusion. Where Smythe finds a dialogic between Barth's assimilation of Paul's so-called apocalyptic thought and Reformation theology's forensic doctrine of justification—each synthetically informing the other—I would be inclined to see a reversal of Paul's polarity in Barth. If we were to follow de Boer, we might acknowledge that Paul's forensic apocalyptic eschatology was subordinate to his cosmic apocalyptic eschatology. Smythe's argument has perhaps demonstrated that while the Barth of *Romans* simply adopted Paul's cosmic apocalyptic eschatology, the Barth of *CD* 4.1 has rather folded it into a reformational doctrine of forensic justification. The implications of such a conclusion should be obvious—Barth was no uncritical Pauline puppet, but rather used the Reformation's insights to tacitly criticize and correct the aporias of Paul's thought. Now that's a conversation I'd like to see!

---

the differing methodological protocols of historical and theological scholars. For an excellent illustration of these differing methodological presuppositions and their importance for defining "apocalyptic," see Wilson, "Dead Sea Scrolls," and especially the response of Collins, "Apocalyptic Theology." For an excellent model for how an analytic category for application to modern thinkers can be drawn from ancient sources, see O'Regan, *Gnostic Return*.

11

Barth and Kegan

Theological Anthropology and Developmental Psychology in Lived Experience

—By Blair D. Bertrand

1. People Matter: Theological Anthropology and Developmental Psychology

FOR BOTH KARL BARTH and Robert Kegan, people matter. As a theologian Barth cares about people and how they relate to God, while as a psychologist Kegan hopes to understand people and how they relate to their own selves. Human beings then are the object of study for two distinct but related perspectives: theological anthropology and developmental psychology. The relationship between these two perspectives is not neat and tidy. Theological anthropology "confines its enquiry to the human creatureliness presupposed" in the relationship between God and humanity.[1] Covenant, the particular relationship that humans have with God, is the essential aspect of humanity because we are created as covenant partners. Creator to creature, Redeemer to redeemed, Sustainer to sustained—the relationship takes form as covenant. We must look to God and God's characteristics within this relationship to understand who we are. Like all knowledge about God for Barth, "as the man Jesus is Himself the revealing Word of God, He is the source of our knowledge of the nature of man as created by God."[2] On the other hand, according to Barth, developmental psychology must limit its inquiry

---

1. *CD* 3.2:19.
2. *CD* 3.2:41.

into humanity to the phenomenal, to the "plenitude of man's possibilities."[3] Someone like Robert Kegan, a developmental psychologist, can make "statements to the effect that man as a phenomenon is to be seen and understood by man according to this or that standpoint and in this or that aspect of his constitution and development, as determined by current knowledge of these facts accessible to human enquiry."[4] Psychology must proceed tentatively, offering the best possible answer in its time without making universal claims. For Barth, theological anthropology describes reality and developmental psychology describes the phenomenon of humanity.

The intersection of these two perspectives concerns practical theology. Practical theology finds its specific purchase where reality as revealed in Jesus Christ encounters our everyday lived phenomenal existence.[5] There is no hard divide between the humanity accessible through Jesus Christ and our lived experience, as if theology and psychology carry on in parallel lines of inquiry but never intersect. Barth himself does not allow this. Besides places in the *Church Dogmatics* where he specifically acknowledges and values what he calls our "psycho-physical development in time," there is a sense that in *CD* 3 he must reconcile our everyday lived experience, our creatureliness, with the christological reality of God's creative grace that makes us covenant partners.[6] Barth will never allow our quotidian existence to determine theological reality but, at the same time, that everyday lived experience is not inconsequential. Our status as covenant partners is given to us in Jesus Christ's full humanity, which means that our human agency bears significance. Jesus Christ as covenant-partner is at "the conjunction of heaven and earth [that] corresponds to the covenant in which the divine and human being and action meet."[7] Because we act as covenant partners to God by exercising our full humanity in the phenomenal realm, disciplines that help us understand that agency may make a contribution to our faithful understanding of God and God's ongoing action in the world.

A conversation between Karl Barth and Robert Kegan will need to include the kind of interdisciplinary methodology talk carried on so far,

---

3. The translation used for this essay consistently uses male pronouns when referring to humanity. For ease of reading I have not noted each use of "man," although I am philosophically and theologically committed to using gender inclusive terminology for humanity.

4. *CD* 3.2:24.

5. For more on the field of practical theology, see Osmer, *Practical Theology*; for more on human and divine action as the generative problematic for practical theology, see Loder, "Normativity."

6. *CD* 3.4:607–18.

7. *CD* 3.2:12.

but it should not end there. To say that people matter for both Barth and Kegan leaves the concept of "people" in the abstract. This speculation is in part necessary since individuals as humans hold characteristics in common with all people. To refer to "people" is to refer to that which is common to all individuals. This commonality can fund interdisciplinary conversations in a way that particularity cannot. Others, such as F. LeRon Shults, have already mined Kegan to construct an interdisciplinary methodology that addresses theological anthropology and Barth.[8] This kind of framing is good as far as it goes, but it does not engage the material insights that both Barth and Kegan bring to understanding lived experiences. Barth and Kegan both care about particular people, about how individuals understand themselves, others, and God both theologically and psychologically. To avoid repeating generalized interdisciplinary conversations here, I begin by looking at a specific situation from both the theological and psychological perspectives. I bring Barth and Kegan into conversation around a specific case study—a young Christian man named Dylan—to reveal how our lived experiences interact with the theological norms and interpretive insights provided by both thinkers. Barth's insights into the form of humanity limit, guide, and ground Kegan's clinical understanding of Dylan. On the other side, Kegan's developmental perspective challenges, interprets, and actualizes Barth's theological understanding. The point of this conversation between Barth and developmental psychologist Robert Kegan is to move past the abstract to the actual lived experience of human-divine interaction.

After describing Dylan and his situation, I turn to Kegan as an interpretive lens. Following that, I reframe Dylan and Kegan's interpretation using a limited portion of Barth's theological anthropology. This reframing does not annihilate Kegan's interpretations but limits, guides, and grounds them in a deeper and richer theological understanding. Finally, I offer a few observations for both practical theologians and Barthians as to the implications for our respective work because of this conversation.

2. Dylan: Larger Than Life

Dylan is large in many ways. He looks big; at age eighteen he is 6'2" and a muscular 220 lbs. His largeness also comes out in his gregarious nature. Along with his faithful side kick Dave, Dylan is often heard hooting, laughing, yelling, and generally carrying on. Dylan is a counselor at a summer Christian camp and he puts his whole large heart into serving. All of his colleagues love this fun loving, party creating attitude. At the same time,

---

8. See Shults, *Reforming*, 39–60.

this love and admiration is tinged with fear. Dylan is both the life of the party and the ring leader for any mischief the staff might get up to. At times he goes too far. Normal pranks get carried one step further than everyone is comfortable with. What is fun at the start borders on cruelty or danger by the time Dylan has taken over. In taking risks, he places others at risk both physically and emotionally. The female staff especially struggle with Dylan, wanting to be within his orbit but also tentative about what might happen by getting too close. Campers have much the same reaction. Boys find it exhilarating to be in Dylan's cabin. They feel Dylan's loyalty to them as he creates experiences filled with fun and risk. Girls on the other hand like to watch from afar but feel excluded and a bit frightened by such a display of "testosterone." Senior staff recognize Dylan's leadership gifts and have spent considerable amounts of time and energy trying to channel them into productive activities. During training it was clear that Dylan lacked critical risk assessment skills, so senior staff attempted to educate the entire staff on proper boundaries. By focusing staff attention on serving campers using the popular servant-leadership model and by using the ministry goals of the camp as the main criteria for determining behavior, senior staff hoped to shift Dylan from what they viewed as a narcissistic attitude to one of selfless service. Senior staff tried to appeal to Dylan's heartfelt but largely unreflective faith, a faith that he associates with his own childhood experiences at camp. These experiences serve as his motivation for working at the camp, more so than any abstract understanding of vocation or mission. He wants children to experience acceptance and fun in a Christian setting, just like he did.

On a day off between camps, Dylan finally went too far. Against a specific prohibition in the standard staff contract that clearly stated no parties and no alcohol on site, Dylan organized a party at a remote part of the camp site. Underage employees purchased alcohol through older members of staff. By the time the party was shut down, more than half of the staff were involved, most underage and many dangerously inebriated. When the first senior staff member initially confronted Dylan at the party, he ignored her command to stop the party. He saw no reason to stop—the party was in full swing and he was in his element. The next morning, per the direct restrictions in the contract that the staff had signed, senior staff had no choice but to fire all the staff involved in the incident, including Dylan. This left the senior staff with a large group of disgruntled teens, a lot of explaining to do, and nobody to look after the camp coming in within hours. In this chaos, Dylan continued to play a leadership role. Now he was the prime agent in subverting anything the senior staff tried. Instead of accepting that his behavior was wrong, Dylan felt aggrieved. In his mind, and soon also in the minds of most of the fired employees, he was the one wronged in this incident. He felt betrayed. In the months to come, only one of the fired staff approached the camp to confess and apologize. It wasn't Dylan.

3. Kegan: Challenging, Interpreting, and Actualizing

For both Kegan and Barth, Dylan matters. More specifically, Dylan matters as an end rather than as a means. Kegan understands Dylan as an individual developing within a particular society and a unique relational matrix. Barth sees in Dylan a human being created as covenant partner. To understand Dylan is to understand more general truths about humanity, to be sure, but that is not the primary reason why he matters to Kegan and Barth. Primarily, Dylan is a human being struggling to make meaning in his world, a person created in relation to a sovereign God struggling to make sense of himself in relation to that createdness. Kegan demonstrates in his writings and teaching a deep care for the individual as individual: as a person who is not just a source of fascination or academic curiosity but a person with inherent value and worth. Leaving aside where this value and worth come from for Kegan, it is clear that Dylan matters.

At first glance, it may appear that Barth values Dylan in a completely different way than Kegan. In contradiction to Kegan's methodology, which relies on case studies, critical incidents, and clinical analysis, Barth contends that scholars cannot generalize results from anecdotes and incidents such as this one. Kegan's kind of argument is the danger that Barth guards against when he argues that the best a developmental psychologist can hope for is a provisional description of the phenomenon and not a more universally valid anthropology. Even a statistically significant sampling of eighteen-year-old North American male experiences would not be sufficient to reveal the theological truth of our createdness within a covenant partnership. This is not a matter of bad qualitative research methodology at work, but rather a limit imposed by theological reality. Even so, as Christians living in this broken and sinful world, we have an obligation to understand our own agency and our own selves so that we might more faithfully participate in our covenant partnership with God. Our own individual living of our covenant partnership has value. Dylan as a creation of God who is in relation to that same God has worth as a person. So while developmental psychology cannot determine the nature of the covenant partnership or—in Barth's terms—the basic form of humanity, it can challenge some of the naïve theological assumptions we might make, interpret our human agency, and provide a thick description of actualized human agency. Kegan and Barth value Dylan differently but not in contradictory terms.

The challenge that Kegan puts to Barth centers on the particularity of human experience. Kegan can account for the uniqueness of Dylan within a complex system whereas Barth makes universally true statements that obscure Dylan's individuality. Barth's generally true statements appear somewhat thin when challenged by a personalism more developed than the one that he employs in *CD* 3.2. It is difficult to see how a theological anthropology influenced by Buber's I-Thou personalism can thoroughly account for the complexity of relationships that Dylan finds himself in. There is no simple dyad, no I-Thou, that Dylan fits into. As noted by Paul Dafydd Jones in his criticism of *CD* 3.2, Barth's theological thinking here "drifts from its moorings, caught in the swell of philosophical, social-scientific and cultural discourses."[9] Because Kegan is moored within the social-scientific discourse of psychological personalism, moving beyond both a vision of humans as "autonomous subjects that stand over against the natural world and other subjects" and a simple dyad of I-Thou, he can challenge some of Barth's more speculative theological meanderings. Kegan can account for Dylan as a human "understood as always and already embedded in relations between self, other, and world."[10] Jones would correct Barth by a return to *sola scriptura* and trinitarian dogmatic reflection as found in *Church Dogmatics* 1 and 2, while Kegan would challenge Barth by offering a more sophisticated personalism. Neither invalidate Barth's basic insights, nor are they mutually exclusive, but they are both necessary for a more faithful understanding of Dylan as a particular human. In other words, Jones holds Barth to account theologically and Kegan challenges Barth anthropologically.

Kegan's first contribution to this conversation consists of challenging naïve personalism and centers on the relationality inherent in the human condition. In his major works, Kegan gives significant time to interpreting and describing this relationality, going far beyond Barth in building a nuanced understanding of the human condition.[11] Kegan's interpretive and descriptive contribution centers on relationships, and more specifically on the fact that there are at least three different relationship constructions in Dylan's scenario. The campers, Dylan and his peers, and the senior staff are all related to each other, but each group understands those relationships differently. For instance, children such as the campers Dylan counsels largely inhabit what Kegan calls

---

9. Jones, *Humanity*, 118.
10. Shults, *Reforming*, 31.
11. See Kegan, *Evolving Self*; and Kegan, *In Over Our Heads*.

the Imperial self.[12] For them, relationships are something given to them by the institutional structures surrounding them. Usually family and school perform this structuring role, but in the incident above a residential Christian camp structures the relationships. Children see the relational world through a series of roles that dictate and determine appropriate behavior. Mothers and fathers, teachers and principals, counselors and directors all have roles and the child figures out how they fit within this relational matrix.

Eventually a figure/ground shift occurs where the child is no longer the role taker but is the relationship between the roles. This is the stage Dylan and most of his peers are in, the Interpersonal.[13] Teenagers "are" their relationships. Teens can exhibit great degrees of self-sacrifice and collaboration within their peer group. Dylan and Dave were fiercely loyal to each other. They have escaped from understanding each other within prescribed institutional roles and can see each other as discrete individuals. What a teen cannot do, though, is to step back and determine which relationship and what components of that relationship she wants to have. In some ways, Dylan's behavior was dictated by the relational expectations of his peers. He could no more stop being gregarious and risk-taking than he could stop breathing because both were necessary to his identity. Certainly, teens exhibit behaviors like risk-taking on a spectrum influenced by many factors that are related to development, such as brain chemistry. The point is not to suggest that Dylan's developmental stage determines his behavior; rather, it is the distinction between "being" risky versus "taking" a risk that is salient. Kegan's schema concerns itself with the capacity to transcend "being" risky in order to "take" a risk, marking this change as a cognitive development. Likewise, teens cannot "have" relationships because their connection to their peer group is the way that they see reality. They do not have the cognitive capacity to construe relationships in any other way than "being."

When the next figure/ground shift occurs, moving the teen into adulthood and from the Interpersonal to the Intrapersonal, an individual can have a relationship using a larger ideological criterion.[14] The senior staff in this incident were committed to the mission of the camp. They determined their relationships to each other, to the staff, and to campers based on this ideological commitment. The introduction of a servant-leadership model, an ideological construct that determines the nature of the relationship, makes sense to the senior staff. You "have" a relationship using the criteria set out within a larger framework. It is this ability to "have" a relationship

12. See Kegan, *Evolving Self*, 161–83.
13. See ibid., 184–220, and Kegan, *In Over Our Heads*, 15–72.
14. See Kegan, *Evolving Self*, 221–54; Kegan, *In Over Our Heads*, 73–136.

that allowed them to subordinate their own feelings for someone and fire him even though it meant destroying the relationship. As evidenced by Dylan's reaction, teens struggle with the dissolution of a relationship for reasons that remain abstract to them. To destroy a relationship is to destroy the self. Children, on the other hand, could understand that this outcome is what the situation demanded. The contract clearly stated the rules and roles all were to assume. Children could not construct the reasons why the contract is like it is, but they clearly understand the roles determined by it. A violation of role means a violation of the social norms that give meaning to the world and must be punished according to those social roles. In many ways, the contract itself was within the Imperial understanding of the world.

Even this thumbnail sketch is suggestive of the depth of interpretation that Kegan could give to this situation and others. Two important points emerge from this analysis other than insights gained on the immediate incident in question. First, it is easy to see that even something as fundamental to humanity as "relationship" changes depending on our developmental stage. Children, teens, and adults are all relational, but the character of those relationships changes significantly depending on life stage. Kegan's work focuses on those situations where there is a mismatch between expectation and ability. To expect Dylan to separate himself from his relationships, a demand that the senior staff implied in trying to shift him away from his narcissism to a more servant-based understanding of leadership, sets Dylan up for failure and the senior staff for disappointment. The appropriate response, according to Kegan, would be for the senior staff to construct "an ingenious blend of support and challenge" that would coach Dylan into a new way of being.[15] Dylan must experience the feeling of being "in over his head" in terms of his own self-understanding and construction of relationships, but must also simultaneously "experience effective support."[16] As someone within the Interpersonal stage, Dylan cannot assume an Intrapersonal perspective. Kegan has much to say on how those in higher developmental stages might help bridge the distance and promote growth, suggestions that may have helped the senior staff before the fateful night of the party.[17] The senior staff obviously needed better interpretive tools in understanding Dylan so that they could help him mature.

Second, there is a larger philosophical or theological dimension to this incident about which Kegan remains silent. Kegan interprets the way that

15. Kegan, *In Over Our Heads*, 42.
16. Ibid., 43.
17. For instance, he sketches the necessary confirmation, contradiction, and continuity, as well as a possible transitional object, needed to move from the Imperial to the Interpersonal self. See Kegan, *Evolving Self*, 165.

we construe the world—in this case, through relationships—but does not determine norms for those constructions. For instance, in this case, Dylan was morally wrong to organize the party. Whatever kind of ethic undergirds this judgment, it includes a criterion partly based on teleological assumptions. Kegan can explain why Dylan did this, i.e., he can interpret it, but he remains silent on the normative question of whether Dylan should have done this. This silence is not from ignorance. Kegan recognizes that at some point "no framework that is strictly psychological" can fully justify itself.[18] For all of Kegan's epistemological sophistication, he lacks a grounding axiology or justifying teleology. Why care about Dylan? Why concern ourselves with the nature of the relationships in the first place? What determines what actually constitutes a "good" or "bad" fit between expectations and behaviors? Kegan attempts a partial philosophical answer to these questions, but his work begs for a fuller theological anthropology that can give value and direction to the development of the human person.

4. Barth: Limiting, Guiding, and Grounding

It is exactly this kind of fuller theological anthropology that Barth can offer to this conversation. If Kegan challenges, interprets, and describes, then Barth limits, guides, and grounds. Kegan—as a Jew and a Harvard psychologist—would not necessarily accept the universality of Barth's normative theological anthropology. He might not want the limits, guidance, or grounding that Barth supplies. But that does not mean that Kegan's work does not demand a robust engagement with philosophical norms beyond what psychology itself can give him. Kegan invites this kind of conversation and is not fearful of his work getting lost if the dialogue partners have a true conversation. The sticking point, as it always is and will be for those who encounter Barth, is his christocentrism. Barth's contribution to the conversation starts and ends with God's self-revelation in Jesus Christ. It is Jesus Christ, as the created covenant partner, who reveals the contours of humanity's basic form, provides fruitful directions to look for a true representation of humanity, and ultimately provides humanity with a theological grounding within God's self. Kegan's challenge to Barth has merit because his psychology fits within the theological limits set out by God in Jesus Christ—they both speak the same language in terms of relationship, and therefore the challenge is not hostile but friendly. Likewise, because Kegan assumes many of the same things as Barth, his interpretation and description find resonance with true humanity as revealed in Jesus Christ.

18. Ibid., 288.

This privileging of Barth's theological anthropology as descriptive of a reality inaccessible to Kegan's developmental psychology need not imply that Kegan's insights are invalid or second best. Nor need it imply that Barth's account is stifling of a fuller understanding of the reality and phenomenon of humanity. In general, the foundational position held by Jesus Christ in Barth's theological anthropology is not some simplistic reading of humanity's essence off the biblical record. Barth does not engage in an exercise of "What Would Jesus Do?" theology, where a naïve reading of Christology determines actual behavior. When Barth does engage in what Jones calls "fairly hackneyed readings of Gen. 2.18-25, Eph. 5.22-33 and so on," he violates his own larger and more comprehensive practice of theological interpretation.[19] Literal readings of specific biblical passages as they relate to gender relations lead Barth down a path where he equates the phenomenon of humanity with the reality of being a covenant partner. Indeed, Barth denies his own argument based on an expansive vision of covenant history by warranting his understanding of gender relations in this simplistic fashion. When Barth does warrant his theological anthropology in a broader christocentrism rather than conflating the theological with the phenomenal, someone like Kegan can make a positive contribution because real conversation is possible.

Therefore, despite strong christological statements, for Barth "Christology is not anthropology."[20] We as humans are not the unique human-divine subject, Jesus Christ. At the same time, we are human and so must look to the truly human Jesus Christ to understand what that means. Christology does play a crucial role in Barth's theological anthropology. We can have true humanity as we correspond to, and have similarity through our common humanness with, Jesus Christ. As Barth makes clear, "we cannot start with the assumption that there is a known and accepted picture of man and humanity before which we can pause and from the contours of which we can read off that which corresponds and is similar in man to the humanity of Jesus."[21] We can no more move from a psychological description to a true image of humanity than we can move from a simplistic biblical reading to a full blown theological anthropology. Instead, we must start with the basic form of humanity revealed in Jesus Christ and then move to interpretations such as Kegan's to help explain that true form. Barth points out the four characteristics of true humanity in *Church Dogmatics* 3.2, §45.2—the basic form of humanity as covenant partner—and so I will use these four to

---

19. Jones, *Humanity*, 119.
20. *CD* 3.2:222.
21. *CD* 3.2:226.

understand what limiting, guiding, and grounding a psychological anthropology might look like for Barth, at least in part.

If we want to have real human relationships with each other, which is to participate in our own real humanity, then any time that we consider someone like Dylan—whether it is in day-to-day interaction or in an analytic situation such as the one I have constructed here—we must start with four basic premises. First, true humanity is "a being in which one man looks the other in the eye."[22] We must see each other. While limited by the fact that images are windows into the person but do not actually communicate the totality of a person, we must start by seeing the other as other: separate, distinct, and autonomous. Second, only where there "is mutual speech and hearing" is true humanity present.[23] We must hear and speak to each other from our depths and not just from the surface of the image. As Nell Morton would say, we must hear each other into speech.[24] Third, "the fact that we render mutual assistance in the act of being" is constitutive of humanity.[25] We must serve each other. It is not sufficient to simply see and hear another. We must use our own agency on the other's behalf. While we see the other as autonomous, humanity does not exist outside of a "with" the other and "on behalf of" the other. Finally, all of these actions must be "done on both sides with gladness."[26] We must delight in each other.[27] This kind of encounter with another is not a duty or obligation, for that implies inequality. Relationships are not an imperative that we can choose to obey or not; rather, our relational nature is a reality. To be human is to see, hear, serve, and delight with and in each other.

These four basic forms of humanity limit our interpretations. Writing during and after the Holocaust, Barth was keenly aware of the fact that even apparently benign ways of seeing each other can ultimately serve evil. We must limit our interpretations using this kind of theological anthropology or our interpretations "might be only a matter of psychology and not the other man, of pedagogics and not the child, of sociological statistics and systematisation and not the individual, of the general and not the particular,

---

22. CD 3.2:250.
23. CD 3.2:252.
24. See Morton, *Journey*.
25. CD 3.2, 260.
26. CD 3.2, 265.

27. I realize that I am stepping away from Barth's original text by using the word "delight." Barth uses the adverb *gerne* (translated as "gladness" but more properly "gladly") to describe how we see, hear, and serve. I have translated the intent of *gerne* as a verb, "delight," in part because Barth describes this gladness as "a decisive, all-animating and motivating dynamic." We see, hear, and serve gladly—or, in my translation, we delight in doing these things. See CD 3.2:265.

which is the only thing that really counts in this respect."[28] Just as Barth's theology in general dynamites pretensions to understanding God through "religion," so his theological anthropology dismisses any interpretation that blurs the basic form of humanity. Kegan's attentiveness to individuals within context—seeing who they are, listening to their story, desiring to help them, and genuinely caring for them—places him within the parameters established by this theological anthropology. Through his work, Kegan can see, hear, serve, and delight in Dylan. It is less clear that the senior staff encountered Dylan in quite the same way. Things like a standard contract limited the ability of the senior staff to really see, hear, serve, and delight in Dylan as they were forced to encounter him as an employee.

Furthermore, these four characteristics should guide our interpretations. In the instance of Dylan, the heuristic category "relationships" suggests itself given Kegan's understanding of meaning making, but also because there is a resonance with the relationality of Barth's anthropology. Inclusion and agency, community and autonomy—poles that Kegan uses to interpret and describe individuals like Dylan—are constantly present within the personalist-influenced anthropology that Barth articulates. Barth considers how we are both determined by God's covenant and thereby included in a relationship that we do not choose, and how we have real human agency within that relationship. We cannot experience humanity in its truest form outside of our neighbor, so all interpretations must account for this. This would more than likely rule out or at least moderate any real conversation between Barth and network structuralism or a social science reliant on variables.[29] At the same time, we are to see and hear the distinct individual, suggesting that the relationship between the particular and the universal will always play a role in understanding humans. Interpretations that reduce us to simple structures or atomized biological animals do not take proper guidance from the true humanity Barth presents. Within the limits set by true humanity, Barth's theological anthropology presents a positive direction by which we might proceed.

Although I previously noted that Barth changes keys in *CD* 3 when compared to *CD* 1 and 2, it is still true that Barth's theological anthropology grounds itself deeply within his theology and therefore can undergird an interpretation such as Kegan's.[30] There are a number of ways to understand how this anchoring happens, any of which are deeper than failing to give a justification for understanding or caring about Dylan. As already alluded to, Barth's anthropology roots itself in his christocentrism and its implications

---

28. *CD* 3.2:252.
29. See Smith, *What Is a Person?*, 220–316.
30. For a short summary of the change, see Jones, *Humanity*, 117–20.

for the creature in relation to the Creator within covenantal history. As God's covenantal partners, humans interact with God in a special and unique way. We depend on God for our being but still have real freedom and agency. God does not partner with a puppet, but it is also mistaken to believe that God partners with the autonomous modern self. Our agency finds both its freedom and limit within God's covenantal grace. Barth's anthropology is an articulation of how this covenantal relationship occurs within creation. Because Dylan is working in a Christian context, we might assume that other ways of understanding his position before God and the rest of humanity also warrant consideration. For instance, Dylan's existence is also grounded in Barth's understanding of sanctification, vocation, and mission. However, these other doctrines assume a different interaction between human and divine. Without specifying whether or not Barth is a universalist, it is clear that when he speaks of all of creation he means all humanity, Christian or not. The interpretation that Kegan puts forward assumes a foundation like this, that is, he assumes that all humans are created equal. It is therefore legitimate to say that grounding Kegan in Barth's theological anthropology rather than another doctrine, such as sanctification, offers a real foundation rather than an alien one. In the end, Barth limits, guides, and grounds a legitimate interpretation of human agency.

5. Swatting At Flies

A reader of an early version of this essay noted that I was swatting at flies throughout, and that this swatting distracted the reader. By this she meant that there were conversations going on in the background that popped up in a stand-alone piece like this but only tangentially. I hope that in reworking this piece since then my intentions have become clearer: while acknowledging that interdisciplinary methodology is necessary, practical theologians need to move on to the material contribution that Barth can make to our understanding of human and divine interaction; that developmental psychologist Robert Kegan challenges, interprets, and actualizes the phenomenon of human experience; that Karl Barth limits, guides, and grounds the actual phenomenon within a christocentric theological anthropology. By presenting the larger than life Dylan, I hope to have drawn the reader's attention away from abstractions to the particular reality of lived human experience within a theological framework. Investigating and interpreting this interaction of human understanding and divine action is—for me—one of the main purposes of practical theology.

The practical theological task would remain incomplete without some move toward pragmatic implications of this work. I have pointed to some implications within the body of the essay itself. For instance, Christian organizations would do well to structure their relationships so as to encourage growth, rather than locking participants into a particular stage of development. Senior staff could have engaged Dylan in a developmental manner, recognizing his full humanity as someone who sees, hears, serves, and delights in others but in a categorically different way than the senior staff do. In light of this interpretation, the senior staff would need to reconsider how they structure staff training, the employer-employee relationship as defined by the contract, and reasonable expectations for teenage counselors in relation to the overall mission of the camp. This is not to say that developmental psychology determines all actions of the senior staff. But it is to argue that because Dylan and his peers are human in seeing, hearing, serving, and delighting in others, and because they construe these relationships in particular ways dependent on their own developmental stage, senior staff have a responsibility to faithfully engage these young people with ministry that meets them as people.

These kinds of pragmatic actions may seem incongruous or inconsequential when compared to the deeper theological conclusions often associated with Barth. These two sentiments—that Barth has little to do with practical matters, or that those practical matters do not have a direct bearing on theological thought—have been flying around in the background of my thought and, admittedly, I have taken some awkward swipes at them. While it is true that a certain school of thought within practical theology uses Barth, there are larger portions that struggle to get past a perception that he never rises above a debilitating form of revelatory fideism.[31] Simply because Barth starts with revelation does not mean there is no place for fields of study that focus on human agency. Barth's theological anthropology is too rich to toss out despite early evaluations of his thought that led to the conclusion that his christological concentration leaves human agency out of the picture. Barth himself grants that other disciplines are "relevant, interesting, important and legitimate," and may go a long way to understanding human agency provided that we do not believe they are describing human reality *in toto*.[32] Since Kegan doesn't believe that his theories describe human reality *in toto*, it does not seem unreasonable for practical theology—in this case at least—to embrace Barth as an important and necessary part of its own ongoing interdisciplinary conversation.

31. Examples of those who use Barth are Anderson, *Shape*; Hunsinger, *Theology*; and Loder, *Logic*. For an example of one who dismisses Barth, see Browning, *Fundamental Practical Theology*.

32. CD 3.2:79.

The work that I have done here highlights the fact that the practical is not inconsequential to Barth's theological concerns. Writing against the backdrop of the Holocaust, it is clear that when Barth calls for a theological anthropology that recognizes the full humanity of others regardless of their ethnicity, age, or gender, he is making a theological statement with practical implications. We cannot confuse the fact that Barth starts his theology with God and God's own self-revelation with indifference to the lived experience of God's covenant partners. Developmental psychology will never serve as a source for theology, nor should it. At the same time, theologians could acknowledge materially in their own work that while Barth may give limits, guidance, and grounding for practical theology, he does not have all of the answers. For instance, Barth assumes an understanding of seeing, hearing, serving, and delighting largely located in the Intrapersonal. This implicit anthropology makes unreasonable demands of someone like Dylan unless reinterpreted by someone like Kegan. A child or a young person can still see, hear, serve, and delight, but they will not do so in the same ways as an adult. The practical can act as a critical filter through which we might appropriate the theology of someone like Barth. Systematic theologians do not need to do the work of practical theologians, but they also need to be aware that their thoughts can fund meaningful and significant action only if they consider the implications in lived reality.

For Kegan and Barth, Dylan matters. How he sees, hears, serves, and delights in the world is specific to his age but universal in its theological grounding. In the end, Kegan and Barth could both discuss Dylan and add significance to understanding him psychologically and theologically with the hope of guiding future actions. Neither needs to be afraid of the other, nor should we as systematic or practical theologians be afraid of having interdisciplinary discussion. Young people like Dylan depend on it.

Kegan and Barth

A Response to Bertrand

—By Katherine M. Douglass

BLAIR BERTRAND PROVIDES A thought-provoking essay exposing the challenge and fruitful benefit of interdisciplinary dialogue when considering real problems faced in ministry. In response, I will expand on Bertrand's criticism of Karl Barth's theological anthropology that I believe limits full humanity to those who have the developmental capacity to participate in relationships of equality and mutuality. Bertrand addresses this challenge through conversation with Robert Kegan, who offers a definition of humanity that includes people, such as Dylan, who are not yet developmentally adults but have the potential to be. I will push this further in order to consider the problems with Barth's theological anthropology when individuals lack the capacity to eventually attain Intrapersonal relationships. I believe Bertrand has a theological answer to this power differential within his essay in the notion of covenant.

As Bertrand shows, both Kegan and Barth give attention to the social dimension of what it means to be human. Kegan is concerned with the changing quality of social relationships as individuals mature and develop throughout a lifetime. Barth is concerned with the social dimension of humans as a uniquely defining characteristic of what it means to be human.

Bertrand poignantly identifies the intersection of tension between Kegan and Barth in his consideration of Dylan. He criticizes Barth's assumption that seeing, hearing, serving, and delighting happen only when individuals have reached the Intrapersonal stage of development. When individuals like Dylan have not yet reached the stage of Intrapersonal development and yet are still held to this demand, they often—predictably—fail. This failure is not one of ability, but rather of degree. While Dylan may not see, hear, serve, and delight to the same degree as an adult, he is still able to see, hear, serve, and delight. It is worthwhile to further consider the implications of Bertrand's criticism and the trajectory of Barth's theological anthropology for those who may be even more limited than Dylan in their ability to see, hear, serve, and delight in others.

As Bertrand implies, Dylan is—like any child or young person—not yet capable of seeing, hearing, serving, and delighting in the same way as an adult. This seemingly excludes him from Barth's theological anthropology because of his inability to participate in the kind of mutually responsive relationship that Barth claims to be definitive of authentically human relationships. Bertrand rightly suggests that through interaction with Kegan, Barth's theological anthropology might be expanded to include those with the future potential for such mutual seeing, hearing, serving, and delighting even if they are not presently capable.

Bertrand's underlying criticism is of the static modernist definition that Barth creates. Barth's theological anthropology is a beautifully written appeal to those living in Germany during the Third Reich to see, hear, serve, and delight in one another based not on religion or ethnicity, but rather on their common humanity. However, as Bertrand shows, when the attempt is made to universalize this theological anthropology, we run into those—like Dylan—who fall outside of this definition of humanity due to power differential, which in this instance is in the form of psychosocial development. Dylan is not an equal with the camp leaders developmentally or in job position. While Dylan does not currently have the intrapersonal skills necessary for the kind of relationship Barth defines, he will one day have the capacity.

My concern is for those who, unlike Dylan, may never have or have lost the capacity to be in the kind of seeing, hearing, serving, and delighting relationship Barth describes. I agree with Barth that being in authentic relationships is central to being human. There must be more to these relationships than mutuality, however, because not all individuals are able to engage in mutually acknowledging and responsive relationships.

The parable of the Good Samaritan (Luke 10) affirms the humanity of a man left for dead by the side of the road. He is unable to actively participate in a relationship with another but, even so, the treatment he receives from a stranger affirms his humanity. For some, relational participation is limited to passively *being* seen, *being* talked to, *being* served, and *being* delighted in despite their lack of ability to respond. I believe this further nuanced definition of intrapersonal relationships creates space to recognize the full humanity of infants and pre-verbal children, those in a coma or with Alzheimer's, as well as individuals with any condition that challenges their ability to respond to or contribute to relationships. In fact, it was most often the blind, the deaf, the "demon possessed," and children—those who were considered less than human in the first-century world—whom Jesus went to, treating them as fully human and thereby affirming their humanity. The relationality central to being human is upheld in these relationships, but further nuance allows for the inclusion and affirmation of individuals who might not otherwise fit into Barth's theological anthropology.

Perhaps a return to Bertrand's initial insights regarding covenant is helpful here. If Jesus is our model for the true nature of humanity, it is only logical that his embodiment of the concept of covenant might inform our social relationships. The power differential between the Creator and created or the Redeemer and the redeemed does not deter the more powerful from electing to be in a covenantal relationship with the less powerful. In a covenantal relationship with God we see and are seen, we hear and are heard, we serve and are served, and we delight in and are delighted in despite the gap in degree to which humanity might relate positively to God. In some, if not many, instances we are blind to God's presence, and yet God faithfully continues to see us. If we consider power in terms of age, race, gender, or developmental capacity rather than "God" versus "not-God," I believe the notion of covenant can further inform the kind of mutual relationships that

Barth believes define humanity. Aware of the difference in ability and power, we can enter into covenantal relationships with others.

It is not Dylan's equality in terms of power that allows him to see and to be seen by the leaders at the camp. Rather, it is the unspoken covenantal relationship between Dylan and the leaders that binds them to one another. While justice is served when Dylan and those attending the party are fired from their summer jobs, grace seems to be lacking. I am left wondering: Would it have been more powerful or transformative (or, dare I suggest, faithful) if the leaders at the camp had sought out a third way in response to Dylan's actions?

Kegan helps us understand the challenge Dylan faces in mutuality—he is in a different developmental stage than his leaders. Bertrand suggests that the camp leaders might have responded better had they been equipped with Kegan's framework. While I agree that this insight helps explain and address the challenge of a theological anthropology based on mutuality, it needs to go a step further to claim that we are covenantally bound to individuals like Dylan despite developmental differences. This binding means we must think creatively about our ministries and how our work is defined less by job contracts and more by the kind of loving accountability that God shows through God's covenant with humanity.

Exactly how this might have played out at camp could have taken a plethora of forms—and it may be that at the end of any one of these Dylan would have still been fired. It is worthwhile, however, to employ our imaginations to consider how an emphasis on a covenantal commitment to Dylan might have changed the outcome of this situation. Perhaps Dylan and the others could have been put on probation and asked to complete duties where they did not interact with campers. Through their service they could earn back the trust of the camp leaders. Perhaps Dylan could be invited to meet with one of the leaders with whom he had a prior relationship to talk through his choices and how they affected not only his job, but also his relationships. Perhaps Dylan's parents could have been invited to camp to talk about how they might all encourage the positive leadership qualities he has, while discussing the impact of his actions on the camp community. Perhaps the camp leaders and counselors could have come together with Dylan and the others who attended the party to plan a time of worship, confession, and reconciliation.

I look forward to hearing how Bertrand further elaborates on what seems to be a preliminary criticism of Barth studies in practical theology, as well as to engaging with his future contributions in this area of the field.

12

No Country for Old Man

Barth Calls the Coen Brothers

—By Jon Coutts

1.

THE PHONE RANG ONE and a half times and cut off. With a glance at the bedside, a bright red 4:37 invaded my bleary eyes. Two dog-eared paperbacks were lit up in the clock's glow.

One was a hot pink and heavily underlined part-volume of Karl Barth's *Doctrine of Reconciliation* (i.e., *CD* 4), the other a coolly bound edition of Cormac McCarthy's *No Country for Old Men*—picked up in my obsession for Joel and Ethan Coen's award winning film adaptation. For those who missed it, *No Country* is a story with three main characters (four if you count the state of Texas, which you should) and one devastating theme. There is Anton Chigurh, the villain; Llewelyn Moss, the cowboy who stumbles across his drug-money; and Ed Tom Bell, the sheriff who finds himself in pursuit of them both. The thematic motor that drives the story is that the bad guy wins. As such, the stories sitting so close on my nightstand could not stand further apart. And yet my dreams had been swirling with resonances between them, as if the novel was a sort of parable for Barth's depiction of the sin of sloth.[1]

Unable to fall back asleep, I picked up the phone. The beep said there was a message. I listened. It was some kind of telecommunications misconnection. You will not believe the conversation I overheard.

---

1. *CD* 4.2, §65.

It began with a ding—the kind you'd hear if you bumped a rotary telephone—followed by a voice in German, curt but relaxed:

"I saw your film last night, the one that won all the awards."[2]

"*No Country for Old Men?*" responded another voice. To my ear it sounded like one of the nihilists in *The Big Lebowski*. "Did you enjoy it?"

"Enjoy! What is to be enjoyed?" shrilled the first voice. "It leaves one with the palpable sense that evil is ultimate, that we are caught in the ebb and flow of the most capricious fate, that the best way forward is every man for himself!" I couldn't believe my ears. It was Barth.

"Granted, *enjoy* may not be the word," chuckled the second voice. "But what you are describing is certainly the lurking darkness of reality captured by the novel we were tapping into." Incredible—it was a Coen. It sounded like Joel, the eldest of the Minnesota-born brothers of film-noir's postmodern revival.

"Reality? If *enjoy* is not the word for it, then neither is *reality*," replied the first voice, continuing no less enigmatically: "It was like Ecclesiastes or Job without the final revelation. There may have been a little light on the silver screen, but on its own it is nothing but dark. The film curves in on itself."

"This sounds like more than a complaint about the lighting," responded Joel. "Hang on and let me get my brother on the line."

The younger Coen holds a philosophy degree from Princeton University, but Joel was not likely looking for conversational backup.[3] I recalled the interviews where the Coens seemed more interested in hearing responses to the film than defending a fixed meaning.[4] Sure enough, a moment later Ethan came on, exchanged pleasantries, and prodded for more:

"Joel tells me that your issue with *No Country* has something to do with the sustainability of the narrative?"

"I assure you my quibble is no mere literary one, but that is a very good way to put it. Your villain is evil personified, is he not?"

"We're not all that interested in evaluating Anton Chigurh, to be honest," said Ethan. "Clearly he's not the good guy, I'll concede that, but I don't even know that I'd describe him as evil. He's a little more complicated and elusive than that."[5]

"That sounds consistent. In the film, evil so eclipses every good that on its own logic there can be no talk of evil. Whatever the case, his is the

---

2. Among its numerous accolades, *No Country* won four Academy Awards, two Golden Globe Awards, and three British Film Academy Awards. The American Film Institute named it their 2007 Movie of the Year. See "Awards."

3. Flint, "Joel Coen, Ethan Coen," paragraph 6.

4. Edelstein, "Coen Heads."

5. Ethan Coen makes a similar point in Hogg, "Absurdity," paragraph 18.

shadow of death, and it encompasses all. Everyone is either trying to hold death at bay or use it to their own gain."

Joel rejoined: "That sounds like a fair way to characterize them doesn't it? Bell on the one hand and Chigurh on the other?"

"Yes. Sheriff and villain alike are ultimately submitted to their fate. The one ends up resigned to it, and the other squeezing the most from it. The rest of the characters are simply caught up in between. It is a startling depiction of what one might call the twin temptations of sloth. The alternatives are passive death and active death. The man in the middle, Moss, tries to beat them both and loses. He can't win."[6]

"We don't do a lot of sitcom endings," chimed in one of the Coens, "where a sentimental sense of basic goodness bubbles up to the surface in the closing scene."

Barth seemed taken aback. "That would be just as dangerous a representation of things! A placebo! Evil should not be treated as if it is nothing to be reckoned with. Nor should it be portrayed as nothing we could not reconcile if we applied ourselves."[7]

The Coens responded one after the other as if they'd had this conversation before: "Our films sometimes get labelled as naturalistic—the way Hollywood defines it—as if we are presenting a kind of depressing realism. We aren't proponents of anything so abstract. We are most interested in telling stories."

"Our films might be a recurring *exercise* in such naturalism, but I think their comedic element should tell you that there is more to it than that. We want our actors to *act as if* it's a true story, for the sake of the story."[8]

"And yet the film is provocative," Barth countered.

"Yes. Many people react strongly to it," came the response, "and that reaction tells us that we told the story well. If people weren't reactionary to the ending, then we would not have done our jobs."[9]

"At the same time," the other explained, "people might also just laugh at the film, and that's okay with us. What matters are the characters, the

---

6. See Barth's hamartiology, particularly when he describes sloth and the un-freedom of such an existence in *CD* 4.2:403–7 and 469–72. The sin of falsehood is similarly described in *CD* 4.3:254.

7. For a description of evil as objectively "nothing," see *CD* 4.3:178. For a description of evil as something to be reckoned with, see *CD* 4.1:407–13 and *CD* 4.3:434. For the intensity required of such reckoning, see *CD* 4.3:570.

8. This paraphrases the Coens regarding the film *A Serious Man*. See Adams, "Interview," question 13.

9. This paraphrases Josh Brolin, who plays Llewelyn Moss. See "Interview," question 13.

country, and the way they interact. You see the feet of the characters a lot. We are more interested in the particulars of people and where they come from."[10]

"And yet the villain, Chigurh, is ambiguous—an interloper. We do not know where he is coming from or where he is taking us. He is your new man." Barth seemed to be probing for something.[11]

"Yeah, I often say he's like the man who fell to earth," Joel said. "He's the thing that doesn't grow out of that landscape. So he is able to frighten on several levels."[12]

"He is an impossible possibility." Barth seemed to be thinking out loud.[13]

Ethan went with it: "Like the bit at the beginning of McCarthy's novel where the sheriff contemplates going any further. Right before the line in the film about putting one's soul at hazard he says: '*It aint just bein older . . . I think it is more like what you are willin to become.*'"[14]

"Yet the problem posed has all the force of a No and none of the force of a Yes," Barth said. "It remains a question mark."[15]

I remembered the scene where Chigurh is about to kill Carson Wells, the private detective who had so resolutely pursued him, and asks: "If the rule you follow brought you to this, of what use was the rule?" I wondered if Barth would see Chigurh as an exposure of the trajectory of the western hero, the dangerous "enticement" of the lone ranger into the "cavern of a fatherless and brotherless isolation."[16]

More of the film's question marks flooded through my mind as they spoke for the next few moments, from that ominous opening monologue to the deepening pathos of its denouement. Just when viewers are tempted by the comforting notion that the sheriff is simply past his prime, the posturing of the younger crime-fighter is quickly exposed as a brave but foolish mask for the fear of death. Just when viewers clamor for shafts of light in

---

10. See the points Joel Coen makes about filmmaking in Tropel, "Joel Coen," and Jacobs, "Joel and Ethan."

11. Barth describes evil as an alien interloper with nothing to contribute in *CD* 4.1:139.

12. This paraphrases a quotation in McFarland, "No Country," 171, which is quoted in Hirschberg, "Coen Brothers," paragraph 2.

13. On sin as an impossible possibility, see *CD* 4.2:495. On sin as a negative "fact," see *CD* 4.1:411.

14. McCarthy, *No Country*, 4.

15. On the mystery of sin without Christ's revelation, see *CD* 4.3:84, 369; *CD* 4.1:139, 360–61.

16. *CD* 4.3:664.

the darkness, the film takes that away too. A visibly injured Llewelyn Moss offers to buy a young man's coat and the man bargains with him over price. On the lookout for a Good Samaritan, later we get a boy on a bicycle arriving on the scene of Chigurh's car accident, willing to give the shirt off his back. But when Chigurh refuses to let him go unpaid, the boy immediately refuses to share with his friend. His gut reaction of self-giving spurred by the horror of the accident dissolves quickly into selfishness in the banality of day-to-day life.

It is as if the self-asserting principle is latent in even the innocent bystander, just waiting to emerge. Even the stereotypically "innocent" shop-owner has his fateful encounter with Chigurh. The more he is drawn in to the villain's game, the more the white lies of his cliché social avoidance strategies are drawn out of him. He too is told: "You've been putting it up your whole life but just didn't know it."

When I snapped out of my reverie, Ethan was agreeing: "Yeah, it is not about young or old. If anything it is a different take on the old west."[17]

"The guy in the white hat doesn't actually ride off into the sunset. It certainly challenges the myth of progress," Barth said. "This film could be seen as a wake-up call, except it has nothing to wake up to. The Yes is absent within which the No could have any meaning."[18]

I was reminded of something Barth had written and later looked it up. "In the modern novel there are not lacking portrayals which give us the impression that the author originally had in mind something like God's pardon of sinful man. But in fact they do not go beyond what is often a strikingly honest depiction of his vileness."[19]

"In the film, to be alive simply means to be not dead yet," Barth continued. "And the closing scenes follow the violence through to the bitter end, sucking the life right out of its viewers. It is a powerful piece, inasmuch as a vacuum can be said to have power."[20]

"But in the end it is not as if this is news," answered Ethan. "We see this in Bell's conversation with his uncle Ellis. The sheriffs have always known

---

17. Ethan Coen is quoted to this effect in Hirschberg, "Coen Brothers," paragraphs 1–2.

18. Barth would allow that the Holy Spirit might utilize things of this world in the awakening of persons to faith in Jesus Christ (and in consequent recognition of sin), but would insist that such awakening is discernible as Christian as opposed to being featureless. As such, the true awakening has not only force but content. See *CD* 4.1:762. Regarding the criteria for discerning the Word of God within "other words," see *CD* 4.3:126–30.

19. *CD* 4.1:594.

20. For Barth's description of evil as a vacuum, see *CD* 4.1:139, *CD* 4.2:421, and *CD* 4.3:84.

what was coming. Supposed to be shields from the worst reality, they feel like sieves."

It is quite a scene. Ellis says: "All the time you spend tryin to get back what's been took from ya, mores goin out the door. After a while, you just have to try and get a tourniquet on it."

"Yes," Barth continued the thought: "Their resignation is simply the tipping point in their struggle to keep it at bay, the crisis experience of the emergence of their ever-present futility. There is certainly no domesticating of the tensions of the human situation going on here. To be fair, I think this might be the closest thing to a point of contact with reality. But it is not. Reality has to present itself to us."[21]

There was a pregnant silence. Joel took the opportunity for a question. "What did you think of Carla Jean Moss and Loretta Bell—the women of the film?"

"They do appear to offer another word," Barth answered, "but this is no country for them, either. Mrs. Bell has a kind of serenity. That she has found a safe place of peace in the midst of the conflict may be to her credit, but we all know it is a false peace, which comes home to her on the increasingly despondent face of her man. She is simply ahead of him in her resignation to what is out there."[22]

"And Mrs. Moss?"

"She is the only one who will not play Chigurh's game. She will not submit to his gods of fate and chance, allowing him to avert responsibility for her death with his coin toss. She won't bow to his principles. She holds on to a shred of belief in something better—which she doesn't seem to know." After a pause Barth continued: "Of course, he wipes his shoes of *her* blood, too. Nonetheless, it is as if hers is the only death not fated, but chosen. She is the closest thing this film has to a Christ-figure."[23]

"But not really," offered one of the Coens.

"No." Barth took a breath and continued. There was no stopping him now. He sounded like he might start preaching. "The advertisement said 'there are no clean getaways,' but the film implies there are no getaways *at all*. And we have no reason to believe otherwise. There is no closing scene

---

21. For a description of the "frontier" that is the closest thing to a point of contact, see *CD* 4.2:475. On the falsehood of "domesticating" sin, see *CD* 4.3:437.

22. Barth adeptly perceives the problem of "false peace" among church people in *CD* 4.3:815. For his description of resignation as the passive side of slothful anxiety (or "care"), see *CD* 4.2:475.

23. Barth represents and proclaims Christ "as one who fell among thieves" in *CD* 4.3:106. He also argues that the cross was taken up as grateful obedience to a living command rather than as bitter fate in *CD* 4.2:604.

with Mrs. Moss having the last laugh. Why should there be? Her fate is the same as her husband's, and everything is tangled up. It is not even clear whether his biggest mistake is taking the money or taking water to a dying man, returning to the scene of the crime. As far as we know, these acts are of one and the same reality. It is the triumph of evil, except the categories by which it can be called that are not available. There is no Christ-figure, and no light to see what is darkness."

I listened to hear if Barth would take this opportunity now to proclaim the death and resurrection of Jesus Christ, whether he'd talk about the Nevertheless that answers the No, the No that is only known in the light of God's Yes. Was this all a set-up for Barth to present one Christ-figure, the Son of God, who came into the *far country*, knowingly took on flesh, and *overcame* it?[24] With baited breath I waited to hear him say "there is no more place for the old man" and "the day of the new has broken."[25]

But all I heard was a beep, as my messaging system reached its allowable time limit.

2.

Some may question the veracity of my story, insisting that either Barth or the Coen brothers would not have said these things in these ways. As even the tellers of true stories must, I take full responsibility for the words I have relayed. However, I find little here that the Coen brothers have not said with film or in interviews. I also find in this interaction with twenty-first century thought a Barth similar to the one who was so generous with both resonance and criticism in *Protestant Theology in the Nineteenth Century*.[26]

---

24. See "The Way of the Son of God into the Far Country," in *CD* 4.1:157–210.

25. *CD* 4.1:557.

26. This is not the place for a full-scale analysis of authorial or directorial intent in film interpretation. Although I have tried here to pay close attention to the perceivable purposes of the directors (as is implicit in the decision to make this Barth's conversation with the Coens rather than simply with the film itself), I take some licensed play-room from Joel Coen's own recognition that a film often takes on a life of its own once released. When asked about the inspiration behind the film *A Serious Man*, he said "it's always really hard to say. Personally we don't really know. The truth of it is you start to think back on it and you impose more order and rationality on it than actually occurred when you were thinking it out" (Jacobs, "Joel and Ethan"). In addition, while there may be some doubt as to whether Barth would ever mix theology and art like he does here, I take considerable support for this conversation's plausibility from Barth's comments on "Hyperion's Song of Fate" (quoted later), where he does almost exactly what I have him doing here. See *CD* 3.2:515–18.

What first struck me in this film was its staggering depiction of the banality and sheer force of evil. Feeling falsely placated by a chicken-soup-for-the-soul approach to Christianity, I have often felt the gospel more alive when portrayals have forced me to face the problem straight on, and wondered if we need these reminders that there are no clean getaways. I have heard it suggested that Barth's lofty Christology has its head too far in the clouds, glosses over the mess, or has little place for lament.[27] Could the Coens have something to say to Barth? Didn't Christ predict difficulty in the same breath as resurrection? Maybe films like this help bring us down to earth so our salt is forced to get in with the meat, potatoes, and gravy.

There may be something to this, but it has more to do with misreading Barth than raising a substantive criticism against him. By the time one reaches the closing volume of the *Church Dogmatics*, it is clear that Barth is no stranger to the human predicament. Sin amounts to nothing and evil is relegated to shadow, but the doctrine of sin is on every page—still there, but put in its place as a misshapen absurdity that futilely mocks the wholeness of life in Christ. The light of life does not blur but sharpens the assessment of darkness, giving a clear conception of the cross to be taken up.[28]

In fact, the more I listened to their voices, the more it was Barth that was speaking—to me. Could such literature and film be for me a veiled attempt at self-soothing sloth? As Augustine suggested in the third book of his *Confessions*, perhaps such theater affords me the opportunity to be a spectator rather than a victim, to stroke my own sense of pity without actually having to get my hands dirty with compassion, and to play the judge and jury rather than be the one standing in the dock. Wasn't even Mel Gibson's *The Passion of the Christ* an opportunity to serve emotional penance? Perhaps I go to the theater to wallow a little bit in the mess so that the relief of grace might feel wonderful to me again. Do we "need aesthetic experiences that impress upon us the horror" of evil?[29] Or is such theater like Mrs. Bell's cup of coffee—a coping strategy to replace the life-hazarding confrontation with evil that is called for and enabled by Christ?

On another note, since when do we *need* the darkness in order to perceive the light? Isn't it the other way around? What more must be said about our human condition once the Son of God has come into this far country

---

27. This was a point of some debate at a conference in 2010 following Brown's claims in this regard. See Brown, "In the Beginning."

28. See an example of this in "The Christian in Affliction," *CD* 4.3:614–47.

29. This quote is from a comment made by Chris E. W. Green during the 2010 Karl Barth Blog Conference (see "2010 KBBC"). I do not mean to single Green out, but he articulated well a view that stood behind much of my own preliminary reflection.

as the true human only to die unrecognized at the hands of humanity?[30] What depiction of evil (or real-life, modern-day tragedy for that matter) provides humanity a wake-up call exceeding that of the Christ event? And what is there to wake up to unless One died and rose again? Thought about in this way, the question may not be whether Barth has room for lament but whether the Coen films have room for laughter. How can even the ironic comedy of such dark films really be laughed at unless, as the revelation of Christ entails, there is no longer any reason to "pay serious respect" to such powers?[31] In one sense, Carla Jean Moss stands in for this disrespect by refusing to play by Chigurh's rules and insisting that she is not a victim of fate. But it seems to me that neither the Coens *nor Barth* would call Carla Jean a Christ-figure since the film presents her rather as a last tragic victim in the triumph of death.[32] She may represent one last gasp of the human spirit, but "why that should be considered anything but naïve is not something the film is willing to offer."[33] As Barth might put it, the church fails pivotally if in surrender to this sin-distorted "picture of the world in place of the reality it ranges itself with the world in its groping."[34]

Of course, Barth himself allowed that things of the world may be used by God as "other words" echoing the Word, "little lights" reflecting the Light, or "parables" of the kingdom of heaven invading earth.[35] Thus, beyond being a well-told and harrowing tale, this film might serve as a parable for the pervasiveness of sin and as a reminder that we are still in the old world.[36]

---

30. I am grateful to John Webster for making this part of Barth's outlook clear to me.

31. *CD* 4.3645.

32. David Tiessen made this case when he suggested that there may be reason to believe "something potentially redemptive is introduced" by the Coen brothers when after Carla Jean's challenge Chigurh "breaks his own general rule and leaves a trail by not killing the boys" who help him in the very next scene ("2010 KBBC"). Brad East's preliminary response and ensuing comments on this issue were compelling, and I look forward to seeing the extent to which he still considers Carla Jean as a Christ-figure.

33. This was my own comment in that discussion ("2010 KBBC"). She could still conceivably be seen as a Christ-figure, if the Coens wished to say that God was dead. They have not been vocal about such a meaning. In fact, as I elaborated in the original discussion, "the Coens seem to dangle Christ-figures in front of us on a number of occasions only to take them away. We have the 'Idiot' in the store, the boy giving up his shirt, Carson Wells, the Sheriff, the dream of the father at the end . . . all falling away and, as Halden Doerge put it, demanding 'that we think redemption in the most radical and truthful way possible.'"

34. *CD* 4.3:772.

35. See *CD* 4.3:110–25.

36. This resonates with what Chris E. W. Green wrote in response when pushed on his claim that we "*need* reminding" of evil's horror. He argued in clarification that films such as this "can function as story-in-service of the gospel" whether they were intended

Surely Barth would agree that denying the old life is not the same as living in denial. Living in the light does not entail blissful ignorance of the darkness. Naiveté is the last thing Barth peddles when he insists that creation is made new and the old is no longer definitive.[37] Attentive readers know that in the climactic pages of the *Church Dogmatics* Barth neither glosses over sin and death nor writes a slick piece of over-realized church propaganda. His emphasis is both on the content of the faith *and* on the fact that this side of full redemption it remains a *faith*. Faith in Christ's triumph should not breed triumphalism.

Nonetheless, it may be true that Barth's accuracy and emphasis on this point might be defended while his *rhythm* might not. Is it not the effect of his rhetoric that lamentation finds little room to breathe? At certain points in Barth's corpus it might do readers some good to put down the book, watch something like *No Country for Old Men*, and let it be the prayerful cry of solidarity with our broken world that Barth recommends.[38] With the Psalms of David and the tearful prayers of Gethsemane, we may not *need* Sheriff Bell's narrations. But certainly they help us give voice to our laments as they arise in the particularity of our place and time. When Jesus and his disciples were questioned for "eating and drinking" while John's disciples and the Pharisees fasted and prayed, Jesus answered that the "guests of the bridegroom" do not "fast while he is with them" (Luke 5:33–34 niv).[39] On two occasions in the *Church Dogmatics* Barth refers to this explicitly as the indication of a change that has taken place and is still effective among the followers of the risen Lord.[40] However, he neglects to make much of Jesus' follow-up comment, which signals a tension: "But the time will come when the bridegroom will be taken from them, and on that day they will fast" (Mark 2:20 niv).[41] Does Jesus refer only to the impending Holy Saturday, or does he also indicate the mixture of praise and lament that befits the time between his ascension and return? If Jesus called the mourners "blessed" and "comforted" (Matt 5:4 niv), there must be both "a time to weep *and* a time to laugh" (Eccl 3:4 niv, my emphasis) in Christian life and worship.[42]

---

that way or not ("2010 KBBC").

37. See *CD* 4.2:560, 570–71.

38. Saints are not removed from the world but have a new kind of "solidarity" with it. As "disturbed sinners," their solidarity with the world brings both "dispeace" and peace. See *CD* 4.2:496, 519, 524; and *CD* 4.3:91.

39. See also Mark 2:18–19, and Matthew 9:14–15.

40. See *CD* 3.2:471–72; and *CD* 4.4:82.

41. See also Matthew 9:15 and Luke 5:35.

42. I agree here with Halden Doerge's comment in the original blog conference discussion that this film "articulates, in the most profound way possible, the reality of

What happens if Christians overdose on praise and laughter while abandoning the world to its weeping? Laments are left hanging in the air, with no one to guide their address in both solidarity and hope. If we have to leave our troubles at the door in order to worship, we handcuff the risen Christ and perform acts of self-solace instead of praying for comfort. Where worshipers compete on the market of "spiritual inspiration," it is little wonder if one feels like the Coen brothers fill a lacuna.

Indeed, the lines that haunt the film's rolling credits still ring in my ears, as if unleashing the groans I mistakenly hid so long at church: "I always thought when I got older God would sort of come into my life in some way," the sheriff says to his uncle, concluding with what might be called a modern cry of dereliction: "but he didn't. I don't blame him." The defensive reaction is: Where is the church in the movie? But the movie asks: Where is the church in the world? Barth is no stranger to this question. He answers it in terms of faith, in terms of both the visible and invisible church, and in terms of the Christian duty to hope.[43] We hope that in the end God *will* come into each life in some way and respond to his call to take part in that eventuality here and now—even if our attempts are fraught with failure. The final scene has the sheriff replaying a hopeful dream that has his father riding ahead in the hard country "*fixin to make a fire out there in all that dark and all that cold.*" Then he wakes up, despondently unconvinced. The questions pile up and are left to linger, begging to be turned heavenward in lament: If it is the Holy Spirit who awakens to faith, and Jesus Christ came for all, then why are there those for whom waking equals dying?

"How long, O Lord, how long?"[44] It remains a good question.

Having said that, the question is better asked than cleverly evaded or reasoned away, and there is a difference between asking questions and expressing complaints. Furthermore, for Barth it is not only the answer but also the question that arises from the self-revelation of true God and true humanity in Jesus Christ.[45] Barth denied in debate with Emil Brunner that

---

Holy Saturday" ("2010 KBBC").

43. See *CD* 4.1:650–739. On universal hope as a "duty" but not an expectation, see *CD* 4.3:477–78.

44. To paraphrase Psalm 6:3.

45. This aligns well with Halden Doerge's suggestion that *No Country* could be read as a "narrative instantiation of Barth's argument against natural theology in response to Brunner" by its "refusal to find any . . . redemptive movement latent in the world" ("2010 KBBC"). Beck poignantly interprets *No Country* as a "theodicy failure" that does not undermine but *undergirds* true faith. Rightly reckoning Sheriff Bell's problem as an epistemological one, Beck suggests that the film gives "three options in living with a failed theodicy": "Bell's *nostalgia*," "Ellis' *stoicism*," and "Carla Jean's *Sisyphian scorn*." A fourth option is Christian faith, but as such this faith excludes the provision of a

anyone can have what he calls "a sinless knowledge of sin, the capacity to do on earth subjectively, *per analogiam*, what God does in heaven *per essentiam*." He insisted that without Christ no one is ultimately able "to sit in judgment on human existence, to inform oneself concerning oneself, to know oneself to be punished with despair, to destroy the fictions of *Weltanschauungen*, [or] to unmask idols."[46] This is the voice I heard on the phone.

I realize that the voice I heard sounds more willing to engage with the Coen brothers than some hearers of his *Nein* to Brunner might find believable. Thus I leave my dreams and reflections aside and conclude with some words from Barth's *Doctrine of Creation*, where he interacts with "Hyperion's Song of Fate" by Friedrich Hölderlin. The poem concludes:

> Harried by pain,
> We grope and fall
> Blindly from hour to hour.
> Like water dashed
> From cliff to cliff,
> In lifelong insecurity.[47]/

Finding in this a "pious song" of fate that "eschews all cheap and easy consolation," Barth proceeds to put such a depiction in the light of the incarnation of the Son of God:

> Jesus is not only God and therefore different from us, but also man and therefore like us ... Hence we cannot escape the contrast by pleading His absolute dissimilarity. Nor can the painful contrast between Him and us be the last word on the subject ... The monstrous nature of this situation may perhaps be overlooked or forgotten, but once seen and remembered, it cannot be denied ... We all run away from this picture. We would all prefer it otherwise ... [But] when we prefer not to look or think, trusting that we can find help in a resolute "as if," what is hidden beneath the surface is definitely something abnormal and

---

"perfect theodicy," says Beck. The film does not include this option, but it does viewers a better service by leaving it out than by offering solace in one of the other options. See Beck, "Theodicy." For my part, I think there is still room to give a Christian answer to the problem of evil, even if it remains in the realm of faith. Though Feuerbach exposed *promeity* as too often a thinly veiled form of "self-interest disguised as virtue," it did not for Barth prevent the possibility that God could be "for us" despite us. In fact he refuses to answer Feuerbach *via* Feuerbach. The question of human need does not create our Christ, but arises from confrontation with his self-revelation. See Feuerbach, *Essence of Faith*, 94–117 and *CD* 4.3:72–86.

46. Brunner and Barth, *Natural Theology*, 121; see also ibid., 56, 82.
47. Quoted as translated in *CD* 3.2:515; see Hölderlin, *Selected Poems*, 25–26.

> unnatural: not an inevitability which we can calmly recognise and accept; but a contradiction in face of which we are powerless, yet which we try to escape by hook or by crook, even by putting it right out of our minds . . . What we have been describing is sinful man in time . . . who has to pay for his rebellion against God by living in contradiction with himself, in contradiction with his God-given nature.[48]

Thus far we can hear in Barth's response to Hölderlin a good deal of resonance with the presentation of Chigurh as some kind of incomprehensible contradiction. But Barth goes further, and we should hear in this a criticism of our attempts to "find God" in such films rather than accepting them as they are and finding their veracity lit up by Christ. After all, just like Hölderlin's song, the sobering effect of the Coens' film wears off.

> And the real reason why we cannot accept it calmly, or gloss it over, or forget it, or effectively deny it, is that man is not left to his own devices in this contradiction, but that in the existence of the man Jesus with His very different being in time a divine protest is made against his perverted and disturbed reality . . . God did not undertake to recognise and accept our monstrous being in time . . . [but] is determined to vindicate and protect his right as Creator and ours as His creatures in face of the monstrous perversion and corruption in which we exist. Because this protest is made, we may look our situation in the face and either handle it with metaphysical profundity or hymn it as our fate, or we may refuse to look it in the face, either glossing it over or simply living on in spite of it, but we cannot escape its monstrous abnormality or accommodate ourselves to it . . . [T]he being of Jesus in time has this power to unmask and sober man . . . because the monstrosity of general human being in time is overcome in Him.[49]

---

48. *CD* 3.2:515–17. As if addressing modern cinema *via* Greek mythology, Barth says that in the persistence of our situation "we should have to resign ourselves to our fate, not hymning it like Hyperion but defying it like Prometheus." I take this excursus as the archetype for Barth's side of the conversation.

49. *CD* 3.2:517–18.

A Response to Jon Coutts on Barth and the Coen Brothers

—By Brad East

HAVING READ THE BOOK in advance, and knowing well the tonal parabola of the Coens's filmography, it was with hesitant openness that I came to the cinematic adaptation of Cormac McCarthy's *No Country for Old Men*. What I discovered was, indeed, an impossible possibility: an adaptation both faithful to its source and enriched by other concerns, a work of undeniable literary consonance, stretched taut with a dissonance peculiar to the visual medium.

Thus it was with gratitude and fitting surprise that I received Jon Coutts's fortuitous eavesdropping report. Like the theater lights dimming in November of 2007, I did not know exactly what to expect—but what a match! A lively conversation overheard between the brothers Coen—that most inscrutably postmodern directing duo—and the prophet of doom to modernity himself, Karl Barth. We are lucky to be in the hands of such a gifted storyteller (ahem, transcriber) as well as interpreter of film, narrative, and theology alike.

In response to the given transcription, I want to take up one particular set of questions raised by Barth and Coutts in relation to both the Coens and McCarthy. However, as something of a preemptive methodological apology, let me comment briefly on my approach to putting these thinkers, and their texts of disparate mediums and genres, into interpretive conversation.

To put it plainly, I am wholly uninterested in interrogating any piece of art, much less those under discussion here, until it relents and gives up the good confession. "Finding" (i.e., arbitrarily inserting) God or the gospel in random texts that, under unprejudiced scrutiny, bear no such trace is not only injurious to the texts and their authors but theologically unhelpful in every respect. The Coen brothers and Cormac McCarthy are, fortunately for us, substantive enough artists to warrant thinking their thoughts after them by way of their creations, and to justify letting those shared thoughts be tinged with the theological. But let it be clear: when I offer a reading of these below, when I mingle their thoughts with Barth's thoughts (by way of my own thoughts), when I probe the texts's surface for depth and substance beneath the immediately apprehensible—I am openly and happily *not* proposing ideas about supposed (theologically Christian!) intentions in the individuals Joel, Ethan, or Cormac. Rather, and more broadly, I am stepping into the worlds of meaning they offer, following their narrative threads and character arcs, asking after the *vision* on display, the way in which it *situates us*. And in the light of Christ, I am wondering about the truths that catch us, the falsehoods that tempt us, the issues that indict us, and the parables that remind us.

In other words: a study in contrast, but also in concord, between lights in the darkness—revealed on the one hand, projected on the other.

And with that, let us begin properly—at the end.

In the film's closing scene, as Coutts notes, Sheriff Ed Tom Bell tells his wife about a dream he had the night before, a dream in which there seem to be hints and sparks of hope, of light and warmth just ahead in the darkness, until the final words are spoken: "And then I woke up." As it is portrayed on the screen, Coutts is right to describe the Sheriff as "despondently unconvinced."

Though this final scene is taken from the book's closing page almost word for word,[50] the impact of the ending in the book is less straightforwardly ominous, indeed more hopeful, in the context of the whole. In the film, it seems that Sheriff Bell's journey—climaxing in and encapsulated by this breakfast table soliloquy with his wife—consists of what we might call *one long awakening from hope to nihilism*. There simply were no good old days, malice and violence cannot be explained, and the vision of a father riding ahead to prepare the way is an illusion. In the book, on the other hand, Ed Tom's final italicized reflection—in this case, the last of many intimate asides and confessions shared with seemingly none but the reader—serves rather as a prophetic coda to the chaos come before: namely, that *such hope, even in a dream, speaks of a reality deeper than and untouched by ten thousand Chigurhs*. It will not seem so, whisper the wisps of flame sheltered in an ancient horn on a cold mountain pass, but all is not lost.

This latter is obviously one of many possible readings, and perhaps unlikely. The Coens's adaptation may get the nihilistic final note just right. As Daniel Oudshoorn suggests, following Amy Hungerford's interpretation of *Blood Meridian*, the façade of Ed Tom's homey, old-timer reflections could be McCarthy's subtle luring of the reader into a warm, nostalgic trustfulness, only for the curtain to be raised and absolutely nothing—literally, *nihil*—unveiled as the "moral" center of the cosmos.[51] This interpre-

---

50. See McCarthy, *No Country*, 309. In the book, Ed Tom shares the dreams not with his wife but with the reader, having experienced them not the previous night—that is, after the events of the book—but many years prior, shortly after his father died.

51. See Dan Oudshoorn's comment on Doerge, "Barth." Note well the subsequent conversation between us on this question, especially the fascinating textual evidence he

tation commends itself on a number of grounds, and it certainly applies to the Coens's film. But I demur—I lay both readings side-by-side for others to decide.

Returning to the two visions, opposed as they are in slight but important ways, it seems as if Barth's objections to the Coens—as reported by Coutts—find a sort of hearing in McCarthy. But surely Barth would go still further. Yes, there is Something deeper than cold personified Fate, impervious to the indiscriminate scythe of Chigurh's coin tossed unblinkingly in the air. But were we to stop there, what kind of word or hope would that ephemeral "Something" be *pro nobis*—that is, *for us*?[52] Is an old man's half-remembered dream in a country now unfit for old men's visions anything but wishful thinking, human grasping for that which might (but ultimately will not) stem the unalterable tide of time and death?

For Barth, and thus for the church, the banal ferocity of Chigurh is neither an awakening jolt[53] nor even a subordinate but presently victorious power. It is, finally, no power at all. Christians confess in the face of *das Nichtige*—indeed, before such a human face as we see in Chigurh—that it is not Fate or Death or Violence or Chance that has swept through this world and carries the final say: it is instead the insurmountable and unaccountable Nevertheless, enfleshed, entombed, and enthroned. God "Himself has become a creature in Jesus Christ. And therefore He has set Himself in opposition to nothingness, and in this opposition was and is the Victor."[54] This divine victory "is the existential determination given to the oppressed Christian by the resurrection of Christ," that "[n]o one and nothing can be

---

adduces from elsewhere in McCarthy's corpus (in this case, The Border Trilogy) regarding moral order and dumb luck. For summaries and videos of Hungerford's lectures, see "Blood Meridian."

52. I am aware of the traditional (and thus Coutts's) use of *promeity*, but following the creed and its right emphasis on the communal character of salvation, I prefer *pronobisity*. Theology's barbarisms know no bounds.

53. Some discussion following the original version of Coutts's piece and my response focused on the extent to which we "need" art like *No Country* in order to remind us of the world's horrors. As I agree in full with Coutts's suitably Barthian (i.e., christocentric) answer, I will only add that it is a serious problem if and when "we" stand in "need" of such a reminder at all. Though the world rendered by this film and others like it may have the (sometimes necessary) secondary effect of "waking us up," the reason it can do this in the first place is that it is fulfilling its primary purpose as art: namely, to tell the truth. *That* is why we need—or rather, are authorized in creating—art. The result of our encounters with the truth thus told will surely depend on variables of context and personal experience.

54. *CD* 3.3:290.

against us, or do us true and serious harm, or finally overcome us—not even the last thing which may threaten, namely, death."[55]

Coutts's Barth is not far from the mark, then, in identifying Carla Jean Moss as the film's nearest approximation to a Christ-figure. To be sure, there is no savior in *No Country for Old Men*, print or film. Redemption is not just over the horizon if we can only be patient. There is perhaps a vaguely perceptible Something; more likely just Nothing. In either case, it is indeed fitting to recognize this depiction as a sort of Holy Saturday writ large.[56] Except here Sunday isn't coming: the restless Sabbath darkness of death's creeping, invariable victories covers the country entire. Sheer night engulfs, reducing people to nostalgia for the light,[57] or merely dreams thereof.

Carla Jean may nonetheless serve as an *indicator*—the frail finger of a gesturing witness—of another way, of something amiss in Saturday's gloom. That "there are no getaways," per the film's tagline, remains as true in the light of Christ as before—if by "getaway" we mean getting away from death's reach. But Carla Jean does not avoid death's reach in the person of Chigurh. She does not turn and run. Rather, she opens the door, takes sight of his intrusion, approaches him directly, and speaks the truth to his face. By not calling the coin toss she refuses to play his game, thereby holding him

---

55. CD 4.3:645.

56. Coutts rightly draws on Halden Doerge's wonderful insight in this regard. In "Barth," Doerge writes: "Precisely by eliminating redemption from the film, the Coen brothers have demanded that we think redemption in the most radical and truthful way possible—if we can bear to do so, wagering on a word of hope that hangs in the air and defies us the moral and religious certainty we so deeply crave." Note that Doerge interprets "no country" in a different way than I do below. Rather than what I take to be the force of the original source of the phrase in Yeats's poem, he—not without intertextual warrant—takes "no country" to be descriptive: the country of the void, the *nihil*, the nothing. And this country, the no-country, is that into which nothing *but* an irruption from the outside, of the radically new in Christ, can bring redemption. The direction I take with the phrase below is, however, offered in harmony with his reading rather than in contradistinction to it, only from another perspective. Finally, I am grateful to Doerge for helping me to think through the way in which Carla Jean is less a Christ-figure and more a witness, literally a *martyr*, in the film.

57. I take this phrase from the title of the 2010 Chilean documentary, *Nostalgia de la luz*.

accountable for his action.⁵⁸ In this way her witness⁵⁹ may represent for us Barth's vision of conversion as, however ironically phrased, "the new life of a new man."⁶⁰ If "the life of the old man" is unconverted life, and therefore "a life which is encircled by death," then "the axis which makes [the life of the new man]"—in this case, that of Carla Jean—"a movement in conversion is the reality which is . . . revealed as the truth, that God is for him and therefore he is for God."⁶¹

On this Barthian reading, Carla Jean's strength, truthfulness, and witness before death testify to a power Chigurh can see only as impotent or futile, but is nevertheless the only real power there is.⁶² (Might this would-

---

58. There are important differences in this scene as portrayed in the book compared to the film (McCarthy, *No Country*, 253–60). Carla Jean has just returned from burying her mother, and it is evening. From the moment she enters the room she is unsure of herself, and McCarthy repeatedly describes her as "sobbing" (257–59). Her conversation with Chigurh is much more extended, and in some ways more explicitly theological, than it is in the film. Regarding Chigurh's so-called promise to Llewelyn that he would kill Carla Jean, she says: "You dont owe nothin to dead people." To which Chigurh responds a few lines later, "Yes. But my word is not dead. Nothing can change that" (255). When Carla Jean answers that *he* could change it, he says, "I dont think so. Even a nonbeliever might find it useful to model himself after God. Very useful, in fact" (256). When he flips the coin, moreover, instead of refusing to call it, she calls heads— and it's tails. About his willingness to give her this apparent out in light of the inevitability of the thing, Chigurh comments, "Yet even though I could have told you how all of this would end I thought it not too much to ask that you have a final glimpse of hope in the world to lift your heart before the shroud drops, the darkness. Do you see?" (259). Finally, to her insistence that he doesn't have to kill her, he replies, "You're asking that I make myself vulnerable and that I can never do. I have only one way to live. It doesnt allow for special cases. A coin toss perhaps. In this case to small purpose. Most people dont believe that there can be such a person. You can see what a problem that must be for them. How to prevail over that which you refuse to acknowledge the existence of. Do you understand? . . . You're asking that I second say the world" (259–60).

59. A worthwhile question to pursue elsewhere would be why the Coens, who wrote the adapted screenplay and otherwise stuck as closely as possible to McCarthy's original text, so altered the tenor of Carla Jean's confrontation with Chigurh. My own theory is that they really are presenting her as something of an enigma and exception to Chigurh's (fatal) encounters so far in the film—all of which are with men. The Coens's odd brand of feminism is thus worth including in this discussion. Consider, for example, the various roles of Frances McDormand, Joel Coen's wife, in their filmography (especially *Fargo*), as well as those of Holly Hunter in *Raising Arizona*, Irma P. Hall in *The Ladykillers*, and Hailee Steinfeld in *True Grit* (2010). I will leave it there for now as more on this question belongs to a different essay altogether.

60. *CD* 4.2:560.

61. *CD* 4.2:560–61.

62. See *CD* 1.2:112: "The man who has to fight and despise the world is the one to whom it still means something, whom it can still tempt and attack . . . [T]he man who hears the New Testament witness . . . is not summoned to battle with, or contempt for, the world, but to belief and awareness that this world is a past world in the death

be power, faced with this would-be weakness, be moved also to question the truth he previously thought he grasped?) True, as Coutts's Barth notes, in "her blood too" does Chigurh wipe his boots (or wash his hands). But this supposedly unstoppable force is rendered no less subject, no less brittle and bloody, when the straight line of a station wagon cuts across his circle of death. The path of such a man "also involves movement," but without the axis of resurrection he "moves straight ahead, and this means straight ahead to the descent—the plunge—to death."[63]

Having said this—while Carla Jean may represent the converted life, may bear witness to an Other whom *we*, the believing audience, know—it is clear that, as presented on the screen and the page, *she* does not know it. Hers is not in any apparent way "the life of the new man." Her witness, we might say, belongs a day earlier in this abbreviated Triduum: a Good Friday martyr without hope for Sunday. She points away from herself, hints of another possibility—another country?—yet dies unceremoniously and alone. Perhaps in this Easterless world there isn't a place for someone like her.

"That is no country for old men," says Yeats.[64] For McCarthy, "that country" is a post-Vietnam morass of inexplicable violence, however dimly lit by hope; for the Coens, "that country" is here, now, always our world in all its dark absurdity and deathly happenstance.

But which is no country, per Coutts's apt title, for *old man*? Before answering, it is important to note that Coutts's question is not only christological, whether relating to issues of theodicy ("Must suffering and death imply a godforsaken world?"[65]) or of soteriology ("What is salvation if it is complicit in the present mess and indefinitely deferred?"[66]). It is also eccle-

---

of Christ, and that its gods and idols have ceased to wield any power. If Christ really fought the fight with the old world and if man already lives with Him in faith in the new, his only business, his only fight is to acknowledge and confirm that the fight in question has already been fought."

63. *CD* 4.2:560.

64. See Yeats, *Collected Poems*, 193–94. The poetry of R. S. Thomas—particularly in his recurring image of the world's darkness as the shadow of God, as well as the constant dialectic of divine absence and presence—would make for a fruitful dialogue partner in the present discussion. See, e.g., Thomas, *Collected Later Poems*, 105, 116 ("a presence illimitable / as its absence"), 119, 156, 331.

65. Though without calling forth the entire book's argument, this question and its relation to Barth recalls Hauerwas's claim that "Karl Barth is the great natural theologian of the Gifford Lectures," so long as it is understood "that natural theology is the attempt to witness to the nongodforsakenness of the world even under the conditions of sin." See Hauerwas, *With the Grain*, 20.

66. Coutts is right to point to Richard Beck's extraordinary reflections on *No Country* as "a world of a failed theodicy," which is, for just that reason, "the only kind of world where true faith and virtue can exist." See Beck, "Theodicy."

siological. And here is where the Easter gospel must give an answer, for Holy Saturday—on whose precipice Ed Tom's final words place us—is not the end of the paschal mystery. Sunday comes. The tomb is emptied. The crucified is risen. The journey to the far country, though full of sorrows, ends in transfigured joy. The old man, the old self, is dead and gone, taken from the cross and placed in the ground, forever. As Coutts suggests, Barth has it just right: "There is no place for the new man alongside the old. He can only crowd him out and replace him. He can only have him behind him. His day can break only when the day of this other is over." More succinctly, "there is no more place for the old man," for "the day of the new has broken."[67]

Moreover, something of this newness and life has been given, granted to the church for the sake of the world that is passing—a glimpse of the new country in the midst of the old. However we parse this delicate subject, ripe for the only fights peace-loving theologians are wont to have, these two commitments cannot be elided: We *are* on this side of Sunday, and though Easter's consummation tarries, its victory lives on however imperfectly, however unpossessed, in the community of the Risen One. Put negatively, the Holy Saturday of *No Country for Old Men* is not the only word about the world, even if it is a partially true one. For those in need of the reminder, let Ed Tom's despair resituate them in the nakedness of expectancy, in the unassuming hope that is the condition of hearing Easter's good news. But there are also those who already know this stance in life, who recognize Chigurh as that ever-present threat encountered every day in the slog of making ends meet, of keeping faith faced with death, of staying alive without losing hope. For them, the sunlessness of Saturday is assumed. They need Sunday's resurrection light.

Two worlds, two kingdoms, two countries do battle from cross, through darkness, to light on that holy weekend. Yeats providing the template, the brothers Coen and Cormac McCarthy have provided their respective (post)modern twists. Which, then, for Karl Barth, is no country for "the old man"? According to the Swiss master, the gospel answers concretely: it is "that country" which welcomes the disposed and dispossessed, which blesses the mighty meek, which reverses in a word the verdicts of Carla Jeans and Galileans. For with the new man—with the new *human*—is a new country. A country whose No turns out, at the last, to be Yes.[68]

---

67. *CD* 4.1:557. Here is the larger passage: "The fact that there is no more place for the old man, that he has been put to death and has perished, shows itself to be true and actual in the fact that he is replaced by the new, that the day of the new has broken, that Jesus Christ has been made the Victor in His resurrection from the dead. Jesus Christ lives as the risen One, as the bearer of the right which God has given to man, as the recipient of His grace, completing the justification of man by His receiving of it."

68. See *CD* 1.2:111–12: The "No" of the New Testament "is a No which cannot be

---

ignored or contradicted, a divine No which reposes upon the divine Yes of revelation, because, in virtue of what happened at Easter, the passion in which it takes its rise is the passion of the only-begotten Son of God, full of grace and truth. It is because all things are become new, and for no other reason, that the old is done away."

Afterword

The Future of Conversing with Barth

—By David W. Congdon

THE CONVERSATION WITH BARTH is still in its infancy. Despite (or perhaps because of) the fact that we are closing in on a century since the publication of *Der Römerbrief*, we are only just now seeing the creative possibilities in Barth scholarship. There are various reasons for this. Besides the sheer volume of his writings, there is the challenge posed by the diverse and complicated history of his reception. For many decades the academic dialogue about Barth focused primarily around the flash points of twentieth-century theology (e.g., "liberal theology," "faith and history," or postliberalism) and often labored under serious misunderstandings (e.g., Barth as neoorthodox, as lacking an account of human agency, or as lacking resources for a theology of culture). Certain confessional and ecclesial communities have had their own barriers to understanding Barth. For example, North American evangelicals received Barth initially through the myopic lens of Cornelius Van Til, and the still-ongoing "battle for the Bible" ends up missing the scriptural forest for the inerrantist trees. Roman Catholics, for their part, have to deal with Barth's rejection of sacramentalism and the *analogia entis*—to name just two issues of theological conflict—in addition to dealing with the ambiguous legacy of Hans Urs von Balthasar within Catholic theology. The point in raising these examples is simply to indicate how difficult it has been to engage in a truly meaningful conversation with Barth.

The essays gathered in this volume signal the promise of a new generation of Barth scholars. A new generation, of course, does not guarantee superior scholarship, nor is it ever free from its own biases and interpretive blind-spots. But it does offer original vantage points, different angles of approach, fresh contextual concerns, and new dialogue partners. Not all of the dialogue partners in this book are new. Some, like Schleiermacher, are old friends. But the conversations are framed in new ways that will hopefully shed fresh light on Barth's enduring significance for contemporary theological reflection.[69]

The purpose of this afterword is threefold. First, I will discuss additional conversations with Barth that we as the editors hope to see others take up in the future. Second, I will identify some of the most significant barriers in the current theological scene, primarily within North America, to a responsible hearing of Barth's theology. Third, I will offer a constructive clarification of three key aspects of his theology—its dialectical character, its understanding of metaphysics, and its basis in a revised supralapsarianism—to aid future conversations with his life and legacy.

Future Conversations

Volumes of this nature are often notable more for what they leave out than what they contain, and this book is no different. Missing are conversations with the reformers—especially Calvin and Luther[70]—as well as conversations with prominent contemporary theologians like Jürgen Moltmann, Wolfhart Pannenberg, and T. F. Torrance. There are many engagements with Barth's theology that we wish could be included here but that we hope others will take up in the years ahead. We can subdivide these as: (a) Barth and patristic theology, (b) Barth and non-European theology, and (c) Barth and contemporary continental philosophy.

Barth and patristic theology

It is obvious that this volume looks at Barth within the context of modernity. The earliest figure represented here is John Wesley. Unfortunately, this leaves unaddressed the scholarly lacuna regarding Barth's relation to

---

69. Especially distinctive about the new generation of Barth scholarship is the relative absence of the old anxieties. There are no illusions about Barth's indebtedness to German idealism, and no attempts to claim that Barth's theology is somehow purely exegetical and free from all extratheological presuppositions. The postliberal concern about the threat of extratextuality is noticeably lacking. Additionally, the new generation has little interest in preserving Barth's orthodoxy or in making him ecumenically attractive. There is less anxiety about emphasizing and developing some of Barth's more radical insights, especially with respect to the doctrine of election. There is also less anxiety about criticizing Barth, particularly on matters related to philosophy and politics.

70. For some aid in conversations between Barth and these two reformers, see Elwood, "Getting Calvin Right," 63–80; and Hunsinger, "What Karl Barth Learned," 279–304.

the church fathers. For a theologian who commented so extensively on the ancient doctors of the church, it is remarkable how little has been written on the topic. Most of the attention, not surprisingly, focuses on Augustine and Thomas Aquinas, with occasional mentions of Athanasius here and Gregory of Nyssa (or Nazianzus) there. But there are very few sustained treatments, especially outside of the major figures, and what has been written is very limited in its scope. The focus tends to be on the doctrines and texts that Barth explicitly mentions (e.g., the *anhypostasia-enhypostasia* doctrine, Augustine's *vestigia trinitatis*, or Thomas's doctrine of analogy). The implicit connections and indirect influences have received very little attention.

One of the more interesting possible conversations would be with Maximus Confessor. The work of Maximus is starting to receive a wider audience, and his work reveals a number of fascinating points of contact with Barth's theology, particularly in the area of christology. Maximus's understanding of Christ as the Second Adam whose obedience to the Father acquires redemption for the cosmos anticipates themes that are central to Barth's christology as well. A comparative analysis of their respective treatments of Gethsemane could make for a fascinating case study in the relation between Barth and patristic theology.[71]

Barth and non-European theology

Barth has long enjoyed a strong global reputation. As a theologian writing expressly against the legacy of Christendom, he often finds more receptive ears outside of the European context within which he worked. He was influential among certain Japanese philosophers and theologians in the mid-twentieth century, for instance, having the philosophical theologian Katsumi Takizawa as one of his more notable students.[72] His *Die kirchliche Dogmatik* is presently being translated into Korean, in addition to Brazilian Portuguese.[73] As global Christianity continues to move South and East,

---

71. Jones has already initiated this conversation in his excellent treatment of Christ's humanity in Barth's *Church Dogmatics*. See Jones, *Humanity of Christ*, 41, 234, 242. He notes, for instance, that Barth "thinks about Christ's human volition with an intensity reminiscent of Maximus Confessor" (41), and with respect to the historical antecedents to Barth's treatment of Gethsemane, he suggests that "archival work on Barth's knowledge of Maximus would be important here" (242).

72. See Kim, "Proclaiming Jesus," 68–80, esp. 74–76. Cf. Takizawa, "Überwindung," 127–71; Takizawa, *Karu Baruto*.

73. Since 1985, portions of the *KD* have been translated into Italian, Russian, Hungarian, Romanian, and Korean. Thanks to Marianne Stauffacher of TVZ for this information.

the theological conversations will necessarily change. New contexts, new dialogue partners, and new problems will demand ever new reflection on the present meaning of the gospel. Dietrich Bonhoeffer's famous question, "Who is Jesus Christ for us today?" will need to be asked again and again. It is within this changing global situation that we can expect Barth to find receptive ears and can expect the conversation about Barth to be invigorated with fresh perspectives. It was never Barth's aim to provide a Christian worldview capable of answering theological problems in advance with a timeless system. On the contrary, he wrote in firm opposition to precisely such a notion of theology. His dogmatics is never "dogmatic," in the pejorative sense of the word. What Barth provides, by contrast, is a way of thinking theologically about God in obedience to Scripture that gives full attention and respect to the particularities of one's sociohistorical location.

With that in mind, future engagements with Barth ought to bring him into conversation with theologians outside of the Euro-American West that presently dominates the academy. I am thinking here of dialogues between Barth and African theologians like John Mbiti, Kwesi Dickson, Lamin Sanneh, Tinyiko Maluleke, and Engelbert Mveng; or between Barth and the *Minjung* theology of South Korea; or between Barth and the mujerista theology of someone like Ada María Isasi-Díaz that seeks a liberative praxis for Latina women. These are just a few examples. Conversations along these lines have rarely taken place, due in large part to the assumption that the two sides diverge so sharply that a productive dialogue is not possible. Barthian theology and contextual theology tend to be construed as theological antipodes. This is an unfortunate situation, and the future of Barth's theology depends on overcoming these kinds of misunderstandings. Important methodological differences notwithstanding, there are unexplored possibilities here for mutual enrichment and ecumenical understanding that could have immense implications for the mission of the church in the twenty-first century.

One final recommendation: sustained attention ought to be given to the way Barthian theology can help inform and learn from the work in intercultural theology. The field of intercultural theology and hermeneutics—whose key proponents include *inter alia* Walter Hollenweger, Theo Sundermeier, Volker Küster, Werner Ustorf, and Robert Schreiter—raises crucial questions about the very nature of theological speech. While intercultural theology is still largely carried out in Euro-American contexts, it does so as a radical disruption of western cultural hegemony, seeking to make hermeneutical understanding of the cultural other determinative of all theological discourse. Barth is not viewed positively by participants in this field of research; intercultural theologians are almost as allergic to dialectical theology as Barth was to natural theology. Nevertheless this is a much-needed dialogical encounter: Barthians may (and, I suggest, should) find in intercultural theology numerous insights to develop Barth's counter-constantinian project; likewise, intercultural theologians may find in Barth an interlocutor far more nuanced than the usual stereotype, whose theology could similarly assist their own project of intercultural understanding for the sake of what Sundermeier calls *Konvivenz* (*convivencia* or coexistence).[74]

Barth and contemporary continental philosophy

Continental philosophy is not entirely absent from this volume, given the essay on Jacob Taubes by Benjamin Myers and the presence of Slavoj Zizek in the contribution from Jones. But that is barely scratching the surface. Considering the sheer volume of interest in figures like Giorgio Agamben, Alain Badiou, Judith Butler, Gilles Deleuze, Julia Kristeva, Catherine Malabou, Jean-Luc Nancy—not to mention older figures like Theodor Adorno, Walter Benjamin, Michel Foucault, Edmund Husserl, and Jacques Lacan—it is quite surprising how little Barthian engagement there has been with these philosophers and theorists. Most of the dialogue is limited to prominent names like Martin Heidegger and Jacques Derrida, and there are occasional efforts to engage Agamben, Badiou, and Foucault, but the conversation between Barth and contemporary continental philosophy is still inchoate. In what follows I will offer two suggestions for future work in this area with respect to Badiou and Butler.

Badiou is a widely-known figure in contemporary philosophy, and for good reason. He has developed a philosophical system rivaling Heidegger, Hegel, and Kant in its scope and significance. Unfortunately, among those writing in theological and religious studies, (a) he is generally not read in a genetic-historical way that understands the major shifts in his thinking over the past several decades and (b) when he is read it is almost always limited to his short book on Paul, with occasional engagements with his major metaontological work, *Being and Event*. The problem is that Badiou's thinking since *Being and Event* has changed again, as indicated by the material in *Logics of Worlds* and *Second Manifesto for Philosophy*. The more recent work takes up existential and phenomenological themes, in conversation with figures like Kierkegaard,[75] and the result is material that augments and corrects his earlier work in a direction that should prove immensely interesting to theological scholars. To give an example, Badiou replaces his earlier (and

74. See Sundermeier, *Konvivenz*, 43–75.
75. Badiou, *Logics of Worlds*, 425–35.

widely criticized) concept of "generic set" with his new concept of "body," which names the new subject incorporated by the irruption of a truth into a world. Whereas the generic identifies "what a truth *is*," a body identifies "what a truth *does*"; the former is a "doctrine of being," while the latter is a "doctrine of doing."[76] Badiou's new concept of the body, and the related notion of the "point" as the moment of decision in which an individual is incorporated into the new subject, offers a profound way of conceptualizing the community of faith in a way that subverts all attempts at what Donald MacKinnon calls "ecclesiological fundamentalism."[77] I would suggest, in particular, a future conversation between Badiou's recent writings and the ecclesiological paragraphs of CD 4 (§§62, 67, 72), as well as Barth's account of human existence in §71, where the "event of vocation" is a kind of Barthian parallel to Badiou's account of the event of subjectivation.

The work of Butler is a less obvious dialogue partner for Barth. What could a Jewish post-structuralist feminist philosopher and queer theorist possibly have in common with a Swiss Reformed dogmatic theologian? More than you might think! Butler is justly famous for her *Gender Trouble* thesis about sexual identity as a performative act. She places her position over against substance metaphysics, specifically what she calls a "metaphysics of gender substances."[78] A metaphysics of this kind posits a static "ontology of gender" that exists prior to the actual practices and rituals of gender identity; it is a being that subsists prior to becoming. Her alternative is what we might call an *actualistic ontology of gender*: "That the gendered body is performative suggests that it has no ontological status apart from the various acts which constitute its reality."[79] Consequently, "there is no preexisting identity by which an act or attribute might be measured," and therefore "*woman* itself is a term in process, a becoming, a constructing that cannot rightfully be said to originate or to end."[80] Barth's theological anthropology rejects a substance ontology of human being just as emphatically as Butler. The difference between them then lies in the nature of the act that constitutes human identity. The actualistic character of Barth's anthropology derives from the history of Christ as the actualization of true humanity: "Human beings do not first have some kind of nature [*Beschaffenheit*], only then to be addressed by God in this nature. They do not have something different, earlier, and more basic, no deeper stratum, no original substance

---

76. Badiou, *Second Manifesto*, 128.
77. MacKinnon, "Kenosis," 23.
78. Butler, *Gender Trouble*, 30.
79. Ibid., 185.
80. Ibid., 192, 45.

of being, in which they are without or prior to the word of God. They are . . . from the very outset 'in the word of God.'"[81] The affinity between Barth and Butler in their definition of human identity as a being-in-act is worthy of sustained scholarly reflection. It may prove to be a conversation that not only demonstrates Barth's internal inconsistency with respect to the question of gender, but also mobilizes a Barthian actualistic anthropology for the sake of subjecting notions of heteronormativity to a thoroughgoing theological critique.

Obstacles to Conversation: The Problematic State of Theology Today

Barth is a thinker of immense complexity whose writings contain an almost inexhaustible potential for new insights when readers approach them with fresh new questions. Barth's profound witness to the freedom of God results in a theology that is correspondingly free for new questions, new encounters, and new possibilities for thinking and speaking about the living God. Unfortunately, the history of Barth scholarship is a history of asking the same two or three questions and receiving the same two or three now-stale answers—or sometimes asking questions with the same set of presuppositions and failing to get the answers that one wants or expects, and so dismissing Barth for not being the theological genie-in-a-bottle who will provide the justification for the views that one already holds.

The history of "neoorthodoxy" is emblematic of this stale approach to the Swiss theologian. For many decades, Barth was (wrongly) viewed in North America as a "neoorthodox" theologian. This had much to do with a reception of Barth's theology mediated through the Niebuhr brothers and the work of Emil Brunner, who taught for a year at Princeton Theological Seminary and was, at least for a time, viewed favorably as a representative of Barth's thinking. It was the burden of Bruce McCormack's magisterial work to disabuse American readers of this myth of the "neoorthodox Barth."[82] And while that has largely succeeded among Barth scholars, many remain unclear just what about neoorthodoxy makes it objectionable. Many have defined neoorthodoxy as that position which rejects both liberalism and fundamentalism, but such a vague definition is of little practical help. Any

---

81. KD 3.2:179.

82. CRDT, 28: "The present study is offered in the hope that through a reconsideration of Barth's development, the 'neo-orthodox' misreading of his theology will at last be seen for what it is and be set aside in the historiography of twentieth-century theology."

number of labels claim to fit that description (e.g., postliberalism). The point is that clarifying this issue will go some way toward explaining what Barth is up to theologically, and what the conditions are for a responsible and productive conversation with Barth.

I am going to propose a rather heterodox definition of neoorthodoxy. The aim here is to gain clarity about *Barth*, not about the historical meaning of the word or the other theologians who are connected with the label. Neoorthodoxy, as I understand it, sought to marshal certain ideas from Barth—mainly, divine transcendence and the notion of revelation as a personal encounter, both abstracted as permanently-valid propositions—and use them to buttress the project of Christian orthodoxy within the modern era, thus making it a new, rather than repristinated, orthodoxy. This quasi-Barthian project rightly recognizes that classical orthodoxy is untenable in its traditional form and therefore aims to reform it. Neoorthodoxy is fundamentally ideological, however, in that it presupposes the absolute validity of something like a Christian orthodox tradition. Having presupposed this tradition (and the institutions that go with it) as something to be preserved and maintained, it then finds in Barth certain concepts that are useful toward that end. Neoorthodoxy does not qualify as dialectical theology for the simple reason that the latter makes no such presupposition; it is in fact the total abolition of ecclesiastical presuppositions. Dialectical theology is a thoroughly destabilizing understanding of the gospel. Neoorthodoxy, by contrast, is basically a species of natural theology, in that it takes for granted something stable and given in the world—in this case, the church and the divine revelation given to the church. It comes as little surprise that Barth (as the representative of dialectical theology) and Brunner (as a representative of neoorthodoxy) would fall out over the issue of natural theology. For Barth, the history of Jesus Christ is a reality that does not give itself as an empirical datum to ecclesiastical and theological traditions any more than it does to the natural world. The saving event of Christ, interpreted dialectically, must always be an offense to those theologies that seek to sustain and prop up the institution of the church, with its dogmas and rituals and polities. True dogma, as Barth insisted, is only ever an *eschatological* reality.[83] As

---

83. See *KD* 1.1:284: "A theology claiming to know and have dogma would be a *theologia gloriae*, which the dogmatics of the church should not want to be . . . Every answer . . . can only be one of two things: *either* the event of the word of God itself, which dogmatics can neither presuppose nor postulate nor produce, *or* one of the great illusions and prolepses of a dogmatics, which is unaware of the fact that there is no presupposing, postulating, or producing with respect to this event. The *real* results of a dogmatics, even when they take the form of positive statements, can only be new *questions* . . . If the questions ceased, . . . then dogmatics, along with the *ecclesia militans*, would be at an end and the reign of God would have dawned . . . In this sense one may

such, there is no orthodox faith in history. And therefore there can be no neoorthodox theology.

I say all this because the present theological context in which people are receiving Barth's theology is dominated by assumptions regarding theology and the church that Barth himself does not share. While Barth is perhaps more popular and more widely studied than ever, the North American churches are currently witnessing a massive reaction to the progressive developments made a half-century ago.[84] The Roman Catholic reactions against certain aspects of the Vatican II period—and, by implication, against the work of people like Balthasar, Rahner, and Schillebeeckx—are well-known and have had an indirect impact on Barth's reception among Catholics. The doctrine of divine impassibility has made a major comeback after decades of dismissal in the twentieth century. Today even the *analogia entis* is all the rage, and not only among the Roman Catholics and Eastern Orthodox. And where the *analogia entis* is not in fashion, virtue ethics almost certainly is. In each case, some version of metaphysics is on offer: whether a metaphysics of the divine being, a metaphysics of creation, or a metaphysics of the human self. It is hardly a surprise, then, that Barth's own postmetaphysical approach to theology is largely seen as a failure, as a threat, or at least as in serious need of supplement.

Less prominent but also influential is the rise of "analytic theology," which is the systematic application of analytic philosophy of religion to the various areas of Christian doctrine.[85] Scholars in this field have made an

---

call . . . dogma an 'eschatological concept.'"

84. The analysis that follows is, by necessity, cursory and largely surface-level, to be sure. The recent developments are by no means limited to North America, but that is my own context and it is where these changes are especially noticeable. I will also focus on the more "conservative" or "orthodox" side of the theological scene, primarily because I do not view theological liberalism to be a threat—at least not any longer. It certainly is not the threat that Barth saw in his day. In the present situation, the churches, academies, and theologies that are thriving are traditional, conservative, and invested in preserving orthodoxy. The problem today is not liberal theology but *evangelical* theology.

85. Rea begins his introduction to *Analytic Theology* with the following statement: "In recent decades, philosophers of religion in the so-called 'analytic tradition' have gradually turned their attention toward the explication of core doctrines in Christian theology. The result has been a growing body of philosophical work on topics that have traditionally been the provenance of systematic theologians" (Rea, "Introduction," 1). We should note, however, that there is a difference between analytic philosophers of religion and analytic theologians. The former, by and large, are concerned only with defending and elaborating some account of theism. The latter are usually more invested in a fuller notion of Christian orthodoxy, and they are often more explicit about belonging to a specific tradition of Christian orthodoxy (e.g., Reformed). However, the two groups share the same basic methodological principles and rhetorical styles. More importantly,

effort to engage Barth critically, finding him wanting on numerous counts. In general this field of literature criticizes Barth for being logically incoherent and self-contradictory.[86] This typically involves either pointing out a conflict between explicit statements by Barth,[87] or evaluating Barth's claims with respect to a "classical orthodoxy" with which he is supposed to be in agreement.[88] Barth's dialectical and paradoxical modes of expression are deemed signs of conceptual confusion, while his revolutionary upheavals

they both share the crucial conviction that the material content of Christian faith can be responsibly translated into the form of propositional statements and modal logic. Both groups presuppose that Christian orthodoxy refers to a set of doctrinal beliefs that can be organized into syllogisms. One can determine whether a theologian is orthodox by evaluating the logical consistency of her propositional claims with those of some assumed classical tradition. This entails an essentially ahistorical approach to Christian theology, because these propositional statements of traditional orthodoxy are treated as timeless. A syllogism is unable to account for the unstated philosophical assumptions behind the claims of Chalcedon, for instance, much less the contextual factors associated with Barth's rejection of natural theology or biblical inerrancy. More importantly, Barth would question whether such an approach is possible in principle, if the event of revelation is in fact a historical event in a particular person, to whom Scripture bears a narratival witness.

86. The usual argument against Barth's analogy of faith from the side of analytic philosophy goes something like this: "Barth's theology is viciously circular, because he claims that God-talk depends upon Christ. But talk about Christ, as the God-human, itself depends upon and presupposes some understanding of God-talk. Therefore, Barth's claim to ground God-talk christocentrically is actually nonsensical. One has to clarify one's conceptual categories before one can explicate the meaning of Christ. And this is the burden of analytic philosophy." What the analytic philosopher does not understand is just how radical Barth's epistemological revolution is. Barth rejects the notion that we have access to a notion of God independently of Jesus Christ, and therefore we cannot speak meaningfully of God in a way that is not thoroughly determined by the history of Christ. For Barth, talk of Christ does not presuppose some prior account of God but actually defines what the word "God" means. This is indeed nonsensical to the analytic philosopher of religion, as it must be. It is impossible to find a middle ground between Barth and analytic philosophy (or analytic theology) here. There is only an either-or.

87. See, for example, Crisp's essays on Barth's universalism, especially Crisp, "On Barth's Denial," and Crisp, "I Do Teach It."

88. See Crisp's essays on the question of Christ's fallen humanity: Crisp, "Did Christ" and Crisp, *Divinity*, 90–117. See also the essay on Barth's doctrine of Scripture by McCall, "On Understanding Scripture." McCall provides a classic example of testing Barth against some assumed orthodoxy. Near the end of his piece, he cites McCormack's claim that Barth's doctrine of Scripture is determined by his Reformed christology. McCall then responds by "assuming (with Barth) that 'Reformed' Christology is in line with classical, Chalcedonian orthodoxy," which he confirms by citing a study of *Calvin* (McCall, "On Understanding Scripture," 184). McCall appears to assume that "Reformed" and "orthodoxy" basically mean one thing, at least where christology is concerned. While this has the advantage of providing a tidy way of defeating creative, modern contributions to Reformed theology, it does so at the expense of historical sensitivity and theological nuance.

in theological ontology and epistemology are seen as heterodox. These conflicts are hardly a surprise, considering Barth's thoroughgoing opposition not only to philosophical starting-points but also to a presupposed notion of "the tradition." So far the analytic treatments of Barth have failed to understand (a) that he makes a certain reformational account of soteriology constitutive of his epistemology and ontology (for more on this point, see the following section); (b) that he views theology to be wholly in service to the church's mission, such that proclamation and doxology are its proper aims, not logical consistency or orthodoxy; and (c) that he sees theology's form as integral to its content. His theology is dialectical and actualistic not out of some abstract commitment to principles of actualism and dialectic; rather they are the modes of thinking and speaking that are proper to the subject-matter itself.

A more subtle problem is the rise of Kuyperian neocalvinism. Dutch Reformed theology is experiencing a rise in popularity, even among those who do not self-identify as Reformed. Whereas analytic theology is attractive for those who want to defend Christianity's rationality, a Kuyperian-neocalvinist approach is attractive to conservative, yet socially conscious, evangelicals for the way it funds the kind of social, political, and cultural engagement that was once seen to be the purview of liberalism. The irony is that Kuyperian theology accomplishes this by making the same kind of theological moves that Barth condemned liberals for a century ago. In short, neocalvinism prides itself on its robust doctrine of creation, which operates independently from (or at least antecedently to) christology as its theological starting-point. Creation is ontologically and epistemologically prior to redemption. In making this move Kuyperian theology aims to construct a Christian worldview, not primarily as a rational apologetic to defeat skepticism, but as a sociocultural apologetic to defeat secularism. The establishment of a general account of revelation—and thus the prior conceptualization of creation apart from new creation—certainly succeeds in providing the foundation for a program of cultural-political transformation, which is precisely why similar moves were so attractive to the *Kulturprotestantismus* against which Barth wrote so vigorously.[89]

---

89. The actual social and cultural aims of neocalvinist theologians are not the issue here. What is under examination are the *theological* moves that allow a Kuyperian thinker to engage in a certain form of culture-making. Neocalvinism, like other theological programs, is premised on a bifurcation between creation and redemption, in which creation is thematized independently of any consideration of Jesus Christ. The underlying motivation for this prior thematization of creation is the desire to influence the general society, that is, to construct an ethical law or moral framework that will apply to people irrespective of faith and religion. Dialectical theology, however, is essentially opposed to culture-making as a legitimate Christian goal. That does *not* mean

The persistent danger is that the New Testament message of Jesus Christ becomes a prop for a program of social reform that one has developed independently of the gospel of God's reconciling incursion in the crucified one. One ends up with a "creational" or "natural law" ethic, which Jesus might help make it possible to fulfill but certainly does not himself define—except perhaps in cases where one turns him into an abstract logos-principle or tries to extract a general ethic from his teachings in the Gospel accounts, which are no better. It does not matter how conservatively or orthodoxly one develops the doctrine of creation and the "Christian worldview" that corresponds to it. The end result remains the same: the deployment of theology for ideological ends. Whether these ends are benign, or even beneficial, is irrelevant; Barth opposed Religious Socialism for its use of Christianity as a political program, even though he agreed with the political goal of socialism until the end of his life. The ever-present threat of Kuyperian theology is that it will result in precisely the culturally-captive Christianity that John Drury and Christian Collins Winn address in their above contributions. A theology that conceives of Christianity as a worldview—even if it is a worldview that seeks to be "countercultural" with respect to the wider society—has already abandoned the real scandal of the gospel and become enslaved to the powers of this world. For it is not *which* worldview one has, but the mere fact *that* one thinks in terms of worldviews, that already indicates one remains trapped within the logic of the old age—a point I develop below in relation to Barth.

The state of American theology presents us with an environment that is often at distinct odds with the theological vision that Barth provides. At the same time there is a growing interest in his writings and a willingness to engage him charitably. My aim here is simply to call for a serious engagement with the *real* Barth. And since Barth is himself an immensely complex figure whose theology developed in major ways throughout his life, I am calling for a historically-sensitive engagement with the full range of his corpus.[90] To be sure, reading widely in Barth (or Barth scholarship) is no

---

dialectical theology is opposed to culture, as Barth's frequent comments about Mozart indicate well. It is instead the very freedom of theology *from* all temptations to influence the culture that makes a theology truly relevant and open to culture.

90. By "full range" I do not mean every single thing that Barth wrote. I am referring instead to the fact that readers need to attend to both early and later Barth, both the Barth of *Epistle to the Romans* and the Barth of *Church Dogmatics*. And the range should not only be chronological. It should also involve a range of genres and doctrines: not just the Barth of the major dogmatic texts, but also the Barth of the exegetical texts, sermons, letters, and interviews; not just the Barth of christology and election, but also the Barth of ethics and ecclesiology. And, ideally, not just Barth in translation, but Barth in German—though I hasten to add that one need not read German in order to

guarantee that one will read him accurately, much less charitably. But in a situation where Barth gets routinely criticized (even praised) for positions he does not hold, it is past time to set some boundaries for the sake of a responsible reading of his theology.

Toward a Responsible Reading of Barth

By way of conclusion, I wish to clarify three key terms that are used often in Barth discourse: (1) dialectical theology, (2) metaphysics, and (3) infra- and supralapsarianism.

1. It is well-known that Barth is a dialectical theologian, but exactly what this means is a topic of much dispute. Dialectical theology is best understood as the theological paradigm that corresponds to the reformational conviction that the world's rectification (or justification) is by divine grace alone. Whereas the reformers themselves isolated the problem of soteriology from ontology and epistemology—that is to say, they failed to think through the implications of their soteriology for the question of the being of God and our knowledge of God—dialectical theology develops a theological ontology and epistemology commensurate with its reformational soteriology. Interpretations of Barth that do not understand his soteriological starting-point often end up thinking that he changed his mind between the "wholly other God" of 1922 and the "humanity of God" of 1956. But such claims misunderstand that Barth was faithful to his dialectical convictions from start to finish; he was a consistently dialectical thinker throughout his life. He changed his understanding of what counts as a properly reformational soteriology—moving from an actualistic election in the present moment to a protological election in the (primal) history of Christ—but he expounded this soteriology in a consistently dialectical way.[91]

Dialectical theology should be understood as having an epistemological component and an ontological component. Both aspects follow from and exist for the sake of the soteriological claim noted above. For the sake

---

understand him accurately. However, anyone hoping to write on Barth in an academic context ought always to consult the German text.

91. I emphasize soteriology not as a contrast to christology, but as the proper clarification of what christology means for Barth. There is an unfortunate tradition of distinguishing between the person of Christ and his saving work. Barth himself actually employs this distinction in his christology of KD 1.2, but he firmly renounces it in his mature christology of KD 4. His later christology is therefore wholly determined by what Christ does; Christ's work *is* Christ's person. What thus unites the early and late Barth is therefore the conviction that the reconciling action of God is our theological starting-point.

of methodological clarity, I will begin with epistemology. Dialectical theology makes a claim that is as revolutionary as it is simple: knowledge of God—and thus the very possibility of meaningful God-talk—is given in the very same event in which we are justified before (or reconciled to) God. Our soteriological relation to God is constitutive of our epistemological relation to God, both of which are established in the person of Christ in the power of the Spirit. The reformational rejection of "salvation by works" becomes the basis for Barth's rejection of "knowledge by natural reason." True knowledge of God is therefore not realized through any method of moving from world to God (i.e., metaphysics), but rather through the faithful acknowledgement of God's gracious movement to the world in Christ (i.e., revelation). Revelation *is* reconciliation, and vice versa. All of this is simply a way of saying that a proper understanding of God, and thus a responsible mode of God-talk, occurs strictly within faith. *Extra fidem nulla scientia dei* ("outside of faith there is no knowledge of God"). The event in which our wills are made free by the Spirit is the same event in which our eyes and ears are opened to the acts and words of God. As stated above, this is merely the epistemological extension of the reformational claim that justification is *sola gratia* and *sola fide*. Dialectical theology is a way of speaking about God that "thinks after" (*Nachdenken*) God's self-giving reality in Jesus of Nazareth.

The ontological corollary of this epistemological-soteriological claim is fairly straightforward: the being of God is determined by the same (christological) event in which God both reconciles the world to Godself and reveals Godself to the world. This ontological claim has two aspects: dissimilarity and similarity.[92] These correspond, respectively, to (a) the emphasis in *Romans* on God's "wholly otherness" and the so-called "infinite qualitative distinction" between God and the world and (b) the emphasis in *Church Dogmatics* 2.2 and following (along with coterminous writings) on the humanity and historicity of God. In the former, God meets the creature as a tangent touches a circle; in the latter, God is one who includes creaturely reality within Godself through the divine self-determination in Jesus Christ. These two dimensions of theological ontology in Barth are a source of much

---

92. These two aspects correspond to the two elements of analogy: similarity within dissimilarity. The Fourth Lateran Council defines the analogy between God and the world as a "greater dissimilarity in the midst of similarity." We need not get into the details of Barth's dispute with the *analogia entis*, or Jüngel's post-Barthian inversion of the Fourth Lateran Council ("greater similarity in the midst of dissimilarity"). All we need to point out here is that both the dissimilarity and similarity, however they are specified, can only occur for Barth *within* the soteriological event that forms the starting-point for all of his theological reflection on ontology and epistemology. It is on this basis that he must reject all doctrines of analogy based on some general datum, that is to say, something *extra fidem*.

confusion, made especially complicated due to Barth's own claim in 1956 that his later understanding of God's humanity corrects his earlier understanding of God's wholly otherness. While it would seem permissible to play the later Barth off against the early Barth, the truth of the matter is that he never renounces the essence of his early position—nor could he do so and remain a dialectical theologian. In fact, both aspects are equally essential and are interwoven throughout his writings.

Both ontological aspects follow from the inbreaking of God's reconciling grace in Christ. The reformational doctrine of justification means that God sovereignly and graciously moves toward the world. There is no movement from the world to God, neither soteriological (works-righteousness) nor epistemological (natural theology) nor ontological (*analogia entis*); instead, the movement is strictly from God to the world, including the soteriological (*sola gratia*), epistemological (divine self-revelation), and ontological (*analogia fidei*). In each case, the agency of the creature can only be thematized *in response to* God's prior agency. Creation is logically and ontologically subordinate to the covenant. This divine sovereignty means, on the one hand, that there is an ontological *diastasis* between God and the world. God's absolute transcendence is necessarily entailed in the confession of God's gracious election.[93] God's wholly otherness means that we are wholly dependent on God coming to the world in Christ. On the other hand, God's reconciling agency posits God's *nearness* at the same time that it posits God's otherness. Divine promeity and aseity coincide as two aspects of a single soteriological event: God's being-for-us necessarily entails that God is absolutely other than us, while God's radical transcendence frees God to be just as radically immanent. God transcends creation in such a way that God is able to be, as Eberhard Jüngel is fond of saying, "nearer to us than we are to ourselves."[94] The triune God is a *human* God, not because of some metaphysical projection of our humanity onto the divine, nor because God is ontologically dependent upon creation, but rather because God eternally determines to be God-for-us in Christ.

---

93. This serves as a correction to the widespread notion that Barth's theology begins with the claim that God is wholly other or qualitatively distinct, as if Barth simply assumes such a statement to be axiomatic for theology. It then becomes quite easy to dismiss Barth's position as begging the question; it appears that he is as beholden to a philosophical (i.e., Kierkegaardian) conceptuality as those whom he criticizes. The truth is that Barth never takes an axiom like this as his starting-point. Though such an axiom functions well as a summation of his earlier position, his theology consistently begins by attempting to tease out the broader systematic implications of a reformational soteriology. Barth's theology is dialectical because it is first actualistic.

94. Jüngel, *Gott als Geheimnis*, 245.

Finally, it should be noted that the vigorous debate in Barth studies over the idea of "actualistic ontology" is really a debate over dialectical theology itself. If, as I have claimed, dialectical theology is fundamentally about conforming our epistemology and ontology to the soteriological work of God in Christ, then an actualistic ontology is necessarily what follows. The term simply takes seriously the claim that what God *does* in Christ is constitutive of who God is and who human beings are (ontology) and what we can meaningfully say about both (epistemology). God is not pure act in some general scholastic sense; God is a particular act in the economy of salvation. Any claim that there is a being that stands behind this act, whose existence we can know regardless of the act ever taking place, is to place ontology before soteriology, and thus to abandon dialectical theology.

2. The concept of metaphysics is a hotly contested one in theological studies after Barth. The term came into prominence in the generation of scholars after Barth who sought to appropriate the later Heidegger's insights—especially Heinrich Ott (Barth's successor at Basel), Ernst Fuchs, and Gerhard Ebeling—and was then taken up further in the generation after that, including Jürgen Moltmann, Robert Jenson, and Jüngel. The concept certainly appears in Barth's own texts, but it is not nearly as dominant as one might expect from the secondary literature. Today there is a sharp impasse between those post-Barthian theologians who remain broadly faithful to the line of inquiry developed by the likes of Ebeling and Jüngel (e.g., McCormack and Kevin Hector), and the wider theological and philosophical world that finds the idiosyncratic usage of the word "metaphysics" to be largely unhelpful, if not incomprehensible. Moreover, there is a resurgence of theological interest in classical metaphysics among thinkers in both continental and analytic traditions. The result is that Barthian critics of metaphysics find themselves continually defending their understanding of the concept. A few words on this issue are in order.

First, we need to clarify what contemporary Barthian critics of metaphysics mean by the word. At the most basic level, the concern is any mode of God-talk that begins with something in the world as the starting-point. The *triplex via* of Dionysius the Areopagite is paradigmatic here: (a) the *via causalitatis* begins with the created world as such and then posits a first cause; (b) the *via eminentiae* begins with a creaturely attribute and raises this to the level of infinite perfection; and (c) the *via negationis* begins with a creaturely attribute and negates it. The problem is that once one begins with the creature, one can never guarantee that one ends with the creator. How does one know that one is not simply projecting a deity in one's own image (Feuerbach)? The epistemological problem is thus a reflection of the soteriological problem: how does one ever find a gracious God if one does not begin with God's gracious action toward us in Christ? Certainty in our knowledge of God is intimately connected with—in fact, we might say, identical with—the assurance of salvation. If we begin with the creature, we end up with the creature, and thus we are trapped in a vicious and hopeless circle. Only the apocalyptic interruption of God's word can break open this circle and free us for a new understanding of God.

For a more nuanced articulation of the metaphysical problem, the work of Jüngel is of special significance. His two most well-known works, *Gottes Sein ist im Werden* (ET *God's Being Is in Becoming*) and *Gott als Geheimnis der Welt* (ET *God as the Mystery of the World*), reflect at length on the metaphysical problem. In the former work from 1965, Jüngel provides the classic definition when he says that metaphysics "divides reality (platonically) into two 'worlds,' in one of which exists a 'God for Godself' and in the other exists a 'God for us.'"[95] This statement locates metaphysics in the context of the debate over the immanent and economic trinity, which is of course a christological debate over the question: how decisive is the history of Jesus for the eternal being of God? Jüngel's challenge does not simply consist in affirming the unity of God's eternal being and economic action. He instead aims at a mode of God-talk that makes the cruciform history of Jesus Christ decisive for the very meaning of the word "God." Our *language* about God remains metaphysical, he claims, unless and until creaturely speech comes to correspond to the crucified one. Jüngel's claim is not the unity of *ad intra* and *ad extra* in God; it is instead that the word "God," including all talk of the immanent trinity and divine aseity, has *no meaning* apart from the concrete history of the man Jesus. All of which is to say, we must free our God-talk from the shackles of a conceptuality alien to this particular event, even if that means breaking fundamentally with the received *regula fidei*. Jüngel calls this binding of our God-talk to a presupposed conceptuality metaphysics or mythology, which he uses synonymously since "the two are close to each other in the Greek tradition."[96] He defines mythology as "an attempt to capture revelation through language," whereas the kerygma is "language captured by revelation." In a way, this remains the best definition of metaphysics (language-captured revelation) and of a theology without metaphysics (revelation-captured language).

The problem of metaphysics is therefore simply the problem of analogy, which is why Jüngel focuses on developing a doctrine of analogy in his 1977 magnum opus, *Gott als Geheimnis der Welt*. Both aspects of metaphysics from his earlier work—viz. the being of God and the human language

95. Jüngel, *Gottes Sein*, 45.
96. Ibid., 33n85.

that corresponds to this being—are developed at length here. For instance, he says early on that "metaphysics assigns the being of God a place fundamentally and exclusively *over us*," whereas death "works under us."⁹⁷ The result is the same split between God's being and act noted above, since it is precisely death that marks the history of Jesus. Metaphysics is incapable of thinking God and perishability (*Vergänglichkeit*) together; it is unable to think and speak of a God who dies, of a God who is the unity of life and death *in God's eternal being*. Jüngel goes on to say, however, that we cannot simply have a "metaphysics-free" theology. Instead, Christian theology "does not refuse to make use critically of the metaphysical tradition," and in doing so it achieves "a thoroughly *ambivalent* relation to this tradition."⁹⁸ Theology that abandons the *deus supra nos* remains profoundly free with respect to metaphysics, and thus free for a new hearing of God's being-for-us in Christ.⁹⁹ Jüngel's insights into the metaphysical problem lie at the heart of what contemporary post-Barthian critics of metaphysics mean by the concept.¹⁰⁰ Any critique of the Barthian analysis of metaphysics will need to take seriously the material concerns of a theologian like Jüngel and examine his texts in detail.

Second, we must acknowledge that this definition of metaphysics is not disqualified simply because it is not how the average philosopher defines the term. It is perfectly legitimate for Barthians to use a word in a uniquely theological way, provided that they carefully define the term, as has been the case. To disallow theologians from speaking about metaphysics in their

---

97. Jüngel, *Gott als Geheimnis*, 62.

98. Ibid., 62–63.

99. Jüngel makes it clear throughout his writings that a theology free with respect to metaphysics is *not* a theology that simply proclaims the death of God. What he calls "modern metaphysics" refers to those thinkers who, like the older metaphysicians, are also incapable of thinking God's unity with perishability. Whereas the older metaphysicians say that God lives because God cannot die, the modern metaphysicians say that God dies because God cannot live. Neither is able to say that God is the unity of life and death, that God lives in dying. For this reason, Jüngel says that the non-dialectical statement that "God is dead" in fact "belongs entirely" to the notion of metaphysics as "theo-onto-logic" that these modern writers intend to reject (Jüngel, *Gott als Geheimnis*, 275). As he puts it in another essay, "The last thought of metaphysics is not the thought of the death of the metaphysical God, but the metaphysical thought of the death of God." See Jüngel, "Vom Tod," 122.

100. Jüngel's conception of metaphysics as revelation captured by language anticipates the work of someone like Hector, who speaks of an "essentialist-correspondentist metaphysics" that captures or fits God into a general framework of meaning. God is conceived as an object that corresponds to our conceptual categories. Like Jüngel, Hector develops his understanding of metaphysics in conversation with Heidegger. See Hector, *Theology*, 9–13.

own way is to beg the question regarding theology's claim to be a distinctive discipline responsive to the word of God. It is identical to the problem surrounding a word like "God." Is theology free to define the meaning of God-talk according to its unique claim regarding God's self-revelation in Christ? Or is it forced to use the word in a way that has general currency either among extratheological disciplines or in the larger society as a whole? This dispute over metaphysics is really over the legitimacy of Christian theological discourse as such. Having said that, Barthians need to acknowledge that this usage is indeed idiosyncratic and will likely be the source of further reaction and misunderstanding. While I do think it serves a necessary purpose in clarifying Barth's contribution to theological epistemology, those making use of the word in a strictly pejorative, post-Barthian sense need to ask themselves whether it is always the best way to communicate the significance of Barth's theological project.

Third, I would contend that in most cases it is *not* the best way to explain what Barth is up to. For one thing, the problem of *Metaphysik* is primarily a Heideggerian contribution that gets picked up by later generations of dialectical theologians. Barth criticizes metaphysics without thematizing it in any detail, except when he is commenting on Heidegger.[101] Barth's writings are certainly antimetaphysical, but what is in view is usually much more than just an issue in epistemology and ontology. If one wishes to identify a more suitable word for what Barth wishes to reject, I would submit that the concept of "worldview" (*Weltanschauung*) is more fitting: Barth uses it frequently throughout the entirety of his career, he gives special attention to it in his mature writings,[102] and most importantly it brings to expression a problem that is not just epistemological or ontological, but is also, perhaps even primarily, *practical* in nature. The concept of worldview refers to something that is essentially social, cultural, and political; it refers to the ideological, and thus the unity of the epistemological and the political.[103]

---

101. See *KD* 3.3:384–90.

102. See, especially, *KD* 3.1:390–94; 3.2:1–20; 3.3:18–19, 23–24, 157–60; and 4.3:293–99.

103. This becomes particularly evident in Nazi propaganda, where the concept of *Weltanschauung* plays a prominent role. For example, on August 24, 1927, Joseph Goebbels gave a talk about the need to move from the idea to the state by way of a *Weltanschauung*: "The more the idea is spread and the more it penetrates all aspects of life, the more it becomes a *Weltanschauung*. If an organization becomes the carrier of this *Weltanschauung*, then at the end of this line stands the state, whose carrier are a whole people. If a concrete state structure is formed on the basis of the *Weltanschauung*, then propaganda has reached its goal" (see Mühlberger, *Hitler's Voice*, 1:270). For another example, see the following passage from a propaganda article on "the victory of faith" in 1939: "The briefest way to describe the misery of the German people before

Since Barth's own theology insists on the practical and political implications of theological speech, it would seem natural to highlight his opposition to worldviews. Barth's rejection of natural theology was never merely a matter of correcting our *language* about God. He was opposing the way Christian faith had been coopted by various forms of what he considered culturally-captive Christianity (especially what became known as *Kulturprotestantismus*) to serve ideological purposes, whether this was the *Kriegstheologie* in support of the war effort in 1914, the religious socialism of Leonhard Ragaz, the missionary natural theologies of Bruno Gutmann and Emil Brunner, the Catholic cultural engagement of Erich Przywara's *analogia entis*, or the existentialist theology of the Bultmann school.[104] Reframing all of these concerns in terms of Barth's denial of worldviews would defuse much of the misunderstanding about Barth and would clarify just what it is about metaphysics, as a species of worldview-thinking, that he opposes.

3. The final term needing clarification is (infra-/supra-)lapsarianism. Of all the terms essential for understanding Barth, this might be the least acknowledged in the literature. And yet its significance for making sense of Barth's theology can hardly be overstated.[105] The term itself is historically rooted in a debate within Reformed scholasticism over the order of the divine decrees in eternity. The infralapsarians presented the order: (a) creation, (b) permission of the fall, (c) election and reprobation, and (d) provision of the mediator. The infralapsarians based their order on the *tem-*

---

the comprehensive and direction-giving uprising of 1933 is this: the German people no longer had a worldview. A worldview is not a subjective standpoint, a personal opinion of what is true, but rather a force that shapes an era, a firm will, 'a view that binds together all deep aspects of life' (as Rosenberg said at the culture rally of the Reich Party Rally of Honor [1936]). Germany had fallen into worldview chaos, from which followed political, economic, cultural and moral decay, since a standard of measurement failed that would have enabled a valid judgment about the value or lack of value of a particular phenomenon . . . The era had lost a central worldview, and thus the measure of character, of style. The chaos of worldviews resulted in chaos in science, education, and all other areas of life. People staggered before the abyss, unsteady, irresolute . . . The National Socialist revolution ended this situation in Germany . . . The worldview decision that came through the creative act of the National Socialist revolution ended a dying and weak age, bringing instead a new era" (see Mehringer, "Sieg des Glaubens," 2–4; English translation available online: http://www.calvin.edu/academic/cas/gpa/schulo1.htm).

104. Of these, I judge Barth to be mistaken only with respect to Bultmann. He saw formal similarities between the Marburg school and previous forms of liberal theology, and he judged the former to be guilty of the mistakes of the latter. This was an error on his part, as I argue in Congdon, "Theology," and which I will argue at length in my forthcoming dissertation. See also Chalamet, *Dialectical Theologians*.

105. For Barth's discussion of the infralapsarian-supralapsarian debate, see *KD* 2.2:136–57.

poral order within the history of salvation. They were also concerned to protect the claim (shared by both groups) that God is not the author of sin. By contrast, the supralapsarians presented the order: (a) election and reprobation, (b) creation, (c) permission of the fall, (d) provision of the mediator. The supralapsarians based their order on the *logical* order within the mind of God. It is the sovereign *will* of God that is finally decisive, not the issue of God's justice in the face of human sinfulness. Each vigorously rejected the other side. Infralapsarians rejected the "supra" position for viewing God as electing and reprobating only possible or hypothetical human beings, and not actual persons who have committed actual sins; supralapsarianism turns God into a monster who creates people solely for the sake of fulfilling a prior decision to reprobate them. Supralapsarians, however, viewed the "infra" position as failing to recognize the sovereignty of God's will; election and reprobation cannot be responses (not even in the sense of divine foreknowledge) to creaturely sinfulness, because God's decision to create can have no other purpose than the one given to it by election and reprobation. Creation is ordered toward (i.e., predestined for) the eschatological judgment.

Barth recognizes that this debate is not a mere artifact of Reformed history. To be sure, he unequivocally rejects both sides for the same reason: they each separate the decree of election and reprobation from the decree to provide a mediator, that is, from Christ. As a result, both of the lapsarian positions are species of double predestination, a position that Barth flatly denies. These doctrinal problems notwithstanding, Barth sees that, when the proper adjustments are made, a modified supralapsarianism becomes not only relevant but actually necessary. The adjustment is simple: identifying the decree of election with Jesus Christ himself. Election and reprobation no longer pertain directly to individual human beings, potential or actual. They pertain to one person, Jesus of Nazareth, in the singular event of his saving history. The new order of decrees is now (a) the decree to elect and be elected in Jesus Christ and (b) the decree to create a world as the theater of this election and to create human beings who are elect in Christ, which includes the permission of the fall as part of this cosmic theater of redemption. Jesus is no longer merely the instrument of a soteriological decision that logically precedes him. And creation now has its ground in nothing above or prior to his reconciling history. There is no *decretum absolutum*, no disincarnate deity, no abstract sovereignty, no arbitrary voluntarist will. The point is that Barth's radically revised christocentric supralapsarianism is no longer a relic of Reformed scholasticism. It now describes the essence of dialectical theology as we defined it above, viz., that all things are ordered by and toward the soteriological truth of the gospel.[106]

The genius of Barth's appropriation of this debate is that it crystallizes what he consistently opposes and what he, in his later years, comes to advocate. The relation between Christ and creation becomes the lens by which one can analyze any theological problem. Every species of natural theology can now be redescribed as a version of infralapsarianism: the attempt to find some natural or general starting-point necessarily entails the subordination of Christ to a logically prior decree of creation. Metaphysical thinking is therefore a mode of infralapsarian thinking. On the other hand, any claim to be an interpretation or development of Barth's theology that does not explicitly uphold his christocentric supralapsarianism is dubious at best. Attempts to find in Barth the resources for a Protestant *analogia entis* or virtue ethic will only have merit if they deal responsibly with his priority of redemption over creation. Most importantly, criticisms of Barth that focus on some subsidiary issue—such as his denial, for example, of general revelation, sacramentalism, casuistry, or apologetics—often end up misreading Barth, especially when they praise him at the same time for his rigorous emphasis on Christ and his rejection of liberal theology.[107] Far too

---

106. For a fuller discussion of this aspect of Barth's theology, see McMaken, *Sign*, 119–24. McMaken there describes Barth's position as a "christologically modified supralapsarianism" (123).

107. As just one among many examples of an irresponsible reading of Barth, take Fitch's analysis in his argument for a "missional political theology." He praises Barth, as many do, for his christocentric interpretation of revelation for the way it reorients the question of scriptural authority and provides a necessary corrective to American evangelicalism. But then he adds: "Of course, Barth presents a problem for a missional political theology. Most obviously, if all knowledge of God comes exclusively in and through the incarnate Christ alone, those who are outside this revelation in Christ can become closed off from the community who believes. The community can view itself as singularly in control of the truth of God. This would be a community closed off from the mission of God, incapable of translating our beliefs beyond our own language" (Fitch, *End of Evangelicalism?*, 134). Such a reading of Barth is not "obvious" at all, despite Fitch's claim. And his acknowledgement that this critique comes from the work of D. Stephen Long does not help. In fact, this interpretation is only possible on the basis of an unfamiliarity with *KD* 4.1–3, esp. §§62, 67, and 72, where Barth develops at length a missionary ecclesiology that accomplishes exactly what Fitch claims Barth denies. It is very hard to understand how anyone could read Barth to be saying that the Christian community gains "control" over revelation, for this is precisely what dialectical theology rejected under the description of liberal theology.

In short, it is clear that Fitch has only a superficial understanding of Barth's actual theology, as evidenced by the fact that his only citations from the dogmatics in this section of his book are from *CD* 1.1. He gives no attention at all to the question of election and the relation between covenant and creation in Barth's christocentric supralapsarianism. It is therefore fitting that Fitch follows up this criticism with an appeal to Hans

often people fail to see the systematic interconnection between the various aspects of Barth's theology. In most cases this is because people overlook the overall architectonic of his dogmatic thought, and what holds this entire structure together is his radically revised supralapsarianism. If one is going to criticize Barth, it should actually be *Barth* that one is criticizing.

Conclusion

In his 1968 second edition of *A Layman's Guide to Protestant Theology*, William Hordern—former professor at Garrett Theological Seminary and then president of Lutheran Theological Seminary in Saskatchewan—concluded his chapter on Karl Barth with the following words:

> Karl Barth has left a rich heritage to theology. For many years to come his *Dogmatics* will inspire new theological research . . . His consistent attempt to build a theology around the act of God in Christ and his joyous expression of Christian faith will win followers for many years. Perhaps those who claim that theology has entered into a post-Barthian period will prove to have been premature. On this continent Barth has been rather consistently misunderstood. (This misunderstanding was shared by the first edition of this book.) Future history may conclude that on this continent, at least, theology in the sixties was still pre-Barthian.[108]

Today we can pronounce that conclusion confirmed. In fact, the Barthian era in North American theology really only began well after the sixties, when the influence of Tillich, Niebuhr, and Bultmann started to fade.[109]

Urs von Balthasar, who provides a "Christological reinterpretation of the analogy of being" that "makes possible the manifestation of God to all humanity in all the various forms of human experience and knowledge in creation" (Fitch, *End of Evangelicalism?*, 134–35). Borrowing from Balthasar's theological aesthetics, Fitch says that "Scripture is part of Christ himself" and thus we participate in Christ "in and through the church and tradition" (ibid., 135). The irony is that, for all of Fitch's talk of ideology and the need to overcome "Constantinian strategies," his ecclesiocentric strategy of assimilating Christ into the church only serves to prop up a new ideological understanding of God's mission in the world. Fitch serves as a lesson: no matter how much one might praise Barth, if one fails to uphold his revised supralapsarianism, one will almost certainly end up endorsing precisely what Barth sought to reject. One cannot cherry-pick from dialectical theology. For a different interpretation of Barth that counters the Radical Orthodoxy underpinning Fitch's reading, see Hector, "Ontological Violence."

108. Hordern, *Layman's Guide*, 148–49.

109. This is an empirical-historical judgment, not a theological or normative one. That is to say, I am not pitting Barth against Tillich, Niebuhr, and Bultmann, but simply

Hordern's words now ring truer today than ever. Indeed, the *Dogmatics* is inspiring new theological research like never before.

For these reasons, the future of *Barth studies* is full of promise. While he is no longer a major interest in contemporary German scholarship, his influence in Anglophone studies is dominant and pervasive. There are a growing number of first-rate monographs on Barth by young scholars who mark the start of a new era of Barthian theological engagement in the twenty-first century.[110] At the same time, the future of *Barth* in North America still remains unclear. There is a widespread Protestant (even evangelical) interest in *ressourcement*, sacramentalism, confessionalism, classical metaphysics, and various forms of *weltanschaulich* thinking. It often seems that Barth is someone one has to know but not necessarily take seriously; or if he is someone to take seriously, it is only because one already knows that we need to get past him. There is a persistent danger that a real conversation with Barth will not take place. They will be like ships passing in the night, or to use one of Barth's favorite images, like a whale and an elephant trying to speak with one another. We offer this volume of essays in the hope that the ships will meet and that the whale and elephant, like the Spirit-filled participants at Pentecost, will come to speak a common language.

---

noting that, historically speaking, Barth's time did not come until after people had lost interest in these other thinkers. Though I myself think Bultmann's true time is still yet to come.

110. In addition to the work of Jones noted above, the following is a representative sample (in alphabetical order): Burnett, *Karl Barth's Theological Exegesis*; Collins Winn, *"Jesus Is Victor!"*; Flett, *Witness*; Greggs, *Barth*; Johnson, *Karl Barth*; Marga, *Karl Barth's Dialogue*; Neder, *Participation*; Nimmo, *Being*.

Appendix

Become Conversant with Barth's *Church Dogmatics*: A Primer[111]

—By David Guretzki

AT THE OUTSET OF the second decade of the twenty-first century, there are few signs that the Karl Barth renaissance is in any danger of waning. Those who are engaged in formal and informal theological study will find that references to the Swiss master abound both in printed and online sources. As a result, there is a sense that even those not at all interested in Karl Barth are forced to know something about him, whether they want to or not! However, it is well known that Barth is a challenging theologian to engage, and diving into his work can be a daunting task. This is compounded by the fact that anyone who wants to get to know Barth from the primary sources (and not just from secondary commentary on Barth) will eventually need to read deeply in his monumental *Church Dogmatics*. There are simply no shortcuts! Consequently, beginners faced with its sheer size (which some have affectionately called "the white elephant") for the first time may have reason to despair, if only because the work is over six million words in length and extends more than ten thousand pages (in English translation)! For those who want to become acquainted with this vitally important work but aren't exactly sure how to start, the following intends to be a short primer that will help those new to Barth ease into one of the greatest theological works of church history.

This primer is divided into three parts. In the first part, I introduce some useful tidbits of information about the *CD*, along with some suggested strategies for reading that will be especially beneficial for the Barth novice.

---

111. I wish to dedicate this little primer to all the participants of my Karl Barth Reading Group at Briercrest College & Seminary in Caronport, Saskatchewan who have met faithfully with me every week for the last eight years, and who have been a source of both stimulation and encouragement.

In the second part, I attempt to introduce three interpretive metaphors that may help to illuminate the larger theological, rhetorical, and literary style of Barth and his *magnum opus*. Finally, I provide a short annotated bibliography of some of the important secondary works which can be of significant aid in moving a reader from being a novice to an intermediate interpreter of Karl Barth.

Reading the *Church Dogmatics*

Understand the nature of the *Church Dogmatics*

As a professor of theology teaching in both undergraduate and graduate contexts, I have occasionally had students who—when first introduced to the *CD*—are offended by its length. Exasperated, they ask, "How could anyone presume to write such a long work that is many times longer than the Bible itself?" I try to lessen the offense by helping my students understand that the *CD* is a thirty-five-year record of Barth's theology lectures to his students. That is to say, nearly all of the content of the *CD* (with the exception of the very last parts of *CD* 4) first came into existence as oral lectures and were only later polished and edited for publication.

Knowing that an oral tradition undergirds the *CD* may help remind readers that these lectures were originally meant to be "heard." We need to keep in mind that we are dealing with an English translation, and some of its original rhetorical beauty and force is consequently lost. Nevertheless, it can be still helpful to read passages out loud (to yourself or to whatever lucky soul happens to be within listening distance!) to highlight the oral element. This doesn't always work, of course, but sometimes when we *hear* a portion of Barth's lecture we may understand it better than when we simply *read* it.

Awareness of the oral tradition underlying the *CD* partially helps to explain some of the repetition that is encountered throughout. The repetition might seem unnecessarily burdensome at one level, but at another level the text may suddenly come alive when read aloud. Also, don't forget that delivering a long lecture lasting over three decades (!) obviously meant that Barth needed continually to remind students of themes he had mentioned earlier. One can only imagine how excited the stream of students coming to Basel must have felt to be the original receptors of this revolutionary theology in the making!

Become familiar with the structure of the *Church Dogmatics*[112]

In just over a decade prior to the start of the *CD*, Barth had already twice attempted to write a "dogmatics," or what we English speakers are more apt to call a "systematic theology." However, Barth considered both endeavors to be "false starts." When he began the *CD* in the early 1930s, already in his late forties (!), he intended to spread the work out over five volumes—a program from which he never again deviated. From then on, he worked doggedly at expanding the basic outline for over thirty-five years. But the work proved to be so expansive that Barth had to resort to releasing part-volumes every two or more years rather than trying to cram everything he wanted into a single binding.

More fundamentally, it is essential to appreciate that the *CD* is deliberately structured around a trinitarian framework. Thus, in *CD* 1 Barth expounds his trinitarian doctrine of revelation as the prolegomenon to his work, and in *CD* 2 he launches into a discussion about the knowledge of God and the fundamental place of the doctrine of election in the knowledge of God in Christ. This was to be followed in *CD* vols. 3–5, speaking broadly about God the Father the Creator, God the Son the Reconciler, and God the Holy Spirit the Redeemer. However, Barth died before *CD* 4 was finished and he never even got started on the fifth volume on the Holy Spirit and redemption. Thus, the main structure is as follows:

- *CD* 1—The Doctrine of the Word of God (consisting of two part-volumes).
- *CD* 2—The Doctrine of God (consisting of two part-volumes).
- *CD* 3—The Doctrine of Creation (consisting of four part-volumes).
- *CD* 4—The Doctrine of Reconciliation (incomplete; consisting of three part-volumes, the third of which is itself in two parts, and one "fragment" volume!).
- *CD* 5—The Doctrine of Redemption (never begun).

It should be noted that most scholarly works today reference the *CD* through a more or less standard set of conventions whereby each part-volume is referenced. Thus, for example, *CD* 2.2 (variations: II/2, II.2, etc.) represents the second volume and second part, while *CD* 4.3.2 (or: IV/3.2, IV.3.2, etc.) references the fourth volume, the third part, and the second half of the third part.

---

112. See Godsey, "Architecture."

Understand how the *Church Dogmatics* works

As already noted, Barth conceived of his *Church Dogmatics* as a single work by necessity spread out in multiple part-volumes. Moreover, the entire work is divided up into chapters and paragraphs, with the paragraphs being marked off with a symbol known as a section sign (§). Barth scholars often deal with these sections as distinct "pericopes" and usually refer to them by their paragraph number, e.g., "In paragraph 10 (or, §10) Barth deals with the doctrine of God as Father." Each paragraph begins with a concise summary—known as a *Diktatsatz* or *Leitsatz* in German—which is a very carefully constructed sentence that Barth would likely have expected students to write down verbatim, and that functioned as the means by which he introduced the basic thesis of the lectures to follow. Consequently, it is a good practice to return to these chapter summaries whenever you find yourself getting lost in the details. Reminding yourself of what *this* particular paragraph is all about can sometimes help in regaining your bearings.

New readers also quickly notice that the whole work is printed in two distinct font sizes. These are usually referred to—unimaginatively!—as the "regular" and "small print" sections. The regular sections are where Barth trots out his main ideas and where the main flow of his argument unfolds. The small print sections are where Barth provides detailed insight into the exegesis, historical background, or theological rationale that undergirded his thinking and which led him to his specific conclusions. In the virtual absence of footnotes from the *CD* (except for the very occasional editorial note), it is appropriate to think of these small print sections as—more or less—Barth's footnotes because they are also the sections most likely to contain references to other works and authors with whom Barth was engaging.

Finally, the regular print sections generally tend to have more of an oral style while the small print sections tend to be more technical or encyclopedic in nature. Thus, Barth would occasionally suggest that people who couldn't afford the time to read the whole *CD* could still benefit from reading the large print sections while simply ignoring the small print sections. However, I would recommend that you not take his advice here! In reality, some of Barth's greatest theological nuggets can be found embedded in these small print sections. One may certainly get to know *what* Barth said when reading the regular print sections, but one has a better chance of understanding *why* Barth said what he said—and why it is significant that he said it—if one is patient enough to read the small print sections carefully. One small warning: if you happen to have one of the original T. & T. Clark editions of the *CD* translations, the Greek, Hebrew, and Latin quotations from biblical and classical authors that are scattered liberally throughout the small print sections, especially in the earlier volumes, are not translated. Those without the ability to read these languages unfortunately will have to rely on someone who has the linguistic training to help them through, though having appropriate dictionaries available can help. Fortunately, a newer edition of the *CD* available both in print and in electronic format now has all the Greek, Hebrew, and Latin sections translated into English.[113]

Get a quick overview before diving in

Because the *CD* is such a massive work, readers would do well to get a broad overview of the whole before engaging the parts. This is a little like consulting a topographical map of an unknown area before beginning a hike. Knowing in advance what you are going to face makes for a more pleasurable journey.

There are at least three ways one can do this. First, I recommend that students *read* the table of contents for each volume before diving in. I know that many people just skip the table of contents altogether. But reading through them for each volume can make a vast difference in understanding where Barth is going. Better yet, get a copy of Godsey and Green's compilation of the major headings outline of the entire *CD*.[114] I personally keep a copy of this outline at my desk, because it serves as a handy map to help me locate where I am within the larger world of the *CD*.

Second, it can be extremely helpful to take the time to read through the summaries compiled and available in the *Church Dogmatics* index volume (i.e., the last volume in the *CD* collection). Although these statements are extremely dense, spending time reading them carefully can be an invaluable way of grasping the whole *CD* in abridged form, as it were. Whatever the case, reading through the summaries will provide significant insight into the fundamentals of Barth's theology.

Third, you may want to consult the appropriate section in Geoffrey Bromiley's book entitled, *An Introduction to the Theology of Karl Barth*.[115] This now classic text provides a section-by-section exposition of the content of the *CD*. Sometimes when starting work on a new section of the *CD* that I haven't read before, I read Bromiley's exposition first. However, be fore-

---

113. Logos Bible Software has the entire *CD* available on CD-ROM or for download. Bloomsbury/T. & T. Clark also has a "Study Edition" of the *CD* which includes English translation of the Greek, Hebrew, and Latin phrases.

114. See Green, *Karl Barth*, 169–70.

115. Bromiley's work has been more recently supplemented by Busch's excellent introduction. See Busch, *Great Passion*.

warned: reading Bromiley's text can in no way replace reading the *Dogmatics* for yourself, any more than reading a biblical commentary can replace reading the Bible for yourself!

If you are still intimidated by the mammoth size of the *CD*, and just aren't sure you either want to read it or have the time to do so, then I would recommend reading Barth's 1946 lectures on the Apostles' Creed which he delivered to theological students and colleagues in Bonn and later published as *Dogmatics in Outline*. While this text is not—as some have mistakenly assumed—an abridged version of the *CD*, reading this little book will nevertheless provide insight into some of Barth's distinctive theological ideas, all of which are greatly expanded upon in the *CD*.

Read a lot and read a little!

Given the massive size of the *Church Dogmatics*, initial forays into the work can be quite discouraging for the beginner. Hours might be spent reading without a significant dent being made in a single part-volume! Add to this the fact that the density of Barth's prose means that it takes three or four times longer to read a paragraph in Barth than most other books, and the beginner can easily be tempted to give up almost before she has started.

My advice: learn to read Barth in both large and small chunks. Force yourself to read large sections, without even pretending to know all that is going on. This approach is a little like the "jumping-into-the-deep-end-of-the-pool" method of learning to swim. Even if you don't catch everything the first time, reading larger chunks of the *CD* will yield a better sense of Barth's rhythm and movements—something which cannot be grasped by reading only a page or two at a time. Then, once you have a feeling for the larger sections, intersperse this large section reading with close or slow reading of smaller sections to become more attuned to the delicate theological nuances that Barth provides.[116] In other words, try to pay attention to both the proverbial trees and the forest.

Finally, don't neglect the prefaces to each work. The prefaces give some of Barth's rarer self-editorial comments and autobiographical details, many of which are sprinkled throughout with his characteristic humor. For starters, you might want to read Barth's lament about Dutch Neo-Calvinist views

---

116. In fact, this is a good strategy to follow in Bible reading as well. We need to read both broadly and narrowly, in large (chapters and books) and small (words and verses) portions. On this concept of the relationship of the whole to the parts in Barth's thought, see Burnett, *Karl Barth's Theological Exegesis*, 78–84.

of Mozart in *CD* 3.4, and one of the closest things you'll see by way of a "retraction" by Barth is in *CD* 4.1.

Start a *Church Dogmatics* reading group

I have personally been involved with a group of students and colleagues in reading slowly and carefully through various volumes of Barth's *Church Dogmatics*, and I have found this to be an enjoyable, stimulating, and spiritually uplifting way to learn and read Barth while being challenged to think through theological issues on my own. It isn't necessary to begin at *CD* 1.1, although that's not a bad place to start, because reading a part of Barth's work often gives insight into the whole. I'll say more about that later.

Our group meets once a week for about sixty to ninety minutes during the academic year to discuss a five- to ten-page section of the *CD*. We've found that fruitful discussion can't cover more than a maximum of ten pages in one week—not to mention that busy people might not be able to finish more than five or ten pages in one week. Now, to be fair, this strategy will not give you much hope of finishing the *CD* even in a lifetime—it took our group three years to read through the doctrine of election!—but in many respects this slow reading of Barth has had the positive side-effect of encouraging us all to read more of Barth on our own.

Most importantly, reading the *CD* in this way has had the positive effect of forcing us all to read our Bibles afresh as we consider ways of reading Scripture that perhaps had not occurred to us before. I have made it a habit to select a scriptural passage that may relate to the section we are reading or which Barth may have mentioned. This often leads to significant discussion about the biblical text and how Barth has helped us to see things about that text in fresh perspective, even when we may not agree with some of the details of his own exegesis. I do believe that Barth would *not* be happy to know that people were getting together only to discuss his thoughts, but I do believe he would be gratified to know readers of his *Dogmatics* are pressed to return to the Bible again and again, and "from the beginning," as Barth was fond of saying.

Beyond all this, we've made it a rule in our own group to start and finish each session with prayer. In his earlier *Göttingen Dogmatics*, Barth began by saying:

> It was significant that Thomas Aquinas put at the head of his *Summa Theologica* the prayer: "Merciful God, I ask that thou wilt grant me, as thou pleasest, to seek earnestly, to investigate carefully, to know truthfully, and to present perfectly, to the

glory of thy name, amen." If there is any mortally dangerous undertaking on earth, any undertaking in which we have reason not only at the beginning but also in the middle and at the end to take the last resort of invoking the name of the Most High, then it is that of a *summa theologica*, a dogmatics, and I must add that in our day and our situation such a prayer will have to be made out of materially much deeper distress and perplexity than in the time of Thomas.[117]

Read Hunsinger's *How to Read Karl Barth*

But don't read it before you've started reading Barth! The title of Hunsinger's book can be slightly misleading, because it suggests that it will serve as a beginner's introduction to Barth. While in certain respects that may be true, in reality this important book is much more profitable once you've gotten through a couple hundred pages of the *CD* yourself. In essence, Hunsinger shows that there are massive difficulties in trying to provide a hermeneutical key which will serve to unlock the mysteries of Barth. On the contrary, Hunsinger argues that there is no single key, no one center or theme that can "get at" Barth. In this regard, Hunsinger points out that at least six motifs or patterns characterize Barth's theology in the *CD*.[118] While I certainly can't expound on these to any great length, the six motifs or patterns that Hunsinger says shapes Barth's thought are:

1. *Actualism*—Actual events of God's action in history shape reality as we experience it. That is, we understand history by how God has *actually* acted, as opposed to interpreting God by how we think God *should* act. We do not, in other words, try to fit God into our conception of history, but seek to understand history in light of God's surprising actions in Jesus Christ's history.

2. *Particularism*—The particular and concrete, logically and theologically, precedes the general and the abstract. That is, the unique particularity of the incarnation must inform the general nature of humanity rather than a general theory of humanity informing the particular nature of a human named Jesus. We do not fit Jesus into humanity, but we seek to understand humanity by reference to *this* particular human.

3. *Objectivism*—Theological claims must be shaped by the object they seek to describe. That is, God must be spoken of in terms of how he

117. Barth, *Göttingen*, 3–4.
118. Hunsinger, *How to Read*, 4–6.

himself objectively presents himself (or "reveals" himself) to us, not in terms of how we *conceptualize* or *speculate* about God.

4. *Personalism*—To know God is to know him as a personal being. "God" is not merely a "control belief" for a theological system, but a living being that is really and personally encountered as he freely makes himself known in Christ and by the power of the Holy Spirit.

5. *Realism*—Language about God is based on Scripture and is neither "literalist" (i.e., theological language cannot be equated directly to God) nor "expressivist" (i.e., theological language is not merely what humans express when thinking about God), but a "real analogy" to God. Theological language says something "real" about God, and is not—contrary to some theologies—merely symbolic or metaphorical.

6. *Rationalism*—The mystery of God can be spoken of coherently without needing to presume that theological language gives an all-encompassing, comprehensive knowledge of God. In other words, theology is a "rational wrestling with the mystery."[119]

Remember that Barth wrote a *church* dogmatics

Barth was a theologian for the pastor. He intended his *Church Dogmatics* to serve the pastor who was faced with the task of preaching week after week. Indeed, Barth insisted that a theology that forgot it was in service to the task of preaching was a theology that had lost its moorings. The *CD* is intended (and whether Barth succeeded or not can only be tested in the pulpit and podium) to help answer the question of what it is that we should *preach* and *teach* concerning God and the gospel, and not simply what we think we can know or prove about God. For Barth, a dogmatics that does not ask how this or that doctrine needs to be preached or taught is a dogmatics that has not yet understood its own task. As Barth explained, "No single item of Christian doctrine is legitimately grounded, or rightly developed or expounded, unless it can of itself be understood and explained as part of the responsibility laid upon the hearing and teaching Church towards the self-revelation of God attested in Holy Scripture."[120]

Barth's intention that the *CD* serve the preacher first and foremost was confirmed in part by the editors of the *CD* who included in the index volume what they call "Aids to the Preacher"—a compendium of about eight hundred extracts drawn from the *CD* volumes, most of which are exegetical

---

119. *CD* 1.1:368.
120. *CD* 2.1:35.

notes on a particular Sunday's selected Scripture passages for the liturgical year as outlined in the 1958 Lutheran lectionary, *Ordnung der Predigttexte*.

Enjoy the journey!

Whatever you do, do not allow yourself to become discouraged if you do not reach your goal of reading a certain number of pages in a year, or fail to finish the whole *CD* in the years you allotted. Remember that not even Barth himself finished the task he set out to accomplish. In one of numerous interviews conducted near the end of his career, Karl Barth quipped, "There is a certain merit to an unfinished dogmatics . . . It points to the eschatological character of theology!"[121] In other words, the goal should not be to worry about finishing the *Church Dogmatics*, but to realize that the work of dogmatics is never finished. So enjoy the journey, learn, grow, and cry out, as Barth often did, "Come, Lord Jesus! *Veni Creator Spiritus*! (Come Spirit Creator!)."[122]

Interpreting Barth: Three Metaphors

Having provided a basic sketch of pertinent information and strategies for reading the *CD*, we now turn to a short exploration of ways to view the ethos of Barth's work. This will be accomplished through attention to three suggestive metaphors: Barth as *theological architect*, Barth as *theological composer*, and Barth as *fractal theologian*. The exploration here will be brief, but my hope is that the metaphors can function as memorable heuristic tools that can easily be recalled while reading Barth over time.

Barth as theological architect

The more deeply one studies Barth the more one becomes aware that the *CD* has both structure and movement, both stability and development. Barth had a master blueprint for the *CD* ("structure"), but he did not allow this structure to become a literary or theological straitjacket as he continued to develop his thought ("movement"). In other words, at the same time that Barth was careful not to deviate too far from his original plan, he also remained open to the need to adapt in the working out of the details.

---

121. Barth, *How I Changed*, 86.
122. *CD* 4.4:210.

As early as 1956, John Godsey—a former student of Barth—described Barth as a theological architect and the *CD* itself as materially displaying an evolving "architecture."[123] Commenting specifically on *CD* 4 ("The Doctrine of Reconciliation"), Godsey notes that though Barth remained faithful to the large-scale structure of the *CD* that he had envisioned from the beginning, the architectural details were constantly undergoing revision as the structure emerged. Even the plan for his doctrine of reconciliation, which Barth announced at the beginning of the first part of the fourth volume, ended up being unreliable in predicting the details. Godsey argues that this is because Barth was a self-critical theologian who consistently and consciously sought to avoid having his dogmatics devolve into a closed or inflexible system. In this regard, Godsey praises Barth for his dogmatic thinking, which allowed him to construct a dogmatics that is "both architecturally beautiful *and* theologically correct."[124]

Describing Barth as a theological architect thus reminds readers of his commitment both to the integrity of his theological program and to openness in following where the evidence of the scriptural witness took him. Similar to how an architect needs to be open for adaptations to his original vision in order to account for unexpected environmental or material limitations, so Barth admitted that he did not always know where his writing would lead him in working out the details. Even in the last years of his life, he was still able to say, "only the angels in heaven . . . actually know in detail what form the material [of the *Church Dogmatics*] will take."[125] This was because Barth was committed to allowing the object of his inquiry—the living reality of a free God revealed in Christ and attested in Holy Scripture—to direct his dogmatic steps.

Interestingly, Barth himself picked up on the architectural motif. In an interview late in his life, Barth compared his unfinished dogmatics to the architectural marvel of the Strasbourg Cathedral—a magnificent Gothic structure built over the course of several hundred years between the tenth and fourteenth centuries. Though the present structure clearly signals that two spires had been intended in the original architectural plan, the second spire was never completed and remains unfinished to this very day. In this regard, though perhaps disappointed that he was likely unable to finish his theological project, Barth recognized that "finishing" was less important than "faithfulness."

123. Godsey, "Architecture," 236–50.
124. Ibid., 248.
125. *CD* 4.2:xi.

Gaining a basic understanding of the architectural structure of Barth's *CD* can serve beginning (and advanced) readers well. Sometimes a reader may wish that Barth would deal with a topic that she has in mind and be frustrated when he appears to avoid the topic altogether. On the one hand, this may simply be a function of better understanding the overall structure of the *CD*. At those times the reader needs to consider where in the *CD* she is reading and what should therefore be expected. For example, a reader may be working his way through *CD* 4.1 and note that Barth talks extensively about "justification" but says very little about "sanctification." Just like understanding the logical organization of a library keeps us from expecting to find books on astronomy in the poetry section, so understanding the architectural plan that Barth employs in his *CD* will help this reader realize that just as Barth deals extensively with justification in *CD* 4.1, so he will deal with sanctification in *CD* 4.2 (and vocation in *CD* 4.3).

On the other hand, Barth's architectural openness also serves the reader well by how it functions in evoking our own theological thinking. If we look at a picture (or happen to be present at) the Strasbourg Cathedral, the architecture clearly suggests that something is "missing" and we are forced imaginatively to "fill in." In this regard, my own experience in reading the *CD* is that as expansive and in depth as Barth's thinking is, its architectural strength prompts my own thinking in theological directions that I may not have followed or explored had I not read Barth in the first place. The architecture of Barth's *CD*, in other words, is both majestic in itself and suggestive of even greater things beyond itself. Barth's *CD*, therefore, empowers attentive readers with a sense of theological anticipation for the work yet to be done.

Barth as theological composer

Another metaphor used to describe Barth's approach to the *CD* comes from the field of music. In 1986, Theodore Gill said, "Mightn't we get farther in understanding Barth in system and method if we began to think of him as fundamentally an artist—or at least more an artist than a scientist? As such, he would be a theologian composer of Mozartean rank. And he would belong exactly to Mozart's classical school of style."[126] The identification of Barth as a "theologian composer" comes as no surprise, given Barth's well-known devotion to Mozart and his music.[127] As Gill explains: "[B]efore

---

126. Gill, "Barth," 403.

127. In fact, Barth is quoted as saying, "When the angels go about their task of praising God, they play only Bach. I am sure, however, that when they are together *en*

Barth turned to each day's tasks—writing, teaching, preaching, counseling, correcting, leading a resistance—he listened every morning for at least a half hour to the music of Mozart . . . He knew Mozart's Köchel [catalogue] listings as well as he did the classification of his own *Dogmatik*."[128]

Gill goes on to suggest that Barth is fruitfully compared to Mozart because "Barth's frame of mind is quintessentially aesthetic."[129] Gill explains: "[Just as] the musician uses counterpoint, changes in harmony, key, rhythm to keep the movement interesting," so Barth, "the theological composer uses references to the same theme in older treatments, arguments with contemporaries, surprising implications, ethical consequences, all to the same end, developing the themes while sustaining interest."[130]

What does this mean for the reader of Barth? At the very least it means try to *listen* to Barth as one would listen to a musical composition rather than as to a recitation of a legal document in which an exacting argument is made. Just as a musical appreciation of one of Mozart's concertos does not merely consist of breaking it down into a series of logical propositions ending in a triumphant "therefore" statement, so Barth must be read with a kind of theological appreciation that attends not only to *what* Barth is saying, but also *how* he is saying it as well. In this regard, while it is legitimate for a reader to ask, "To what extent do I *understand* Barth?" an appreciation of Barth as a theological composer will ask, "To what extent am I *captured* by that which Barth is captured by?" So how might this theological appreciation of Barth as theological composer work in practice?

It has already been noted that Barth tends to repeat themes over and over again, and this was partially explained as a function of the orality that underlies the *CD*. But there is also something deeper at stake if the reader pays close attention to these repetitions. Barth engages in repetition not as mere reiteration of previously mentioned material, but as a means of filling out or thickening what he has said with a subtle nuance, perspective, or angle not covered earlier. As George Hunsinger explains, "Part of what Barth seems to share with Mozart . . . is a certain taste for thematic interplay, a taste which includes the custom of complex recapitulation, modification, and allusion. The more deeply one reads in Barth, the more one senses that his use of repetition is never pointless. Rather, it serves as a principle of

---

famille they play Mozart and that then too our dear Lord listens with special pleasure" (quoted in Green, *Karl Barth*, 322).

128. Gill, "Barth," 403.
129. Ibid., 408.
130. Ibid., 409.

organization and development within an ever forward spiraling theological whole."[131]

Readers of Barth would do well to realize that just as Mozart (and other composers) might repeat a theme (or *leitmotif*) throughout a piece of music in different keys, harmonies, volume, etc., so does Barth replay his theological themes throughout the expanse of the *CD*, but usually from a slightly different angle or with a subtle twist. Beginning to notice these subtleties takes significant practice, but pays rich dividends in a manner similar to the practice of careful listening to a complex musical composition.

Barth as fractal theologian

Perhaps some readers of this primer are uncomfortable with my use thus far of "aesthetically oriented" metaphors, rather than metaphors that get at the level of theological precision with which Barth was also concerned. In this regard, I offer one more metaphor to describe Barth, a metaphor unexplored elsewhere in the literature. Certainly Barth can be described as a theological *architect* or *composer*, but let me suggest that he is also a theological mathematician, or more precisely, a *fractal theologian*. Let me explain.

Readers may be more or less familiar with the field within mathematics called fractal geometry. What exactly is a "fractal"? One classic text defines it as follows: "a rough or fragmented geometric shape that can be split into parts, each of which is (at least approximately) a reduced-size copy of the whole."[132] Or as another author puts it, "A fractal is a geometrical figure in which an identical motif repeats itself on an ever diminishing scale."[133] Thus, the field of fractal geometry seeks to explore the mathematical predictability of apparently random objects or shapes—the shapes which we usually find in the natural world of rocks, plants, and landscapes—which otherwise might appear to be random or complex, and therefore incapable of being described easily (or at all) by Euclidean geometry (i.e., the geometry that we all learned in high school that deals with lines, circles, squares, etc.).

As I write this paragraph, I am looking out my window at a pine tree. If we were to attempt to assign a mathematical formula which would account for the shape of this tree in all its detail, it would quickly become clear that no simple Euclidean formula would suffice and we may be tempted to

---

131. Hunsinger, *How to Read*, 28.

132. Mandelbrot, *Fractal Geometry*. A quick internet search will provide you with graphic representations of fractals.

133. Lauwerier, *Fractals*, xi.

suggest that the shape of a pine tree is mathematically "random." Nevertheless, if one were to look carefully at the tree's branches in detail, we would realize that an interesting pattern emerges such that upon closer examination, each branch—indeed, each twig of each branch—looks like a miniature pine tree itself. Fractal geometry thus recognizes that the basic shape of the twig corresponds nearly (or least roughly) to the geometric shape of the tree as a whole, and *vice versa*. In other words, fractal mathematicians would insist that each needle or twig of a pine tree is a self-contained version of the whole tree.

The parallel to Barth's view of dogmatics can therefore be observed as follows. Early on in the writing of the *CD* Barth makes the following axiomatic statement: "Strictly speaking, in dogmatics and in Church preaching every single statement is at once the basis and the content of all the rest."[134] In other words, Barth believes that any faithful and true theological statement coheres with and corresponds to the totality. Indeed, the failure of a statement to serve as the "basis and content of all the rest" is probably an indicator of its theological deficiency. Here are two examples of how this plays out in Barth's work in the *CD*.

First, and perhaps even most fundamentally for Barth, it becomes evident in *CD* 1 that the primal Christian confession—"Jesus is Lord"—summarizes not only what Barth calls the "root of the doctrine of the Trinity,"[135] but the totality of the Christian faith itself. Wrapped up in itself, the confession simultaneously functions as a fundamental geometric shape of the doctrine of the Trinity, and also as the linguistic microcosm (to mix my own metaphors) of the real relationship that exists between the creator Lord God and his creation in and through the man Jesus Christ. The short statement is capable of being fractally expanded, so to speak, to represent the whole.

A second example is just as illuminating and is found in Barth's famous exposition of the doctrine of election in *CD* 2.2. Barth undertakes to take up and reshape the classical Reformed doctrine of double-predestination with the insistence that the doctrine of election cannot be isolated from the announcement of the gospel itself. Indeed, Barth is most critical in his engagement with his Reformed forebears concerning the isolation of the doctrine of election from the rest of the church's proclamation of Christ as the Savior of the world. It is unacceptable, Barth argues, to view election as something inscrutably hidden from human view—behind the back of God, as it were—nor is it acceptable to view election as something disconnected from the announcement of the gospel itself. In this regard, Barth points to

134. *CD* 1.1:257.
135. *CD* 1.1:304.

the problem of the doctrine of election as it has been sometimes understood, especially in the Reformed tradition, as a doctrine for believers and not as a doctrine used in the presentation of the gospel itself to those outside of the faith. On the contrary, Barth insists, a serviceable doctrine of election will be judged to be true and faithful as it corresponds to and actually finds reiteration in the public proclamation of Jesus Christ.

Barth is so insistent about the relationship of the doctrine of election to the totality of the gospel that he writes, "The doctrine of election is the sum of the Gospel because of all words that can be said or heard it is the best: that God elects man; that God is for man too the One who loves in freedom."[136] The doctrine of election—that Jesus Christ is both the electing God and the elected human being—functions for Barth, to use our metaphor, as a theological fractal that can be both infinitely expanded in the totality of the theology and proclamation of the church and tightly compacted as the simplest statement of the gospel. Whether expanded over thousands of pages or contracted into a single sentence, the shape of the gospel is the same, and the test of the integrity of gospel proclamation is whether it can be reduced or expanded without losing its basic shape in which Jesus is central.

Practically speaking, reading Barth the fractal theologian means keeping the relationship of the parts to the whole constantly in mind and therefore resisting the temptation to isolate one small section of Barth from the rest of his dogmatic work. As each pine twig does not stand on its own but is nevertheless representative of the whole tree, so all of Barth's dogmatic statements need to be understood relative to the larger whole. But note also that just as in the real world (and in fractal geometry) each pine twig is not an *exact* replica of the whole pine tree in every detail, so too in Barth's *CD* we should not abstract a detailed passage from its larger whole—in which case we may be in danger of losing the forest for the trees—and expect that we now know all there is to know about Barth. Nor should we assume that a basic knowledge of the whole outline of the *CD* is a sure predictor of the minute dogmatic details.

In this regard, I've sometimes been disheartened when I've heard or read individuals who make a grand statement about some aspect of Barth's theology based on a detailed reading of a small portion of the *CD*. While it is entirely appropriate and necessary to make evaluations of these sorts, the fractal complexity of the *CD* requires a degree of chastening and humility on the reader's part. Amazingly, looking at one pine twig may give real insight into the shape of the pine tree, but humility requires an examination of all the pine twigs together in their organic unity to make a confident

---

136. *CD* 2.2:3.

assertion about what the pine tree really looks like. Of course, this is a fundamental principle of any sound hermeneutic employed when reading any large text, and it is a hermeneutic which we do well to heed as we read Barth as a fractal theologian.

A Selection of Secondary Sources: An Annotated Top 10

It nearly goes without saying that the secondary source bibliography on Barth is so massive that no mortal is ever likely to read everything that has been written on Barth, nevermind the challenge of reading everything that Barth himself has written![137] Literally not a month goes by without new books and articles being published on Barth. But do not despair: there are still some enduring classics in the secondary literature. The following ten sources are what I consider to be some of the more important secondary works on Karl Barth that readers who want to go further with Barth *must* eventually read. But believe me when I say that selecting only ten was a challenge! Here they are listed in alphabetical order, not necessarily in any order of importance.

1. Hans Urs von Balthasar's *The Theology of Karl Barth*. This book is a classic Roman Catholic interpretation and interaction with Barth. Even though aspects of Balthasar's interpretation of Barth have been challenged by some newer scholarship, it is still a magisterial work with which to be reckoned.
2. G. C. Berkouwer's *The Triumph of Grace in the Theology of Karl Barth*. The renowned Dutch Calvinist theologian provides a respectful interpretation and criticism of Barth's theology. It is a tribute to the importance of this work that Barth spends considerable space in the *CD* responding to Berkouwer's treatise.[138]
3. Richard Burnett's *Karl Barth's Theological Exegesis*. Though focusing on Barth's early work in his commentary on Romans, Burnett's study is the best available for getting a handle on Barth's hermeneutical theory and practice, and it will serve readers well to understand Barth's method of theological exegesis. This book is especially fascinating in how Burnett examines the multiple prefaces (including unpublished editions) to the various editions of the *Romans* commentary.

---

137. For the standard bibliography on Barth, covering primary and secondary literature only up to 1984, see Wildi, *Bibliographie*.

138. See *CD* 4.3:173–79.

4. Eberhard Busch's *Karl Barth: His Life from Letters and Autobiographical Texts*. Technically speaking, there is no standard critical biography of Barth yet available. Nevertheless, Busch's work is the *de facto* biographical authority on Barth. Apart from being an excellent theologian in his own right, Busch had the distinct advantage of being one of Barth's last students, even living in the Barth household for several years, so his knowledge of Barth's life and thought comes from close acquaintance. There are many, many biographical nuggets of interest here.

5. Eberhard Busch's *The Great Passion: An Introduction to Karl Barth's Theology*. While not as easy to read as Bromiley's classic *Introduction to the Theology of Karl Barth*, Busch's work is bound to become the standard intermediate level introduction to Barth's theology.

6. George Hunsinger's *How to Read Karl Barth: The Shape of His Theology*. I noted Hunsinger's book already and included above a short summary of some of his important themes. As mentioned, this book is probably best read after gaining some first-hand acquaintance with the *CD*. I consider Hunsinger to be the foremost English-speaking authority on the shape and content of the *CD*.

7. Robert Jenson's *God After God: The God of the Past and the God of the Future, Seen in the Work of Karl Barth*—Jenson provided an important interpretation of Barth's doctrine of God shortly after the latter's death. He is a sympathetic Lutheran reader of Barth who over the years has continually engaged Barth's writing with respect, even while pointing out what he feels to be some of Barth's shortcomings. Jenson's lively style, especially in his later works, is very enjoyable to read, even though—in my opinion—he is sometimes wrong!

8. Eberhard Jüngel's *God's Being Is in Becoming: The Trinitarian Being of God in the Theology of Karl Barth*. Although Jüngel's book is a highly significant interpretation of Barth's trinitarian doctrine of God, it also functions as an important constructive work of systematic theology in its own right. This one is a much more difficult book to read than some of the others listed here, but it is relatively short and worth the effort.

9. Bruce L. McCormack's *Karl Barth's Critically Realistic Dialectical Theology: Its Genesis and Development, 1909–1936*. You can't get very far in the current literature on Barth without encountering reference to McCormack's magisterial and seminal study on the development of Barth's early theology. This book is a benchmark work in helping to see historical and theological continuities and discontinuities between

the earlier and later Barth. I tell students that they avoid McCormack at their own peril.

10. Thomas F. Torrance's *Karl Barth, Biblical and Evangelical Theologian*. Torrance was arguably the most important English interpreter and sympathetic critic of Barth, and provided vital editorial oversight of the transformation of Barth's *Die kirchliche Dogmatik* into the *Church Dogmatics*. His *Karl Barth* provides a delightful theological vignette on Barth as a theologian. In many respects, the English-speaking world owes a debt of gratitude to Torrance for making available and disseminating Barth to English readers.

Bibliography

"2010 KBBC: Week 2, Day 1." *Der Evangelische Theologe.* Online: http://derevth. blogspot.com/2010/10/2010-kbbc-week-2-day-1.html.
Ables, Travis. "A Pneumatology of Christian Knowledge: The Holy Spirit and the Performance of the Mystery of God in Augustine and Barth." PhD diss., Vanderbilt University, 2010.
Adams, Sam. "Interview: Joel and Ethan Coen." *A. V. Club.* Online: http://www.avclub. com/articles/joel-and-ethan-coen,33937.
Albrecht, Christian. *Schleiermachers Theorie der Frömmigkeit.* Berlin: de Gruyter, 1994.
Anderson, Ray S. *The Shape of Practical Theology: Empowering Ministry with Theological Praxis.* Downers Grove, IL: InterVarsity, 2001.
Anrich, Ernst, ed. *Die Idee der deutschen Universität.* Darmstadt: Wissenschaftliche Buchgesellschaft, 1964.
Augustine. *Confessions.* Trans. Henry Chadwick. Oxford: Oxford University Press, 1991.
"Awards for No Country for Old Men." *International Movie Database.* http://www. imdb.com/title/tt0477348/awards.
Badiou, Alain. *Logics of Worlds: Being and Event 2.* Trans. Alberto Toscano. London: Continuum, 2009.
———. *Saint Paul: The Foundation of Universalism.* Trans. Ray Brassier. Stanford, CA: Stanford University Press, 2003.
———. *Second Manifesto for Philosophy.* Trans. Louise Burchill. Cambridge: Polity, 2011.
Balthasar, Hans Urs von. *Apokalypse der deutschen Seele.* 3 vols. Salzburg: Pustet, 1937–1939.
———. *Karl Barth: Darstellung und Deutung seiner Theologie.* 2nd ed. Cologne: Hegner, 1962.
———. *The Theology of Karl Barth.* Trans. Edward T. Oakes. San Francisco: Communio, 1992.
Barth, Karl. "Brechen und Bauen-eine Diskussion." In *"Der Götze wackelt": Zeitkritische Aufsätze, Reden und Briefe von 1930 bis 1960,* ed. Karl Kupisch, 108–23. Berlin: Käthe Vogt, 1961.
———. *Briefe 1961–1968.* Karl Barth Gesamtausgabe 5. Ed. Jürgen Fangmeier and Hinrich Stoevesandt. Zürich: TVZ, 1979.
———. "The Christian Community and the Civil Community." In *Against the Stream: Shorter Post-War Writings 1946–52,* ed. Ronald Gregor Smith, 13–50. London: SCM, 1954.

———. *The Christian Life: Church Dogmatics IV, 4: Lecture Fragments*. Grand Rapids: Eerdmans, 1981.

———. "The Christian's Place in Society." In *The Word of God and the Word of Man*, trans. Douglas Horton, 272–327. New York: HarperCollins, 1957.

———. "The Church between East and West." In *Against the Stream: Shorter Post-War Writings, 1946–1952*, ed. Ronald Gregor Smith, 125–46. London: SCM, 1954.

———. *Church Dogmatics*. Ed. G. W. Bromiley and T. F. Torrance. 4 vols. in 14 parts. Edinburgh: T. & T. Clark, 1956–1975.

———. *Community, State, and Church: Three Essays*. Garden City, NY: Doubleday, 1960.

———. *Dogmatics in Outline*. New York: Harper Torchbooks, 1959.

———. *The Epistle to the Romans*. Trans. Edwyn C. Hoskyns. London: Oxford University Press, 1933.

———. *Ethics*. Ed. Dietrich Braun. Trans. Geoffrey W. Bromiley. New York: Seabury, 1981.

———. *Evangelical Theology: An Introduction*. Grand Rapids: Eerdmans, 1963.

———. "From a Letter of Karl Barth to Landessuperintendent P[astor] W[alter] Herrenbrück, 21 December 1952." In *World Come of Age*, ed. Ronald Gregor Smith, 89–92. Philadelphia: Fortress, 1967.

———. *Gespräche 1959–1962*. Karl Barth Gesamtausgabe 4. Ed. Eberhard Busch. Zürich: TVZ, 1995.

———. *Gespräche 1963*. Karl Barth Gesamtausgabe 4. Ed. Eberhard Busch. Zürich: TVZ, 2005.

———. *Gespräche 1964–1968*. Karl Barth Gesamtausgabe 4. Ed. Eberhard Busch. Zürich: TVZ, 1996.

———. *Göttingen Dogmatics*. Ed. Hannelotte Reiffen. Trans. Geoffrey W. Bromiley. Grand Rapids: Eerdmans, 1991.

———. *How I Changed My Mind*. Ed. John D. Godsey. Richmond, VA: John Knox, 1966.

———. "Jesus Christ and the Movement for Social Justice (1911)." In *Karl Barth and Radical Politics*, ed. George Hunsinger, 19–37. Philadelphia: Westminster, 1976.

———. *Die kirchliche Dogmatik*. 4 vols. Munich: Kaiser, 1932; Zürich: TVZ, 1938–65.

———. *Letters 1961–1968*. Ed. Jürgen Fangmeier and Hinrich Stoevesandt. Trans. Geoffrey W. Bromiley. Grand Rapids: Eerdmans, 1981.

———. *Offene Briefe 1909–1935*. Karl Barth Gesamtausgabe 5. Ed. Diether Koch. Zürich: TVZ, 2001.

———. "Poverty." In *Against the Stream: Shorter Post-War Writings 1946–52*, ed. Ronald Gregor Smith, 241–46. London: SCM, 1954.

———. *Revolutionary Theology in the Making: Barth-Thurneysen Correspondence, 1914–1925*. Trans. James D. Smart. Richmond, VA: John Knox, 1964.

———. *Der Römerbrief (Erste Fassung) 1919*. Karl Barth Gesamtausgabe 2. Ed. Hermann Schmidt. Zurich: TVZ, 1985.

———. *The Theology of Schleiermacher*. Ed. Dietrich Ritschl. Trans. Geoffrey W. Bromiley. Edinburgh: T. & T. Clark, 1982.

———. *The Word of God and the Word of Man*. Trans. Douglas Horton. New York: Harper, 1957.

———. "Das Wort Gottes als Aufgabe der Theologie (1922)," in *Vorträge und kleinere Arbeiten, 1922-1925*, ed. Holger Finze, 144-75. Karl Barth Gesamtausgabe 3. Zürich: TVZ, 1990.
———. *Das Wort Gottes und die Theologie*. Munich: Kaiser, 1924.
Barth, Karl, and Rudolf Bultmann. *Karl Barth-Rudolf Bultmann Letters, 1922-1966*. Ed. Bernd Jaspert. Trans. Geoffrey W. Bromiley. Grand Rapids: Eerdmans, 1981.
Bayer, Oswald. *Theologie*. Gütersloh: Gütersloher, 1994.
Beck, Richard. "Theodicy and No Country for Old Men." *Experimental Theology*. http://experimentaltheology.blogspot.com/2010/10/theodicy-and-no-country-for-old-men.html.
Beker, J. Christiaan. *Paul the Apostle: The Triumph of God in Life and Thought*. Philadelphia: Fortress, 1984.
Bence, Clarence Luther. "John Wesley's Teleological Hermeneutic." PhD diss., Emory University, 1981.
Benjamin, Walter. "Theological-Political Fragment." In *Selected Writings*, ed. Howard Eiland and Michael W. Jennings, 3:305-6. Cambridge, MA: Harvard University Press, 2002.
Berkouwer, G. C. *The Triumph of Grace in the Theology of Karl Barth*. Grand Rapids: Eerdmans, 1956.
Bethge, Eberhard. *Dietrich Bonhoeffer: A Biography*. Ed. Victoria Barnett. Trans. Eric Mosbacher et al. Minneapolis: Fortress, 2000.
Betz, John R. "Beyond the Sublime: The Aesthetics of the Analogy of Being (Part One)." *Modern Theology* 21, no. 3 (2005) 367-411.
"Blood Meridian—The Open Yale Lectures." Biblioklept. http://biblioklept.org/2010/09/29/blood-meridian-the-open-yale-lectures.
Bonhoeffer, Dietrich. *Act and Being: Transcendental Philosophy and Ontology in Systematic Theology*. Ed. Clifford J. Green. Trans. H. Martin Rumscheidt. Dietrich Bonhoeffer Works 2. Minneapolis: Fortress, 2000.
———. *Berlin: 1932-1933*. Dietrich Bonhoeffer Works 12. Minneapolis: Fortress, 2009.
———. *The Communion of Saints: A Dogmatic Inquiry into the Sociology of the Church*. New York: Harper & Row, 1963.
———. *Conspiracy and Imprisonment: 1940-1945*. Ed. Mark S. Brocker. Trans. Lisa E. Dahill and Douglas W. Stott. Dietrich Bonhoeffer Works 16. Minneapolis: Fortress, 2006.
———. *Creation and Fall: A Theological Exposition of Genesis 1-3*. Ed. John W. de Gruchy. Trans. Douglas Stephen Bax. Dietrich Bonhoeffer Works 3. Minneapolis: Fortress, 1997.
———. *Discipleship*. Ed. Geffrey B. Kelly and John D. Godsey. Trans. Barbara Green and Reinhard Krauss. Dietrich Bonhoeffer Works 4. Minneapolis: Fortress, 2001.
———. *Ethics*. Ed. Clifford J. Green. Trans. Reinhard Krauss, Charles C. West, and Douglas W. Stott. Dietrich Bonhoeffer Works 6. Minneapolis: Fortress, 2005.
———. *Letters and Papers from Prison*. Ed. John W. de Gruchy. Trans. Isabel Best et al. Dietrich Bonhoeffer Works 8. Minneapolis: Fortress, 2010.
———. *London: 1933-1935*. Ed. Hans Goedeking et al. Trans. Isabel Best and Douglas W. Stott. Dietrich Bonhoeffer Works 13. Minneapolis: Fortress, 2007.
———. *Sanctorum Communio: A Theological Study of the Sociology of the Church*. Ed. Clifford J. Green. Trans. Reinhard Kraus and Nancy Lukens. Dietrich Bonhoeffer Works 1. Minneapolis: Fortress, 1998.

———. *A Testament to Freedom: The Essential Writings of Dietrich Bonhoeffer*. Ed. Geffrey B. Kelly and F. Burton Nelson. San Francisco: HarperSanFrancisco, 1995.

———. *The Way to Freedom, 1935–1939: From the Collected Works of Dietrich Bonhoeffer*. Ed. Edwin H. Robertson. His Letters, Lectures and Notes 2. New York: Harper & Row, 1966.

Bromiley, Geoffrey W. *An Introduction to the Theology of Karl Barth*. Grand Rapids: Eerdmans, 1979.

Brown, David. "In the Beginning Was the Image: Why the Arts Matter to Theology." Paper presented at the annual meeting for the Society for the Study of Theology, Manchester, UK, April 12–15, 2010.

Browning, Don. *A Fundamental Practical Theology: Descriptive and Strategic Proposals*. Minneapolis: Fortress, 1991.

Brunner, Emil, and Karl Barth. *Natural Theology: Comprising "Nature and Grace" by Professor Dr. Emil Brunner and the reply "No!" by Dr. Karl Barth*. Trans. Peter Fraenkel. London: Geoffrey Bles, 1946. Reprint, Wipf and Stock, 2002.

Burnett, Richard E. *Karl Barth's Theological Exegesis. The Hermeneutical Principles of the Römerbrief Period*. Grand Rapids: Eerdmans, 2004.

Busch, Eberhard. *The Great Passion*. Trans. Geoffrey Bromiley. Grand Rapids: Eerdmans, 2004.

———. *Karl Barth: His Life from Letters and Autobiographical Texts*. Trans. John Bowden. Philadelphia: Fortress, 1976.

———. *Unter dem Bogen des einen Bundes: Karl Barth und die Juden, 1933–1945*. Neukirchen-Vluyn: Neukirchener, 1996.

Butler, Judith. *Gender Trouble: Feminism and the Subversion of Identity*. New York: Routledge, 2006.

Calvin, John. *Calvin's Commentaries*. Trans. and ed. John King et al. 45 vols. in 22. Grand Rapids: Baker, 1993.

———. *Institutes of the Christian Religion*. Ed. John T. McNeill. Trans. Ford Lewis Battles. Library of Christian Classics 20–21. Louisville: Westminster John Knox, 1960.

Chalamet, Christophe. *Dialectical Theologians: Wilhelm Herrmann, Karl Barth and Rudolf Bultmann*. Zürich: TVZ, 2005.

Christian, William A. *Doctrines of Religious Communities: A Philosophical Study*. New Haven: Yale University Press, 1987.

Collins, John J. "Apocalyptic Theology and the Dead Sea Scrolls: A Response to Jonathan Wilson." In *Christian Beginnings and the Dead Sea Scrolls*, ed. John J. Collins and Craig A. Evans, 129–33. Grand Rapids: Baker Academic, 2006.

Collins, Kenneth J. "John Wesley's Platonic Conception of the Moral Law." *Wesleyan Theological Journal* 21 (1986) 116–128.

———. *The Theology of John Wesley: Holy Love and the Shape of Grace*. Nashville: Abingdon, 2007.

Collins Winn, Christian T. *"Jesus Is Victor!": The Significance of the Blumhardts for the Theology of Karl Barth*. Eugene, OR: Pickwick, 2009.

Cone, James H. *God of the Oppressed*. Rev. ed. Maryknoll, NY: Orbis, 1997.

Congdon, David W. "The No-God and God's No: Barth's Exegesis of Romans 1 in Romans II." With a response by Halden Doerge. Karl Barth Blog Conference 2009. http://derevth.blogspot.com/2009/08/2009-barth-blog-conference-day-3.html.

———. "Theology as Theanthropology: Barth's Theology of Existence in Its Existentialist Context." Paper presented at the 2012 Barth Conference: "Karl Barth's Visit to America: A Celebration of the 50th Anniversary of *Evangelical Theology.*" Princeton Theological Seminary, June 19, 2012.

Congdon, David, and W. Travis McMaken, "Theo-Blogging and the Future of Academic Theology: Reflections from the Trenches." *Princeton Theological Review* 17, no. 2 (2010) 91–100.

Crisp, Oliver D. "Did Christ have a *Fallen* Human Nature?" *International Journal of Systematic Theology* 6, no. 3 (2004) 270–88.

———. *Divinity and Humanity: The Incarnation Reconsidered.* New York: Cambridge University Press, 2007.

———. "'I Do Teach It, but I Also Do Not Teach It': The Universalism of Karl Barth." In *"All Shall Be Well": Explorations in Universalism and Christian Theology from Origen to Moltmann,* ed. Gregory MacDonald, 305–24. Eugene, OR: Cascade, 2011.

———. "On Barth's Denial of Universalism." *Themelios* 29, no. 1 (2003) 18–29.

Dalferth, Ingolf U. *Theology and Philosophy.* Oxford: Blackwell, 1988.

Dayton, Donald W. "'Good News to the Poor': The Methodist Experience after Wesley." In *From the Margins: A Celebration of the Theological Work of Donald W. Dayton,* ed. Christian T. Collins Winn, 77–108. Eugene, OR: Pickwick, 2007.

de Boer, Martinus C. "Paul and Apocalyptic Eschatology." In *The Encyclopedia of Apocalypticism,* ed. John J. Collins, 1:345–83. New York: Continuum, 2006.

Dempsey, Michael. *Trinity and Election in Contemporary Theology.* Grand Rapids: Eerdmans, 2011.

Deschner, John. *Wesley's Christology: An Interpretation.* Grand Rapids: Asbury, 1960.

Doerge, Halden. "Barth and the 'No Country.'" Inhabitatio Dei. http://www.inhabitatiodei.com/2010/10/11/barth-and-the-no-country.

Dole, Andrew C. *Schleiermacher on Religion and the Natural Order.* New York: Oxford University Press, 2010.

Dramm, Sabine. *Dietrich Bonhoeffer and the Resistance.* Trans. Margaret Kohl. Minneapolis: Fortress, 2009.

Edelstein, David. "Coen Heads." *New York Movies.* http://nymag.com/movies/filmfestivals/newyork/2007/38025.

Ellis, Daryl T. "Moral Action in the Midst of Havoc: Karl Barth and Dietrich Bonhoeffer on the Divine Command." MA thesis, Wheaton College Graduate School, IL, 2006.

Elwood, Christopher. "Getting Calvin Right: How Karl Barth Changed Our Reading of the Reformer." *The Princeton Theological Seminary Bulletin* 30 (2009) 63–80.

Fargo. DVD. Directed by Joel Coen. 1996. Santa Monica, CA: MGM, 2000.

Feuerbach, Ludwig. *The Essence of Faith According to Luther.* Trans. Melvin Cherno. New York: Harper & Row, 1967.

Fischer, Hermann. *Friedrich Daniel Ernst Schleiermacher.* Munich: Beck, 2001.

Fitch, David E. *The End of Evangelicalism? Discerning a New Faithfulness for Mission: Towards an Evangelical Political Theology.* Eugene, OR: Cascade, 2011.

Flett, John G. *The Witness of God: The Trinity, Missio Dei, Karl Barth, and the Nature of Christian Community.* Grand Rapids: Eerdmans, 2010.

Flint, Rebecca. "Joel Coen, Ethan Coen." *Coenesque.* http://www.coenbrothers.net/coens.html.

Forsyth, P. T. *The Cruciality of the Cross*. London: Hodder and Stoughton, 1910. Reprint, Wipf and Stock, 1997.

Foucault, Michel. "What is Enlightenment?" In *The Essential Foucault: Selections from the Essential Works of Foucault 1954–1984*, ed. Paul Rabinow and Nikolas Rose, 43–57. New York: New, 2003.

Funk, Robert W., ed. *Apocalypticism: Journal for Theology and the Church 6*. New York: Herder, 1969.

Gaventa, Beverly Roberts. "God Handed Them Over." In *Our Mother Saint Paul*, 113–23. Louisville: Westminster John Knox, 2007.

Gemmer, Anders, and August Messer. *Sören Kierkegaard und Karl Barth*. Stuttgart: Strecker and Schröder, 1925.

Gerrish, Brian. "Friedrich Schleiermacher on the Task of Theology." In *Tradition and the Modern World*, 13–48. Chicago: University of Chicago Press, 1978.

———. "*Ubi theologia, ibi ecclesia?* Schleiermacher, Troeltsch, and the Prospect for an Academic Theology." In *Continuing the Reformation*, 249–73. Chicago: University of Chicago Press, 1993.

Gill, Theodore. "Barth and Mozart." *Theology Today* 43, no. 3 (1986) 403–11.

Göckel, Matthias. *Barth and Schleiermacher on the Doctrine of Election: A Systematic-Theological Comparison*. Oxford: Oxford University Press, 2006.

———. "Mediating Theology in Germany." In *The Blackwell Companion to Nineteenth-Century Theology*, ed. David A. Fergusson, 301–19. Oxford: Wiley-Blackwell, 2010.

Godsey, John D. "The Architecture of Karl Barth's Church Dogmatics." *Scottish Journal of Theology* 9 (1956) 236–50.

———. "Barth and Bonhoeffer: The Basic Difference." *Quarterly Review* 7, no. 1 (1987) 9–27.

———. Review of *Reclaiming Dietrich Bonhoeffer: The Promise of His Theology*, by C. Marsh. *Theological Studies* 56, no. 1 (1995) 195.

———. *The Theology of Dietrich Bonhoeffer*. Philadelphia: Westminster, 1960.

Gollwitzer, Helmut. "Kingdom of God and Socialism in the Theology of Karl Barth." In *Karl Barth and Radical Politics*, ed. George Hunsinger, 77–120. Philadelphia: Westminster, 1976.

Gould, Joshua Robert. "Jacob Taubes: Apocalypse from Below." *Telos* 134 (2006) 140–56.

Green, Clifford J. *Karl Barth: Theologian of Freedom*. San Francisco: Collins, 1989.

Greggs, Tom. *Barth, Origen, and Universal Salvation: Restoring Particularity*. Oxford: Oxford University Press, 2009.

———. *Theology Against Religion: Constructive Dialogues with Bonhoeffer and Barth*. London: T. & T. Clark, 2011.

Harink, Douglas. *Paul among the Postliberals: Pauline Theology Beyond Christendom and Modernity*. Grand Rapids: Brazos, 2003.

Hart, David Bentley. *The Beauty of the Infinite*. Grand Rapids: Eerdmans, 2003.

Hart, Kevin. "Bonhoeffer's 'Religious Clothes': The Naked Man, The Secret, and What We Hear." In *Bonhoeffer and Continental Philosophy: Cruciform Thought*, ed. Brian Gregor and Jens Zimmermann, 177–97. Bloomington: Indiana University Press, 2009.

Hauerwas, Stanley. *Character and the Christian Life: A Study in Theological Ethics*. Notre Dame: University of Notre Dame Press, 1985.

———. *Christian Existence Today: Essays on Church, World, and Living in Between.* Grand Rapids: Brazos, 2001.
———. *A Community of Character: Toward a Constructive Christian Social Ethic.* Notre Dame: University of Notre Dame Press, 1981.
———. *The Hauerwas Reader.* Ed. John Berkman and Michael G. Cartwright. Durham, NC: Duke University Press, 2001.
———. *The Peaceable Kingdom: A Primer in Christian Ethics.* Notre Dame: University of Notre Dame Press, 1983.
———. *Vision and Virtue: Essays in Christian Ethical Reflection.* Notre Dame: University of Notre Dame Press, 1986.
———. *With the Grain of the Universe: The Church's Witness and Natural Theology.* Grand Rapids: Brazos, 2001.
Healy, Nicholas M. "Practices and the New Ecclesiology: Misplaced Concreteness?" *International Journal of Systematic Theology* 5, no. 3 (2003) 287–303.
Hector, Kevin W. "Ontological Violence and the Covenant of Grace: An Engagement between Karl Barth and Radical Orthodoxy." In *Karl Barth and American Evangelicalism*, ed. Bruce L. McCormack and Clifford B. Anderson, 323–46. Grand Rapids: Eerdmans, 2011.
———. *Theology without Metaphysics: God, Language, and the Spirit of Recognition.* Cambridge: Cambridge University Press, 2011.
Higton, Mike, and John C. McDowell, eds. *Conversing with Barth.* Aldershot: Ashgate, 2004.
Hirschberg, Lynn. "Coen Brothers Country." *New York Times Magazine.* http://www.nytimes.com/2007/11/11/magazine/11portfolio-t.html.
Hoekendijk, J. C. *The Church Inside Out.* Trans. Isaac C. Rottenberg. Philadelphia: Westminster, 1966.
Hogg, Trevor. "Absurdity & Carnage: A Coen Brothers Profile." *Flickering Myth.* http://flickeringmyth.blogspot.com/2010/02/absurdity-carnage-coen-brothers-profile_17.html.
Hölderlin, Friedrich. *Selected Poems and Fragments.* Trans. Michael Hamburger. London: Penguin, 1994.
Holmes, Christopher R. J. "Karl Barth on the Economy: In Dialogue with Kathryn Tanner." In *Commanding Grace: Studies in Karl Barth's Ethics*, ed. Daniel L. Migliore, 198–215. Grand Rapids: Eerdmans, 2010.
Holmes, Stephen. *The Bonhoeffer Legacy: Post-Holocaust Perspectives.* Minneapolis: Fortress, 2006.
Hordern, William. *A Layman's Guide to Protestant Theology.* Rev. ed. New York: Macmillan, 1968.
Howard, Thomas Albert. *Protestant Theology and the Making of the Modern German University.* Oxford: Oxford University Press, 2006.
Hughes, Carl. "Subversive Revelation: Kierkegaard on Unknowing Christ in Desire." Paper presented at the annual meeting for the American Academy of Religion, November 19, 2011.
Hunsinger, Deborah van Deusen. *Theology and Pastoral Counseling: A New Interdisciplinary Approach.* Grand Rapids: Eerdmans, 1995.
Hunsinger, George. "After Luther: How Barth Socialized the Evangelical 'As.'" *Karl Barth Society Newsletter* 33 (Fall 2006) n.p.

———. "Election and the Trinity: Twenty-Five Theses on the Theology of Karl Barth." *Modern Theology* 24, no. 2 (2008) 179–98.

———. *How to Read Karl Barth: The Shape of His Theology*. Oxford: Oxford University Press, 1993.

———. "Karl Barth's Christology: Its Basic Chalcedonian Character." In *The Cambridge Companion to Karl Barth*, ed. John Webster, 127–42. New York: Cambridge University Press, 2000.

———. "Torture *Is* the Ticking Time-Bomb: Why the Necessity Defense Fails." *Dialog* 47, no. 3 (2008) 228–39.

———. "What Karl Barth Learned from Martin Luther (1998)." In *Disruptive Grace: Studies in the Theology of Karl Barth*, 279–304. Grand Rapids: Eerdmans, 2000.

Hütter, Reinhard. "Karl Barth's 'Dialectical Catholicism': Sic et Non." *Modern Theology* 16, no. 2 (2000) 137–58.

"Interview: Josh Brolin on 'No Country for Old Men.'" *Cinema Confidential*. http://www.cinecon.com/news/1142/interview-josh-brolin-no-country-for-old-men.

Jacobs, Jay S. "Joel and Ethan Coen: Two Serious Men Gaze Into Their Past." *Pop Entertainment*. http://www.popentertainment.com/coenbros.htm.

Jennings, Theodore W., Jr. *Good News to the Poor: John Wesley's Evangelical Economics*. Nashville: Abingdon, 1990.

Jenson, Robert W. *Alpha and Omega: A Study in the Theology of Karl Barth*. New York: Nelson, 1963.

———. "Christian Civilization." In *God, Truth, and Witness: Engaging Stanley Hauerwas*, ed. L. Gregory Jones, Reinhard Hütter, and C. Rosalee Velloso Ewell, 153–63. Grand Rapids: Brazos, 2005.

———. *God after God: The God of the Past and the God of the Future, As Seen in the Work of Karl Barth*. Minneapolis: Fortress, 2010. 1969.

———. "The Hidden and Triune God." *International Journal of Systematic Theology* 2, no. 1 (2000) 5–12.

———. "How the Word Lost Its Story." *First Things* 36 (1993) 19–24.

———. *Systematic Theology*. 2 vols. Oxford: Oxford University Press, 1997–99.

———. *The Triune Identity: God According to the Gospel*. Philadelphia: Fortress, 1982. Reprint, Wipf and Stock, 2002.

———. "You Wonder Where the Spirit Went." *Pro Ecclesia* 2, no. 3 (1993) 296–304.

Johnson, Keith. *Karl Barth and the Analogia Entis*. London: T. & T. Clark, 2010.

Jones, Paul Dafydd. *The Humanity of Christ: Christology in Karl Barth's Church Dogmatics*. London: T. & T. Clark, 2008.

———. "The Rhetoric of War in Karl Barth's Epistle to the Romans: A Theological Analysis." *Journal for the History of Modern Theology / Zeitschrift für Neuere Theologiegeschichte* 17, no. 1 (2010) 90–111.

Jüngel, Eberhard. *God as the Mystery of the World: On the Foundation of the Theology of the Crucified One in the Dispute between Theism and Atheism*. Trans. Darrell L. Guder. Grand Rapids: Eerdmans, 1983.

———. *God's Being Is in Becoming: The Trinitarian Being of God in the Theology of Karl Barth*. Trans. John Webster. Grand Rapids: Eerdmans, 2001.

———. *Gott als Geheimnis der Welt: Zur Begründung der Theologie des Gekreuzigten im Streit zwischen Theismus und Atheismus*. Tübingen: Mohr, 1977.

———. *Gottes Sein ist im Werden: Verantwortliche Rede vom Sein Gottes bei Karl Barth: Eine Paraphrase*. 4th ed. Tübingen: Mohr, 1986. 1965.

———. *Karl Barth: A Theological Legacy.* Trans. Garrett E. Paul. Philadelphia: Westminster, 1986.

———. "Die Möglichkeit theologischer Anthropologie auf dem Grunde der Analogie." *Evangelische Theologie* 22 (1962) 541–42.

———. "The Mystery of Substitution: A Dogmatic Conversation with Heinrich Vogel." In *Theological Essays II*, edited and trans. John Webster, 145–62. Edinburgh: T. & T. Clark, 1995.

———. "Vom Tod des lebendigen Gottes: Ein Plakat [1968]." In *Unterwegs zur Sache: Theologische Bemerkungen*, 105–25. München: Kaiser, 1972.

Kant, Immanuel. *Religion and Rational Theology.* Ed. Allan Wood and George Di Giovanni. Cambridge: Cambridge University Press, 1996.

Kantzer Komline, Han-luen. "Finitude in the Beauty of the Infinite: A Theological Assessment and Proposal." *The Heythrop Journal* 50, no. 5 (2009) 806–18.

Käsemann, Ernst. "The Beginnings of Christian Theology." In *New Testament Questions of Today*, 82–107. Philadelphia: Fortress, 1969.

———. *Commentary on Romans.* Trans. and ed. Geoffrey W. Bromiley. Grand Rapids: Eerdmans, 1980.

———. "On the Topic of Primitive Christian Apocalyptic." In *New Testament Questions of Today*, 108–37. Philadelphia: Fortress, 1969.

———. "'The Righteousness of God' in Paul." In *New Testament Questions of Today*, 168–93. London: SCM, 1969.

Kegan, Robert. *The Evolving Self: Problem and Process in Human Development.* Cambridge, MA: Harvard University Press, 1982.

———. *In Over Our Heads: The Mental Demands of Modern Life.* Cambridge, MA: Harvard University Press, 1994.

Kellerman, Bill Wylie, ed. *A Keeper of the Word: Selected Writings of William Stringfellow.* Grand Rapids: Eerdmans, 1994.

Kerr, Nathan. *Christ, History, and Apocalyptic: The Politics of Christian Mission.* Theopolitical Visions. Eugene, OR: Cascade, 2009.

Kierkegaard, Søren. "Om Forskjellen mellem et Genie og en Apostel." In *Samlede Værker*, ed. Peter P. Rohde, 15:49–64. Copenhagen: Gyldendal, 1963.

———. *Works of Love.* Trans. Howard and Edna Hong. New York: Harper Perennial, 1962.

Kim, Sung-Sup. "Proclaiming Jesus in a Strange Land: Possibilities and Limits of an Asian Christology." *Koinonia* 20 (2008) 68–80.

Kline, Peter. "Participation in God and the Nature of Christian Community: Robert Jenson and Eberhard Jüngel." *International Journal of Systematic Theology* 13, no. 1 (2011) 38–61.

Kotsko, Adam. *Žižek and Theology.* London: T. & T. Clark, 2008.

Lacan, Jacques. *Écrits.* Trans. Bruce Fink in collaboration with Héloïse Fink and Russell Grigg. New York: Norton, 2005.

The Ladykillers. DVD. Directed by Joel Coen and Ethan Coen. 2004; Burbank, CA: Walt Disney Video, 2004.

Lauwerier, Hans. *Fractals: Endlessly Repeated Geometrical Figures.* Trans. Sophia Gill-Hoffstadt. Princeton: Princeton University Press, 1991.

Lehmann, Paul L. "The Concreteness of Theology: Reflections on the Conversation Between Barth and Bonhoeffer." In *Footnotes to a Theology: The Karl Barth*

Colloquium of 1972, ed. H. Martin Rumscheidt, 53–76. Waterloo, ON: Corporation for the Publication of Academic Studies in Religion in Canada, 1974.

Levinas, Emmanuel. *Totality and Infinity*. Trans. Alphonso Lingis. Pittsburgh: Duquesne University Press, 1969.

Loder, James. *The Logic of the Spirit: Human Development in Theological Perspective*. San Francisco: Jossey-Bass, 1998.

———. "Normativity and Context in Practical Theology: The Interdisciplinary Issue." In *Practical Theology—International Perspectives*, ed. Friedrich Schweitzer and Johannes A. van der Ven, 359–81. Berlin: Lang, 1999.

Long, D. Stephen. *John Wesley's Moral Theology: The Quest for God and Goodness*. Nashville: Kingswood, 2005.

Loughlin, Gerard. "Introduction: The End of Sex." In *Queer Theology: Rethinking the Western Body*, ed. Gerard Loughlin, 1–34. Oxford: Blackwell, 2007.

Luther, Martin. *Vorlesung über den Römerbrief 1515/1516*. Ed. Johannes Ficker. Leipzig: Dieterich, 1908.

Macken, John. *The Autonomy Theme in the Church Dogmatics: Karl Barth and His Critics*. Cambridge: Cambridge University Press, 1990.

MacKinnon, Donald. "Kenosis and Establishment." In *The Stripping of the Altars*, 13–40. London: Fontana, 1969.

Malysz, Piotr. "From Divine Sovereignty to Divine Conversation: Karl Barth and Robert Jenson on God's Being and Analogy." *Concordia Theological Quarterly* 71, no. 1 (2007) 29–55.

Mandelbrot, Benoit B. *The Fractal Geometry of Nature*. San Francisco: Freeman, 1982.

Mangina, Joseph. "Bearing the Marks of Jesus: The Church in the Economy of Salvation in Barth and Hauerwas." *Scottish Journal of Theology* 52, no. 3 (1999) 269–305.

Marga, Amy. *Karl Barth's Dialogue with Catholicism in Göttingen and Münster: Its Significance for His Doctrine of God*. Tübingen: Mohr/Siebeck, 2010.

Marquardt, Friedrich-Wilhelm. "Socialism in the Theology of Karl Barth." In *Karl Barth and Radical Politics*, ed. George Hunsinger, 47–76. Philadelphia: Westminster, 1976.

Marquardt, Manfred. *John Wesley's Social Ethics: Praxis and Principles*. Nashville: Abingdon, 1992.

Marsh, Charles. *Reclaiming Dietrich Bonhoeffer: The Promise of His Theology*. New York: Oxford University Press, 1994.

Marshall, Bruce. "Absorbing the World: Christianity and the Universe of Truths." In *Theology and Dialogue: Essays in Conversation with George Lindbeck*, ed. Bruce Marshall, 69–102. Notre Dame: University of Notre Dame Press, 1990.

Martyn, J. Louis. *Galatians*. Anchor Bible 33A. New York: Doubleday, 1997.

Matlock, Barry. *Unveiling the Apocalyptic Paul: Paul's Interpreters and the Rhetoric of Criticism*. Sheffield, UK: Sheffield Academic, 1996.

McCall, Thomas. "On Understanding Scripture as the Word of God." In *Analytic Theology: New Essays in the Philosophy of Theology*, ed. Oliver D. Crisp and Michael C. Rea, 171–86. Oxford: Oxford University Press, 2009.

McCarthy, Cormac. *Blood Meridian or the Evening Redness in the West*. New York: Vintage, 1985.

———. *No Country for Old Men*. New York: Knopf, 2005.

McCormack, Bruce L. "Election and the Trinity." *Scottish Journal Theology* 63 (2010) 203–24.

———. "Karl Barth's Christology as a Resource for a Reformed Version of Kenoticism." *International Journal of Systematic Theology* 8, no. 3 (2006) 243–51.
———. *Karl Barth's Critically Realistic Dialectical Theology: Its Genesis and Development 1909–1936.* Oxford: Clarendon, 1995.
———. "Karl Barth's Historicized Christology: Just How 'Chalcedonian' Is It?" In *Orthodox and Modern: Studies in the Theology of Karl Barth*, 201–33. Grand Rapids: Baker Academic, 2008.
———. *Orthodox and Modern: Studies in the Theology of Karl Barth.* Grand Rapids: Baker Academic, 2008.
———. "Seek God Where He May Be Found: A Response to Edwin Chr. van Driel," *Scottish Journal of Theology* 60, no. 1 (2007) 62–79.
McFarland, Douglas. "No Country for Old Men as Moral Philosophy." In *The Philosophy of the Coen Brothers*, ed. Mark T. Conard, 163–78. Lexington: University Press of Kentucky, 2008.
McKenny, Gerald. *The Analogy of Grace: Karl Barth's Moral Theology.* New York: Oxford University Press, 2010.
McMaken, W. Travis. "Religion, Reformation, and Sacred Space." Public Lecture presented at Lindenwood University. St. Charles, MO. October 18, 2011.
———. *The Sign of the Gospel: Toward an Evangelical Doctrine of Infant Baptism after Karl Barth.* Emerging Scholars. Minneapolis: Fortress, 2013.
———. "Why I Support #OWS as a Reformed Theologian." *Unbound: An Interactive Journal of Christian Social Justice* (Feb/Mar 2012). http://justiceunbound.org/journal/ current-issue/why-i-support-ows-as-a-reformed-theologian.
Mehringer, H. "Sieg des Glaubens. Zum 30. Januar." *Der Schulungsbrief* (1939) 2–4. http://www.calvin.edu/academic/cas/gpa/schulo1.htm.
Milbank, John. *Theology and Social Theory: Beyond Secular Reason.* Oxford: Blackwell, 1993.
Miles, Rebekah L. "Happiness, Holiness, and the Moral Life in John Wesley." In *The Cambridge Companion to John Wesley*, ed. Randy L. Maddox and Jason E. Vickers, 207–24. Cambridge: Cambridge University Press, 2010.
Molendijk, Arie L. *Aus dem Dunklen ins Helle: Wissenschaft und Theologie im Denken von Heinrich Scholz, mit unveröffentlichten Thesenreihen von Heinrich Scholz und Karl Barth.* Amsterdam: Rodopi, 1991.
Morton, Nelle. *The Journey Is Home.* Boston: Beacon, 1985.
Mühlberger, Detlef. *Hitler's Voice: The Völkischer Beobachter, 1920–1933.* 2 vols. Oxford: Lang, 2004.
Myers, Benjamin. "From Faithfulness to Faith in the Theology of Karl Barth." In *The Faith of Jesus Christ: Exegetical, Biblical, and Theological Studies*, ed. Michael F. Bird and Preston M. Sprinkle, 291–308. Carlisle, UK: Paternoster, 2009.
Neder, Adam. *Participation in Christ: An Entry into Karl Barth's Church Dogmatics.* Louisville: Westminster John Knox, 2009.
———. Review of *Being in Action* by Paul T. Nimmo. *International Journal of Systematic Theology*, 10, no. 2 (2008) 233–36.
Newman, John Henry. *An Essay on the Development of Doctrine.* Notre Dame: University of Notre Dame Press, 1989.
Niebuhr, H. Richard. *Faith on Earth: An Inquiry into the Structure of Human Faith.* Ed. Richard R. Niebuhr. New Haven: Yale University Press, 1989.

Nietzsche, Friedrich. *Thus Spoke Zarathustra*. Ed. Adrian Del Caro and Robert B. Pippin. Trans. Adrian Del Caro. Cambridge: Cambridge University Press, 2006.

Nimmo, Paul T. *Being in Action: The Theological Shape of Barth's Ethical Vision*. London: T. & T. Clark, 2007.

No Country for Old Men. DVD. Directed by Joel Coen and Ethan Coen. 2007; Burbank, CA: Walt Disney Video, 2008.

Oakes, Kenneth. "The Question of Nature and Grace in Karl Barth: Humanity as Creature and as Covenant Partner." *Modern Theology* 23, no. 4 (2007) 595–616.

O'Donovan, Oliver. *The Desire of the Nations: Rediscovering the Roots of Political Theology*. Cambridge: Cambridge University Press, 1996.

O'Regan, Cyril. *Gnostic Return in Modernity*. Albany: State University of New York Press, 2001.

———. "Žižek and Milbank and the Hegelian Death of God." *Modern Theology* 26, no. 2 (2010) 278–86.

Osmer, Richard. *Practical Theology: An Introduction*. Grand Rapids: Eerdmans, 2008.

Pangritz, Andreas. "Dietrich Bonhoeffer: 'Within, not Outside the Barthian Movement.'" In *Bonhoeffer's Intellectual Formation*, ed. Peter Frick, 245–82. Tübingen: Mohr/Siebeck, 2008.

———. *Karl Barth in the Theology of Dietrich Bonhoeffer*. Trans. Barbara and Martin Rumscheidt. Grand Rapids: Eerdmans, 2000.

Pannenberg, Wolfhart. *Theology and the Philosophy of Science*. Trans. Francis McDonagh. Philadelphia: Westminster, 1976.

Park, Chang Hoon. "The Theology of John Wesley as 'Checks to Antinomianism.'" PhD diss., Drew University, 2002.

The Passion of the Christ. DVD. Directed by Mel Gibson. 2004: Beverly Hills, CA: Newmarket Films, 2004.

Pound, Marcus. *Žižek: A (Very) Critical Introduction*. Grand Rapids: Eerdmans, 2008.

Price, David J. *Karl Barth's Anthropology in Light of Modern Thought*. Grand Rapids: Eerdmans, 2002.

Raising Arizona. DVD. Directed by Joel Coen. 1987; Beverly Hills, CA: 20th Century Fox Home Entertainment, 2002.

Rea, Michael C. "Introduction." In *Analytic Theology: New Essays in the Philosophy of Theology*, ed. Oliver D. Crisp and Michael C. Rea, 1–30. Oxford: Oxford University Press, 2009.

Redeker, Martin. *Schleiermacher: Life and Thought*. Trans. John Wallhausser. Philadelphia: Fortress, 1973.

Rose, Matthew. *Ethics with Barth: God, Metaphysics, and Morals*. Farnham, UK: Ashgate, 2010.

Rowland, Christopher. *The Open Heaven: A Study of Apocalyptic in Judaism and Early Christianity*. New York: Crossroad, 1982.

Rowland, Christopher, and Christopher Morray-Jones. *The Mystery of God: Early Jewish Mysticism and the New Testament*. Leiden: Brill, 2009.

Schelling, F. W. J. *Vorlesungen über die Methoden des Akademischen Studiums*. Vol. 3 of *Schellings Werke: Münchner Jubiläumsdruck*, ed. Manfred Schröter. 6 vols. Munich: Beck, 1958.

Schlegel, Thomas. *Theologie als unmögliche Notwendigkeit*. Göttingen: Neukirchener, 2007.

Schleiermacher, F. D. E. *Brief Outline of Theology As a Field of Study: Translation of the 1811 and 1830 Editions*. Trans. Terrence Tice. Lewiston, NY: Mellen, 1990.

———. *The Christian Faith*. Edinburgh: T. & T. Clark, 1999.

———. *Der christliche Glaube: Nach den Grundsätzen der evangelischen Kirche im Zusammenhange dargestellt (1830/31)*. Ed. Rolf Schäfer. Berlin: de Gruyter, 2008.

———. *Dialektik*. Ed. Manfred Frank. 2 vols. Frankfurt: Suhrkamp, 2001.

———. *Kurze Darstellung des theologischen Studiums zum Behuf einleitender Vorlesungen (1811/1830)*. Ed. Dirk Schmid. Berlin: de Gruyter, 2002.

———. *On the Glaubenslehre: Two Letters to Dr. Lücke*. Trans. James Duke and Francis Fiorenza. Atlanta: Scholars, 1981.

———. *On Religion: Speeches to Its Cultured Despisers*. Ed. Richard Crouter. Cambridge: Cambridge University Press, 1996.

Schmitt, Carl. *The Concept of the Political*. Chicago: University of Chicago Press, 1996.

———. *Legality and Legitimacy*. Trans. Jeffrey Seitzer. Durham, NC: Duke University Press, 2004.

———. *Political Theology*. Trans. George Schwab. Chicago, IL: University of Chicago Press, 1985.

Shults, F. LeRon. "A Dubious Christological Formula: From Leontius of Byzantium to Karl Barth." *Theological Studies* 57 (1996) 431–46.

———. *Reforming Theological Anthropology: After the Philosophical Turn to Relationality*. Grand Rapids: Eerdmans, 2003.

Smith, Christian. *What Is A Person? Rethinking Humanity, Social Life, and the Moral Good from the Person Up*. Chicago, IL: University of Chicago Press, 2010.

Sturm, Richard E. "Defining the Word 'Apocalyptic': A Problem in Biblical Criticism." In *Apocalyptic in the New Testament*, ed. Joel Marcus and Marion L. Soards, 17–48. Sheffield, UK: JSOT Press, 1989.

Sundermeier, Theo. *Konvivenz und Differenz: Studien zu einer verstehenden Missionswissenschaft*. Ed. Volker Küster. Erlangen: Verlag der Ev.-Luth. Mission, 1995.

Takizawa, Katsumi. *Karu Baruto kenkyu*. 2 vols. Takizawa Katsumi chosakushu. Tokyo: Hozokan, 1975.

———. "Die Überwindung des Modernismus—Kitaro Nishidas Philosophie und die Theologie Karl Barths." In *Reflexionen über die universale Grundlage in Buddhismus und Christentum*, 127–71. Frankfurt: Lang, 1980.

Tanner, Kathryn, "Barth and the Economy of Grace." In *Commanding Grace: Studies in Karl Barth's Ethics*, ed. Daniel L. Migliore, 176–97. Grand Rapids: Eerdmans, 2010.

———. *Christ the Key*. Cambridge: Cambridge University Press, 2010.

———. "Creation and Providence." In *The Cambridge Companion to Karl Barth*, ed. John Webster, 111–126. New York: Cambridge University Press, 2000.

———. *Economy of Grace*. Minneapolis: Fortress, 2005.

———. *God and Creation in Christian Theology: Tyranny or Empowerment?* Oxford: Blackwell, 1988.

———. "Incarnation, Cross, and Sacrifice: A Feminist-Inspired Reappraisal." *Anglican Theological Review* 86, no. 1 (2004) 35–56.

———. *Jesus, Humanity and the Trinity: A Brief Systematic Theology*. Minneapolis: Fortress, 2001.

———. *The Politics of God: Christian Theologies and Social Justice*. Minneapolis: Fortress, 1992.

———. *Theories of Culture: A New Agenda for Theology*. Minneapolis: Fortress, 1997.
Taubes, Jacob. *Ad Carl Schmitt: Gegenstrebige Fügung*. Berlin: Merve, 1987.
———. "Christian Nihilism." Review of *Against the Stream*, by Karl Barth. *Commentary* 18 (1954) 269–72.
———. *Occidental Eschatology*. Trans. David Ratmoko. Stanford, CA: Stanford University Press, 2009.
———. "On The Nature of the Theological Method: Some Reflections on the Methodological Principles of Tillich's Theology." In *From Cult to Culture: Fragments Toward a Critique of Historical Reason*, ed. Charlotte E. Fonrobert and Amir Engel, 195–213. Stanford, CA: Stanford University Press, 2010.
———. *The Political Theology of Paul*. Trans. Dana Hollander. Stanford, CA: Stanford University Press, 2004.
———. "Theodicy and Theology: A Philosophical Analysis of Karl Barth's Dialectical Theology." In *From Cult to Culture: Fragments Toward a Critique of Historical Reason*, ed. Charlotte E. Fonrobert and Amir Engel, 177–94. Stanford, CA: Stanford University Press, 2010.
———. "Theology and Political Theory." In *From Cult to Culture: Fragments Toward a Critique of Historical Reason*, ed. Charlotte E. Fonrobert and Amir Engel, 222–32. Stanford, CA: Stanford University Press, 2010.
Terpstra, Marin, and Theo de Wit. "'No Spiritual Investment in the World As It Is': Jacob Taubes's Negative Political Theology." In *Flight of the Gods: Philosophical Perspectives on Negative Theology*. Ed. Ilse N. Bulhof and Laurens ten Kate. New York: Fordham University Press, 2000.
Thomas, R. S. *Collected Later Poems: 1988–2000*. Tarset, Northumberland, UK: Bloodaxe, 2004.
Thompson, Geoff. "Salvation beyond the Church's Ministry: Reflections on Barth and Rahner." In *God of Salvation. Soteriology in Theological Perspective*, ed. Ivor J. Davidson and Murray A. Rae, 137–54. Farnham, UK: Ashgate, 2011.
Torrance, Thomas F. *Karl Barth, Biblical and Evangelical Theologian*. Edinburgh: T. & T. Clark, 1990.
Tracy, David, *The Analogical Imagination: Christian Theology and the Culture of Pluralism*. New York: Crossroad, 1982.
Troeltsch, Ernst. "Die Dogmatik der 'Religionsgeschichtlichen Schule.'" In *Gesammelte Schriften Band 2: Zur religiösen Lage, Religionsphilosophie und Ethik*, 500–524. Tübingen: Mohr/Siebeck, 1913.
Tropel, Fred. "Joel Coen on No Country for Old Men." *The Can Magazine*. http://www.canmag.com/nw/9576-no-country-for-old-men-joel-coen.
True Grit. DVD. Directed by Joel Coen and Ethan Coen. 2010; Hollywood, CA: Paramount Pictures, 2011.
Webb, Stephen H. *Refiguring Theology: The Rhetoric of Karl Barth*. Albany: SUNY Press, 1991.
Webster, John. *Barth*. New York: Continuum, 2000.
———. "Reading the Bible: The Example of Barth and Bonhoeffer." In *Word and Church: Essays in Church Dogmatics*, 87–110. Edinburgh: T. & T. Clark, 2006.
Werner, Martin. *Das Weltanschauungsproblem bei Karl Barth und Albert Schweitzer: Eine Auseinandersetzung*. Münich: Beck, 1924.
Wesley, John. *Explanatory Notes Upon the New Testament*. Niagara Falls, NY: Wesleyan Heritage, 2009.

———. *Thoughts Upon Slavery*. 4th ed. Dublin: Whitestone, 1775.
———. *The Works of John Wesley*. Ed. Thomas Jackson. Grand Rapids: Baker, 1978.
———. *The Works of John Wesley*. Bicentennial ed. 17 vols. Nashville: Abingdon, 1984–.
Wigley, Stephen. *Karl Barth and Hans Urs von Balthasar: A Critical Engagement*. New York: T. & T. Clark, 2007.
Wildi, Hans. *Bibliographie Karl Barth*. 3 vols. Zurich: TVZ, 1984.
Williams, Rowan. "Barth on the Triune God." In *Karl Barth: Studies of His Theological Method*. Ed. S. W. Sykes. Oxford: Clarendon, 1979.
Wilson, Jonathan R. "The Dead Sea Scrolls and Christian Theology." In *Christian Beginnings and the Dead Sea Scrolls*, ed. John J. Collins and Craig A. Evans, 123–28. Grand Rapids: Baker Academic, 2006.
Yeats, William Butler. *The Collected Poems of W. B. Yeats*. Ed. Richard J. Finneran. 2nd ed. New York: Scribner Paperback Poetry, 1996.
Yoder, John Howard. *The Original Revolution: Essays on Christian Pacifism*. Scottsdale, PA: Herald, 2003.
Ziegler, Philip. *Doing Theology When God Is Forgotten: The Theological Achievement of Wolf Krötke*. New York: Lang, 2007.
Ziolkowski, Theodore. *German Romanticism and Its Institutions*. Princeton: Princeton University Press, 1990.
Žižek, Slavoj, and John Milbank. *The Monstrosity of Christ: Paradox or Dialectic*. Ed. Creston Davis. Cambridge, MA: MIT Press, 2009.

Contributors

Sigurd Baark, PhD (Princeton Theological Seminary). His dissertation is entitled, "Seeking out the Enemy in his own Camp: problems and proofs in dialectical theology."

William T. Barnett, doctoral candidate (Princeton Theological Seminary), and assistant pastor at Highrock Covenant Church in Arlington, MA. His dissertation is entitled, "'At Once Believing and Enlightening': The Theology of Robert W. Jenson and the Problem of Modernity."

Blair D. Bertrand, doctoral candidate (Princeton Theological Seminary), and pastor at Calvin Presbyterian Church in Abbotsford, BC. His research interests are theological anthropology, vocation, prayer, and how these intersect in the everyday life of young people.

Matthew J. Aragon Bruce, PhD (Princeton Theological Seminary), and assistant professor of religion at Lindenwood University in St. Charles, MO. His dissertation is entitled, "Theology without Voluntarism: Divine Agency and God's Freedom for Creation."

Christian T. Collins Winn, PhD (Drew University), and professor of historical and systematic theology and chair of the biblical and theological studies department at Bethel University in St. Paul, MN. His publications include, *'Jesus is Victor!' The Significance of the Blumhardts for the Theology of Karl Barth* (Pickwick, 2009), and (as editor) *The Pietist Impulse in Christianity* (Pickwick, 2011).

David W. Congdon, PhD (Princeton Theoloigcal Seminary), and associate editor of academic books at IVP Academic. His dissertation is entitled, "The Mission of Demythologizing: Rudolf Bultmann's Dialectical Theology," and he blogs at *The Fire and the Rose* (http://fireandrose.blogspot.com/). He is author of the forthcoming book, *The God Who Saves: A Dogmatic Sketch* (Cascade).

Jon Coutts, PhD (University of Aberdeen), and pastor of Richmond Alliance Church in Greater Vancouver, BC. His dissertation is entitled, "As We Forgive: Forgiveness and the Church in Karl Barth's Doctrine of Reconciliation." He blogs at *This Side of Sunday* (http://thissideofsunday.blogspot.com/) and *Out of Bounds: Theology in the Far Country* (http://theologyoutofbounds.wordpress.com/).

Halden Doerge, teacher and theologian at the Church of the Servant King in Portland, Oregon. He is currently working on a book with Nathan Kerr and Ry Siggelkow entitled, *Kingdom-World-Church: A Theological Manifesto* (Cascade Books). He blogs at *Inhabitatio Dei* (http://www.inhabitatiodei.com/).

Katherine M. Douglass, PhD (Princeton Theological Seminary). Her dissertation is entitled, "The Transformative Role of the Arts in the Faith Lives of Young Adults."

John L. Drury, PhD (Princeton Theological Seminary), and assistant professor of systematic theology and Christian ministry for Wesley Seminary at Indiana Wesleyan University in Marion, IN. His dissertation is entitled, "The Resurrected God: Karl Barth's Trinitarian Theology of Easter."

Brad East, doctoral student (Yale University). His research interests include ecclesiology, theologies of scripture and its interpretation, and the ethics of peace, war, and nonviolence. He blogs at *Resident Theology* (http://resident-theology.blogspot.com).

Matthias Gockel, PhD (Princeton Theological Seminary), and Wissenschaftlicher Mitarbeiter at Friedrich-Schiller-Universität in Jena, Germany. He is the author of *Barth and Schleiermacher on the Doctrine of Election: A Systematic-Theological Comparison* (Oxford, 2007).

Andrew R. Guffey, doctoral candidate (University of Virginia). His dissertation explores the book of Revelation's imagery in light of the visual culture of ancient Asia Minor, and he blogs at *Seeing the Form* (http://www.seeingtheform.blogspot.com).

David Guretzki, PhD (McGill University), and professor of theology, church and public life at Briercrest College and Seminary in Caronport, SK. He is the author of *Karl Barth on the Filioque* (Ashgate, 2009) and is currently writing a book on trinitarian theology for InterVarsity Press. He blogs at *Theommentary* (http://dguretzki.wordpress.com/).

J. Scott Jackson, PhD (University of Chicago). His dissertation is entitled, "Jesus Christ as the God who Loves in Freedom: Election, Covenant and the Trinity in the Thought of Karl Barth," and he blogs at *Theology of Freedom* (http://www.theologyoffreedom.blogspot.com).

Paul Dafydd Jones, PhD (Harvard University), and associate professor of religious studies at the University of Virginia. His first book, *The Humanity of Christ: Christology in Karl Barth's Church Dogmatics* (T & T Clark, 2008), was honored with a Templeton Award for Theological Promise. He is also the coeditor of the *Oxford Handbook of Karl Barth* (forthcoming, 2016).

Peter Kline, doctoral student (Vanderbilt University). He is a fellow in the Theology and Practice Program, and writes for the online journal *Gaga Stigmata* (http://gagajournal.blogspot.com/).

Han-luen Kantzer Komline, doctoral candidate (University of Notre Dame), and Fulbright Fellow (2008–09). Her dissertation addresses Augustine's conception of will.

W. Travis McMaken, PhD (Princeton Theological Seminary), and assistant professor of religion at Lindenwood University in St. Charles, MO. He is the author of *The Sign of the Gospel: Toward an Evangelical Doctrine of Infant Baptism after Karl Barth* (Fortress, 2013), and he blogs at *Die Evangelischen Theologen* (http://derevth.blogspot.com).

Benjamin Myers, PhD (James Cook University), and lecturer in systematic theology at Charles Sturt University's School of Theology in Sydney, Australia. He is author of *Christ the Stranger: The Theology of Rowan Williams* (Bloomsbury T&T Clark, 2012) and *Milton's Theology of Freedom* (De Gruyter, 2006). He blogs at *Faith and Theology* (http://faith-theology.com).

Matthew Puffer, doctoral candidate (University of Virginia), and dissertation fellow at the Institute for Advanced Studies in Culture. His dissertation is entitled, "Augustine and Barth on the Image of God."

Contributors

Andy Rowell, doctoral candidate (Duke Divinity School), and assistant professor of ministry leadership at Bethel Seminary in St. Paul, MN. His dissertation addresses Barth's ecclesiology. He blogs at *Church Leadership Conversations* (http://www.andyrowell.net) and tweets at @AndyRowell.

Ry O. Siggelkow, doctoral candidate (Princeton Theological Seminary). He is currently working on a book with Halden Doerge and Nathan Kerr entitled, *Kingdom-World-Church: A Theological Manifesto* (Cascade Books), and he blogs at *Rain and the Rhinoceros* (http://rainandtherhinoceros.wordpress.com).

Shannon Nicole Smythe, PhD (Princeton Theological Seminary). Her dissertation is entitled, "Forensic Apocalypticism of a Reformed Order: Karl Barth's Exegetically Grounded Doctrine of Justification."

Keith Starkenburg, PhD (University of Virginia), and associate professor of theology at Trinity Christian College in Palos Heights, IL. He is writing a book based on his dissertation which examines connections between Karl Barth's doctrine of glory and his ecclesiology.

Derek Alan Woodard-Lehman, doctoral candidate (Princeton Theological Seminary). He works broadly on historical and theoretical issues of normativity in religion, ethics, and politics, and his dissertation is entitled, "Free in Deed: Agency and Accountability in Karl Barth's Ethics."

Index of Names

Ables, Travis, 92
Adams, Sam, 236
Albrecht, Christian, 41
Althaus, Paul, 54
Althouse, Peter, 21
Anderson, Ray S, 229
Anrich, Erst, 27–28
Aquinas, Thomas, 129, 135, 181, 257, 285
Aristotle, 14
Augustine, Saint, 51, 80, 181, 241, 257

Badiou, Alain, 180, 184, 259–60
Balthasar, Hans Urs von, 26, 40, 50, 70, 152, 156, 255, 263, 277, 295
Bayer, Oswald, 27
Beck, Richard, 244–45, 252
Beker, J. Christiaan, 211
Bence, Clarence Luther, 5
Bender, Kimlyn, 21
Benjamin, Walter, 71, 75–76, 78, 84, 259
Berkhof, Hendrikus, 59, 67
Berkouwer, G. C., 295
Bethge, Eberhard, 46–48, 58, 60, 64–68
Betz, John, 152–53, 165
Bonhoeffer, Dietrich, 46–69, 113, 258
Boulon, J., 59
Bromiley, Geoffrey W., 283–84, 296
Brown, David, 241
Browning, Don, 229
Brunner, Emil, 54, 113, 244–45, 261–62, 274
Burnett, Richard, 278, 284, 295

Busch, Eberhard, 46, 58, 84, 202, 283, 296
Butler, Judith, 259–61

Calvin, John, 6–7, 11, 21, 51, 60, 202, 210, 256, 264
Chalamet, Christophe, 274
Collins, John J., 215
Collins, Kenneth J., 12, 14
Collins Winn, Christian, 266, 278
Cone, James, 130
Congdon, David W., 121, 274
Crisp, Oliver D., 264

Dalferth, Ingolf U., 44
Dayton, Donald W., 11, 20–21, 24
de Boer, Martinus, 196–97, 213–15
Dempsey, Michael, 161
Deschner, John, 15
Doerge, Halden, 242–44, 248, 250
Dole, Andrew C., 40, 42, 45
Dramm, Sabine, 58

Ebeling, Gerhard, 270
Edelstein, David, 235
Ellis, Daryl T., 61–62
Elwood, Christopher, 256

Feuerbach, Ludwig, 162, 176, 179, 182, 191, 245, 270
Fischer, Hermann, 43
Fitch, David E., 276–77
Flett, John G., 278
Flint, Rebecca, 235
Forsyth, P. T., 182
Foucault, Michel, 114, 259

Index of Names

Fuchs, Ernst, 270
Funk, Robert W., 214

Gaventa, Beverly Roberts, 195, 209
Gerrish, Brian, 29, 37
Gill, Theodore, 290–91
Gockel, Matthias, 40, 203–204
Godsey, John D., 47, 55–56, 64–65, 281, 283, 289
Gollwitzer, Helmut, 132
Gould, Joshua Robert, 71
Green, Clifford, 65, 283, 291
Green, Chris E. W., 241–42
Greggs, Tom, 61, 278

Harink, Douglas, 195–96, 213
Hart, David Bentley, 57, 152–67
Hart, Kevin, 57
Hauerwas, Stanley, 116–28, 252
Healy, Nicholas M., 127
Hector, Kevin W., 270, 272, 277
Hegel, G. W. F., 15, 51, 97–98, 110, 134, 154–55, 172–74, 178–79, 182, 184, 189–91, 259
Heidegger, Martin, 80, 259, 270, 272–73
Hirschberg, Lynn, 237–38
Hoekendijk, J. C., 148
Hogg, Trevor, 235
Hölderlin, Friedrich, 245–46
Holmes, Christopher, 130–31, 133, 146, 149
Holmes, Stephen, 58
Hordern, William, 277–78
Howard, Thomas Albert, 27, 29
Hughes, Carl, 100
Hungerford, Amy, 248–49
Hunsinger, Debora van Deusen, 229
Hunsinger, George, 7, 51, 136, 176, 184, 256, 286, 291, 296
Hütter, Reinhard, 125

Jacobs, Jay S., 237, 240
Jennings, Theodore W., 24
Jenson, Robert W., 15, 19, 91–115, 270, 296
Johnson, Keith, 62, 95, 156, 278

Jones, Paul Dafydd, 173, 183, 221, 225, 227, 257, 259, 278
Jüngel, Eberhard, 15, 17, 47, 52, 61, 161, 185, 191, 268–72, 296

Kant, Immanuel, 15, 28, 111, 173, 259
Kantzer Komline, Han-luen, 166
Käsemann, Ernst, 195–96, 198–200, 212–14
Kegan, Robert, 216–33
Kellerman, Bill Wylie, 142
Kerr, Nathan, 108–10, 126
Kierkegaard, Søren, 20, 108–110, 173, 189, 194, 259, 269
Kim, Sung-Sup, 257
Kline, Peter, 105
Kotsko, Adam, 174

Lacan, Jacqus, 171, 173–74, 190, 259
Lauwerier, Hans, 292
Lehmann, Paul, 59, 64
Levinas, Emmanuel, 110
Loder, James, 217, 229
Long, D. Stephen, 14
Loughlin, Gerard, 187
Luther, Martin, 15, 21, 48, 51, 54, 60, 65, 202, 256

Macchia, Frank, 21
Macken, John, 15
MacKinnon, Donald, 81, 260
Malysz, Piotr, 92
Mandelbrot, Benoit B., 292
Mangina, Joseph, 125
Marga, Amy, 278
Marquardt, Friedrich-Wilhelm, 132
Marquardt, Manfred, 24
Marsh, Charles, 64–65
Marshall, Bruce, 10
Martyn, J. Louis, 195–96, 207, 213–14
Matlock, Barry, 196, 213–14
Maury, Pierre, 203–4
McCall, Thomas, 264
McCarthy, Cormac, 234, 237, 247–53
McCormack, Bruce L., 94–95, 99, 101, 105, 184, 203–204, 211, 261, 264, 296–97
McFarland, Douglas, 237

Index of Names

McKenny, Gerald, 111–14
McMaken, W. Travis, 150, 276
Mehringer, H., 274
Milbank, John, 171–94
Miles, Rebekah L., 24
Molendijk, Arie L., 34
Morray-Jones, Christopher, 213
Morton, Nelle, 226
Moltmann, Jürgen, 256, 270
Mozart, Wolfgang Amadeus, 266, 285, 290–92
Mühlberger, Detlef, 273
Myers, Benjamin, 81

Neder, Adam, 7, 112, 278
Newman, John Henry, 10
Niebuhr, H. Richard, 187, 261, 277
Nietzsche, Friedrich, 153, 174, 177
Nimmo, Paul T., 7, 278

Oakes, Kenneth, 152, 165–66
O'Donovan, Oliver, 77
O'Regan, Cyril, 174, 215
Osmer, Richard, 217
Ott, Heinrich, 59, 270
Oudshoorn, Dan, 248

Pangritz, Andreas, 46, 57, 65
Pannenberg, Wolfhart, 27, 29–31, 256
Park, Chang Hoon, 19
Plato, 14, 15, 19, 145, 162, 166, 271
Pound, Marcus, 174
Price, David J., 51
Przywara, Erich, 48–50, 93, 274

Rea, Michael C., 263
Redeker, Martin, 30
Rose, Matthew, 112
Rowland, Christopher, 213
Richardson, Kurt Anders, 21

Schelling, F. W. J., 27–28, 39, 45, 173

Schlegel, Thomas, 34
Schleiermacher, F. D. E., 26–45, 48, 115, 127, 129, 180, 255
Schmitt, Carl, 70, 77, 85–86
Seeberg, Reinhold, 51, 56, 65
Shults, F. LeRon, 212, 218
Smith, Christian, 227
Söhngen, Gottlieb, 156
Sturm, Richard E., 214
Sundermeier, Theo, 258–59

Takizawa, Katsumi, 257
Tanner, Kathryn, 129–51, 186
Taubes, Jacob, 71–87, 259
Terpstra, Marin, 77
Thomas, R. S., 252
Thompson, Geoff, 45
Thurneysen, Eduard, 93, 104
Tiessen, David, 242
Tillich, Paul, 277
Tindal, Matthew, 14
Torrance, Thomas F., 256, 297
Tracy, David, 131
Troeltsch, Ernst, 19, 29, 31, 51
Tropel, Fred, 237

Webb, Stephen H., 173
Webster, John, 61, 137, 242
Wesley, John, 3–25, 256
Wigley, Stephen, 152
Wildi, Hans, 295
Williams, Rowan, 110
Wilson, Jonathan R., 215

Yeats, William Butler, 250, 252–53
Yoder, John Howard, 86, 118

Ziegler, Philip, 61
Ziolkowski, Theodore, 27
Zinzendorf, Nicolas von, 18, 21
Žižek, Slavoj, 171–94, 259